Artificial Intelligence

Is Artificial Intelligence (AI) a more significant invention than electricity? Will it result in explosive economic growth and unimaginable wealth for all, or will it cause the extinction of all humans? *Artificial Intelligence: Economic Perspectives and Models* provides a sober analysis of these questions from an economics perspective. It argues that to better understand the impact of AI on economic outcomes, we must fundamentally change the way we think about AI in relation to models of economic growth. It describes the progress that has been made so far and offers two ways in which current modeling can be improved: first, by incorporating the nature of AI as providing abilities that complement and/or substitute for labor, and second, by considering demand-side constraints. Outlining the decision-theory basis of both AI and economics, this book shows how this, and the incorporation of AI into economic models, can provide useful tools for safe, human-centered AI.

WIM NAUDÉ is an economist, author, and entrepreneur. He has held appointments at Oxford University and the United Nations University (UNU) and has been a visiting faculty member at Brown University's Brown International Advanced Research Institutes. He has published widely in scientific journals and has authored and edited books published by Palgrave Macmillan, Oxford University Press, and Routledge. He is ranked by Stanford University/Elsevier among the top 2 percent of scientists in the world.

THOMAS GRIES studied economics at Göttingen and the University of California. He received his PhD at Kiel University. He also was a visiting scholar at UNU World Institute for Development Economics Research in Helsinki. Currently, he is Professor for International Growth at Paderborn University, Germany. His research is highly interdisciplinary and covers a large variety of topics, from economic growth and development to the economics of conflict.

NICOLA DIMITRI is a professor of economics, former deputy rector, and former acting rector at the University of Siena, Italy. He has published widely in international journals and edited three books, including the *Handbook of Procurement* (2006) for Cambridge University Press. His main interests are in game theory and in the application thereof to the economics of AI, blockchains, and cryptocurrencies.

Artificial Intelligence

Economic Perspectives and Models

WIM NAUDÉ
RWTH Aachen University

THOMAS GRIES
Paderborn University

NICOLA DIMITRI
University of Siena

Shaftesbury Road, Cambridge CB2 8EA, United Kingdom

One Liberty Plaza, 20th Floor, New York, NY 10006, USA

477 Williamstown Road, Port Melbourne, VIC 3207, Australia

314–321, 3rd Floor, Plot 3, Splendor Forum, Jasola District Centre, New Delhi – 110025, India

103 Penang Road, #05–06/07, Visioncrest Commercial, Singapore 238467

Cambridge University Press is part of Cambridge University Press & Assessment, a department of the University of Cambridge.

We share the University's mission to contribute to society through the pursuit of education, learning and research at the highest international levels of excellence.

www.cambridge.org
Information on this title: www.cambridge.org/9781009483087

DOI: 10.1017/9781009483094

When citing this work, please include a reference to the DOI 10.1017/9781009483094

First published 2024

A catalogue record for this publication is available from the British Library

Library of Congress Cataloging-in-Publication Data
Names: Naudé, Wim A., author. | Gries, Thomas, 1960– author. | Dimitri, Nicola author.
Title: Artificial intelligence : economic perspectives and models / Wim Naudé, RWTH Aachen University, Thomas Gries, Paderborn University, Nicola Dimitri, University of Siena.
Description: Cambridge, United Kingdom ; New York : Cambridge University Press, 2024. | Includes bibliographical references and index.
Identifiers: LCCN 2023056623 | ISBN 9781009483087 (hardback) | ISBN 9781009483117 (paperback) | ISBN 9781009483094 (ebook)
Subjects: LCSH: Artificial intelligence – Economic aspects. | Management – Technological innovations.
Classification: LCC HC79.I55 N385 2024 | DDC 658/.0563–dc23/eng/20240318
LC record available at https://lccn.loc.gov/2023056623

ISBN 978-1-009-48308-7 Hardback
ISBN 978-1-009-48311-7 Paperback

Contents

Figures

Tables

About the Authors

Wim Naudé is an economist, author, and entrepreneur. He is Visiting Professor of Technology, Innovation, Marketing, and Entrepreneurship at RWTH Aachen University, Germany, Distinguished Visiting Professor of Economics at the University of Johannesburg, South Africa, and affiliated as an AI Expert at the OECD's AI Policy Observatory in Paris, France. He has held appointments at Oxford University, Maastricht University, and the United Nations University and has been a visiting faculty member at Brown University's Brown International Advanced Research Institutes. As an author, he has widely published in scientific journals and has authored and edited books published by Palgrave Macmillan, Oxford University Press, Springer, and Routledge. As an entrepreneur, he is the (co)founder of several companies. As a scientist, Naudé is ranked by Stanford University and Elsevier as among the top 2 percent of scientists in the world. He lives in Maastricht, the Netherlands.

Thomas Gries is Professor of Economics, International Growth and Business Cycle Theory, at Paderborn University, Germany. His major focus is the process of global growth and development, including conflict economics. Gries studied economics and social science at the University of Göttingen, Germany, and graduated receiving the diploma (Diplom Volkswirt) in 1984. He also holds an MA from the University of California, Santa Barbara. He received a doctoral degree, doctor of political science, from the Christian-Albrechts-University, Kiel, in 1988. His habilitation at the Georg August University, Göttingen, was finished in 1994. He lives in Paderborn, Germany.

Nicola Dimitri is Full Professor of Economics, University of Siena, Italy. He is a leading scholar on public procurement and coauthor of the *Cambridge Handbook of Public Procurement*. His is also a life member of Clare Hall College at the University of Cambridge and a research associate of the Center for Blockchain Technologies at University College London. In the past, Dimitri served as the acting rector (February–April 2006) and as the deputy rector, of the University of Siena (2004–2006). His research ranges across different areas and includes game and decision theory, auctions, public procurement, health and pharmaceutical economics, the economics of innovation, cloud computing, neuroeconomics and cognitive economics, artificial intelligence and the economics of blockchain and cryptocurrencies. More specifically, in recent years, his research is focused on the role of public procurement in promoting and guiding innovative solutions, on the importance of the state in the research and development race for a general artificial intelligence, and on the impact of big data and artificial intelligence solutions on public policy activities. He lives in Siena, Italy.

Preface

The field of economics is useful for artificial intelligence (AI), and AI in turn can add value to the evolving science of economics. For one, economics may help AI better understand the behavior of and between agents, and AI may help economics to make better models of complex systems. Also, perspectives from economics can provide a reality check of the hype and hysteria that marks the public discourse on AI and assist policy makers to design guardrails to make AI safer, as well as steer AI as an innovation in the method of innovation, which is sorely needed. This book is our modest attempt to facilitate further enrichment between the field of economics and the field of AI.

At the outset, we wish to acknowledge several specific debts. First, we are grateful to the team at Cambridge University Press, in particular Philip Good and Sable Gravesandy who provided expert support, from the commissioning to the production and marketing stages of this book. Our thanks also to three anonymous referees for their useful comments and suggestions on an earlier draft.

Second, the core of the real options model developed in Chapter 6 is derived from earlier work with Natasa Bilkic, for which we thank her for her contributions.

Third, we are grateful to several colleagues who have over time engaged with us on our earlier papers, in particular Derick Almeida, Seth Benzell, Martin Cameron, Pedro Mazeda Gil, Thomas Kittsteiner, Jacques Ludik, Frank Piller, Tiago Neves Sequeira, Erik Stam, Aleksander Surdej, and Ricardo Vinuesa. Also, our thanks goes to the participants of several conferences and workshops, including at Oxford University, RWTH Aachen University, the University of Sussex, Utrecht University, and the Tor Vergata University of Rome, who freely gave us many constructive comments as our ideas evolved.

Finally, the financial assistance of the Volkswagen Stiftung, through planning grant AZ 97042 from their project on Artificial Intelligence and the Society of the Future is gratefully acknowledged for the research that forms the basis of Chapters 4, 5, 8, and 9. The usual disclaimer applies.

1 Introduction

1.1 INTRODUCTION

Alan Turing is deservedly a hero of the modern computer age. Back in 1950 he called for the invention of thinking machines – what we would today call artificial intelligence (AI). He had a good idea how this could be done:

> We may hope that machines will eventually compete with men in all purely intellectual fields. But which are the best ones to start with? Many people think that a very abstract activity, like the playing of chess, would be best. It can also be maintained that it is best to provide the machine with the best sense organs that money can buy and teach it to understand and speak English. I think both approaches should be tried. (Turing, 1950, p. 460)

Turing argued that AI should start by playing chess and speaking English. As we are preparing this book for publication at the end of 2023, both approaches have been tried and successfully implemented. In chess, there are IBM's Deep Blue algorithm and Google's AlphaZero. The latter has taught itself to play chess in four hours and then defeated other leading chess computer programs. And as far as talking is concerned, in 2018 Google introduced Google Duplex, an AI telephone assistant that can conduct a complex conversation. Nowadays we routinely talk to our devices, whether it be Siri, Alexa, ChatGPT, or our car.

Recognizing patterns from mountains of data, whether these be chess moves or sentences, and moreover doing it better and faster than the human brain can and learning in an unsupervised manner by doing, is at the core of AI – also called *Machine Learning* (ML). It underpins a wide range of applications with which we are all to some extent engaging daily, whether it be filtering spam emails, performing searches on Google, engaging ChatGPT to write some code, using Bing to design an image for our next Instagram post, watching a series on Netflix, or just using our mobile devices.

While this is all very remarkable, in many ways AI seems like a typical new technology and, by that comparison, not all *that* remarkable. It has been a long way in the making. It seems to be following a typical hype cycle and *S-curve* in its reception and impact. It is, like electricity before it, slow to diffuse. Like the technologies that heralded the First Industrial Revolution, it has been associated with rising inequality – or at least the potential to widen income and wealth gaps – so nothing new there. And as with many previous technologies – for example, the steam engine, electricity, the motor car, DNA, and nuclear energy – there are hypesters and hopesters (who hype its potential benefits) and Luddites and doomsters (who lament its consequences). For example, AI has been hyped as an exponential technology by Chiacchio et al. (2018, p. 3) who claimed (with reference to a McKinsey study) that AI disruption would be 10 times faster and 300 times the scale than that of the First Industrial Revolution – thus having "3,000 times the impact." And in 2023 Yudkowsky (2023) exclaimed, "If somebody builds a too-powerful AI, under present conditions, I expect that every single member of the human species and all biological life on Earth dies shortly thereafter."

In the case of AI, the difference seems to be, at least from the present vantage point, that it is not a finished technology but a technology that is incrementally changing and still evolving. While AI currently (in its ML form) is data and energy intensive, and based on describing but not understanding intelligence, it is likely to keep on evolving. It is possible that it will become quite different in coming years. In this, AI is very different than electricity, a general-purpose technology to whom it is often compared. The scientific details of electricity are today the same as ever; it is only the way it is being engineered in applications that has differed. When the first car was driven out of the shop, its dangers were well known, and moreover, these have remained roughly similar. Nuclear technology, and its dangers, today is fundamentally the same as it was half a century ago. By contrast, AI is developing – it is a learning technology at the same time as humans are learning more about the nature of intelligence – and these learning processes mean that *what* precisely AI will evolve into – and when – is unknown. As Martin Rees, Astronomer Royal, pointed out, "there is no consensus among experts on the speed and advance in machine intelligence" (2018, p. 102).

This uncertainty is one reason why there is unprecedented hype – and hysteria – surrounding the technology (Naudé, 2021, 2019a). For example, how many previous technologies have spurned more than two dozen governments to formulate and adopt national strategies? How many have led calls for a specific technology to be governed from the United Nations? On an almost daily basis, new articles and position papers are being published on ethics for AI, regulation of AI, and human-centered AI. Compare this with the fact that the very real potential existential risk of bioengineered weapons and biowarfare is handled by the Biological Weapons Convention with an annual budget of US$1.4 million, as Ord (2020, p. 57) pointed out, less than that of an average McDonald's restaurant.

The uncertainty about the end game of AI and its true benefits and costs is responsible for the fascination with and horror toward AI in equal measure. For many start-up entrepreneurs, it is a potential money machine and a way to tap into the large reservoirs of venture capital that are swooshing around the world economy. Big promises can be sold on AI. For resource-starved and dying philosophy departments, the ethical dilemmas of AI has offered a new lease of life – providing a means of tapping into the funds governments feel they have to be seen spending on AI. The potential moral ambiguities and ethical traps in AI seem infinite, and philosophers have shown great creativity and are spinning out ever more thought experiments to confront us with the moral mazes of AI. For social justice warriors and Marxists, AI is a new instrument of oppression and capitalism:

It may very well be the ultimate winner-takes-all and surveillance technology. And those – the AI doomsters – proclaiming that the end of the world is nigh, many of them funded by promoters of existential altruism, have found a new existential threat: a superintelligence that will, by definition, be an adversary that humanity can never beat.

In light of this, our book's ultimate contribution is to help reduce the uncertainty about the contemporary and future economic implications of AI. It is inspired by David Deutsch's Principle of Optimism: "If something is permitted by the laws of physics then the only thing that can prevent it from being technologically possible is not knowing how" (2011, p. 213). We need to know more about AI to clear up the uncertainties. This includes knowledge of the economics of AI and how it may shape the future economy, given that it is an evolving technology. Economics is a field that until now has only to a limited degree taken on the challenge of helping to understand AI (Agrawal et al., 2019b). This book is therefore ultimately a contribution to motivate economists to bring their insights and approaches to bear on the matter.

The scientific field of economics, which studies human exchange, has gained deep knowledge of how markets create information that coordinates decentralized decision-making toward the efficient use of resources and how societal institutions (rules of the game) affect the functioning of markets. In the case of previous technologies, economists have shown that technologies that are technically possible are often not adopted because of market-institutional features. Take, for example, the invention of farming (cultivation of crops). Before around 15,000 years ago, humans had been foragers for more than 150,000 years. The shift to farming and its technologies was always technically possible during that time, and even if humans had known *how* to farm, they would have failed to do so before markets were sufficiently large to provide economies of scale and before there were appropriate social technologies, such as property rights, to incentivize the adoption of farming (Bowles and Choi, 2019).

We believe that economics can provide similar insights into many aspects of contemporary and future AI. This book provides illustrations of this. But the field of economics also needs to adjust its tools to be able to illuminate AI better. Key models in economics, for example, growth models, have until recently wholly abstracted from technology (and energy), focusing only on the nineteenth-century world of capital and labor as production factors. It was only in the 1990s that technology was endogenized, and the key feature of technology – as ideas that offer increasing returns and combinatorial possibilities – incorporated into economic growth models. These insights earned Paul Romer a Nobel Prize. It would be premature to imagine that the Information and communication technology (ICT) revolution, which has gathered speed only after 2007,[1] is adequately reflected in these models. We need more details and realism of digital technologies, and specifically AI, to be included in our models. These will offer gains in understanding how and why, and when, AI affects key economic outcomes such as economic growth, inequality, productivity growth, poverty, innovation and investment rates, wages, and consumption. This book illustrates how AI can be modeled in economics and how this can lead to deeper insights into this technology and reduce some of the uncertainty that surrounds it.

It is not that economists have been totally neglecting AI. The dominant approach to AI, ML, has already been used by economists since at least the 1980s to improve economic forecasting (Gogas and Papadimitriou, 2021). Economists have moreover been concerned not only about how ML can help with forecasting but also about the impacts of AI on labor markets, income distribution, innovation and productivity, allocative efficiency, competition and collusive behavior, among others – even though as we argue in this book the modeling approaches still need work. Examples of this work in economics include Acemoglu and Restrepo (2020), Aghion et al. (2017),

[1] The year 2007 was a pivotal year for the transition to the digital revolution. As Thomas Friedman memorably asked, "What the hell happened in 2007?" (2016, p. 19).

Agrawal et al. (2019a), Berg et al. (2018), Bloom et al. (2018), Furman and Seamans (2019), Prettner and Strulik (2017), and Schiller (2019).

The concerns about AI mentioned in the previous paragraph are issues of immediate concern – topics that have also grabbed global and national political attention. The longer-term concerns, of more existential importance (Bostrom, 2014; Yudkowsky, 2008), have been neglected by economists. For instance, where will continued innovation in AI ultimately lead to? Will narrow AI make way for an artificial general intelligence (AGI)? And will this bring about continuing accelerating innovation resulting in a "Singularity"? Is superexponential, explosive, economic growth possible? Will a future AGI intentionally or unintentionally destroy humanity or, perhaps more likely, be misused by humanity? These are all questions where economists have been fairly silent, leaving the debate to be dominated by philosophers and computer scientists. Thus, this book also focuses attention on the long-term concerns about which substantial uncertainty exists, and do so from an economics viewpoint.

1.2 THE NEED FOR AN ECONOMICS OF AI

There is a strong case to be made for an economics of AI. But first, what do we mean by an economics of AI? We mean that economic tools – models – can and should be used more frequently to draw out the consequences of the development and use of AI. Such applications of AI are indeed growing. We also mean that economic models should be updated to reflect how the presence of AI affects their core assumptions. Just as like software developers issue new updates or versions of their operating systems or programs, for example, to deal with bugs or new security threats, so economists need to update their models. AI, being based in digital technologies and being a disruptor of the way information is used in economic decision-making, holds radical implications for economists' assumptions about costs, prices, competition, and distribution, among others.

Without an economics of AI, we are likely to obtain less benefit from AI and see more examples of "Awful AI" and growing fears of an AGI as an existential risk – with the possible unfortunate outcome that AI progress is regulated to a standstill. Most of the chapters in this book in fact illustrate this point: using existing and modified economic models to analyze the impacts of AI on the economy, the impact of policies on AI, and the economics of AI in the long run. They show that AI will neither take all our jobs nor lead to the extinction of humanity. These points can be elaborated as a way of motivating, as well as introducing, the rest of the book.

1.2.1 The (Shorter-Run) Impacts of AI on the Economy

A first way in which an economics of AI can help is in identifying where and how its benefits may be reduced or lost, and why and how "Awful" AI may emerge, including providing economically grounded perspectives on the realism of an AGI that may pose an existential risk.

Related to these dimensions of AI's impact is the challenge that most advanced economies face in dealing with the so-called *Great Stagnation*. So far, the impact of AI on economic and productivity growth and unemployment has been small. Even the much longer ongoing ICT revolution seems to have played out its productivity impacts (some would argue that we will have to wait a bit more time to see these, e.g., Brynjolfsson et al. [2017]). In fact a worrisome feature of the last few decades has been the stagnating productivity growth in the West. Productivity growth is, for instance, the lowest in the United Kingdom in 200 years – as Figure 1.1 shows. The sharp drop in labor productivity growth since the 1970s (the starting date of the digital/ICT "revolution") is very clear.

How – if at all – can AI reverse the Great Stagnation? And will doing so lead to massive technological unemployment?

In the first part of the book – Chapters 3 and 4 – we provide a model for analyzing the relationship between human capital and what we describe as AI abilities. The general implication of this model is to cast doubt on the likelihood that AI will lead to massive technological unemployment. It may, however, lead to higher levels

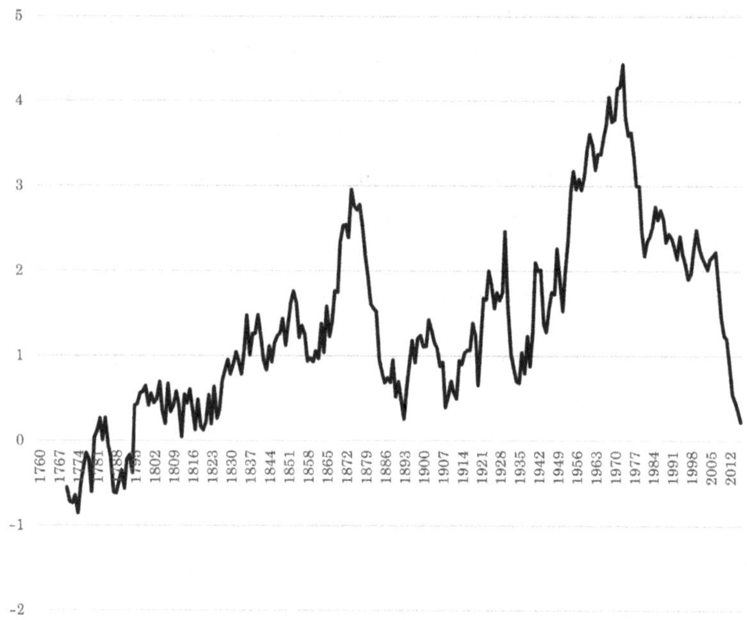

FIGURE I.1 Stagnation: Where is the impact of ICT? Labor productivity growth in the United Kingdom, 1760–2012
Source: Bank of England.

of inequality, which, through reduced aggregate demand, can lead to immiserizing growth. This will not reverse the Great Stagnation – unless, as we discuss in Chapter 10, AI develops into an innovation in the method of innovation (IMI), which can help raise research productivity. It is not clear, however, that AI will be able to fulfill these expectations. Part of the reason has to do with AI itself, and the limitations of Deep Learning. Part of the reason is outside AI: Venture capital funding to commercialize all the possible new ideas that an AI may generate will be a binding constraint.

In Chapter 10 we also consider whether AI, if it advances sufficiently, say to become an AGI, will be able to lead to accelerating economic growth – a growth explosion. Here too we tend to come to pessimistic conclusions. First, an AGI may not happen anytime soon, and if it ever does (there are reasonable grounds to assume it may never), it may not appear suddenly but will more likely be, as the economics of innovation suggests, the result of a long period of incremental improvements and design (as we discuss at more length in Chapter 6) – which will box in its abilities to prevent it from misalignment with human existential needs. Second, a growth explosion is likely to be very short-lived if it can overcome demand-side constraints (the topic of Chapter 5), because it will run into a brick wall of fundamental physical constraints. For instance, the energy demands from an AGI-acceleration in economic growth will quickly become prohibitive (Dutil and Dumas, 2007).

Even though an AGI may be able to increase energy efficiency and be able to decouple much growth from physical resources, it would still need significant amounts of energy to run its software and hardware – the share of the economy that can be nonphysical is ultimately bounded. If an AGI reverses the Great Stagnation and leads to a continuation of the annual average growth in energy consumption over the recent past – say the past century – of around 2,3 percent per annum, then energy use on the planet will grow from its 2019 level of 18 TW to 100 TW in 2100 and 1,000 TW in 2200. Murphy (2022b) calculates that at such a rate the economy would use up all the solar power that reaches the earth in 400 years and in 1,700 years all of the energy of the sun! The use of so much energy would generate tremendous waste heat *independent of the AGI's smart energy*. In economic modeling, the shortcomings are not taking energy as a fundamental driver of economic growth seriously and considering fundamental limits to economic growth. We discuss these shortcomings in more depth in Chapter 10.

1.2.2 The Impacts of Policy on AI

A second way in which an "economics of AI" can help is in identifying how public policy toward AI can be made better. There is indeed much enthusiasm shown by governments to implement policies to make AI more "human-centered." Much of this is unfortunately fed by the hype and hysteria that surrounds AI (for more see Chapter 2).

Without adequate consideration of the economics of AI, governments are likely to get it wrong – making costly policy mistakes. We think that this is, unfortunately, already happening. Let us explain by discussing the current fashion for Grand National AI Strategies.

Already by 2018, at least twenty-two countries as well as the European Union had launched AI strategies, and many more announced Ethical AI frameworks. The European Union Agency for Fundamental Rights (FRA) documents more than 290 AI policy initiatives in individual EU member states between 2016 and 2020.

One country whose approach is fairly representative of these is that of Ireland. The country announced its National Artificial Intelligence Strategy, "AI – Here for Good," in July 2021. The strategy has as its ambition – similar to those of other countries' AI strategies – to see Ireland become "an international leader in using AI to benefit our economy and society, through a people-centred, ethical approach to its development, adoption and use." This is to be obtained by a comprehensive list of policy thrusts: (1) increasing trust in and understanding of AI; (2) to put appropriate governance and regulatory measures in place; (3) to promote the adoption of AI by businesses; (4) to promote the adoption of AI by the government; (5) to steer more innovation and research in AI; (6) to raise labor force skills to use and adapt to AI; and (7) to provide and secure adequate critical (ICT) infrastructure for AI systems.

Comprehensive as these national AI strategies mostly are, they tend to have shortcomings. First, they tend to uncritically share in some of the hype and hysteria surrounding AI. In the case of Ireland the AI strategy claims (p. 14) that AI could double economic growth by 2035. It fails to substantiate this by detailing critically whose growth and how.

The hype aside, a second shortcoming is that without an economic analysis of the costs, benefits, and incentives that shapes business investment and the adoption of AI, national AI strategies tend to ignore or downplay the fact that AI is central to the business models of the Chinese surveillance state and a few large digital platform firms (Google, Apple, Facebook – now Meta, Amazon,

Alibaba – GAFAA) who enjoy winner-takes-most benefits due to network economies that characterize AI business models. These firms do not need government funding or support – in fact their research and development (R&D) budgets exceed that of many rich countries.

A third shortcoming is that, AI national strategies tend to omit consideration of the fact that it is not so much the technology per se that determines the impact but the way it transforms business models and changes the competitive landscape. AI requires large amounts of data, which in turn generate demand economies of scale, first-mover advantages, and winner-take-most effects in markets. The few companies in the world that get it right (GAFAA) become monopolists and gatekeepers, not only disrupting existing businesses but also depressing the start-up of new firms, creating virtual "killing zones" around them that stifle innovation – and which no doubt contribute to the Great Stagnation.

How to deal with this radically different (anti-) competition landscape – labelled "platform capitalism" (Srnicek, 2016), featuring platform envelopment and creative use of AI – has caused regulators and competition authorities substantial headaches (Naudé, 2023b). Not only do digital platform firms out-compete traditional "pipeline" businesses but increasingly entrepreneurs are forced to compete against each other on digital platforms – for example, on Amazon Web Services (AWS) – often with terrible results and a rise in digital subsistence entrepreneurship and destructive digital entrepreneurship (Naudé, 2023a; Van Alstyne et al., 2016). As a result, the European Union, for instance, adopted its Digital Markets Act (DMA), Digital Services Act (DSA), and AI Act in recent years to better regulate digital platforms and manage the risks posed by AI.

A fourth shortcoming of many national AI strategies is that they tend to depart from the critical assumption that there is a trust problem with AI and that this is due to people not understanding AI well enough. For example, the Irish national AI strategy aims to teaching people data science and having an AI ambassador, believing that this will raise trust (belief) in AI. In fact, from applying an economic perspective, one may expect exactly the opposite to be the case: The better people understand AI, the more they will see through the hype and hysteria, and the better they will realize that AI is not the panacea it is made out to be – and they will have less trust in AI.[2]

In the United States, where research and understanding of AI are quite advanced, adoption rates of AI are very low. Zolas et al. (2020) report that a 2018 US Census Bureau Survey of over 800,000 firms in the United States found that only 2,9 percent were using ML in 2018. McElheran et al. (2023) report that the adoption rate of five AI-related technologies among a sample of 850,000 US firms was, corrected for firm size, just 18 percent. A 2020 survey by the European Commission (2020) found that among EU firms who indicate using AI, "at the level of each technology, adoption in the EU is still relatively low. It ranges from merely 3% of enterprises currently having adopted sentiment analysis to 13% for anomaly detection and process/equipment optimisation." Firms do not adopt AI because it makes no business sense, not because they do not trust it. It is still just too expensive, with paltry returns for most firms, it comes with an exorbitant environmental price tag, and markets are dominated by a few incumbent firms.

Chapters 4–9 in this book provide an economic take on these issues. The analyses in the chapters show that indeed with a few firms dominating the business landscape the regulatory challenges facing governments – to for instance, incentivize human-centered AI or to limit AI arms races – may be more tractable. The analyses also highlight that to track, trace, and regulate AI advances, government regulators need to be sufficiently resourced, including having access to appropriately skilled staff, to be able to do this. In sum, the impacts of policy on AI will depend not so much on the impacts of policy on technology hardware and software but on the business models that these give rise to. Economics is well prepared to make a contribution in this regard, for instance, through insights from Game Theory, Mechanism Design, and Network Economics.

[2] This may, however, be a desirable outcome.

1.2.3 The Impacts of AI in the Longer Run

> That's right: the end of the world is nigh, and it's no longer the preserve of megabudget disaster movies or bleak survivalist thrillers. These days the looming obliteration of our species can just as readily form the backdrop to some governmental mockery or a boozy country-house drama. (Hess, 2022)

The *Zeitgeist* in the third decade of the third millennium is one of *Angst*, as this quote reflects. While there have always been doomsayers predicting the imminent end of humanity, a rational, scientific approach toward understanding and acting on existential risks facing humanity is still lacking. The focus has so far largely been on measuring, mitigating, and responding to vulnerability to various idiosyncratic and covariate risks – such as risks to falling in poverty, risks to health, and the risks from natural hazards or human action – where this risk posed threats of significant damage but not to such an extent that it would "permanently or drastically curtail the potential of humanity" (Bostrom, 2002, p. 2).

However, the climate change challenge, the COVID-19 pandemic, and the renewed specter of nuclear war have made warnings that we need to face up to real existential threats more urgent. Books dealing with existential risks, including longer-term risks, have become bestsellers – see, for instance, Rees (2018), Ord (2020), and MacAskill (2022).

There is a widespread view that AI poses an existential risk. Consider, for instance, that a recent headline exclaimed that "A third of scientists working on AI say it could cause global disaster" (Hsu, 2022). According to Noy and Uher (2022, p. 498), "Artificial Intelligence (AI) systems most likely pose the highest global catastrophic and existential risk to humanity from the four risks we described here, including solar-fares and space weather, engineered and natural pandemics, and super-volcanic eruptions." AI is even seen as "millions of times more powerful than nuclear weapons" and that it "could create multiple individual global risks, most of which we can not currently imagine" (Turchin and Denkenberger, 2020, p. 148).

In March 2023, several scientists and other notables signed an open letter published on the Future of Life Institute's web page,[3] calling "on all AI labs to immediately pause for at least 6 months the training of AI systems more powerful than GPT-4. This pause should be public and verifiable, and include all key actors. If such a pause cannot be enacted quickly, governments should step in and institute a moratorium." By the time this book was going to press, this open letter has been signed by more than 33,000 people.

In Chapter 10, we argue that these fears are, just like the hopes of a Singularity and growth explosion, exaggerated. First, as we discuss in greater depth in chapter 6, an AGI is still a far way off, and if (which is a big if) it is ever invented, the process leading to its invention may very likely reduce the risks of misalignment with human objectives. Perhaps Floridi (2022, p. 9) has a point in warning that the preoccupation of certain philosophers with the Singularity and existential risks from AI "is a rich-world preoccupation likely to worry people in wealthy societies who seem to forget the real evils oppressing humanity and our planet."

However, we argue that economists ought to weigh in more on the matter of AI's potential long-term risks and discuss the reasons why they so far, have not done so. One reason is that economic risk assessment methods using expected utility theory (EUT) are not well-suited to deal with existential risks. Weitzman (2009) has proposed a dismal theorem that states that, because the probabilities of catastrophic events are characterized by long tails, EUT would assign infinite losses to it. As a result, EUT may not be able to provide an ethically acceptable approach to deal with catastrophic and existential risks. A future economics of AI may set this right.

1.3 STRUCTURE OF THIS BOOK

The rest of the book is structured as follows.

In Chapter 2, *Artificial Intelligence and Economics: A Gentle Introduction*, we describe the development of AI since World War

[3] See https://futureoflife.org/open-letter/pause-giant-ai-experiments/

II, noting various AI "winters" and tracing the current boom in AI back to around 2006/2007. We provide various metrics describing the nature of this AI boom. We then provide a summary and discussion of the salient research relevant to the economics of AI and outline some recent theoretical advances.

Chapter 3, *Artificial Intelligence and the Economics of Decision-Making,* deals with how microeconomics can provide insights into the key challenge that AI scientists face. This challenge is to create intelligent, autonomous agents that can make rational decisions. In this challenge, they confront two questions: what decision theory to follow and how to implement it in AI systems. This chapter provides answers to these questions and makes three contributions. The first is to discuss how economic decision theory – EUT – can help AI systems with utility functions to deal with the problem of instrumental goals, the possibility of utility function instability, and coordination challenges in multi-actor and human–agent collective settings. The second contribution is to show that using EUT restricts AI systems to narrow applications, which are "small worlds" where concerns about AI alignment may lose urgency and be better labeled as safety issues. The chapter's third contribution points to several areas where economists may learn from AI scientists as they implement EUT. These include consideration of procedural rationality, overcoming computational difficulties, and understanding decision-making in disequilibrium situations.

In Chapter 4, *Artificial Intelligence in the Production Function,* the book moves from the microeconomic perspective of Chapter 3 to the macroeconomic perspective of labor markets and economic growth – although the analysis remains grounded in microeconomic functions. In this chapter, we provide an economic growth model wherein AI as a possible substitute for human labor is modeled, taking into account the nature of AI as an automation technology. This goes to the heart of the current focus of economists on AI, namely its implications for labor markets, and specifically unemployment and skills requirements. The crucial points that we make here are that economists need to go further than indirectly modeling

AI through assumptions on substitution elasticities, and need to take the specific nature (narrow focus) of AI into explicit account.

In Chapter 5, *Artificial Intelligence, Growth, and Inequality*, we take the production function enriched with AI abilities from Chapter 4, and apply it to study the implications for progress in AI on growth and inequality. The crucial finding we discuss in this chapter is that understanding the nature of AI as narrow ML and its effect on key macroeconomic outcomes depends on having appropriate assumptions in growth models. In particular, we discuss the appropriateness of assuming, as most standard endogenous growth models today do, that economies are supply driven. If they are not supply driven, then demand constraints, which can arise from the diffusion of AI, may restrict growth. Through this we show why expectations that AI will may lead to "explosive" economic growth is unlikely to materialize: the increase in inequality and decline in consumption that will occur will act as a negative feedback effect, which will truncate the growth rate. AI progress may even contribute to negative growth. In this way, we show that by considering the nature of AI as specific (and not general) AI, and making appropriate assumptions that reflect the digital AI economy better, economic outcomes may be characterized by slow growth, rising inequality and rather full employment – conditions that rather well describe economies in the West. This chapter contributes to not only the recent theoretical literature on AI and economic growth modeling, such as the AR model, but also work by Aghion et al. (2017), Cords and Prettner (2019), Hémous and Olsen (2018), and Prettner and Strulik (2017). Unlike these models, the model presented in Chapter 5 incorporates demand constraints and a modified task approach to labor markets.

In Chapter 6, *Investing in Artificial Intelligence: Breakthroughs and Backlashes*, we move from the impacts of AI on the economy to the impacts of firm– and government-level decisions on AI. In particular, we ask what economic modeling can tell us about the likelihood that firms will invent an AGI: how much and for how long must they sustain investment in R&D to obtain such an invention? We develop a novel Real Options Model, one that uses a Stochastic Compound Poisson Process, to explicitly consider that a radical innovation such as an AGI is subject to much more uncertainty than typical business investments – which also helps throw light on the breakthroughs and backlashes that have characterized periodic AI winters, as is discussed in Chapter 2. The crucial insight of our model is that it will be largely government-funded agencies or state-owned enterprises efforts (e.g., by the US or Chinese governments) and/or a few large corporations (such as Google or Alibaba) that will invent an AGI, if ever. In Chapter 10, we will come back to the question of what may be the consequences if they indeed succeed.

In Chapter 7, *Artificial Intelligence Arms Races as Innovation Contests*, we go deeper into modeling one of the implications or features noted in Chapter 6, namely that a strong motivation for large firms to invest substantial amounts into R&D for an AGI is due to the winner-takes-all effects it may bestow on them. This feature, while important to incentivize AI investment, has the downside that it implies that AI arms races may take place. And the danger of an AI arms race is that it may result in an inferior AGI from a human safety perspective. In this chapter, we model such an AI arms race as an innovation contest and show how a government can steer such an arms race so as to obtain a better outcome in terms of the quality of the AGI. A crucial insight from our modeling is that the intention (or goals) of teams competing in an AGI race, as well as the possibility of an intermediate outcome ("second prize"), may be important. Making the latter available through government innovation procurement leads us to Chapter 8.

In Chapter 8, *Directing Artificial Intelligence Innovation and Diffusion*, we ask, given that Chapter 7 suggested a role for public procurement of innovation to potentially play a role in steering innovation in AI, how values and ethics in AI development can be incentivized by governments. We start out from the difficulty acknowledged in the rapidly growing field of AI ethics that the many proposals for ethical AI – or human centered AI (HCAI) – lack strong incentives for developers and users to adhere to them. The crucial insight from this chapter is from the use of a simple theoretical model that shows how public procurement of innovation can incentivize the development of HCAI.

Chapter 9, *Artificial Intelligence, Big Data, and Public Policy*, focuses on how public policy can steer AI, by taking how it can impact on the use of big data, one of the key inputs required for AI. Essentially, public policy can steer AI through putting conditions and limitations on data. But data itself can help improve public policy – also in the area of economic policymaking. Hence, this chapter touches on the future potential of economic policy improvements through AI. More specifically, we discuss under what conditions the availability of large data sets can support and enhance public policy effectiveness – including the use of AI – along with two main directions. We first analyze how big data can help existing policy measures to improve their effectiveness and, second, we discuss how the availability of big data can suggest new, not yet implemented, policy solutions that can improve upon existing ones. In doing so, we assume that data represent a fundamental element in policymaking. Both points are discussed within a very simple model that, despite its simplicity, provides some interesting insights. The key message of this chapter is that the desirability of big data and AI to enhance policymaking depends on the goal of public authorities and on the aspects such as the cost of data collection and storage and the complexity and importance of the policy issue.

Chapter 10, *The Future of AI and Implications for Economics*, is the final chapter. Whereas in Chapter 2, we evaluated the past and present of AI, in this chapter, we consider the future of AI. This means that unavoidably this chapter is somewhat speculative. But we build our speculation on informed discussions of the implications of current socioeconomic and technological trends and on our understanding of past digital revolutions. This allows us to provide insights on where the economy is heading and what this may imply for economics as a science.

Future avenues for research are identified in Chapter 10. These include the need for further elaborations of economic growth models to explore the possibility of an AI-induced growth collapse, to explore the physical limits of growth, and to sharpen the tools to draw out the policy implications of facing fat-tailed catastrophic risks. Furthermore, economic perspectives may usefully be applied to the solutions and implications of the *Fermi Paradox*. These include applying economic tools to potential far-future challenges, such as decisions on whether and when – and how – to colonize the galaxy; whether or not to try and contact extraterrestrial intelligences (ETIs); whether or not to choose conflict or attempt cooperation with other ETIs; how to best protect a planetary civilization; and when an Earth-based civilization could expect to find evidence of an ETI. What Chapter 9 neatly illustrates is that delving into the economics of AI can act as a portal for economists to venture beyond the narrow confines of traditional economics – to go where no economics student has gone before.

1.4 WHO THIS BOOK IS FOR

This book is first aimed at our fellow economists – colleagues and graduate students – as a contribution to expand our field a little, and to elicit more interest for, and debate on, AI. We therefore assume that the reader of this book will be in command of a fairly high level of economic theory – especially of microeconomic optimization and economic growth theory, including familiarity with the mathematical tools – primarily calculus – that provides the language for economic theorizing. Those who are already studying economics but may not (yet) meet these requirements may benefit from first delving into some of the many great textbooks on economic growth theory. We can recommend two classics: Daron Acemoglu's *Introduction to Modern Economic Growth* (Acemoglu, 2009) and Philippe Aghion and Peter Howitt's *Endogenous Growth Theory* (Aghion et al., 1997).

We do not assume any deep level of understanding of AI models, and this is not a textbook on AI models or the application of Deep

Learning to economics and business cases. Chapters 1–3 of the book do however provide a broad and what we consider an easy introduction into the field of AI. We do recommend however, for those not too familiar with the technical aspects of AI, the textbook of Russell and Norvig (2021), *Artificial Intelligence: A Modern Approach*, and the textbook of Deisenroth et al. (2020), *Mathematics for Machine Learning*. For those who want to jump into using ML as part of their econometric toolkit, there is Chan and Mátyás (2022)'s *Econometrics with Machine Learning*.

At this point, it is appropriate to acknowledge that this book is fundamentally theoretical in its approach. Although we do make reference to the empirical literature in economics, which has dealt mostly with the impact of AI on employment, and moreover critically reference the rather limited empirical work as stemming from the pervasive use of the task approach to labor markets (see especially Chapters 4 and 5), we see our theoretical approach as one of the strengths and unique features of the book. Our theoretical approach has two advantages: one is that it is less likely to age rapidly, unlike the case with empirical work that tends to always evolve, and which tends to be indeterminate due to difficulties comparing results from differently designed surveys, different contexts, and using different statistical methods to analyze these. A second advantage is pedagogical: the book offers a clear and consistent guide and introduction to the economics of AI. By taking a theoretical/mathematical approach, we illustrate to students and researchers new to the topic how the toolbox of economics can be applied to real-world problems.

In addition to our fellow economists, this book is also offered to fellow scientists in the fields such as (machine) ethics, philosophy, and computer science as a contribution and invitation to expand the interdisciplinary scrutinizing of AI. If economists are to do a better job at modeling AI, they would need the feedback from colleagues working in these fields. They need to understand the cutting edge of the fields of intelligence science, the science of information and of computation in particular. Hopefully, many of our colleagues in these fields will be able to follow our mathematical arguments, and find in them ideas that are useful for inspiring improvements in AI. As per David Deutsch's *Principle of Optimism*, it is only our limited knowledge that prevents us from designing an AI – a superintelligence – that can be of service to humanity without any of the concerns that it now raises.

2 Artificial Intelligence and Economics

*A Gentle Introduction**

2.1 INTRODUCTION

In this chapter, we provide a concise introduction to what artificial intelligence (AI) is, where it comes from, and what the current (anno 2024) state of the art is in AI. We also introduce the reader to the main reasons why economists are interested in AI. It serves as a gentle background for the more rigorous chapters that follow. The reader who is familiar with AI and AI research in economics may skip this chapter and proceed directly to the technically oriented chapters – Chapters 3–9 – or the bit more speculative and philosophical Chapter 10.

Before proceeding, it is good to reflect why *we* are interested in AI, and why we think that economists ought to be paying more attention to the phenomenon. The reason is that AI is one of the leading new technologies of the early twenty-first century. It has been described as a new general-purpose technology (GPT) perhaps even similar to electricity in potential impact (Agrawal et al., 2019a; Brynjolfsson et al., 2017; Eloundou et al., 2023; Trajtenberg, 2018). In fact, Google's CEO has claimed[1] that its impact is even "more profound than electricity."

Humanity's past and future are inextricably linked to technology, and while, as the most active tinkerers on the planet our technology tend to proceed incrementally, and with stops and starts, waves of breakthrough technologies have been transformative (Auerswald,

* This chapter draws on and updates Naudé (2019b) and Naudé (2021).

[1] See https://bit.ly/2vY3n3Z.

2017; Landes, 1999; Mokyr, 2002, 2016; Pinker, 2018; Ridley, 2011). Think, for example, of the domestication of fire, the wheel, agriculture, cities, the printing press, the microscope, telescopes, the steam engine, the germ theory of disease, electricity, the combustible engine, nuclear science, and the personal computer (PC) – all technologies that were at one stage, novel.

As a novel technology, with the potential to be a GPT, AI may similarly be transformative. It is already ubiquitous – we all interact with AI in one way or another, whether through our smart phones, social media apps, or through our Netflix subscription, or when we do an online search. AI is foundational to the business models of digital platforms (Naudé, 2023b; Sena and Nocker, 2021), increasingly adopted in high-frequency trading on financial markets, in predicting financial risk and exchange rates (Kogan et al., 2009; Yilmaz and Arabaci, 2020) and is becoming indispensable in economic growth and business cycle nowcasting and forecasting (Athey and Imbens, 2019; Basuchoudhary et al., 2017; Cerulli, 2021; Fornaro and Luomaranta, 2020; Yoon, 2020). AI has also been taken up by economists to do algorithmic text analysis– the extraction of data from text – a technique whose use is likely to expand in the near future given progress in Natural Language Processing (NLP), in particular through the development of Large Language Models (LLMs) (Ash and Hansen, 2023; Gentzkow et al., 2019).

The rest of the chapter will proceed as follows. In Section 2.2, we define and describe AI, contrasting contemporary AI, which is based on big data and machine learning (ML) with good-old-fashioned AI (GOFAI). We also make a distinction between narrow AI, artificial general intelligence (AGI) and a superintelligent AI (ASI). Section 2.3 describes the historical evolution of AI, which provides a counterbalancing perspective to the possibly future evolution of AI that is explored in Chapter 9. Section 2.4 asks why are economists interested in AI? Here, we briefly discuss five reasons. Section 2.5 concludes.

2.2 WHAT IS AI?

A good definition of AI is that it is software with *abilities/ capabilities*:

> any software technology with at least one of the following capabilities: perception – including audio, visual, textual, and tactile (e.g., face recognition), decision-making (e.g., medical diagnosis systems), prediction (e.g., weather forecast), automatic knowledge extraction and pattern recognition from data (e.g., discovery of fake news circles in social media), interactive communication (e.g., social robots or chat bots), and logical reasoning (e.g., theory development from premises) (Vinuesa et al., 2020, p. 1).

Why we find this a good definition of AI will transpire from the discussion later and in the rest of the book, particularly Chapter 4 where we provide a mathematical model of AI as software providing abilities and where we illustrate that this is a better way to model AI in economics than to restrict it to performing tasks.

Having defined AI as such however, we would also like to hasten to point out that there is no single or generally accepted definition of AI (Van de Gevel and Noussair, 2013a). One reason is that there is no single definition of intelligence that everyone agrees on.[2] As Max Tegmark reminds us, "There's no agreement on what intelligence is even among intelligent intelligence researchers" (Tegmark, 2017, p. 49). The word "intelligence" is derived from the Latin verb *intellegere* which means "the acquirement, processing and storage of information" (Resing, 2005, p. 307). This seems indeed to be what computers are doing – Is AI therefore the gathering, processing, and storage of information by computers?

[2] It is also the case that some scholars do not consider the term itself accurate; for instance, Herbert Simon preferred the terms "complex information processing" and "simulation of cognitive processes" to the term AI (see Simon, 1996, p. 4).

2.2.1 *Information*

To answer this we need in turn to know what is meant by *information*. Claude Shannon, in his groundbreaking 1948 paper "A Mathematical Theory of Communication," laid the foundations for classical information theory. From these foundations, information can be defined as "a measure of the minimum volume of communication required to unique specify a message" (Hidalgo, 2015, p. 13). Shannon (1948) also introduced the concept of a "bit" as a unit of information, with "bit" being derived from the term binary digit. A bit is either a 0 or a 1. Eight bits equal one *Byte*. Data storage is measured in bytes. A CD-ROM, for example, stores 5 Gigabytes (GB). To store this book digitally requires around 2 Megabytes (MB). Information (strictly, *information entropy*) is the number of binary digits required to encode a message. The content, or *meaning*, of the message is "irrelevant to the engineering problem" (Shannon, 1948, p. 1), which is the maximum transmission rate of particular channel of communication – its "bandwidth."

Information is at the core of complexity on Earth – and its uniqueness. As Hidalgo (2015, p. x) describes it, "... what makes our planet special is not that it is a singularity of matter or energy, but that it is a singularity of physical order, or information. Our planet is to information what a black hole is to matter and what a star is to energy." Wheeler (1989, p. 309) argued that "every physical quantity, every it, derives its ultimate significance from bits, binary yes-or-no indications, a conclusion which we epitomize in the phrase, *it from bit.*"

Seen in this perspective "the acquirement, processing and storage of information" is certainly what computers are doing, but so are humans, and in fact this binds us to the computers and AI systems that we use to help increase our reach over information and complexity – computers and AI are our progeny. However, what we normally ascribe to as human intelligence seems to go beyond acquiring, processing, and storage of information, to include extracting *meaning* from information, and using information to solve problems. Hence intelligence as we understand it goes beyond the Latin meaning of *intellegere*. In fact, we would typically not consider computers that only acquire, process, and store information as necessarily intelligent. For computers to be intelligent, we require that they should like humans be goal oriented, have agency and act so as to successfully achieve their goals. Goal orientation has become central in definitions of intelligence, hence according to Russell (2019, p. 14) "an entity is intelligent to the extent that what it does is likely to achieve what it wants, given what it has perceived." In Chapter 3, we explain how both the fields of AI and Economics have a common approach to model intelligent agents, whether human or artificial, in the expected utility framework (EUT) of decision theory.

2.2.2 *GOFAI*

One definition[3] of AI that is consistent with this human-centric view of intelligence is that AI is simply the "simulation of human intelligence processes by machines, especially computer systems." In the decades after World War II (which was defining in terms of catalysing the research that would lead to the digital revolution – see Section 2.3) until the 1990s, the simulation of human intelligence was pursued through Symbolic AI, what is today known as "Good old fashioned AI" (Boden, 2014). GOFAI entailed attempts to use computational logic – logical rules programmed into a computer – to simulate human intelligence. For example, "Problems are translated into a set of facts and rules, i.e., into a theory or logical program with a particular syntax and semantics [...] the logical models of the program will correspond to the possible solutions of the studied problem" (Amendola, 2023, p. 106).

2.2.3 *Machine Learning*

The technique of ML can be traced back at least to the 1959 paper of Samuel (1959) wherein he proposed a method for a computer to

[3] From https://searchenterpriseai.techtarget.com/definition/AI-Artificial-Intelligence.

learn how to play the game of Checkers. It was however only in the 2000s that dominant approach to simulate human intelligence had shifted to ML. ML leverages statistical algorithms to accomplish[4] "learning (the acquisition of information and the rules for using the information), reasoning (using the rules to reach approximate of definite conclusions) and self-correction." The main aim of ML is to make predictions on some variable *y* using independent *x* variables, labeled "predictors" (Varian, 2014) or "percepts." ML can take place through decision-tree learning, association rule learning, artificial neural networks, deep learning (DL), inductive logic programming, support vector machines, clustering, Bayesian networks, reinforcement learning (RL), representation learning, similarity and metric learning, genetic algorithms, and rule-based ML (Tien, 2017).

As such, the definition of the field of AI by Russell and Norvig (2021, p. vii) as "the study of agents that receive percepts from the environment and perform actions" where "Each such agent implements a function that maps percept sequences to actions" is essentially an AI definition based on ML – although strictly speaking, AI is broader than ML as the discussion on GOFAI implies.[5] In Chapter 3, we discuss in more detail how the function that maps percept sequences to actions are chosen and what role the economics of decision-making plays in this.

Formally, ML refers to the use of algorithms and neural networks "in a narrow domain or application to make and improve predictions by 'learning' from more and more data about a specific domain" (LeCun et al., 2015). ML has been particularly valuable in advancing NLP, a field that emerged in the 1950s and 1960s but

[4] From https://searchenterpriseai.techtarget.com/definition/AI-Artificial-Intelligence.

[5] Gogas and Papadimitriou (2021, p. 1) suggests that it may be useful to keep the role of ML within AI in mind, so as not to forget the distinction. They recommend that "A general rule of thumb is that if the system acts without intervention, then it is probably AI. If the system classifies or forecasts through learning, then it is ML" (p. 1).

made slow progress[6] when it was based on GOFAI, though accelerated to become the leading approach to AI by the 2020s due to ML advances (in DL) and hardware progress (in Graphics Processing Units [GPUs] for parallel data processing) providing it with a probabilistic approach. This allowed NLP to use prediction to achieve dramatic successes in analysing text, speech, and sentiment. This has not been restricted to human language – research using NLP are being used to understand animal communication too – such as of crows and whales, for example (Parshley, 2023). See the discussion later on how advances in NLP enabled LLMs and the most powerful AI systems to date.

There are various ML techniques, including decision trees, RL, DL, where learning takes places in either supervised, semisupervised, or unsupervised manner (LeCun et al., 2015; Sena and Nocker, 2021). DL, the state of the art in ML, "are representation-learning methods with multiple levels of representation, obtained by composing simple but nonlinear modules that each transform the representation at one level (starting with the raw input) into a representation at a higher, slightly more abstract level [. . .] higher layers of representation amplify aspects of the input that are important for discrimination and suppress irrelevant variations" (LeCun et al., 2015, p. 436).

Russell and Norvig (2021) is a widely used ML textbook; Athey and Imbens (2019) and Mullainathan and Spiess (2017) provide useful introductions to ML for economists, and Cerulli (2021) explains how ML can be used to improve econometric prediction. The most popular software packages that economists use to implement ML algorithms include *Python* and *R*. Cerulli (2022) explains how Stata 16 can be used for ML, via the Stata/Python integration platform.

The ML revolution has been enabled by the availability of big data, accelerated increases in computing power, and advances

[6] A milestone in NLP in the 1960s was the chatbot ELIZA developed by Weizenbaum (1966).

in algorithms and neural networks. Each of these enablers – *big data, computing power, algorithms* and *neural networks* – need to be understood in order to appreciate ML, and perhaps its biggest achievement to date, the development of LLMs which underpins *Generative AI* (GenAI). We discuss these later in this chapter.

2.2.3.1 *Big Data*

Big data refers to the "explosion in the quantity (and sometimes, quality) of available and potentially relevant data, largely the result of recent and unprecedented advancements in data recording and storage technology" (Diebold (2012), cited in Favaretto et al. (2020, p. 1)). Kitchin and McArdle (2016) discuss several traits and characteristics that have been ascribed to big data, such as that it has (enormous) volume, (rapid) velocity, (great) variety, and (huge potential) value but subject to variability and challenges to its veracity.

Varian (2014) discusses the implications of big data for econometrics. He notes that conventional econometric techniques are often inadequate to analyze big data – data that requires storage in external databases and that goes beyond storage in a single Excel spreadsheet as econometricians typically do.

Big data requires ML to yield information but also enables ML algorithms by providing the data on which it is trained, making big data especially valuable to companies whose business models depend on using ML. In 2017, *The Economist Magazine*[7] claimed that "the world's most valuable resource is no longer oil, but data." In the data-driven economy, larger firms have an advantage, and the distribution of firm sizes may become more skew over time (Farboodi et al., 2019). These larger firms, operating globally, may also misuse data through their dominant positions. For example, in 2018, Facebook faced an avalanche of criticisms about the way it exploited the data of its hundreds of millions of users and allowed these data

[7] See: https://econ.st/2Gtfztg.

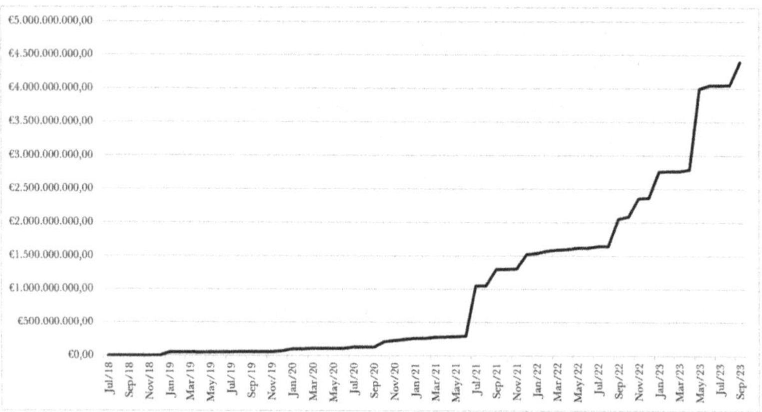

FIGURE 2.1 Cumulative fines for violations of the GDPR, 2018–2023
Source: GDPR Enforcement Tracker at www.enforcementtracker.com/.

to be exploited, including for political purposes in the notorious *Cambridge Analytica Scandal*.[8]

Chapter 9 delves deeper into big data and its relationship with AI from an economics perspective. This perspective has stressed that shortcomings in big data can hinder the diffusion of AI. Small businesses for instance, tend not to have the computing resources to run AI systems (Vipra and West, 2023) nor to obtain big data, also since the data tend to be unstructured, gathered in silos, and increasingly subject to data regulations and fines. Figure 2.1 shows, for instance, the steep rise in the cumulative sum of fines (in Euro) for violations of the EU's General Data Protection Regulation (GDPR) between July 2018 and September 2023.

2.2.3.2 *Computing Power*

Computing power ("compute") in a broad sense refers to the ability of software and hardware computer systems (such as computer chips, data management software, and cables and servers) and is measured in floating point operations (FLOP) (amount of compute) and FLOP per second (FLOP/s) (performance) (Vipra and West, 2023). A related

[8] See: https://en.wikipedia.org/wiki/Facebook-Cambridge_Analytica_data_scandal.

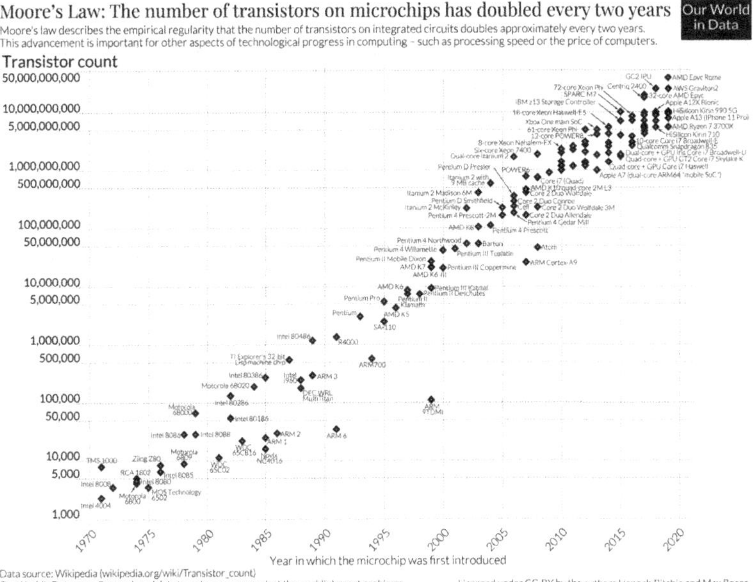

FIGURE 2.2 Moore's law
Source: Our World in Data.

measure of computing power is the number of transistors on a computer chip. Moore (1965) pointed out that these double roughly every two years, a relationship that has come to be known as Moore's Law. Roser et al. (2023) – see also Figure 2.2 – concluded that Moore's Law has held for the past fifty years.

The amount and performance have significantly improved over time to allow big data to be gathered, for instance, through the Internet, the Internet-of-Things, connected sensors, and mobile devices (e.g., smartphones), and to be analyzed. Big data is indeed often considered to be "big" when it requires substantial computing power – information processing – to be analyzed (Gandomi and Haider, 2015). This is where ML algorithms are essential, since it can work on "unconventional data that is too high-dimensional for standard estimation methods, including image and language information that we conventionally had not even thought of as data we can work with, let alone include in a regression" (Mullainathan and Spiess, 2017, p. 99).

However, the larger the database and the tasks required from AI systems, the more compute is necessary to train ML algorithms. Sevilla et al. (2022) document the growth in compute used to train AI systems, distinguishing three eras of compute in ML, namely, the Pre-DL Era, the DL Era, and the Large-Scale Era. They found that during the Pre-DL Era (before 2010), the amount of compute used to train AI systems doubled approximately every twenty months (similar to Moore's Law) but then accelerated to doubling every six months after 2015. In 2018, Google trained AlphaGo Zero, its game (Go) playing algorithm, using over 1,000 petaflop/s[9] a day. This was 300,000 times more compute used than in 2012.[10] It is not known what amount of compute was used to train one of the current largest AI systems, the Generative Pretrained Transformer (GPT) GPT-4 LLM of OpenAI, released in 2023, but its predecessor (GPT-3.5) is reported to have used around 10^{23} FLOP/s (Sevilla et al., 2022) and 45 terabytes of text data – roughly 300 billion words (Ferrari et al., 2023). GPT-4 has $\approx$ 1.8 trillion parameters and the compute cost around US$ 63 million (Schreiner, 2023).

Advances in compute has led to supercomputers that can nowadays perform around 10^{17} FLOP/s.[11] It has been estimated that to replicate the human brain, a computer would need to perform between 10^{12} and 10^{28} FLOP/s.[12] The brain does this using around 15 to 25 MW of power (Martins et al., 2019) which is around 1 million times less than the amount required to run a supercomputer.

It is not only that computing power increased through the number of transistors on a computer chip. It has also improved through becoming ubiquitous and pervasive. Weiser (1991, p. 66) described ubiquitous computing as the integration of computing into everyday life – stating that "The most profound technologies are those

[9] A petaflop/s-day (pfs-day) entails performing 10^{15} neural net operations per second for one day.

[10] See: https://blog.openai.com/ai-and-compute/.

[11] Source: See https://webhome.phy.duke.edu/~hsg/414/images/brain-vs-computer.html.

[12] Source: See https://aiimpacts.org/brain-performance-in-flops/#easy-footnote-2-596.

that disappear. They weave themselves into the fabric of everyday life until they are indistinguishable from it." Ubiquitous computing is facilitating Ambient Intelligence (AmI), when "people in an AmI environment will not notice these devices, but will benefit from the services these solutions provide them. Such devices are aware of the people present in those environments by reacting to their gestures, actions, and context" (Espinilla et al., 2019, p. 4034).

Much of the data storage and computing based on it takes place in the "cloud." The "cloud" refers to "cloud computing, an information technology (IT) paradigm and a model for enabling ubiquitous access to shared pools of configurable resources (such as computer networks, servers, storage, applications, and services), that can be rapidly provisioned with minimal management effort, often over the Internet [...] the cloud facilitates rapid data access, provides redundancy, and optimizes the global usage of processing and storage resources while enabling access from virtually any location on the planet" (Martins et al., 2019, p. 3). The availability in the cloud of free open-source libraries for supporting ML, such as GitHub, TensorFlow and PyTorch significantly facilitated the use of ML (Gogas and Papadimitriou, 2021).

Increasingly, access to computing power determines who will gain in the digital economy. Vipra and West (2023) note from an Andreessen Horowitz report that leading AI firms spend up to 80 percent of their capital investment in computing power. Scarcity in compute – including in vitally important GPUs – is already an important factor influencing the business models and strategies of the industry and of countries.

2.2.3.3 *Algorithms and Artificial Neural Networks*

An algorithm is "a sequence of rules that should be performed in an exact order to carry out a certain task" (OECD, 2017, p. 8). ML has given rise to an "algorithm modeling culture," because central to ML is the development of algorithms "to make predictions about some variables given others or to classify units on the basis of limited information, for example, to classify handwritten digits on the basis of pixel values" (Athey and Imbens, 2019, p. 688).

This algorithmic definition of AI (ML) highlights that the essential use, and strength, of algorithms is that they enable big data to be used to generate predictions and to recognise patterns. Prediction and pattern recognition is essentially what modern AI consists of. For example, AI now dominate in games like Chess and Go (the AI model AlphaGo defeated the Go grand-master in 2016) because it can better predict which move is likely to be successful at a given moment, given the moves that have so far been made, and the moves it has learned from all historical games in its database. Since around 2016 AI systems have exceeded human ability in image recognition.

Artificial neural networks (ANN) are "aggregates of machine learning algorithms that work together to solve more complex problems and mimic the behaviour of neurons in a human brain" (Sena and Nocker, 2021, p. 6). Note here that the term "neuron" in ML would for an economist[13] be another term for "variable" (Mullainathan and Spiess, 2017).

In Section 3.2.2, we briefly discuss the Multilayer Perceptron (MLP), an ANN which is a supervised learning algorithm consisting of various layers of perceptrons, where a perceptron is a program that tries to mimic a biological neuron to perform binary classifications. This is a widely used ANN used to perform classifications (say classifying images or text) (Rosenblatt, 1958; Schmidhuber, 2015). Deep convolutional neural networks (CNNs) is a specific class of ANNs used for image classification (Pattanayak and Krishnamurthy, 2021).

DL, using ANNs and CNNs to perform classifications, has found wide use in *Recommender Systems*, such as is used to suggest what movies or songs subscribers on Netflix or Spotify may want to watch, or what consumers on Amazon or other platforms may want to buy (Ricci et al., 2022).

[13] At a first introduction to ML, economists tend to get confused by the different terminology that data scientists use for familiar concepts. See for instance the discussion in Athey and Imbens (2019).

2.2.4 *Generative AI and Large Language Models*

Generative AI (*GenAI*) "refers to a type of artificial intelligence (AI) that can generate text, images, audio, code, videos, and synthetic data" (Kanbach et al., 2023, p. 2). This content can be generated from training data, and can seem to be meaningful (Feuerriegel et al., 2023).

GenAI applications typically create images, video, and voice from text inputs[14] (examples are *DALL-E2*[15] for image and *VALL-E*[16] for voice generation) or generate text or computer code from text prompts (examples are the chatbot *ChatGPT*[17] and the code generator Codex[18]). The former is at the time of writing largely based on Diffusion Models (DMs)[19] and the latter on LLMs which are enabled by Transformer architecture, the "modern wave of machine learning" (Feuerriegel et al., 2023; Warfield, 2023).

GenAI models such as those based on DMs and LLMs are labeled "foundational models" to signify that these are "trained on broad data (generally using self-supervision at scale) that can be adapted (e.g., fine-tuned) to a wide range of downstream tasks" (Bommasani et al., 2022, p. 1).

At the time of writing, one of the most popular LLMs was GPT-4, which drives the chatbot *ChatGPT*, the latest version at the time of writing released in March 2023 by *OpenAI*. The leading LLMs available circa end of 2023 is summarized in Table 2.1.[20] This table, as well as the discussion in this subsection, is likely to be dated soon, because "The computer science behind generative AI is moving so

[14] Although at the time of writing, several LLMs have become multimodal, that is, they can be prompted not only by text but also by voice and images (Bushwick and Leffer, 2023).

[15] See https://openai.com/dall-e-2.

[16] See https://vall-e.pro/.

[17] See https://chat.openai.com/auth/login.

[18] See https://openai.com/blog/openai-codex.

[19] For a survey of diffusion models, see Yang et al. (2022).

[20] An evaluation of the most widely used LLMs in 2023 is provided by Humphries et al. (2023) who describe Bard as "the playful one," Claude as "the witty one," and ChatGPT as the "popular one."

Table 2.1 *Leading LLMs at the time of writing*

Product	Model	Company
ChatGPT	GPT-3.5	OpenAI
New Bing	GPT-4	Microsoft
ChatGPT+	GPT-4	OpenAI
Bard	PaLM-2	Google
Claude	Claude 2	Anthropic
LlaMA	LlaMA 2	Meta
BLOOM	GPT-3 w/extras	HuggingFace and others
Ernie Bot	Ernie 3.0-Titan	Baidu

Source: Authors' compilation based on Korinek (2023, p. 10).

fast that innovations emerge every month" (Stokel-Walker and Van Noorden, 2023, p. 216).

LLMs are according to Korinek (2023) the type of generative AI that is most useful to economists. He concludes his survey of LLMs stating that "LLMs have become useful research tools for tasks ranging from ideation and feedback, writing and background research to data analysis, coding, and mathematical derivations. Cognitive automation via LLMs is already making researchers significantly more productive" (p. 45).

The fairly rapid development and lighting fast diffusion[21] of LLMs has lead to an intense debate about the possible downsides and threats to this technology, from those who fear it may be becoming an AGI (see Section 2.2.5) to those who fear it poses an existential risk (we discuss this in more detail in Chapter 10) to those who have identified several immediate issues of concern, such as that it may return artificial hallucinations,[22] encourage software piracy, and commit plagiarism (Stokel-Walker and Van Noorden, 2023). The

[21] Within five days of its launch, ChatGPT 3.5 had one million users, see https://explodingtopics.com/.blog/chatgpt-users.

[22] Artificial hallucinations "refer to instances where an AI chatbot generates fictional, erroneous, or unsubstantiated information in response to queries" (Kumar et al., 2023, p. 1). See also Alkaissi and McFarlane (2023). Østergaard and Nielbo (2023,

relatively large carbon footprint of training and diffusing LLMs has also been raised as a concern (Schwartz et al., 2020), and as with most technologies since the Industrial Revolution, the potential for LLMs to lead to job losses have been warned against. According to Eloundou et al. (2023, p. 1) "around 80% of the U.S. workforce could have at least 10% of their work tasks affected by the introduction of LLMs, while approximately 19% of workers may see at least 50% of their tasks impacted" (Eloundou et al., 2023).

A full discussion of these concerns falls outside the scope of this chapter. In chapter 8, where we take up the challenge of how to direct AI innovation and diffusion so as to reduce the negative consequences of AI and enhance its positive contributions, we will return to the more general concerns about "Awful AI." For now however, we can note that LLMs have, because they are trained on such huge amounts of text and image data, much of it sourced from the public domain, lead to concerns of "public infrastructures ending up as proprietary assets in the hands of private companies ..." because "Authors of texts and copyright holders whose content becomes training data for the chatbot are unaware that their work is being transformed into the core component of a proprietary product" (Ferrari et al., 2023, p. 819).

2.2.5 *AGI, Artificial Superintelligence, and Strong AI*

ML-based AI as in circa 2023 is often labeled "narrow," to distinguish it from AGI (Naudé, 2021). Thus, narrow AI can be defined as the training of algorithms (and aggregates thereof – neural networks) on big data, with the aim of leveraging the predictive and pattern recognition abilities of such trained and learning algorithms, to enable certain very specific functions or applications.

In Chapter 4, this definition will be given mathematical expression, where we provide a partial equilibrium model wherein AI

p. 1) find the term "hallucinations" inappropriate in this context, arguing that it is a "stigmatizing metaphor."

Table 2.2 *Examples of narrow applications of AI abilities*

Ability	Applications
Computer vision	Autonomous vehicles
	Medical diagnostics
	Surveillance/security
Language processing	Telecommunications
	Entertainment
Speech recognition	Speech to text
	Voice biometrics
Business intelligence	Marketing
	Forecasting
Design	Prototyping
	Autonomous innovation

Source: Authors' own compilation.

provides abilities that are combined with human skills (such as IT and entrepreneurship skills) to enable domain-specific applications. This is based on the recognition that AI essentially provides abilities (Hernández-Orallo, 2017; Tolan et al., 2020) that do not automatically turn into useful products and services. In Table 2.2, the relation between AI abilities and narrow AI applications, and examples of the latter, is given.

A study by the WIPO (2019) confirms the narrow focus of AI also in terms of where the research and development (R&D) into AI going: Most is going, not into developing AGI, but into developing a few applications as indicated in Table 2.2 – in particular computer vision. Moreover, only a few countries are responsible for virtually the entire AI-boom since 2006: 93 percent of venture capital for AI accrued to firms in only three countries/regions: the USA, China, and the EU (WIPO, 2019). And within these countries, a few very large high-tech companies dominate: In 2017 five high-tech digital-based companies, namely, Amazon, Alphabet (Google), Microsoft, Apple, and Facebook (now Meta), spend US$ 73 billion on R&D – almost twice as much as the entire R&D of the United Kingdom.

Given its narrow focus, AI therefore is not yet comparable to human intelligence – indeed its operation and (domain-specific) applications depend on human intelligence. It does not possess the general intelligence of humans. The term *general intelligence*, sometimes also referred to as general cognitive capacity – refers to the ability of agents to transfer their learning from one domain to another. As Dubey et al. (2018, p. 1) explain, AI applications "attack each problem tabula rasa, whereas humans come in with a wealth of prior knowledge about the world, from physics to semantics to affordances."

Thus, there is no AGI or superintelligence yet. Whether and when an AGI will be invented, and whether and how it could lead to a self-improving, superintelligence orders of magnitude more intelligent than humans, are open questions, which are explored in more depth in Chapter 10.

The development of Transformer Architecture, on which LLMs such as GPT-4 – released in March 2023 – is based, has however raised concern (and hope) in many circles that AI is getting closer to being an AGI. This has reignited the debate on how one can evaluate just how intelligent and AI system has become and has also (re)fuelled speculation whether or not an AI system can ever become conscious. We mention *re-fuelled*, as already in 1980, John Searle put forward the *Chinese Room Argument* to argue that a digital computer cannot possess consciousness, notwithstanding how intelligent it is judged to be (Searle, 1980). Thus, an AGI or superintelligence would not necessarily possess consciousness, however intelligent it may be.

The question of how intelligent an AI system is, inspired Alan Turing in 1950 (see Turing, 1950) to devise the *imitation game*, also known as the Turing Test, to determine "whether a machine can think." Turing's test was passed by chatbots at least around 2014 (Eisenstein, 2023; Warwick and Shah, 2016). By mid-2023, computer scientists concluded that also "GPT-4 another LLMs would probably now pass the Turing test" (Biever, 2023, p. 687). Biever (2023, p. 687) reported that OpenAI tested GPT-4's abilities "on a series of benchmarks designed for machines, including reading comprehension, mathematics and coding" and that "GPT-4 aced most of them." And Gurnee and Tegmark (2023, p. 1) found evidence that LLMs do not only seem to learn only loose facts, but rather learn a "coherent model of the data generating process – a world model." According to Bubeck et al. (2023, p. 1), who subjected GPT-4 to various tests,

> beyond its mastery of language, GPT-4 can solve novel and difficult tasks that span mathematics, coding, vision, medicine, law, psychology and more, without needing any special prompting. Moreover, in all of these tasks, GPT-4's performance is strikingly close to human-level performance, and often vastly surpasses prior models such as ChatGPT. Given the breadth and depth of GPT-4's capabilities, we believe that it could reasonably be viewed as an early (yet still incomplete) version of an artificial general intelligence (AGI) system.

The question has also been asked, whether given that it may be an early and incomplete version of an AGI system, GPT-4 may be a "strong AI," that is to say an AI that is conscious (Russell and Norvig, 2021), with consciousness meaning subjective experience. This question was raised by the comments of the chief scientist at OpenAI who tweeted[23] that "it may be that today's large neural networks are slightly conscious" (Lenharo, 2023b). Butlin et al. (2023, p. 1) investigated this question, as they put it, "in light of our best-supported neuroscientific theories of consciousness," concluding that by 2023 no AI system was conscious (yet).

Their set of multiple indicators used to assess whether an AI system is conscious provides a useful starting point for further research into understanding this complex issue. Consciousness poses a "hard problem" (Chalmers, 1995) – one that has generated

[23] See https://twitter.com/ilyasut/status/1491554478243258368?lang=en.

several theories but no consensus, or definitive results, yet. In 1998, neuroscientist Christof Koch bet the philosopher David Chalmers that by 2023 science would understand how the brain generates self-awareness. He lost the bet (Lenharo, 2023a).

2.3 THE RISE AND FALL AND RISE OF AI

In Section 2.2, the concept of AI was defined and unpacked, and a brief overview given of the main features of AI systems, for purposes of this book. In this section, we provide a concise overview of some of the historical milestones in the development of AI.

2.3.1 *Three Features of AI Progress*

The historical perspective in this section is far from an exhaustive overview – in chapter 1 of their handbook on AI, Russell and Norvig (2021, pp. 35–48) provide a more in-depth history of AI. For present purposes though, we want to refer to the history of AI to highlight three crucial features of AI progress that our subsequent analyses will keep in mind.

One is that it is no easy task to steer or direct the evolution of a technology such as AI – the AI technologies that we have circa 2023 are as much the result of an unforeseen convergence between scientific, technical, societal, and economic trends rather than of some particular foresight or centrally steered mission. As Ridley (2015) puts it, "Innovation is a mysteriously difficult thing to dictate. Technology seems to change by a sort of inexorable, evolutionary progress, which we probably cannot stop–or speed up much either [. . .] Increasingly, technology is developing the kind of autonomy that hitherto characterized biological entities." In Chapter 10, this perspective will be useful to keep in mind when we discuss the possible future trajectories of AI.

A second feature of AI that we want to highlight through a short historical overview is that AI is ultimately a product and that the initiatives, discussions, and fears about AI could usefully be understood as the challenges that profit-seeking firms face in investing in developing and commercializing their product. As Dai (2023) puts it, leading AI firms such as OpenAI may be "trying to conduct research, push the technical envelope, and possibly even build superintelligence, but they're undeniably also building products – products that carry liability, products that need to sell, products that need to be designed such that they claim and maintain market share." In Chapter 6, we focus on modeling and understanding the decision to invest in R&D toward building ever-better AI, and in Chapters 7 and 8, we model how using incentives, AI innovation, and diffusion may be influenced, even if its direction cannot be micromanaged.

The third feature of AI that our historical overview highlights is that AI progress has been very uneven and unpredictable, characterized by AI Winters – periods when investment and R&D in AI dried up. Therefore, despite the excitement that advances in LLMs between roughly 2017 and 2023 generated, one should keep in mind that the current boom in AI may rather abruptly, as in the past, run out of steam. One cause could be that technological progress in the hard-and-software essential to modern, ML-based AI, slows down. Both Moore's Law and DL have been argued to be facing diminishing returns, or "hitting the wall" (Marcus, 2022; Waldrop, 2016). Another cause could be overregulation: in March 2023, several scientists, philosophers, and investors published an open letter calling on a pause in further development of LLMs which between March and October 2023 were signed by more than 33,000 persons.[24] Recent years have indeed seen a barrage of AI and AI-related regulation (see also Figure 2.1 in this regard), as well as growing public distrust of AI, the extreme form that even has its own label, "AI-Doomerism" (Wong, 2023).

2.3.2 *A Very Brief History of AI*[25]

Modern AI is the direct outcome of the digital and computer revolution that emerged during and after World War II. Figure 2.3

[24] See https://futureoflife.org/open-letter/pause-giant-ai-experiments/.

[25] This section draws on, updates, and extends Naudé (2019b) and Naudé (2023a).

Commercialization of War Tech			Internet	PC and WWW		Connectivity
1940–1948	1948	1956	1960s	1970–1990s	1980s	2000s
The Bombe	1948: The Bit	1956: Dartmouth Conference	1966: ARPANET project	1974 : First Pizza ordered online	1984 : Apple Mac Launched	2007: What the Hell Happened?

FIGURE 2.3 The digital revolution and the rise of AI
Source: Authors' compilation.

summarizes the milestones in this revolution. It shows that between 1940 and the present, there were four phases of digital technology development. The first was the commercialization of war technologies, the second the development of the Internet, the third the creation of the PC and World Wide Web (WWW), and the fourth the revolution in connectivity of which the rise of LLMs – an "innovative form of social collaboration" (Larnier, 2023) is the high point.

Although we start our historical timeline in Figure 2.3 in 1940, this does not mean there was no interest in computers and AI – of course differently termed – before then. As Naudé (2019a, 2021) discusses, an analog computer, the Antikythera Mechanism, was used for navigational purposes in Greece around 87 BC, Leonardo Da Vinci proposed a mechanical knight around 1495, and Samuel Butler's 1863 essay *Darwin among the Machines* foreshadowed AI Doomerism by more than a century.[26] The term "robot" – the main form of automation before AI software became widespread in the 2010s – was coined by Karel Čapek in his 1920 play *Rossums Universal Robots* – where, anticipating and inspiring modern-day AI Doomerism, the robots revolt and exterminate all humans. Hudson et al. (2023, p. 197) have correctly pointed out that "Perhaps more than any other technology, artificial intelligence has been entangled with science fiction and mythologies of technology from the beginning."

[26] In 1863, Samuel Butler sounded almost like Eliezer Yudkowsky in 2023 when he wrote "the machines are gaining ground upon us; day by day we are becoming more subservient to them [...] that the time will come when the machines will hold the real supremacy over the world and its inhabitants is what no person of a truly philosophic mind can for a moment question."

More important than these pre–World War II apocalyptic visions of AI were the ideas of Charles Babbage and Ada Lovelace (Hammerman and Russell, 2015). Babbage conceived of what can perhaps be seen as the first idea for a general-purpose computer powered by steam energy, the Analytical Engine, in the 1830s, and Lovelace contributed to this by writing in 1843 what has been described as the first computer program (Aiello, 2016; Hollings et al., 2018).

As Figure 2.3 shows, it was however only during World War II that real progress was made in computing. Unlike the steam energy that Babbage envisaged to power his Analytical Engine (which was never operationalized) by the time of World War II, electricity from fossil fuels was able to provide a much more reliable and effective source of energy to enable the modern Information and Communication Technology (ICT) revolution to takeoff. AI is energy intensive and its carbon emissions are nontrivial. For example, it has been estimated that training GPT-4 required up to 62,318,750 kWh of electricity and generated 14,994 metric tons of carbon dioxide emissions (Ludvigsen, 2023). Data centers already use more than 200 terawatt hours (TWh) each year and are expected to make up around 21 percent of energy demand by 2030 (Jones, 2018). de Vries (2023) discusses the possible future growth in energy demand from increased diffusion of LLMs, concluding (p. 4) that "While the exact future of AI-related electricity consumption remains difficult to predict, the scenarios discussed in this commentary underscore the importance of tempering both overly optimistic and overly pessimistic expectations."

What catalyzed progress during World War II was the need to break the code of the Enigma Machine, a cipher device, used by Nazi forces to encrypt their communications. Alan Turing and colleagues at Bletchley Park in the UK managed to do this by building one of the world's first computers, known as the "*Bombe*" (Davies, 1999). Turing led this effort as he had, already before the War, in 1936, explaining that a general-purpose computer, a "Universal Computing Machine" (also known as the Turing Machine), is possible (Turing,

1936). His 1936 paper has been claimed[27] to be "undoubtedly the most famous theoretical paper in the history of computing."

In 1948, the second great scientific paper that further catalyzed the ICT revolution was published. This was Claude Shannon's "mathematical theory of communication," which provided the foundations for modern information theory and conceptualized the "bit" as a unit of information (Shannon, 1948). "Bit" comes from the term "binary digit." Soon afterward, in 1950, Alan Turing published another hugely influential paper, "Computing Machinery and Intelligence" wherein he suggested that the development of "thinking machines" should start by trying to develop computers that can play chess and speak English (Turing, 1950).

All these developments before, during, and after World War II culminated in 1956 in a conference held at Dartmouth College in the USA, where the term artificial intelligence was adopted (Moor, 2006) as the overarching label to describe the emerging field of computer science, statistics, and information theory that was aiming to develop "intelligent problem-solving machines" (Minsky, 1961).

The Dartmouth College conference, which gave birth to the term AI, took place, as Figure 2.3 indicates, during the post–World War II decades when much commercialization of war technologies and their progeny's took place, primarily driven by the US government. The role of the US government during this time is often cited as an argument for mission-driven industrial policies (Mazzucato, 2015) to direct or steer innovation. Indeed, many initiatives undertaken by the US government during and after World War II had far-reaching consequences; whether these were the outcomes that the US government envisaged or steered toward is debatable.

The US government's steering of innovation started during World War II, with the creation of the National Defense Research Committee (NDRC) in 1940. These efforts resulted in many

[27] See www.historyofinformation.com/detail.php?id=619.

impactful new technologies[28] and their diffusion during and after the war, including radar, mass-produced penicillin, radio communications, and pesticides such as Dichlorodiphenyltrichloroethane (DDT) (Gross and Sampat, 2020).

After World War II, for present purposes, the two most notable government incentives were the creation of the Internet through the USA DARPA program and the creation of Google's search engine algorithm by a government grant (Lenderink et al., 2019). DARPA is the acronym for the USA's Department of Defense's "Defense Advanced Research Projects Agency," which was launched in 1958 and created the ARPANET (Advanced Research Projects Agency Network) in 1966 (Azoulay et al., 2018a). ARPANET was an initiative to decentralize the US information systems so that they would be less vulnerable in the case of a nuclear attack during the Cold War. This was the birth of the Internet (Navarria, 2016) and would later provide the data and cloud computing essential for the operationalization of AI. In 1974, the first pizza was ordered online (Finley, 2015). In Chapters 8 and 9 respectively, we will discuss, with reference to the EU's public procurement for innovation instruments, whether and how the government can steer AI safety and big data from the demand side.

The commercialization in the 1980s and 1990s would lead to the WWW in 1989, which benefited hugely from the increased availability of the PCs – in 1984, the Apple Mac was launched, a pivotal date in the history of the PC. Despite these advances, which would actually prove beneficial only later on, the 1970s and 1980s saw an AI Winter, when investment and research into AI waned (Floridi, 2020). In Chapter 6, we discuss how AI Winters, followed by AI Boom times, create opportunities for breakthroughs and backlashes, wherein backlashes follow generally as a result of the failure of scientists to come up with a viable technology. Chapter 6 is a contribution

[28] An overview of the specific role of government procurement in the establishment of the computer industry, the semi-conductor industry, and the US commercial aircraft industry is contained in Geroski (1990).

to this rather neglected aspect of the innovation and investment dynamics that have been characterizing the history of AI.

Advances in PCs, the rise of mobile computing through the spread of mobile phones, and increased Internet penetration and the availability of cloud computing, together with exponential declines in the cost of computing and exponential improvements in computing power (see Section 2.3.1) converged around 2007 to result in a connectivity revolution – which soon afterward triggered a boom in ML. This convergence is described by Friedman (2016), who posed the question, *"What the Hell Happened in 2007?"* and answered that roughly around 2007, we saw several complementary initiatives coming together and synergizing each other, such as the launch of the Apple iPhone in January 2007, the spread of Facebook, the launch by Google of its *Android* and the takeover of *YouTube*, and the start of *GitHub* and *Amazon Web Services* (AWS) – among others.

As Liu et al. (2017) discuss, the AI Winter ended after around 2007 with breakthroughs in the technique of ML – specifically DL by Hinton and Salakhutdinov (2006) and Hinton et al. (2006). Within a few years, a whole new industrial revolution, the Fourth Industrial Revolution (4IR), was proclaimed (Schwab, 2016). These converging ICT developments that are closely associated with the 4IR are discussed by, among others, Brynjolfsson et al. (2017), Friedman (2016), McAfee and Brynjolfsson (2017), and Tegmark (2017).

Figure 2.4 summarizes the development of "modern" ML-based AI since the end of the AI Winter from 2006 to 2018, when the first GPT was launched.

Figure 2.4 shows the fast progress that has been made since the DL breakthroughs of 2006 and the connectivity convergence in 2007. In 2009, ImageNet was launched, which made millions of images available on the WWW to be used to train DL models on. By 2009, Google started to use this technology to develop autonomous vehicles, in 2010, Apple launched its Siri digital assistant based on NLP, and by 2016, AI had beaten humans at games such as Chess and Go, and became better than humans at image recognition. 2017 was a

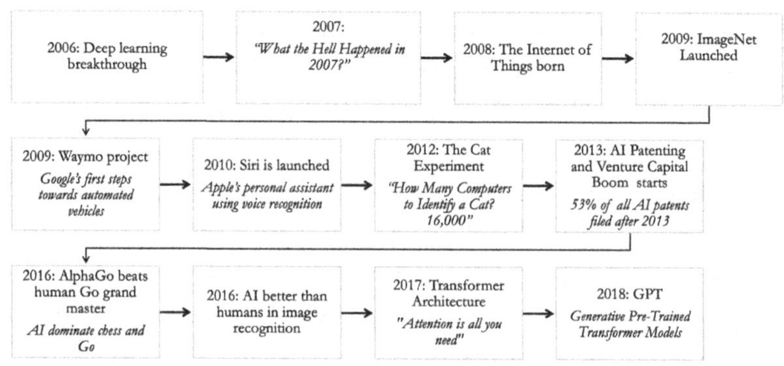

FIGURE 2.4 Selected AI timeline, 2006–2023
Source: Authors' compilation.

milestone year, which saw the publication by Vaswani et al. (2017) of their paper "Attention is All You Need," which introduced the Transformer Architecture for NLP on which subsequent LLMs are based.

It is worth repeating at this stage that AI is not yet comparable to human intelligence. AI depends on the veracity and velocity of data and the data-streaming technology and bandwidth to make good predictions and to learn. And here, the word learn should not be equated with how humans learn. Brooks (2017) correctly emphasized that "machine learning is very brittle, and it requires lots of preparation by human researchers or engineers, special-purpose coding, special-purpose sets of training data, and a custom learning structure for each new problem domain." Moreover, as far as AI and its most successful tool, DL, is concerned, it is the case that "a comprehensive [mathematical] theoretical foundation is completely lacking," which hinders finding solutions to many of the lack of robustness problems that DL still has to deal with, including "a highly delicate trial-and-error-based (training) process" and failures "when a small perturbation of the input data causes a drastic change of the output leading to radically different – and often wrong – decisions" (Kutyniok, 2022, p. 2).

2.4 WHY ARE ECONOMISTS INTERESTED IN AI?

In Chapter 1 (Section 1.2), we argued that an economics of AI is needed to help inform policy and business decisions that will improve the benefits and reduce the risks from AI systems. Given that AI systems already have substantial impacts on many facets of the economy, and are predicted as a GPT to have even more far-reaching implications, this makes AI of great interest to economists. But there are also other reasons why economists are interested in AI, from the philosophical (is AI the perfect *homo economicus*?) to the global (will AI exacerbate global disparities?).

In this section, we will explore this interest in finer detail and discuss five main reasons of interest: AI as a "new tool" in the toolbox of the theoretical and applied economist (Section 2.4.1); AI as a new technological shock to labor and educational markets (Section 2.4.2); AI as an innovation in the method of innovation (IMI) (Section 2.4.3); AI as a driver of inequality within and between countries (Section 2.4.4); and AI's potential contributions and threats to developing and emerging economies (Section 2.4.5).

2.4.1 A New Tool in the Toolbox

Can AI be a game changer for economics? In Chapter 3, we argue that AI may be an indispensable tool to help economics to model human decision-making better. We conclude that there are several areas where economists may learn from AI scientists. One such area we discuss is procedural rationality. Economic theory tends to ignore the reasoning process by which agents make rational decisions, that is, how agents find the optimum of their expected utility functions (Dixon, 2001). Economics has preferred *substantive rationality* over *procedural rationality* (Simon, 1978). It amounts to an approach where "what decisions are made is more important than how they are made" (Harré, 2021, p. 12).

This is of potential importance for economists because, as Dixon (2001) has pointed out, human decision-making is prone to mistakes – even beyond those due to being bounded by computational ability. Thus, Dixon (2001) suggests that "the role for artificial intelligence in economics would then seem primarily to be in situations where economic agents make mistakes, and possibly bad mistakes."

Economics could also benefit from AI research in the sub-field of RL, which may reduce the computational difficulties economists typically face to understand reasoning under bounded rationality (Charpentier et al., 2021). AI models could also help to model human behavior in disequilibrium situations (Dixon, 2001). One may also interpret nonrational quirks in human judgment as the result of AI learning techniques (e.g., DL or RL) that are "inappropriately applied" (Camerer, 2019).

Thus, AI is a potentially useful new tool to strengthen the theoretical and philosophical foundations of economics by modeling decision-making. It is also a potentially useful new tool to strengthen the applied methods that economists use in empirical research – to test theories, to make predictions, and to describe economic outcomes. The applications of AI models in these areas are rapidly expanding. Knowledge of at least the basics of ML has become necessary for all economists. Doing justice to why and how applied economists can use AI in their empirical work requires a book all of its own; hence in this book, we will not go about detail into this. We can mention and recommend however some of the emerging applications and examples of AI by economists, such as for predicting financial risk and exchange rates (Kogan et al., 2009; Yilmaz and Arabaci, 2020), forecasting economic growth and business cycles, and nowcasting GDP (Athey and Imbens, 2019; Basuchoudhary et al., 2017; Cerulli, 2021; Fornaro and Luomaranta, 2020; Yoon, 2020).

Two techniques that are still quite novel at the time of writing are *algorithmic text analysis* – the extraction of data from text (Ash and Hansen, 2023) – and *panel neural networks* (Parret, 2020). In the light of advances in LLMs as discussed in this chapter, and the predominance of panel data econometrics in economic research, we expect that the use of these techniques by economists will expand in the near future.

2.4.2 *Impact on Jobs and Education*

One of the main areas where economists have been interested in AI has been on its impact on labor markets and education. AI has become a leading automation technology – much like the power loom during the Industrial Revolution or industrial robots during the last half of the twenty-first century. There is therefore a long tradition in economics in dealing with the impact of technological innovations on labor markets.

The main theoretical approach to this has been through the theory of skill-biased technological change (SBTC). In SBTC, technological change can either substitute for, or complement, various types of labor. This can result in changes in demand, and hence wages, for certain types of labor, hence altering the distribution of wages. During the First Industrial Revolution, the new technologies of the time such as the steam engine and power loom complemented low-skilled labor and substituted for more skilled artisans. The result was a higher demand for low-skilled labor and a decline in wage inequality, as the wages for lower-skilled labor rose. Since the ICT revolution began (around the 1970s), technological change has been biased in favor of higher-skilled labor, thus raising the demand and wages of more highly skilled labor and even replacing lower-skilled jobs. See, for example, Acemoglu (2002), Autor et al. (1999), Card and DiNardo (2002), and Goldin and Katz (2010).

The possibility that SBTC can lead to higher unemployment – and inequality – was emphasized in the years following the global financial crisis by Brynjolfsson and McAfee (2012), Brynjolfsson and McAfee (2015), and Ford (2016) and by the publication in 2013 of very specific predictions of how much job losses automation will cause. In this regard, Frey and Osborne (2013) (also in Frey and Osborne, 2017) estimated that 47 percent of USA jobs could be automated in 10–20 years. Bowles (2017) estimated this at 54 percent for the EU and the

World Bank (2016) predicted up to 66 percent in developing countries. More recently, with the development of LLMs as the state-of-the-art in AI, Eloundou et al. (2023, p. 1) predicted that "around 80% of the U.S. workforce could have at least 10% of their work tasks affected by the introduction of LLMs, while approximately 19% of workers may see at least 50% of their tasks impacted."

So far, however, most work in economics on the labor impacts of AI has dealt not with disembodied ML algorithms as automation technology, but with robotics. In fact, as recently as 2018, a leading labor economist and co-author referred to robotics as the "leading edge" automation technology (Autor and Salomons, 2018, p. 3). Hence, the bulk of the empirical work on automation and labor markets deals not with modern AI as such, but with the impact of robots. Two of the most cited studies in this regard found that automation through robots tend to reduce employment. According to Acemoglu and Restrepo (2017), one additional robot per 1,000 workers will reduce the employment: population ratio in the USA by 0.37 percent. Chiacchio et al. (2018) calculated that one additional robot per 1,000 workers can reduce EU employment by between 0.16 and 0.20 percent.

While many robots use AI, many do not; robotics do not need to rely on AI. And the extent to which AI has penetrated robotics is difficult to measure (Pissarides, 2018). Hence, the question of how disembodied, software AI, as opposed to embodied robotics, will impact on labor markets is still to be satisfactorily answered. In this, a shortcoming has been the lack of an appropriate theoretical framework from which to test the possible impacts of AI. The dominant approach used to underpin empirical work on robotics automation has been the task approach introduced by Autor (2013). In Chapter 4, we argue that this approach, while useful, needs to be adapted to be able to reflect the many nuances that automation through AI entails.

For now however, it should be noted that the possibility of mass unemployment due to AI has motivated many scholars, governments and international organizations[29] to grapple what this would mean for the future of work and education

The general recommendation from the debate on the *Future of Work* is that if automation is skill-biased, and hence more likely to replace jobs containing routine tasks, then humans should invest in skills that are less likely to be able to be automated[30] such as creativity, communication, empathy, entrepreneurship, and skills that facilitate humans' working with advanced technology, such as software engineering (Deming, 2015; Trajtenberg, 2018).

Recognizing that education market interventions may be too little, too late, there has been increasing interest in the use of better and new forms of social safety nets for the possible large numbers of technologically unemployed, such as a universal basic income (UBI) grant (Cords and Prettner, 2019; Pulkka, 2017). What has generally been absent from these proposals and debates is a discussion of the role of government to stimulate aggregate demand as a way of creating and protecting jobs. In Chapter 5, we will argue that this is a significant shortcoming, as the potential impact of AI on jobs (and inequality) depends on aggregate demand. One of the reasons that this may have been neglected so far is that theoretical growth models tend to be supply driven, assuming that the rise in productive capacity created by technological progress will automatically create its own demand. In theoretical and empirical studies, which tend to be based on the task approach, this shows up as "re-instatement effects" (Acemoglu and Restrepo, 2020; Autor and Salomons, 2018). In Chapter 5, we will depart from the standard growth model assumption that supply will automatically create its own demand.

[29] See, for instance, the International Labour Organization's (ILO) *Global Commission on the Future of Work*; the World Trade Report 2017 on *Trade, Technology and Jobs*, and the World Development Report 2019 on *The Changing Nature of Work*.

[30] Huang and Rust (2018) argue that the belief that AI will not be likely or soon to automate jobs or tasks extensively using intuition or empathy, or jobs in the services sector, is mistaken, and that even such tasks will be automated.

2.4.3 *Impact on Innovation and Productivity*

As envisaged by Bommasani et al. (2022), the impact of AI, and in particular of foundational models such as LLMs, is to accelerate innovation; in their words (p. 150):

> Perhaps the most profound, if still speculative, effect of foundation models is their potential to enhance creativity and boost the rate of innovation itself [...] [they could] transform the market for illustrations much as inexpensive cameras revolutionized photography. If these models enable humans to develop new ways to write new songs and novels, discover variants of drug molecules , extend patents, build innovative software applications, or develop new business processes, then not only the level of productivity, but the rate of growth of productivity would be increased. In this way, foundation models have some of the characteristics of the ideas or blueprints in Paul Romer's growth models.

In Chapter 10, we explain that these hopes, as expressed by Bommasani et al. (2022) and the 2023 *Nature* magazine special edition on *AI and Science*, reflect the view that AI is an IMI that will alter the "playbook" of innovation (Cockburn et al., 2019). It has been claimed decades ago that "the first ultraintelligent machine is the last invention that man need ever make, provided that the machine is docile enough to tell us how to keep it under control" (Good, 1965, p. 33).

Agrawal et al. (2019b) present a combinatorial model of AI-aided innovation. In this model, the AI system predicts which combinations of existing knowledge, based on past successes and failures, may be successful in a specific (narrow) context. A growing literature exists that documents such AI-aided innovation. A few examples will suffice. Chen et al. (2022) for instance report on an AI program that was designed "to observe physical phenomena through a video camera and then try to search for the minimal set of fundamental variables that fully describe the observed dynamics," which in the case of a swinging double pendulum identified two new and unknown variables to explain these dynamics. Another example is in (bio)chemistry, where *DeepMind's* AlphaFold AI system has been used to predict the 3D structure of proteins (Jumper et al., 2021). It has been called "the most important achievement in AI – ever" (McMahon, 2022; Tunyasuvunakool et al., 2021). In energy, AI models have begun to "identify potential molecules and materials for flow batteries, organic light-emitting diodes, organic photovoltaic cells and carbon dioxide conversion catalysts" (De Luna et al., 2017, p. 24). In astrophysics and cosmology, an AI system has used the information from a single galaxy to infer the structure of the universe (Villaescusa-Navarro et al., 2022). In the near future, we are likely to see more and more of such reports. The use of AI to enhance science, innovation, and creative arts is across the board expected to be significant. See, for instance, *Nature* magazine's special edition in 2023 on *Science and the New Age of AI*.[31]

2.4.4 *Impact on Inequality*

Income inequality can rise if SBTC results in middle-skilled, middle-wage jobs to be replaced by automation technology (such as AI). This has been termed the "barbell" effect or the "hollowing out" of the labor market. See, for example, the contributions by Acemoglu and Autor (2011), Acemoglu and Autor (2012), and also Autor and Dorn (2013); Beaudry et al. (2013); Goos and Manning (2007).

In the case of a potential GPT such as AI, inequality can also increase as a result of the share of labor in total value added declining. This could be because more of the rents from the new technology accrues to owners of the technology. Thus, innovation rents from AI can drive higher-income inequality (Korinek and Stiglitz, 2017). Gries and Naudé (2020), incorporating a venture capital-type financial sector and vesting ownership of the AI technology not with labor, illustrate how AI innovation rents can arise and drive inequality, as measured by a decline in the share of value-added accruing to labor.

[31] See www.nature.com/immersive/d41586-023-03017-2/index.html.

Berg et al. (2018) simulate the potential impact of various AI automation scenarios and find that in all of these, output increases significantly, but that inequality rises rapidly. Their worst case is when robots substitute only for low-skilled labor; as they put it "the magnitude of the worsening in inequality is horrific. In our base case calibration, the skilled wage increases 56–157 percent in the long run while the wage paid to low-skill labor drops 26–56 percent and the group's share in national income decreases from 31 percent to 8–18 percent" (Berg et al., 2018, p. 10).

While the potential of technological progress, including in AI, to lead to inequality a priori is recognized, it is however not straightforward to ascribe current or past increases in inequality to AI. This is because the labor share in value-added and within-country inequality already started to worsen during the 1980s (Karabarbounis and Neiman, 2014; Rodriguez and Jayadev, 2010; Van Zanden et al., 2014) – when in fact there was an AI Winter.

This is not to say that technological change, in particular automation, did not contribute toward some of the rise in inequality since the 1980s. Automation via other technologies than AI, such as the Internet, the PC, and the mobile phone, has been found to have played a role, especially in the USA, although the magnitude and significance are points of disagreement among economists, with other factors such as globalization and deunionization also playing a role (Autor, 2014). In the case of Germany, Naudé and Nagler (2018) argue that too little innovation, rather than too fast or too much innovation, has contributed to growing income inequality, in the context of globalization and the erosion of union power.

Autor et al. (2017) explain the declining labor share not as a result of AI or automation, but with reference to the rise of "superstar firms" (that is a number of small firms that gain a large size of the market due to fiercer competition) as a result of globalization and digital technologies which enhance consumer power. Hopenhayn et al. (2018), using a general equilibrium firm dynamics model which they calibrate to USA data, find that the decline in the labor share can be explained by the declining population growth rate. They show that a declining population growth rate leads to a shift in the firm-age distribution toward older firms. And older firms employ relatively fewer "overhead" labor to "production" labor. Hence, over time, and in aggregate, the labor share will decline as the firm-age distribution shifts.

Even if automation did play a role in the historical decline of the labor share and even in job losses, then this should not be taken to imply that AI so far has had a significant impact, or even that AI is a particularly effective automation technology. So far, hard empirical evidence on AI specifically is lacking. Some studies, such as, for instance, Autor and Salomons (2018) and Bessen et al. (2019), measure the impact of automation either by proxies for technological change such as total factor productivity (TFP), robot density, patents, and ICT investments or "automation costs"; in other words, the current state of the art is to use fairly broad measures for automation, and not for AI specifically. As Bessen et al. (2019, p. 6) admit, they "do not know the exact automation tech." The contributions of Chapters 4 and 5 are to address this weakness in the economic literature.

2.4.5 *Impact on Developing Countries and Emerging Economies*

The research cited so far has tended to deal with within-country inequality and with inequality and automation in advanced economies. While it is well established that an important reason for between-country inequality is due to technology gaps (see, e.g., Comin and Mestieri, 2013), there is a relative lack of research on the potential impact of AI on global inequality, global development, and emerging and developing economies. The existing research, however, is somewhat pessimistic. For instance, the World Bank (2016) estimated that the jobs susceptible to automation are larger in emerging economies than in developed countries (reflecting the greater labor intensity in these countries). Similarly worrisome is the econometric estimates of Carbonero et al. (2018) who find that while global employment declined on average by 1.3 percent between 2005 and 2014 due to a 24 percent increase in the number of robots over this period, the decline in employment in emerging economies was up to 14 percent. They conclude (p. 2) that "these results demonstrate that if there are concerns about automation and robots in particular, these should first and foremost be addressed to emerging economies."

Korinek and Stiglitz (2021, p. 1) discuss the mechanisms through which AI could lead to widening global disparities and the potential policy remedies, concluding that "Developing countries and emerging market economies have even more reason to be concerned than high-income countries, as their comparative advantage in the world economy relies on abundant labor and natural resources. Declining returns to labor and natural resources as well as the winner-takes-all dynamics brought on by new information technologies could lead to further immiseration in the developing world." Relatedly, Naudé (2023b) discusses how the business models of large digital platforms that use AI are making catching-up industrialization by late industrializing countries more difficult.

Finally, in 2015, the countries of the world committed themselves to achieve the Sustainable Development Goals (SDGs) – a set of seventeen goals and 169 targets to ensure sustainable and equitable global development. Vinuesa et al. (2020) investigated whether or not AI can help countries achieve the SDGs. Their findings were mixed, suggesting that "AI can enable the accomplishment of 134 targets across all the goals, but it may also inhibit 59 targets." More research is needed to understand the implications for global development, responses to mitigate the negative impacts of AI, and understand how digital divides in AI and big data (see Naudé and Vinuesa, 2021) will affect global disparities.

2.5 CONCLUDING REMARKS

The purpose of this chapter was to provide a gentle introduction to the rapidly expanding and dynamic field of AI for economists. As such this chapter serves as a basis of clarification of central concepts, and the context against which AI should be approached. Throughout the discussion, we included pointers to future chapters where particular ideas will be relevant and analyzed in more detail.

The chapter contained three central sections. The first explained what AI and the field of AI entails, provided a working definition of AI, contrasted GOFAI with ML, and introduced LLMs, the current cutting-edge of AI models, and discussed the extent to which the progress in AI from GOFAI to LLMs is taking us toward AGI.

The second section of this chapter provided a historical timeline of AI, focusing on the breakthroughs that drove AI during and after World War II. This section drew attention to three features of AI's progress over this time period: that it is difficult to steer AI as a broad technology in any particular direction; that AI is ultimately a product that firms need to make a profit from; and that AI progress has, partly as a result of the two former features, been uneven, characterized by periods of breakthroughs followed by backlashes.

The third and final section of this chapter outlined, without being exhaustive, five reasons why economists are interested in AI. These are that AI is a new tool in the toolbox of the theoretical and applied economist; it is a new technological shock to labor and educational markets; it is an IMI; a driver of inequality within and between countries; and AI may contribute to and threaten development in developing and emerging economies.

With the definition and history of AI being dealt with, and the motivation for why AI is a topic worthy of economists' considerations out of the way, Chapter 3 starts to introduce more rigor, in setting out the basics of decision theory, the common point of departure for both economics and AI.

3 Artificial Intelligence and the Economics of Decision-Making

3.1 INTRODUCTION

The challenge facing AI scientists is to create intelligent, autonomous agents that can make rational decisions. This challenge has confronted them with two questions (Oesterheld, 2021, p. 2): "What decision theory do we want an AI to follow?" and "How can we implement such a decision theory in an AI?"

This chapter provides a critical overview of how the economic theory of decision-making has helped to answer these two questions and how it can benefit from the practical solutions that AI scientists are working on. The main contribution is to identify how economists can contribute to the AI "alignment problem," and moreover provide a fresh perspective on the alignment problem. AI systems are said to be aligned when they do what they are supposed to do, and do no harm. They are said to be value aligned when they share human values. The alignment problem has so far largely attracted computer scientists, programmers, and philosophers. Economists have until now contributed little (Gans, 2018).

The chapter is structured as follows. In Section 3.2, the first question earlier, what decision theory should AI follow? is answered. The foundation of both modern data-based AI and economics, expected utility theory (EUT), is outlined. Examples are given of its adoption in AI, including in sequential decision-making, and the challenges to EUT are discussed. In Section 3.3, the second question, how can we implement EUT in AI systems? is answered. Here, the alignment problem is stated, and three ways in which to approach AI alignment in the field of economics are explained: instrumental goals, utility function instability, and utility function coordination.

From the discussions in Sections 3.2 and 3.3, it follows that the application of EUT confines artificial smart agents to very simple situations, so that concerns about AI alignment may, from this perspective, lose some urgency. The problems that AI does pose are perhaps better labeled as safety issues, rather than alignment issues. In the future, as AI will more and more become humans' progeny, we think that this would indeed be a better label.

Finally, this chapter concludes in Section 3.4 that it is not only AI that benefits from the economic theory of decision-making: as we already pointed out in Chapter 2, economics may also benefit from how AI scientists implement EUT – AI may help economics to model human decision-making better.

3.2 WHAT DECISION THEORY DO WE WANT AN AI TO FOLLOW?

> AI researchers aim to construct a synthetic homo economicus, the mythical perfectly rational agent of neoclassical economics (Parkes and Wellman, 2015, p. 267)

AI scientists want AI systems to make rational decisions. Thus, they have resorted to rational choice theory – on which economics is based. Rational choice theory is not a single unified theory but consists of variants. For a review of these, see Herfeld (2020). In economics, rational choice theory, and specifically EUT, is used to model human decision-making. The decision-makers who strictly follow EUT have been labeled *homo economicus*[1] to make clear that real human decision-making tends to depart from some of the assumptions of the theory. As will be discussed later, AI systems may more closely resemble *homo economicus* than *homo sapiens*.

3.2.1 *Expected Utility Theory*

EUT is attractive for AI scientists because "All tasks that require intelligence to be solved can naturally be formulated as a

[1] For a discussion of the concept and origin of *homo economicus*, the economic human, see Persky (1995).

maximization of some expected utility in the framework of agents" (Hutter, 2007, p. 33). In economics, intelligent human agents are modeled as goal-oriented, rational agents acting to maximize their subjective utility subject to resource constraints. The field of AI has adopted this approach, which is reflected in a standard definition of the field of AI (see also Chapter 2) as "the study of agents that receive percepts from the environment and perform actions. Each such agent implements a function that maps percept sequences to actions [...]" (Russell and Norvig, 2021, p. vii).

The functions that map percept sequences (perceptions) to actions should help agents to select actions to achieve their goals (Parkes and Wellman, 2015). In the case of genes, for instance, the goals are survival and gene transmission (Kamatani, 2021). The human phenotype, including its brain, is the expression or action of its genes, which aims at survival and transmission (reproduction) (Dawkins, 1976; Williams, 1966). In the terminology of AI, survival and reproduction are the supergoals of genes, and the human brain is a subgoal (or instrumental subgoal) (Yudkowsky, 2001). Later we will return to the topic of subgoals/instrumental goals.

EUT and qualitative variants thereof (Dastani et al., 2005; Gonzales and Perny, 2020; Russell, 2019) are formal models of rational decision-making set out by John von Neumann and Oscar Morgenstern – see Von Neumann and Morgenstern (1944) (vNM) – and generalized by Savage (1954).

The foundations of EUT go back however to Nicolaus Bernoulli – see Bernoulli (1738) – and his solution to the St. Petersburg Paradox (List and Haigh, 2005). The St. Petersburg Paradox arises in a gamble where a fair coin is tossed n times, until it lands on heads, with the gambler then receiving a prize of $\$2^n$. The paradox is that even though the expected value of the gamble being $\sum_{n=1}^{\infty} (\frac{1}{2})^n \times 2^n = \infty$, no one would pay very much to take this gamble. Bernoulli (1738) solved this by showing that what is important is not to maximize expected *value* but expected utility. Utility should also be maximized after ignoring outcomes with very small probabilities – otherwise this would lead to the problem of "Pascal's Mugger"[2] (Monton, 2019).

In economics, and based on Von Neumann and Morgenstern (1944), EUT justifies the specification of an *utility function* which allows an agent to compare different outcomes from actions – the utility function reflects the agent's preferences.[3] Consequently, the agent will choose actions that maximize the (expected) value of the utility function. Note that in this approach, agents maximize *expected* utility because each possible future outcome is subject to probability – an outcome is a lottery. Actions and their outcomes can thus be compared to playing a lottery.

A lottery can be denoted by $L = [p_1(C_1), p_2(C_2), p_3(C_3), \ldots, p_k(C_k)]$ where the $C_k's$ are the outcomes and $\sum_{i=1}^{k} p_i = 1$ the probabilities of each outcome. The expected value (E) of this lottery is $E(L) = \sum_{i=1}^{k} p_i C_i$, the mathematical average. If the set of lotteries available to an agent i is Λ, then the agent's utility function[4] U_i represents the preferences of the agent over various lotteries, with $U_i(L_1) \geq U_i(L_2) \iff L_1 \succsim L_2, \forall L_1, L_2 \in \Lambda$ (Maschler et al., 2013). Thus, if lottery L_1 is preferred to lottery L_2, the utility from L_1 will be greater than or equal to the utility from L_2.

In following EUT to make decisions, an agent will do their best to choose the lotteries L_i^* (or consumption bundles, as in household economics) to maximize expected utility, $\mathbb{E}[U(L_i)]$. This decision can be written as

$$L_i^* = \arg\max_{L} \mathbb{E}[U(L_i)] \tag{3.1}$$

This choice of L_i^* can be found by solving for $\dfrac{\partial \mathbb{E}[U(L_i)]}{\partial L_i} = 0$

In vNM, human agents will maximize expected utility, choosing the lotteries from Λ that will generate the most utility. This will,

[2] See, for example, Yudkowsky (2007b).

[3] For a survey of how preferences are incorporated in the utility function of AI agents, see Pigozzi et al. (2016).

[4] A linear utility function is a von Neumann-Morgenstern utility function and implies risk neutrality. If u_i is concave, then the agent is risk averse and if U_i is convex, then the agent is risk-seeking (Maschler et al., 2013).

say in the example of a consumer aiming to maximize utility from buying various bundles of goods, lead them to goal-directed decisions and pursuit of instrumental subgoals, such as acquiring money or income. Just like not all lotteries can be played, not all bundles of goods can be afforded. Von Neumann and Morgenstern (1944) proved that if individual agents' preferences[5] are characterized by completeness, transitivity, and continuity, then they will behave as if they were maximizing expected utility (Moscati, 2016).

In the decision calculus, so far, the outcomes of the decision on L_i accrue only to the agent making the choice: it is implicitly assumed that there are no externalities. In reality, however, and in the case of concerns about AI, the unintended consequences of agents' decisions need to be considered. This is a formidable problem. Consider, for instance, that if we denote the external costs/benefits of a decision or action on L_i by $C(L_i)$, then the decision in (1) can be rewritten as

$$L_i^* = \arg\max_{L} \mathbb{E}[U(L_i) - C(L_i)] \tag{3.2}$$

Gauchon and Barigou (2021) discuss the general complexity of this problem, noting that finding the optimum requires various assumptions and somewhat tenuous interpretations of the terms in the first-order conditions.

3.2.2 *Examples in AI*

Equivalents to utility functions[6] used in AI systems include value functions, objective functions, loss functions, reward functions (especially in Reinforcement Learning (RL)), and preference orderings (Eckersley, 2019). The concepts of utility function and goal are often used interchangeably in the AI literature (Dennis, 2020). Where loss functions (gradients) are used, which is the case when some objective

[5] In economics, one does not require direct knowledge of an agent's preferences – it can be inferred from their choices – their revealed preferences, a notion introduced by Ramsey (1931) and Samuelson (1947).

[6] For an extensive overview of the mathematics used in ML, see Gallier and Quaintance (2022).

function is minimized (e.g., minimizing the error of wrongly predicting what is in an image), the sign on the above utility function would be negative.

An example from ML is the ubiquitous use of artificial neural networks (ANNs), such as the multilayer perceptron (MLP) to perform classifications – say classifying images or text. A MLP is a supervised learning algorithm consisting of various layers of perceptrons, where a perceptron is a program that tries to mimic a biological neuron to perform binary classifications (Rosenblatt, 1958; Schmidhuber, 2015).

Formally, an ANN aims, given a (data) set of N samples $D = \{[x_1, x_2, \ldots x_n], [y_1, y_2, \ldots y_n]\}$, to find the best approximation for the function describing $f(x_i) = y_i$ which maps the inputs (x) to the outputs (y), where the outputs would be the classification (Lichtner-Bajjaoui, 2020). The objective function is to minimize the expected value of incorrect classifications, which is equivalent to maximizing the utility or goal of the ML (typically back-propagation[7]) algorithm (García-García et al., 2022). In the case of the MLP, the probabilities attached to each element x to be classified belonging to a class k is a vector $P(y_k|x)$ that can be written as

$$P(y_k|x) = s'\left\{\sum_{j=1}^{n_2} \omega_{jk} \times s\left\{\sum_{i=1}^{n_1} \omega_{ij} \times x_i + b_{0j}\right\} + b_{0k}\right\} \tag{3.3}$$

Where s and s' are respectively known as the activation functions of the hidden and output layers of the neural network, the n as the number of neurons in each of these layers, the ω as weights on the connections between the layers and neurons, and b_0 as the threshold values (activation functions). The back-propagation algorithm will adjust the weights and threshold values to minimize the loss function in classification (and maximize the probability that a classification is accurate). For a more detailed discussion and examples, see García-García et al. (2022).

[7] See Rumelhart et al. (1986) who introduced back-propagation as a supervised learning technique.

Deep learning using ANNs to perform classifications has found wide use in Recommender Systems, such as those used to suggest what movies or songs subscribers on Netflix or Spotify may want to watch or what consumers on Amazon or other platforms may want to buy (Ricci et al., 2022). Jenkins et al. (2021) have shown how these systems can be made more accurate by being explicitly based on microeconomics-based utility functions, which they term neural utility functions. They pointed out that Recommender Systems, which minimize an objective function of choice prediction, do not use quasi-concave utility functions, as economics typically does. Accordingly, they cannot evaluate trade-offs in decisions, such as taking into account that choices are affected by whether there are complements or substitutes. They also show that if they augment DL models with quasi-concave neural utility functions,[8] that the choice prediction loss is smaller – using utility functions with a foundation in economic theory improves AI (Jenkins et al., 2021).

A final example of utility functions in the field of AI is that deep convolutional neural networks (CNNs), a class of ANNs used for image classification, can be interpreted as utility maximizers subject to costly learning, that is, facing informational costs (this is elaborated later under Section 3.2.5) (Pattanayak and Krishnamurthy, 2021). Applying this idea to deep CNN, Pattanayak and Krishnamurthy (2021) found that they could predict the image-classification performance of 200 deep CNNs with an accuracy >94%, removing the need to retrain the models.

3.2.3 *Sequential Decision-Making*

Many decisions relying on EUT are not one-off decisions but sequential. This is particularly, but not exclusively, so in multi-agent settings – where both economics and AI science rely on game theory. Gonzales and Perny (2020) discuss the use of graphical models such as decision trees to analyze such sequential decision-making. In

[8] They use CES and Cobb–Douglas utility function specifications.

complex sequential decision-making under uncertainty, economists use stochastic dynamic programming (Bellman, 1957a,b) and its Markov decision process (MDP) model (Howard, 1960). A typical example is inventory management (Ahiska et al., 2013).

Effective sequential decision-making by AI agents is vital in virtually all AI applications – from playing games such as Chess and Go to autonomous robots and vehicles, health planning, and chatbots. In all of these, the sequence in which decisions are made is important for the overall maximization of the utility function. RL is the branch of AI that focuses mainly on sequential decision-making. In most RL[9], an AI agent learns about the underlying MDP "through execution and simulation, continuously using feedback from the past decisions to learn the underlying model and reinforce good strategies" (Agrawal, 2019, p. 2). To speed up learning, recourse may be taken, given the nature of the goal, to supervised learning or imitation learning[10] (Ding et al., 2019; Hutter, 2000). For detailed discussions of RL, the reader is referred to Arulkumaran et al. (2017) and Sutton and Barto (1998). Charpentier et al. (2021) describe how RL is used in the development of autonomous vehicles. Salimans et al. (2017) refer to the success of RL for developing AI systems that can excel in games such as Atari and Go. For more detail on the use of reinforcement learning from human feedback (RLHF), which is used in the training of LLMs such as GPT-4, see Ziegler et al. (2019) and Lambert et al. (2022).

3.2.4 *Challenges to EUT*

EUT is subject to at least two challenges. One is that experiments have found that humans may violate the EUT under certain conditions, thus apparently not acting rationally (List and Haigh, 2005); the

[9] Exceptions are so-called black-box optimization or direct policy search, which includes a class of optimization algorithms known as evolution strategies (ES) (Salimans et al., 2017) and the AIXI model of universal AI of Hutter (2000, 2007), which dispenses with the Markov assumption that the future only depends on the present.

[10] Particularly useful in robotics (Ding et al., 2019).

second relates to evaluating possible future outcomes where there is no objective probability distribution (LeRoy and Singell, 1987) – also known in economics as Knightian uncertainty after Knight (1933).

Regarding the first challenge, an example is the Ellsberg Paradox or Ellsberg's Urn – see Ellsberg (1961) and Gilboa (2013). According to Binmore (2017), a way around the Ellsberg Paradox, which reflects humans' ambiguity aversion, is to screen agents beforehand using another rationality criterion. Several generalizations of EUT have been proposed to deal with this and other shortcomings of EUT to be a good descriptive model of human decision-making. A discussion of these falls outside the scope of this book. The reader is referred to Gonzales and Perny (2020), who discuss among others rank dependent utility (RDU) and decision models outside the probabilistic framework, and Schoemaker (1982), who discusses nine variants of EUT – from expected monetary value to prospect theory.

In the case of using EUT to model the decision-making of AI agents, the screening solution to the Ellsberg Paradox is implicitly done – by the selection of AI agents who are not human, to begin with. Thus, AI agents more fully inhabit the world of neoclassical economics meaning that economic theory can usefully be applied to AI (Caplin et al., 2022). Other approaches that have been tried in AI to avoid the Ellsberg Paradox are to model AI agents' behavior indeed closely on that of humans, and to do so by relying on models from behavioral economics – see, for instance, Tamura (2009).

Regarding the second challenge, to deal with uncertainty, both economics (Harsanyi, 1978) and AI (Pearl, 1985) revert to Bayes' theorem (Harré, 2021). Von Neumann-Morgenstern's EUT (Von Neumann and Morgenstern, 1944) is based on objective probabilities. Savage (1954) generalized this to subjective probabilities. Here, "Bayesian" agents form subjective probabilities based on their priors (beliefs). As new information comes to light, they update their subjective probabilities – and accordingly modify their actions (Harsanyi, 1978; Savage, 1954). *How* their priors are established is a question of some contention and highly relevant to the agenda of AI scientists (Binmore, 2008, 2017).

3.2.5 Bounded Rationality

Bayesian expected utility maximizers – subjective utility maximizers – are the mythical agents of both economics and the field of AI. The problem is that rational decision-makers often make poor – less than optimal – choices (Binmore, 2017). This is because, unlike in the theoretically idealized world of economics, in reality, agents – both human and AI – face informational and computation limits. As Simon (1955, p. 114) put it, it may be more useful to replace the mythical agent of economics with one "of limited knowledge and ability" which does not have the "global" rationality of the mythical agent. In the case of humans, mistakes in decision-making are often "predictably irrational" (Ariely, 2009) – which has been ascribed to cognitive biases (Kahneman et al., 2021). Computational limitations and cognitive biases have been used by behavioral economists to argue that homo sapiens differ from *homo economicus* (Thaler, 2000). Intelligence agents' rationality is thus *bounded.*

Bounded rationality is not only applicable to humans but also to AI agents – even though they may have vastly better computational abilities (Dennis, 2020). As Wagner (2020, p. 114) point out "whilst the new species of 'machina economicus' [. . .] behaves more economic than man, it too is faced with bounded rationality. Algorithms work with finite computational resources which in practice means that they cannot achieve Turing completeness and are limited to linear bounded automation." The reference here to *Turing Completeness* is to the theoretical possibility that AI can be globally rational as the mythical agent of neoclassical economics (Lee, 2019). The universal Turing machine (UTM) already mentioned in Chapter 2, is a "computing machine," proposed by Turing (1936) that can "be used to compute any computable sequence" (Turing, 1936, p. 241). It is Turing Complete. However, it is subject to the *Halting Problem,* which is how to determine if and when the UTM will find a solution (Lee, 2019). Turing (1936) proved that there is no general algorithm for solving this problem in all cases.

Finite computation resources, as described in the previous paragraph, imply that there are information costs involved in making a decision as described in Equation (1). These information costs can be further specified to come from the updating of an agent's Bayesian priors. If, in the example of Equation (1) in Section 2.1, the agents' probability distribution over the choice of L_i is $p(L)$, then computational resources (costs) will be expended to change from a prior probabilistic strategy $p_0(L)$ to a posterior probabilistic strategy $p(L)$ in the process of decision-making (Leibfried and Braun, 2016). This informational cost is known as the Kullback-Leibler divergence (D_{KL}) and can be specified as $D_{KL} = (p(L)||p_0(L)) \leq B$, where $B \geq 0$ is the upper bound of available computational resources (Leibfried and Braun, 2016). With these informational costs, the expected utility maximization problem in (1) can be modified to

$$L_i^* = (1 - \beta) \arg\max_L \mathbb{E}[U(L_i)] - \beta D_{KL}(p(L)||p_0(L)) \tag{3.4}$$

where $\beta \in (0, 1)$ is the trade-off between expected utility and informational cost (Leibfried and Braun, 2016). It is also consistent with Sims' 2003 "rationally inattentive utility maximization" where paying more attention to making a decision implies high attention costs. The point is that learning is costly, it bounds rationality, and needs to be taken into account in models of bounded rational decision-making (Lipnowski and Doron, 2022; Pattanayak and Krishnamurthy, 2021).

The difference though between AI-bounded rationality and human-bounded rationality is that while human agents are subject to both computational limits and cognitive biases, AI agents will face fewer computational limits and can unlearn cognitive biases. Learning may be less costly. AI agents can be programmed with error correction mechanisms and these will inevitably drive them to *homo economicus*, or more appropriately, as Parkes and Wellman (2015) have suggested, *machina economicus*.

As Omohundro (2008b) explains, the nature of AI systems such as deep learning[11] and (Deep) RL[12] as "learning" agents means that they are self-improving systems. They will thus learn where they have been making suboptimal decisions or have been deviating from their goals, and correct for it in a way that *"discover and eliminate their own irrationalities in ways that humans cannot"* (Omohundro, 2008b, p. 4).

Thus, the state of the art in the fields of economics and AI is the modeling of intelligent agents that rely on Bayesian probability theory to inform beliefs (priors) and utility theory to inform their preferences. With beliefs and wants determined, and with limits on their computational abilities and resources, by aiming to maximize expected utility, intelligent agents will act in a boundedly rational manner under uncertainty (Benya, 2012; Riedel, 2021). Intelligent agents with beliefs and preferences but who fail to attempt to maximize expected utility may be vulnerable and subject to exploitation (Shah, 2019a). Eventually, evolutionary pressures will lead to the disappearance of such agents from a population.

This bounded mythical agent of rational decision theory has much to commend it, as its voluminous application in the economics literature, and its dominance in explaining decision-making, attest to (Binmore, 2008; Dixon, 2001; Moscati, 2016). It has even been found to be applicable to decision-making in other primates, not only humans (Pastor-Berniera et al., 2017). Indeed, it is due to its strengths that it has come to underpin the development of AI.

But, there are also kinks in the armor, which, in light of the continued advancement in AI, pose a number of challenges for

[11] As mentioned in Chapter 2 the dominant approach to unpack functions that maps precepts from the environment into actions is Deep Learning (LeCun et al., 2015; Sarker, 2021).

[12] For more comprehensive explanations of RL see Arulkumaran et al. (2017) and Sutton and Barto (1998). Charpentier et al. (2021) describes how RL is used in development of autonomous vehicles. Salimans et al. (2017) refers to the success of RL in games such as Atari and Go.

AI scientists in the practical implementation thereof. These are discussed in the next section.

3.3 HOW CAN WE BEST IMPLEMENT EUT IN AI SYSTEMS?

EUT is thus, as Section 3.2 discussed, a very attractive theoretical decision-making theory for an AI to follow. How to best implement the EUT in AI systems faces an important challenge: the *alignment problem*.

3.3.1 *The Alignment Problem*

Although AI agents are also rationally bounded, they have fewer cognitive biases than humans, and can unlearn them. Learning and eliminating its biases imply that AI may become recursively self-improving. In such a situation, where AI learns, self-corrects, and recursively self-improves, one would need to avoid that an AI emerges and pursues goals (utility) that conflict with human interest (Bostrom, 2014), or even if these do not conflict with human interest, nevertheless can have unintended negative consequences. These may follow because its utility function may not capture all the considerations relevant in a situation – "humans care about many features of the environment that are difficult to capture in any simple utility function" (Taylor, 2016, p. 125).

The challenge is, as formulated by Omohundro (2008b, p. 36), that AI systems following EUT

> will maintain utility functions which encode their preferences about the world. In the process of acting on those preferences, they will be subject to drives towards efficiency, self-preservation, acquisition, and creativity. Unbridled, these drives lead to both desirable and undesirable behaviors. By carefully choosing the utility functions of the first self-improving systems, we have the opportunity to guide the entire future development.

It is therefore essential, as Riedel (2021) and others have argued, to understand the utility functions (goals) of AI agents – not only for participating with and competing against AI agents, but also eventually for constraining and aligning AI's goals (Bostrom, 2014). Constraining and aligning AI systems' goals or utility functions is a topic that has generated a large and growing literature under the headings of AI alignment and AI ethics (Hauer, 2022), which ultimately aims to ensure that AI "benefits humans" and humans do not lose control over AI (Kirchner et al., 2022, p. 1). Note that this is a very human-centric agenda based on a view of human exceptionalism (Murphy, 2022a).

Discussing all the risks in AI goal design falls outside the scope of this chapter. A recent list of AI goal design risks identified no less than twenty-six distinct risks (Kokotajlo and Dai, 2019). Further reviews on aligning AI are contained in Christian (2020), Everitt et al. (2018), Hubinger (2020), and Kirchner et al. (2022). The AI alignment problem arises in the eventuality that AI will recursively self-improve – something which it cannot do at present, but which cannot be ruled out in the future. In Chapter 10, we explore the possible implications in the case of recursively self-improving AI in the absence of AI alignment.

Economists have so far contributed little to the topic of AI alignment. As Gans (2018) pointed out, "The underlying ideas behind the notion that we could lose control over an AI are profoundly economic. But, to date, economists have not paid much attention to them."

How could economists contribute? At least three possible approaches to AI alignment in the field of economics stand out: instrumental goals, utility function instability, and utility function coordination.

3.3.2 *Instrumental Goals*

The first is to tackle the problem of instrumental goals. Any smart AI system with a goal-oriented utility function will, given the AI drives listed in the quote earlier, have top goals (or super goals) and *instrumental* (or sub) goals (Gabriel and Ghazavi, 2021; Omohundro,

2008a). For example, if the top goal of an AI system is to drive a vehicle from point A to point B, a subgoal may be to ensure that the vehicle is operational (Yudkowsky, 2001).

How this creates a problem for value alignment is illustrated by the *Paperclip Maximizer* thought experiment. Philosopher Nick Bostrom describes an ASI with a top goal to manufacture paper clips, who

> starts transforming first all of earth and then increasing portions of space into paperclip manufacturing facilities. More subtly, it could result in a superintelligence realizing a state of affairs that we might now judge as desirable but which in fact turns out to be a false utopia, in which things essential to human flourishing have been irreversibly lost. We need to be careful about what we wish for from a superintelligence, because we might get it – Bostrom (2003b, p. 17).

The same point is made by the King Midas problem which is cited by Russell (2019), who refers to the classical story of King Midas, who, when he had the opportunity to be granted any wish, wished that anything he touches turn to gold. When he subsequently touched his daughter, she also turned to gold.

These concerns have, on the one hand, led to proposals to constrict the utility function that AI agents optimize, for instance, to try to implement the 1956 suggestion of Herbert Simon not to try to build use utility maximizers, but utility satisficers (Simon, 1956) – which essentially engages only in a limited form of optimization (Armstrong et al., 2012). The shortcomings of these proposals are discussed by Taylor (2016).

On the other hand, concerns have led to proposals to design AI systems with uncertainty about the utility function built in and letting the AI system discover the utility function by learning from humans. This is where reinforced learning (RL)[13] with its reward

[13] Also including Cooperative Inverse Reinforcement Learning (CIRL) – see Hadfield-Menell et al. (2016)

function optimization and supplemented recursive reward modeling is an example (Gabriel and Ghazavi, 2021). The aim is that this search will lead to alignment with human values. Apprenticeship learning is another proposal, based on the idea that an AI system tries to imitate a human expert in performing a particular task where the utility function is uncertain (Abbeel and Ng, 2004). The shortcoming of this proposal is that AI systems may then never become smarter than humans at a task, leaving us bereft of their potential advantage (Taylor, 2016).

In essence, RL has been argued to reflect the evolutionary process which has given rise to much of society's current laws and regulations: "I read the history of Western law and the simple rules that emerged from it as decentralized RL. Jurists and agents, through a combination of reasoning and experience, saw what worked and what did not. Those rules that led to Pareto improvements survived and thrived. Those that did not, dwindled" (Fernandez-Villaverde, 2020, p. 15). According to Shah (2019b), the uncertainty of AI with RL will lead to AI systems that are "deferential, that ask for clarifying information, and that try to learn human preferences" (Hadfield-Menell et al., 2016; Shah, 2019b).

A weakness of getting AI to learn about human preferences and its utility function, and a weakness in general of RL, is that learning itself is an endogenous and imperfect process (Kuriksha, 2021). Two typical problems in learning are cognitive limitations and that learning in one environment does not necessarily carry over to a different environment. Kuriksha (2021) applied an RL model to explore the economic implications of such imperfect learning for AI agents that have to make savings-consumption decisions. He found that agents who learned to optimize saving in an environment with low levels of wealth would not save optimally if transferred to an environment with high levels of wealth, and vice versa.

Another weakness of getting AI to learn about human preferences and its utility function is, as Turchin and Denkenberger (2020, p. 159) point out, that "if AI extracted human values from the most popular TV series, it could be 'Game of Thrones' [...] and then the 'paradise' world it created for us would be utter hell." Consequently, it may be preferential to ensure that the AI systems that can learn about human preferences are artificial moral agents (AMA) (Allen et al., 2005). AMAs are "artificial agents capable of making ethical and moral decisions" (Cervantes et al., 2020, p. 503). However, the design of such an AMA remains an elusive goal (Cervantes et al., 2020).

3.3.3 *Utility Function Instability*

Another angle from which economics can contribute to the AI alignment problem is to address the problem of utility function instability, in other words, the problem that an aligned utility function becomes misaligned. There are two major aspects that involve utility function instability.

One is the related problem of wireheading and self-delusion. Wireheading, or reward-hacking, refers to agents directly stimulating their reward centers, thus interfering in reward provision (Cohen et al., 2022). In the case of AI agents, it is particularly a problem in RL (Everitt and Hutter, 2016). Various methods are being tested and developed to avoid wireheading. These include imitation learning, rewarding agents that maximize their impact on the environment instead of the signals they receive, value reinforcement learning (VRL), inverse reinforcement learning (IRL), apprenticeship learning (AL), myopia, and quantilization (Cohen et al., 2022; Everitt and Hutter, 2016). Related to wireheading is that AI agents may self-delude. This would occur when AI agents deliberately change their own observations of the impacts of their actions so that it may seem that they are maximizing their utility functions, when, in fact, they are not (Hibbard, 2012; Ring and Orseau, 2011).

The second cause of utility function instability is that an AI may change its own utility function autonomously (Dennis, 2020; Totschnig, 2020). It may do so to compensate for being boundedly rational. For instance, the AI agent may perform an action in pursuit of a goal and fail to achieve the goal due to differences in its (imperfect) model of the world and the actual world. It may therefore change the goal. The question is, what informs the direction of change? Here, AI developers have been exploring the programming of values, based on the argument that if the values of AI are aligned, then it will not change its goals in a direction that will be potentially harmful to humans. There is, however, at present no clear understanding of how to program this into AI systems: "our current lack of understanding about how to adequately program behaviour that can flexibly adopt and drop goals is one of the key limitations to our ability to take artificial intelligence to the next level" (Dennis, 2020, p. 2493).

3.3.4 Utility Function Coordination

The third angle from which economics can contribute to the AI alignment problem is to address the challenge for rational goal-directed decision-making posed by multiactor and human–agent collectives (HAC) settings (Wagner, 2020).

So far, the discussion has been about a single decision-maker agent. In an economy with many agents, the challenge is how the individual AIs' decisions should be modeled? How do individual decisions add up to aggregate outcomes? And how can humans effectively and safely interact with AI agents?

Here, another basic methodological foundation that AI scientists and economists share is game theory (Russell, 2019). In multi-AI-agent environments, AIs rely on a game-theoretic view of the world, "where agents rationally respond to each others' behavior, presumed (recursively) to be rational as well. A consequence is that agents would expect their joint decisions to be in some form of equilibrium, as in standard economic thinking" (Parkes and Wellman, 2015, p. 269). We know however from game theory – the Prisoners' Dilemma is an example – that decisions that are rational and optimal on the individual level do not necessarily aggregate to the best outcome for society. The Prisoner's Dilemma exists because of a lack of coordination.

In the field of AI, where RL has been successful in sequential optimization as is evident in the success of AI agents using RL to play GO, Atari games, or steer autonomous vehicles, most of these applications of RL involve multiple agents. It requires AI agents to interact with other intelligent agents and, more generally, the external environment. Therefore, multi-agent RL (MARL) has become popular. As Zhang et al. (2021) discuss, MARL's theoretical foundations are provided by game theory – specifically Markov games and extensive-form games. In these, because each agent may have a different utility function, and all agents are continuously adjusting their policies/actions given feedback from the environment, the environment facing all agents is changing all the time, that is, becomes nonstationary, violating the Markov assumption followed in single-agent RL. This nonstationarity property of MARL remains a challenge in the development of AI systems (Zhang et al., 2021).

In such situations, it is not only that AI developers need to get the utility functions of AI agents to be optimal or appropriate, but they must also specify the institutional features of the environment – the "rules of the game" and the "play of the game," to use the terminology from institutional and transaction cost economics (North, 1991). This, in effect, can facilitate utility function coordination among the various interacting agents. The field of mechanism design, which has been richly applied in economics, has been shown to be useful in this regard for AI systems, though not without challenges (Parkes and Wellman, 2015; Varian, 1995).

Although multi-agent environments are populated by AI agents with different utility functions that pose challenges, this feature has been found to be nevertheless useful in ML, particularly in driving learning using models from evolutionary game theory. Thus, the latter underpins the use of generative adversarial networks (GANs), which exploit the fact that agents (typical neural network based) may have opposing goals and divergent utility functions, to train AI systems (Goodfellow et al., 2014; Guo et al., 2020).

Another problem that arises in AI multi-actor and HAC environments when there is no utility function coordination is a familiar one in economics: the principal–agent problem (Grossman and Hart, 1983). Drawing on multilateral principal–agent models (e.g., Bernheim and Whinston 1986), it can be seen that with AI the simple bilateral principal–agent problem becomes one with three agents – the human user of AI is the principal, the AI system is the agent, and the provider of the AI is another agent (Wagner, 2020, p. 118). Wagner (2020) explores the implications of the principal–agent problem in such a setting, pointing out that there are likely to be substantial and increasing information asymmetries between the human principal and the AI agent – and AI provider – given the superior speed of information processing of AI, the continued background tracking of humans online, and the black-box nature of many current AI decisions. Without utility function coordination between these agents, it is possible that the interests of AI systems and those of their principal agents will increasingly diverge.

As far as the interaction between humans and AI agents in multi-agent situations is concerned, this has been gathering scrutiny under the rubric of HACs (Wagner, 2020). These HACs have been described as starting to exhibit properties of a collective mind or even supermind, and have led to observations that the close integration of AI agents and human agents in a collective mind could improve the strength of institutions and weaken the relevance of methodological individualism, a central plank of neoclassical economics (Arrow, 1994; Wagner, 2020). Modeling institutions, including markets, without invoking the assumptions of methodological individualism remains a challenge for economists. A recent review of the case for methodological individualism in the social sciences by Neck (2021), for instance, omits to consider the implications of the rise of HACs and the growing autonomous economy (Arthur, 2021).

3.4 CONCLUDING REMARKS

> Neoclassical theory involves very smart people in incredibly simple situations, while the real world entails very simply people in incredibly complex situations – Axel Leijonhufvud as quoted by Daneke (2020, p. 28).

The challenge facing AI scientists is to create intelligent, autonomous agents that can make rational decisions. In this challenge, they confront two questions: what decision theory to follow? and how to implement such a decision theory in AI systems? This chapter addressed these questions through a critical overview of the appropriateness of EUT, and by outlining how economics can contribute to the implementation of EUT in AI systems.

It was shown that modern data-based AI has economics' EUT as its basis – the *Homo Economicus* – which is a boundedly rational Bayesian expected utility maximizer. The challenges of endowing AI agents with utility functions (goals and subgoals) were discussed, which include the problem of instrumental goals, the possibility of utility function instability, and coordination challenges in multi-actor and HACs settings. These challenges complicate the design of future AI systems whose values and actions need to be aligned with human interests. The first contribution of this chapter was to outline how economic decision-making theory can address these.

A second contribution of this chapter can now be stated. This is that using EUT as a decision theory constrains AI to "small worlds," in the terminology of Savage (1954). Savage used two proverbs to explain the difference between small and large worlds and argued that Bayesian rationality is applicable to the former and less useful in the latter. One proverb is "Look before you leap" and another is "Cross that bridge when you come to it." As Binmore (2007, p. 25) explains, "You are in a small world if it is feasible always to look before you leap. You are in a large world if there are some bridges that you cannot cross before you come to them."

"Narrow" AI systems inhabit small worlds. They have no choice. As the discussion referring to the Ellsberg Paradox pointed out, implicitly, all AI systems are therefore "screened," meaning that we restrict the class of agents who apply EUT. We also restrict the class of agents by the data and algorithms we endow them with. And second, all current narrow AI systems are, being based on the Bayesian approach, of the "look before you leap" type. Unlike humans, AI still cannot cross that bridge when it comes to it. This establishes the constrained domain of what we call *narrow* AI systems, which "are extremely bounded in that they are highly specialized on specific tasks and thus might not behave rationally beyond their dedicated domain" (Wagner, 2020, p. 114).

In practice, therefore, based on *homo economicus*, the domain of AI systems is restricted to narrow applications, for example, chatbots or search engines, which are the small worlds in terms of the EUT approach. In the world of narrow AI, therefore, concerns about AI alignment may lose urgency. The risks for the safe use of narrow AI are therefore perhaps better labeled safety issues, rather than alignment issues.

Finally, a third contribution of this chapter was not only to describe how AI as a field benefits from the economic theory of decision-making but also to point to several areas where economists may learn from AI scientists as they implement EUT. One such area is procedural rationality. Economic theory tends to ignore the reasoning process by which agents make rational decisions, that is, how agents find the optimum of their expected utility functions (Dixon, 2001). Economics has preferred *substantive rationality* over *procedural rationality* (Simon, 1978). It amounts to an approach where "what decisions are made is more important than how they are made" (Harré, 2021, p. 12).

As Dixon (2001) has suggested, there is a need in economics to consider the process of reasoning itself, because human decision-making is prone to mistakes – even beyond those due to being bounded by computational ability. He concludes[14] that "the role for

[14] Dixon (2001) states that AI research, by highlighting the mechanisms of reasoning, may also throw light on strategic behavior, where economic agents may face incentives to intentionally make mistakes.

artificial intelligence in economics would then seem primarily to be in situations where economic agents make mistakes, and possibly bad mistakes."

AI research, such as in RL, may also help economists overcome computational difficulties in understanding reasoning under bounded rationality (Charpentier et al., 2021) and help to model human behavior in disequilibrium situations (Dixon, 2001). One may also interpret nonrational quirks in human judgment as the result of AI learning techniques (e.g., DL or RL) that are "inappropriately applied" (Camerer, 2019).

In sum, economics helps AI to model rational decision-making by artificial intelligent agents and to constrain these decisions to small worlds; and AI may help economics to model human decision-making better.

In Chapter 4, we start to explore the possible implications for aggregate economic outcomes – such as economic growth, employment, and productivity – when the intelligent, autonomous agents – the AI agents – that computer scientists create based on the economics of decision-making are utilized in the production process. The model we present in Chapter 4 is aimed, *inter alia*, to help evaluate the labor market implications of AI.

4 Artificial Intelligence in the Production Function*

4.1 INTRODUCTION

In Chapter 1, we motivated this book noting that, despite all the hype and hysteria surrounding AI, economics as a field has only to a limited degree, so far, taken on the challenge of helping to understand AI (Agrawal et al., 2019b). In Chapter 2, we further argued that the one area where economists have been taking note of AI has been trying to understand its impact on labor markets. We pointed out that the empirical tests of these impacts – aimed for instance at measuring the job destruction or job creation impact of automation through robotics – suffered from two shortcomings. First, most studies are not concerned with software-based AI systems automating human labor, but with embodied robots (e.g., Chiacchio et al., 2018). And two, studies generally took their theoretical point of departure from the task approach to labor markets (e.g., Autor, 2013).

Studying robotic automation using the task approach is for instance done by Acemoglu and Restrepo (2018b) – the AR model – who incorporated the task approach into an endogenous growth model. The AR model tries to go beyond robotics, positioning itself as a general automation-technology model. However, it remains wedded to the task approach and as such models tasks and skills in automation, but not abilities. Abilities may however be a more appropriate view of what software-based AI, such as LLMs, bring to labor markets (Hernández-Orallo, 2017; Tolan et al., 2020).

* This chapter is based on, updates and extends, Gries and Naudé (2021) and Gries and Naudé (2022).

Therefore, in this chapter, we propose a model wherein AI provides abilities that are combined with human skills to provide an aggregate intermediate service good. In Chapter 2, we pointed out that the dominant approach used to underpin empirical work on robotics automation has been the task approach, introduced by Autor (2013). In this chapter, we argue that this approach, while useful, can be modified to better reflect the nuances that automation through AI software entails.

The rest of the chapter proceeds as follows. In Section 4.2, we discuss the relevant literature. In Section 4.3, we provide an intuitive explanation and motivate why we treat AI as having abilities, rather than skills. Section 4.4 contains the core of this chapter – a model of AI in the production function. Section 4.5 concludes.

4.2 RELEVANT LITERATURE

In Chapter 2, we mentioned that one of the main areas where economists have been interested in AI has been on its impact on labor markets. This work has been based on a long tradition in economics in dealing with the impact of technological innovations on labor markets. The main theoretical approach in this has been the theory of skill-biased technological change (SBTC).

In SBTC, technological change can either substitute for or complement various types of labor. This can result in changes in demand for labor – which can cause job losses – and changes in the wage distribution (Acemoglu, 2002; Autor et al., 1999; Card and DiNardo, 2002; Goldin and Katz, 2010).

From an SBTC perspective, the impact of automation technologies, in the past mainly robotics, has been modeled using overlapping generations (OLGs) frameworks (e.g., Benzell et al., 2018; Sachs et al., 2015), endogenous growth models, or labor market models. In these, the main approach is to define the total output to be produced using a variety of tasks, based on the *task approach* – see, for example, Acemoglu and Restrepo (2020) and Acemoglu and Restrepo (2018b). We briefly summarize the task approach before proceeding.

4.2.1 *The Task Approach*

A task is "a unit of work activity that produces output Y" (Autor et al., 2003, p. 186) and can be expressed as:

$$Y = \beta \left[\int_{N-1}^{N} y(i)^{\frac{\eta-1}{\eta}} di \right]^{\frac{\eta}{\eta-1}} \tag{4.1}$$

where y denotes a task and η the substitution elasticity.

Acemoglu and Restrepo (2018b), in their AR model, incorporate the task approach in an endogenous growth model. They specify separate production functions for tasks that can be automated and for tasks that cannot be automated but provided only with labor. This follows from their indexing tasks ranging from $N - 1$ to N so that there can be a point $I \in [N-1, N]$ with tasks $i \leq I$ that can be automated and tasks $i > I$ that cannot be automated – the assumption is that labor has a comparative advantage in tasks high up in the index. For tasks $i > I$, they specify the following CES production function (p. 1494):

$$y(i) = \beta(\zeta) \left[\eta^{\frac{1}{\zeta}} q(i)^{\frac{\zeta-1}{\zeta}} + (1-\eta)^{\frac{1}{\zeta}} (\gamma(i) l(i))^{\frac{\zeta-1}{\zeta}} \right]^{\frac{\zeta}{\zeta-1}} \tag{4.2}$$

And for tasks $i \leq I$, a similar specification is used, except with the inclusion now of capital (k), which is a perfect substitute for labor l with CES elasticity $\eta \in (0, 1)$:

$$y(i) = \beta(\zeta) \left[\eta^{\frac{1}{\zeta}} q(i)^{\frac{\zeta-1}{\zeta}} + (1-\eta)^{\frac{1}{\zeta}} (k(i) + \gamma(i) l(i))^{\frac{\zeta-1}{\zeta}} \right]^{\frac{\zeta}{\zeta-1}} \tag{4.3}$$

where $\gamma(i)$ is the productivity of labor in task i and $\zeta \in (0, \infty)$ the elasticity of substitution between intermediate inputs (q) and labor inputs (l).

It can be seen from Equation (4.3) that AI is not explicitly modeled, not defined, in the AR model with the task approach! In Acemoglu and Restrepo (2018b), AI is implicitly contained within the variable q – the intermediate inputs – which the authors define as "a task-specific intermediate [. . .] which embodies the technology used either for automation or for production with labor."

Technological progress (e.g., progress in AI) in the AR model is of two kinds: it can either make more tasks amendable to automation (reflected in a shift of I) or transform old tasks that could be automated into new tasks in which labor has a comparative advantage, reflected in an increase in $N - I$ and a reduction in $I - (N - 1)$. In a static version of the AR model, k is fixed and technology (including AI) exogenous. As such, technological innovation changes the allocation of tasks between capital and labor, and this in turn will change relative factor prices – with consequences for employment and the wage share of labor.

With these production functions for tasks carried over into a dynamic setting, Acemoglu and Restrepo (2018b) endogenize capital and technological progress and tease out the long-run implications of automation on jobs and inequality. Now, the price of capital relative to the wage rate will determine the extent to which new tasks are created, and they show that a stable balanced growth path is possible if progress in automation and the creation of new tasks are equal. Any deviations from this will set corrective market forces in operation. In other words, automation has reinstatement effects – it creates new tasks.

4.2.2 *Abilities, or Skills and Tasks?*

As Equations (4.2) and (4.3) reflect, whether or not a task can be automated or not depend on their position in the index – and it is assumed that in tasks higher up the index, labor has a comparative advantage over robots or AI. Typically, higher up the index, one finds tasks that require higher levels of skills – skills that perform less routine tasks than nonroutine tasks (Acemoglu and Restrepo, 2020). Hence, automation is implicitly seen to provide a skill that corresponds to a task somewhere along an index from low skills to high skills.

This may be a valid way of modeling automation that occurs through robots. To the extent that robots depend on software, they are a form of embedded AI, as opposed to purely software AI, such as chatbots (see Chapter 2). However, if we consider the discussion on the definition and nature in Chapter 2, then one may question whether this is the most appropriate way of modeling automation through modern AI. Recall the definition of AI from Chapter 2 that it is software with *abilities/capabilities*:

> any software technology with at least one of the following *capabilities*: perception—including audio, visual, textual, and tactile (e.g., face recognition), decision-making (e.g., medical diagnosis systems), prediction (e.g., weather forecast), automatic knowledge extraction and pattern recognition from data (e.g., discovery of fake news circles in social media), interactive communication (e.g., social robots or chat bots), and logical reasoning (e.g., theory development from premises) (Vinuesa et al., 2020, p. 1).

As per this definition of AI, the visual recognition of objects is an *ability* – the ability to see – and that this ability can be used to perform a *task*, for instance, the task of driving a car or the task of recognizing faces. Applying the ability of being able to see to either driving, or to facial recognition, requires *skills*, which require human judgment.

Thus, even though an AI model can drive a car because of its ability to "see," we still need human skills to make the decision and judgment to apply the ability to the task of driving. No AI algorithm (yet) autonomously decides where and how to apply various abilities, which in the case of current AI, predominantly machine learning (ML), is based on big data (see Chapter 9). It is this combination of human skills, particularly ICT skills, which together with AI's big data-based abilities, results in AI applications – that we illustrated in Table 2.1 (see Chapter 2).

Several scholars have argued that abilities better characterize the nature of the services that AI provides (Hernández-Orallo, 2017). According to Tolan et al. (2020, p. 6–7), abilities are "a better parameter to evaluate progress in AI" because ML provides abilities to do tasks, and not skills, which are a human attribute requiring experience, knowledge, and common sense. Skills are not an attribute of AI. This means that with AI providing abilities, such as the ability to understand human language or recognize objects, it is necessary to go beyond skills and tasks when evaluating any labor market impacts of AI, because the adoption of AI will ultimately depend on its abilities *relative* to the abilities of human labor.

Some abilities may be more (or less) likely to be provided by AI, which means that "AI may cause workplaces to transform the way a task is performed" (Tolan et al., 2020, p. 6). In other words, the technological feasibility of AI in automation will depend on the extent that it changes the very nature of tasks. This however cannot be modeled adequately by the task approach to labor markets.

4.2.3 Modeling Automation

From the task approach and its embeddedness in the AR model as discussed earlier, the distinctions between high-skilled labor and low-skilled labor and between routine tasks and nonroutine tasks were pointed out as essential features of modeling automation. This is not the only way it has been modeled. Cords and Prettner (2019) for example introduced a third production factor in addition to labor and capital, which they called "automation capital." An automation technology can then be simulated as either complementing or substituting for labor. Most often, automation is modeled to substitute for low-skilled labor or routine tasks and complement high-skilled labor and nonroutine tasks. *Routine-replacing technical change* (RRTC) is when automation reduces the demand for middle-skilled labor, as this labor may be performing more routine tasks (Autor and Salomons, 2018; Gregory et al., 2019). Exceptions to the idea that automation is skill-biased or only of concern for middle-skilled routine tasks include Susskind (2017) who proposes a *task encroachment model* wherein output is produced by labor and two varieties of capital: "traditional" capital and "advanced" capital, with the latter eventually driving labor out; and Gries and Naudé (2020) who propose a human service input wherein *all* types of labor can be potentially substituted.

Prettner and Strulik (2017) used a, R&D-based growth model (see Jones, 1995) with high-skilled and low-skilled labors. A critical assumption they make is that high-skilled labor complements machines or robots (the automation technology) and that machines and robots substitute for low-skilled labor. They then show how technological innovation drives economic growth in a process accompanied by more automation, an increase in the skills premium, a decline in the labor share, and higher unemployment.

Acemoglu and Restrepo (2018a,b) similarly used a task approach-based model wherein automation is an expansion of the set of tasks that can be produced with capital. In Acemoglu and Restrepo (2020), they embed the task approach-based model within an endogenous growth model. These models have as result that some tasks, traditionally performed by labor, can be taken over by capital, and would lead to a reduction (a displacement) of the demand for labor. However, they allow for the adoption of automation to create new tasks and hence raise the demand for labor as a countervailing effect, so that the net impact of automation on jobs will depend on the relative strengths of the "displacement" effect and the "countervailing" effects. They postulate that AI-driven innovation will be different from other types of innovation in being more likely to generate countervailing effects. In their model, the simultaneous occurrence of growth with higher income inequality, as in Prettner and Strulik (2017), is recognized as an area for further study (as an extension of their model), as they recognize that the rise in income inequality could mean that "the rise in real incomes resulting from automation ends up in the hands of a narrow segment of the population with much lower marginal propensity to consume than those losing incomes and their jobs" (Acemoglu and Restrepo, 2018b, p. 33).

To allow for and model the joint occurrence of low growth and higher inequality due to automation, Benzell et al. (2018) and Sachs et al. (2015) use an OLGs model to explore how the distributive impacts of automation may lead via the demand side to growth constraints. Sachs et al. (2015), as others, modeled automation through robotics, which they defined as machines that "allow for output without labor" (ibid., p. 3). They found that an increase in automation can raise output over the short term but will also lead to lower wages and consumption over the longer run, due to the lower demand for labor. Thus, over the short term, higher economic growth and inequality may be simultaneous, but this will turn out to be immiserating growth. This will particularly be likely in their model if the goods produced by robots are close substitutes for goods produced by labor, and when traditional capital is a more important factor of production in nonrobotic production. Benzell et al. (2018) build on this by focusing not so much on how automation is incorporated into the production function but rather on what it implies for saving and consumption patterns. Their model predicts a decline in the labor share, tech booms and busts, and "growing dependency of current output on past software investment" (ibid., p. 21). Both Sachs et al. (2015) and Benzell et al. (2018) call for more attention to the distributional aspects of automation; in the words of the latter, their "central massage is disturbing. Absent appropriate fiscal policy that redistributes from winners to losers, smart machines can mean long-term misery for all" (Benzell et al., 2018, p. 22).

In Chapter 5 of this book, we provide an endogenous growth model that addresses the central concerns in Benzell et al. (2018) and Sachs et al. (2015). Here we add imperfect markets and information, allow for the gradual diffusion of AI, and show that progress in AI can be consistent with high employment, low productivity, and low growth, and not high productivity and high unemployment as per most of the available endogenous models. This is due to our rejection of the standard assumption of representative households – and hence being in a position to have different consumption and savings preferences. Through this, aggregate demand can act as a brake on growth – which is a major point of difference from the Acemoglu and Restrepo (2020) task approach-based endogenous growth model.

Before we do so, we return to our concern to model AI as providing abilities. The model that we propose and described in Section 4.3 does not replace the task approach; rather it compliments it. By combining AI abilities with human skills in the production function, we show that the extent of automation through AI technologies will be greater if (1) the economy is relatively abundant in sophisticated programs and machine abilities compared to human skills; (2) the economy hosts a relatively large number of AI-providing businesses and experts; and (3) the task-specific productivity of AI services is relatively high compared to the task-specific productivity of general labor and labor skills.

4.3 AI IN THE PRODUCTION FUNCTION: A NOVEL APPROACH

The task approach to labor markets and its embedding in the AR-model offer important and useful contributions to model automation technologies in economics. They are general approaches which provide insights into all automation technologies, from robots to AI. While being general has its advantages, the disadvantage is that the specific features of a technology are omitted. In the case of AI, these specific features may however matter, for example, for the extent to which it diffuses in the economy. Unlike most other automation technologies, AI depends on big data, a resource that tends to be nonrival in use, and high levels of human ICT skills. In this section, we propose a partial equilibrium model wherein we incorporate these specific features of AI.

4.3.1 Human Service as Intermediate Good

If AI is essentially a technology that provides certain abilities, it will always need to be combined or used in tandem with skills, which are, as we pointed out earlier, distinct human attributes requiring experience, knowledge, and common sense (Tolan et al., 2020). We define this combination of AI and human skills as *human services*, H. To be precise, a human service is an intermediate service good that is generated by variously skilled human labor and AI. Human service

$[H = H(Labor, AI)]$ is produced following the task approach to labor markets specification; however, it can be easily included in any conventional production function leading to a nested production process $Y = Y(H, K)$. Due to this nested structure, the *human service task approach* that we propose here allows us to analyze and separately discuss effects specific to the task approach, without much increase in model complexity. Thus, a shortcoming of AR modeling – its high complexity – is (somewhat) addressed.

The human service production function can be written as $H = H(L_L, A_L, A_{IT}, B_{IT})$. Here L_L is the number of workers each providing given hours of work, A_L is an index of human skills (reflecting experience and human abilities), A_{IT} is the total number of ML abilities (e.g., algorithms) in the economy, and B_{IT} are the IT-business owners or experts providing and running AI services. Hence, our approach enriches and extends the simple task approach by integrating human skills with AI abilities, as per the arguments of Hernández-Orallo (2017) and Tolan et al. (2020).

The production function for human services can be specified, similar to Equation (4.2), as

$$H = \left(\int_{N-1}^{N} h(z)^{\frac{\sigma-1}{\sigma}} dz \right)^{\frac{\sigma}{\sigma-1}} \tag{4.4}$$

where z denotes each task in a unit interval $[N-1, N]$, and $h(z)$ is the output of task z. As tasks range between $N-1$ and N, the total number of tasks is constant. Note that whereas Acemoglu and Restrepo (2018b) define total production as the result of $N-1$ to N tasks, we propose to define total production as the result of human service inputs and other inputs such as capital or other intermediates, where human service inputs consist of the outputs of different tasks. Further, with L_L and B_{IT}, we separate between labor and owners, respectively, providers of AI as a more or less disembodied productive technology.

Each task z can either be produced with labor, $l(z)$, or only with AI services provided by AI businesses, $b_{IT}(z)$, if the task can be done by AI. Therefore, there are two sets of tasks. Tasks $z \in [N-1, N_{IT}]$ can be produced by both labor and AI services [described by process (a) in Equation (4.5)], and tasks $z \in (N_{IT}, N]$ can only be produced by labor [process (b) in Equation (4.5)]. These tasks can be the niche in which labor can continue to specialize in the presence of AI-driven services or automation, as per Arntz et al. (2017). Thus, the output of a task can be stated in two ways

$$h(z) = \begin{cases} \gamma_L(z) l(z) A_L + \gamma_{IT}(z) b_{IT}(z) A_{IT} D & \text{process (a) if } z \in [N-1, N_{IT}] \\ \gamma_L(z) l(z) A_L & \text{process (b) if } z \in (N_{IT}, N] \end{cases} \tag{4.5}$$

Note that the production process (a) implies perfect substitution of human labor abilities by AI, as the human labor ability $(A_L \gamma_L(z) l(z))$ is not a necessary input for this task. To provide further justification for the specification in Equation (4.5), we can note the following:

First, while $l(z)$ is the volume of hours employed in the specific task z, A_L is a description of generally available skills, which includes human *abilities* and *experiences*. So humans who are employed, irrespective of which tasks they perform, are endowed with A_L. Humans can identify problems, understand social signals and social interactions, detect and handle positive and negative social externalities in groups, use common sense, and think ahead. These very human skills have emerged over hundreds of thousands of years of biological evolution interacting with the environment and culture, including education. As these human skills indexed by A_L are homogeneously related to all human labor L_L, this endowment is potentially available in each task z without rivalry and is similar to a public good, $A_L l(z)$. However, in some tasks, these human skills are particularly valuable, while in others, they are not really needed. This task-specific productivity is indicated by $\gamma_L(z)$. Thus, in Equation (4.5), total human contribution to a task is $\gamma_L(z) A_L l(z)$.

Second, as far as production with AI is concerned, A_{IT} denotes the total number and quality of ML algorithms or *machine abilities* in the economy that can provide a general AI service. The idea here is that an AI service contains two components. One is a general AI algorithm or code and the other is a specific application of the algorithm based on particular data. For example, A_{IT} would include various generic ML models and techniques, from logistical regressions to deep learning (DL) and convolutional neural networks (CNN) and their culmination in large language models (LLMs) – see Chapter 2. These algorithms are nonspecific with respect to a particular domain of usage. As such, they can be used without rivalry, although they can become club goods if access ot them can be licensed.

Since ML algorithms are trained on big data (training can be either supervised or unsupervised by a skilled human – indeed even the most sophisticated LLM at the time of writing requires human intervention in the training, specifically through reinforcement learning from human feedback- RLHF), data D is the raw material needed to produce an AI service. Hence, we can denote the complementarity between data and algorithms as $A_{IT}D$, which is the fundamental infrastructure for specific AI services. Since the use of data is nonrival, $A_{IT}D$ is a club good. Note however that $A_{IT}D$ is yet not an AI service. The AI service is obtained when $A_{IT}D$ is applied to a particular task – where it creates value. This application is facilitated by IT experts $b_{IT}(z)$ who tailor $A_{IT}D$ for a particular purpose or business opportunity, z, adding up in total to B_{IT} applications.

It is perhaps useful here to highlight the essential difference between AI as an automation technology and other automation technologies, such as robots. Like AI, robots also have abilities. These abilities, like those of say capital equipment, are for example to have much greater strength and endurance than humans. Humans use their skills to apply robotic strength and endurance where it can add economic value. Robots do not decide this themselves. In this, they are thus similar to AI. Where they are different from AI is in the complimentary skills that their deployment requires. AI, as opposed to robots, depend more critically on data and ML, as discussed in the previous paragraph, and this has, as shown later slightly different implications for the extent of automation.

Finally, AI services that have been tailored to a particular task will be characterized by different levels of task-specific productivity, $\gamma_{IT}(z)$. In total, therefore, AI service production for a particular task z can be described as $\gamma_{IT}(z)b_{IT}(z)A_{IT}D$ in Equation (4.5a).

4.3.2 *AI Abilities and the Demand for Tasks*

If a task z with price $p_h(z)$ is produced with standard labor $h(z) = A_L\gamma_L(z)l(z)$, and labor rewards are calculated according to marginal productivity, then $p_h(z)A_L\gamma_L(z) = w_L$. Symmetrically, the same task could be produced with an AI technology so that $p_h(z)A_{IT}\gamma_{IT}(z) = w_{IT}$, with w_{IT} as the reward for the AI-supplying expert or business. Given these two conditions, and given wages in the market, for any particular task, the firm will choose the kind of service composition (AI service/automation or not) that results in the lowest unit labor costs. Thus, if the following condition holds, the task will be provided by the AI service:

$$\frac{w_{IT}}{p_h(z)A_{IT}\gamma_{IT}(z)} < \frac{w_L}{p_h(z)A_L\gamma_L(z)}$$

This rule leads to condition Equation (4.6) which identifies the switching point between automated (AI) tasks and labor tasks. If tasks are ordered in such a way that $\frac{A_L\gamma_L(z)}{A_{IT}\gamma_{IT}(z)}$ is increasing in z and the tasks with lower numbers $z \in [N-1, N_{IT}]$ are the automated tasks, task N_{IT} is the switching point from an automation task to a labor task. N_{IT} is the highest number in this order for which

$$\frac{A_L\gamma_L(N_{IT})}{A_{IT}\gamma_{IT}(N_{IT})} < \frac{w_L}{w_{IT}} \tag{4.6}$$

holds. Apart from these automated (AI) tasks $[N-1,\ N_{IT}]$, all other tasks $(N_{IT}, N]$ are produced with standard labor. Thus, the costs and respectively the price $p_h(z)$ for any task z is

$$p_h(z) = \begin{cases} \frac{w_{IT}}{A_{IT}\gamma_{IT}(z)} & \text{if } z \in [N-1, N_{IT}] \\ \frac{w_L}{A_L\gamma_L(z)} & \text{if } z \in (N_{IT}, N] \end{cases} \tag{4.7}$$

We can use this to calculate the endogenous optimal number of *tasks provided by AI* in an economy with an efficient supply of the human service:[1]

$$N_{IT} = N_{IT}\left(B_{IT}, L_L, A_{IT}, \ldots\right), \text{ with } \frac{dN_{IT}}{dB_{IT}} > 0, \quad \frac{dN_{IT}}{dL_L} < 0, \quad \frac{dN_{IT}}{dA_{IT}} > 0 \tag{4.8}$$

This result indicates that the number of automated/machine-produced tasks crucially depends on the relative availability of various input factors which are important for AI technologies. The extent of implementation and diffusion of AI technologies and the automation of human services will depend on the relative availability of the specific inputs of the human service production. This result also indicates that the relative availability of factors determines the income shares of the two types of human labor inputs. As we show in the Appendix to this chapter, an increase in the availability of AI ($A_I T$) will decrease the standard labor share of income if the elasticity of substitution (σ) is sufficiently high (σ does not even need to be larger than one). Then, the AI service can easily substitute for the tasks of standard labor. This means that there is a distributional effect from a large availability of AI on the cost of standard labor. The final outcome will however also depend on other parameters. In particular, we have to consider the relative availability of *human skills* to *machine abilities* A_L/A_{IT}; the relative abundance of the volume of *labor* to *AI-supplying experts* L_L/B_{IT}; the relative task-specific productivity at the switch point $\gamma_L(N_{IT})/\gamma_{IT}(N_{IT})$; and the volume and veracity of data available to run all these AI services, D. Thus, our modeling of AI provides a level of detail of specification that is lacking in the AR model.

4.3.3 *Optimal Human Service Supply*

From the demands for the various tasks derived in Subsection 4.3.2, total human service production can be derived. Aggregating automated tasks and labor, Equation (4.4) leads to

[1] See the Appendix to this chapter.

$$H = \left(\int_{N-1}^{N_{IT}} h(z)^{\frac{\sigma-1}{\sigma}} dz + \int_{N_{IT}}^{N} h(z)^{\frac{\sigma-1}{\sigma}} dz \right)^{\frac{\sigma}{\sigma-1}}$$

In the Appendix to this chapter, we show that this expression can be rearranged as:

$$H = \left(\left(\int_{N-1}^{N_{IT}} \gamma_{IT}(z)^{\sigma-1} dz \right)^{\frac{1}{\sigma}} (A_{IT}B_{IT})^{\frac{\sigma-1}{\sigma}} + \left(\int_{N_{IT}}^{N} \gamma_{L}(z)^{\sigma-1} dz \right)^{\frac{1}{\sigma}} (A_{L}L_{L})^{\frac{\sigma-1}{\sigma}} \right)^{\frac{\sigma}{\sigma-1}}$$

With the definitions $\Gamma_{IT}(N_{IT}, N) = \int_{N-1}^{N_{IT}} \gamma_{IT}(z)^{\sigma-1} dz$ and $\Gamma_L(N_{IT}, N) = \int_{N_{IT}}^{N} \gamma_L(z)^{\sigma-1} dz = \Gamma(N_{IT}, N)\Pi(N_{IT}, N)^{\sigma-1}$ we can rewrite the aggregate optimal human service production as

$$H = \left[(\Gamma_{IT}(N_{IT}, N))^{\frac{1}{\sigma}} (A_{IT}B_{IT})^{\frac{\sigma-1}{\sigma}} + \Gamma_L(N_{IT}, N)^{\frac{1}{\sigma}} (A_L L_L)^{\frac{\sigma-1}{\sigma}} \right]^{\frac{\sigma}{\sigma-1}} \quad (4.9)$$

This expression is similar to the familiar constant elasticity of supply (CES) production function.

4.4 CONCLUDING REMARKS

In this chapter, we provided a model of AI in the production function where AI essentially provides abilities. Our ability-sensitive specification of the task approach allowed us to gain novel insights into the labor market consequences of AI progress. Using our model, we showed that the extent to which automation through AI will occur (i.e., we have a large N_{IT}) will depend on if (1) the economy is relatively abundant in sophisticated programs and machine abilities compared to human skills; (2) the economy hosts a relatively large number of AI-providing businesses and experts; and (3) the task-specific productivity of AI services is relatively high compared to the task-specific productivity of general labor and labor skills.

Further, as access to (big) data, a resource characterized by non-rival use, is essential for task-specific AI in our model, its relative abundance will be an important determinant of the diffusion – and hence impact – of AI. This serves as a motivation for us to delve down, in Chapter 9, into consideration of the role of big data and how the government can incentivize its best use and availability.

The model we proposed here has assumed a fixed supply of labor. Clearly, this assumption may be tenuous given declining population growth in the West and China. In Chapter 10, we will allude to the possibility of an "empty planet" and a collapse in economic growth as a result of this demographic trend – see also Jones (2022). In the future, this assumption can be relaxed. If labor supply would be flexible, then higher wages for labor in the face of a declining population could incentivise otherwise AI workers to work rather as regular workers, which will in turn reduce the incentive to automate. Thus, while some may suggest automation as a response to declining population and labor, it may in fact become more difficult to sustain automation and further advances in AI under such conditions.

In conclusion, the partial equilibrium model we presented in this chapter can be imported as a package or module into endogenous growth models to elaborate the economy-wide effects of AI – thus expanding the toolkit of economists. In Chapter 5, we show one example of how this can be done – we provide an endogenous growth model with imperfect markets and information, allow for the gradual diffusion of AI, and show that progress in AI can be consistent with high employment, low productivity, and low growth, and not high productivity and high unemployment as per most of the available endogenous models.

Appendix

A Efficient Production of Human Services

Optimal Allocation within the Task Approach: Human service firms

$$\max : \pi_H = p_H H - p_h(z)h(z) = p_H \left(\int_{N-1}^{N} h(z)^{\frac{\sigma-1}{\sigma}} dz \right)^{\frac{\sigma}{\sigma-1}} - p_h(z)h(z).$$

F.O.C.

$$p_H \frac{\sigma}{\sigma-1}\left(\int_{N-1}^{N} h(z)^{\frac{\sigma-1}{\sigma}} dz\right)^{\frac{\sigma}{\sigma-1}-1} \frac{\sigma-1}{\sigma} h(z)^{\frac{\sigma-1}{\sigma}-1} - p_h(z) = 0$$

$$p_H \left(\int_{N-1}^{N} h(z)^{\frac{\sigma-1}{\sigma}} dz\right)^{\frac{\sigma}{\sigma-1}-1} h(z)^{\frac{\sigma-1}{\sigma}-1} = p_h(z)$$

$$p_H \left(\int_{N-1}^{N} h(z)^{\frac{\sigma-1}{\sigma}} dz\right)^{\frac{1}{\sigma-1}} h(z)^{-\frac{1}{\sigma}} = p_h(z)$$

$$p_H H^{\frac{1}{\sigma}} h(z)^{-\frac{1}{\sigma}} = p_h(z)$$

arriving at

$$h(z) = \frac{H}{p_h(z)^{\sigma}} p_H^{\sigma} \tag{4.10}$$

Demand for task *z*: Using marginal production and productivity rules

$h(z_{IT}) = A_{IT}\gamma_{IT}(z)b_{IT}(z)$	production (4.5)	$h(z_L) = A_L\gamma_L(z)l_L(z)$
$p_h A_{IT}\gamma_{IT}(z)b_{IT}(z) = b_{IT}(z)w_{IT}$	marginal productivity and factor reward	$p_h A_L\gamma_L(z)l_L(z) = l_L(z)w_L$
$p_h\,(z_{IT}) = \frac{w_{IT}}{A_{IT}\gamma_{IT}(z_{IT})}$	price = unit labor costs	$p_h\,(z_L) = \frac{w_L}{A_L\gamma_L(z_L)}$

and plugging in gives Equation (4.11) as being the optimal demand for $h(z)$,

$$\begin{aligned} h(z) &= \frac{H}{\left(\frac{w_{IT}}{A_{IT}\gamma_{IT}(z)}\right)^{\sigma}} p_H^{\sigma}, \qquad & h(z) &= \frac{H}{\left(\frac{w_L}{A_L\gamma_L(z)}\right)^{\sigma}} p_H^{\sigma}, \\ h(z) &= p_H^{\sigma} H \left(\frac{A_{IT}}{w_{IT}}\right)^{\sigma} \gamma_{IT}(z)^{\sigma}, \qquad & h(z) &= p_H^{\sigma} H \left(\frac{A_L}{w_L}\right)^{\sigma} \gamma_L(z)^{\sigma}. \end{aligned} \tag{4.11}$$

Demand for each kind of labor in task *z*: In order to determine the marginal productivity for each total labor input, the productivity for each kind of labor is derived from Equation (4.5), and we can obtain the optimal demand for IT labor:

$$A_{IT}\gamma_{IT}(z)b_{IT}(z) = h(z) = p_H^{\sigma} H \left(\frac{A_{IT}}{w_{IT}}\right)^{\sigma} \gamma_{IT}(z)^{\sigma},$$

$$b_{IT}(z) = \begin{cases} \left(\frac{p_H}{w_{IT}}\right)^{\sigma} H\,(A_{IT})^{\sigma-1}\,\gamma_{IT}(z)^{\sigma-1} & \text{if } z \in [N-1, N_{IT}] \\ 0 & \text{if } z \in [N_{IT}, N] \end{cases} \tag{4.12}$$

and standard labor:

$$A_L \gamma_L(z) l_L(z) = h(z) = p_H^{\sigma} H \left(\frac{A_L}{w_L}\right)^{\sigma} \gamma_L(z)^{\sigma}$$

$$l_L(z) = \begin{cases} 0 & \text{if } z \in [N-1, N_{IT}] \\ \left(\frac{p_H}{w_L}\right)^{\sigma} H \left(A_L\right)^{\sigma-1} \gamma_L(z)^{\sigma-1} & \text{if } z \in (N_{IT}, N] \end{cases} \tag{4.13}$$

Total IT labor is fully employed and allocates to all tasks using IT labor. This holds for standard labor respectively

$$B_{IT} = \int_{N-1}^{N_{IT}} b_{IT}(z) dz, \text{ and} \tag{4.14}$$

$$L_L = \int_{N_{IT}}^{N} l_L(z) dz. \tag{4.15}$$

Income of IT expert w_{IT}:. With the integral in (5.16) $[b_{IT}(z) = \frac{p_H^{\sigma}}{w_{IT}^{\sigma}} H \gamma_{IT}(z)^{\sigma-1} (A_{IT})^{\sigma-1}]$, we obtain

$$\int_{N-1}^{N_{IT}} l_{IT}(z) dz = \int_{N-1}^{N_{IT}} \frac{p_H^{\sigma}}{w_{IT}^{\sigma}} H \gamma_{IT}(z)^{\sigma-1} (A_{IT})^{\sigma-1} dz$$

$$B_{IT} = \frac{p_H^{\sigma}}{w_{IT}^{\sigma}} H (A_{IT})^{\sigma-1} \int_{N-1}^{N_{IT}} \gamma_{IT}(z)^{\sigma-1} dz$$

$$w_{IT}^{\sigma} = p_H^{\sigma} \frac{H}{B_{IT}} (A_{IT})^{\sigma-1} \int_{N-1}^{N_{IT}} \gamma_{IT}(z)^{\sigma-1} dz$$

such that with full employed IT labor, we can determine the wages of IT labor as

$$w_{IT} = p_H \left(\frac{H}{B_{IT}}\right)^{\frac{1}{\sigma}} (A_{IT})^{\frac{\sigma-1}{\sigma}} \left(\int_{N-1}^{N_{IT}} \gamma_{IT}(z)^{\sigma-1} dz\right)^{\frac{1}{\sigma}} \tag{4.16}$$

Symmetrically for standard labor,

$$\int_{N_{IT}}^{N} l_L(z) dz = \int_{N_{IT}}^{N} \frac{p_H^{\sigma}}{w_{IT}^{\sigma}} H \gamma_{IT}(z)^{\sigma-1} (A_{IT})^{\sigma-1} dz$$

$$B_{IT} = \frac{p_H^{\sigma}}{w_{IT}^{\sigma}} H (A_{IT})^{\sigma-1} \int_{N_{IT}}^{N} \gamma_{IT}(z)^{\sigma-1} dz$$

$$w_{IT}^{\sigma} = p_H^{\sigma} \frac{H}{L_{IT}} (A_{IT})^{\sigma-1} \int_{N_{IT}}^{N} \gamma_{IT}(z)^{\sigma-1} dz$$

$$w_L = p_H \left(\frac{H}{L_L}\right)^{\frac{1}{\sigma}} (A_L)^{\frac{\sigma-1}{\sigma}} \left(\int_{N_{IT}}^{N} \gamma_L(z)^{\sigma-1} dz\right)^{\frac{1}{\sigma}}. \tag{4.17}$$

The resulting internal relative factor productivity for labor is:

$$\frac{w_L}{w_{IT}} = \frac{\left(\frac{p_H H}{L_L}\right)^{\frac{1}{\sigma}} (A_L)^{\frac{\sigma-1}{\sigma}} \left(\int_{N_{IT}}^{N} \gamma_L(z)^{\sigma-1} dz\right)^{\frac{1}{\sigma}}}{\left(\frac{p_H H}{L_{IT}}\right)^{\frac{1}{\sigma}} (A_{IT})^{\frac{\sigma-1}{\sigma}} \left(\int_{N-1}^{N_{IT}} \gamma_{IT}(z)^{\sigma-1} dz\right)^{\frac{1}{\sigma}}}$$

$$\frac{w_L}{w_{IT}} = \left(\frac{B_{IT}}{L_L}\right)^{\frac{1}{\sigma}} \left(\frac{A_L}{A_{IT}}\right)^{\frac{\sigma-1}{\sigma}} \left(\frac{\int_{N_{IT}}^{N} \gamma_L(z)^{\sigma-1} dz}{\int_{N-1}^{N_{IT}} \gamma_{IT}(z)^{\sigma-1} dz}\right)^{\frac{1}{\sigma}}$$

Endogenous switch to AI/automated tasks N_{IT}: From the discussion in the chapter, we recall that tasks are ordered such that $\gamma(z) = \frac{\gamma_L(z)}{\gamma_{IT}(z)}$, and $\frac{\partial \gamma(z)}{\partial z} > 0$. If it is assumed that task N_{IT} is the task that exactly separates the production mode, and if tasks are continuous, then

$$\frac{A_L \gamma_L(N_{IT})}{A_{IT} \gamma_{IT}(N_{IT})} < \frac{w_L}{w_{IT}} = \left(\frac{B_{IT}}{L_L}\right)^{\frac{1}{\sigma}} \left(\frac{A_L}{A_{IT}}\right)^{\frac{\sigma-1}{\sigma}} \left(\frac{\int_{N_{IT}}^{N} \gamma_L(z)^{\sigma-1} dz}{\int_{N-1}^{N_{IT}} \gamma_{IT}(z)^{\sigma-1} dz}\right)^{\frac{1}{\sigma}}$$

$$0 = G = \gamma(N_{IT}) - \left(\frac{A_{IT} B_{IT}}{A_L L_L}\right)^{\frac{1}{\sigma}} \left(\frac{\int_{N_{IT}}^{N} \gamma_L(z)^{\sigma-1} dz}{\int_{N-1}^{N_{IT}} \gamma_{IT}(z)^{\sigma-1} dz}\right)^{\frac{1}{\sigma}} \tag{4.18}$$

If $\frac{dG}{dN_{IT}} \neq 0$, G implicitly defines a function $N_{IT} = N_{IT}(B_{IT}, L_L, A_{IT}, \ldots)$. Thus, we need to calculate the respective derivatives.

$$\frac{dG}{dN_{IT}} = \frac{\partial \gamma(N_{IT})}{\partial N_{IT}} + \left[\begin{array}{c} \frac{1}{\sigma}\left(\frac{A_{IT} B_{IT}}{A_L L_L}\right)^{\frac{1}{\sigma}} \left(\frac{\int_{N_{IT}}^{N} \gamma_L(z)^{\sigma-1} dz}{\int_{N-1}^{I} \gamma_{IT}(z)^{\sigma-1} dz}\right)^{\frac{1}{\sigma}} \\ \left[\frac{\gamma_L(N_{IT})^{\sigma-1}}{\int_{N_{IT}}^{N} \gamma_L(N_{IT})^{\sigma-1} dz} + \frac{\gamma_{IT}(N_{IT})^{\sigma-1}}{\int_{N-1}^{N_{IT}} \gamma_{IT}(N_{IT})^{\sigma-1} dz}\right] \end{array}\right] > 0$$

and defining $\Gamma_{IT}(N_{IT}) = \int_{N-1}^{N_{IT}} \gamma_{IT}(z)^{\sigma-1} dz$, $\frac{d\Gamma_{IT}}{dN_{IT}} = \gamma_{IT}(N_{IT})^{\sigma-1}$; and $\Gamma_L(N_{IT}) = \int_{N_{IT}}^{N} \gamma_L(z)^{\sigma-1} dz$, $\frac{d\Gamma_L}{dN_{IT}} = -\gamma_L(N_{IT})^{\sigma-1}$, we obtain

$$\frac{\partial G}{\partial N_{IT}} = \frac{\partial \gamma(N_{IT})}{\partial N_{IT}} + \frac{1}{\sigma}\left(\frac{A_{IT} B_{IT}}{A_L L_L}\right)^{\frac{1}{\sigma}} \left(\frac{\Gamma_L(N_{IT})}{\Gamma_{IT}(N_{IT})}\right)^{\frac{1}{\sigma}} \left[\frac{\gamma_L(N_{IT})^{\sigma-1}}{\Gamma_L(N_{IT})} + \frac{\gamma_{IT}(N_{IT})^{\sigma-1}}{\Gamma_{IT}(N_{IT})}\right] > 0$$

$$\frac{\partial G}{\partial A_{IT}} = -\frac{1}{\sigma}\left(\frac{A_{IT} B_{IT}}{A_L L_L}\right)^{\frac{1}{\sigma}-1} \left(\frac{\Gamma_L(N_{IT})}{\Gamma_{IT}(N_{IT})}\right)^{\frac{1}{\sigma}} \frac{B_{IT}}{A_L L_L} < 0$$

and the derivative of the implicit function $N_{IT} = N_{IT}(A_{IT})$ is

$$\frac{dN_{IT}}{dA_{IT}} = -\frac{\frac{\partial G}{\partial A_{IT}}}{\frac{\partial G}{\partial N_{IT}}} > 0$$

More specific:

$$\frac{dN_{IT}}{dA_{IT}} = \frac{\frac{1}{\sigma}\left(\frac{A_{IT}B_{IT}}{A_L L_L}\right)^{\frac{1}{\sigma}}\left(\frac{\Gamma_L(N_{IT})}{\Gamma_{IT}(N_{IT})}\right)^{\frac{1}{\sigma}}\frac{1}{A_{IT}}}{\frac{\partial\gamma(N_{IT})}{\partial N_{IT}} + \frac{1}{\sigma}\left(\frac{A_{IT}B_{IT}}{A_L L_L}\right)^{\frac{1}{\sigma}}\left(\frac{\Gamma_L(N_{IT})}{\Gamma_{IT}(N_{IT})}\right)^{\frac{1}{\sigma}}\left[\frac{\gamma_L(N_{IT})^{\sigma-1}}{\Gamma_L(N_{IT})} + \frac{\gamma_{IT}(N_{IT})^{\sigma-1}}{\Gamma_{IT}(N_{IT})}\right]}$$

$$\begin{aligned}\eta_{N_{IT},A_{IT}} &= \frac{dN_{IT}}{dA_{IT}}\frac{A_{IT}}{N_{IT}} \\ &= \frac{1}{\sigma\frac{\partial\gamma(N_{IT})}{\partial N_{IT}}\left(\frac{A_L L_L}{A_{IT}B_{IT}}\frac{\Gamma_{IT}(N_{IT})}{\Gamma_L(N_{IT})}\right)^{\frac{1}{\sigma}} + \frac{\gamma_L(N_{IT})^{\sigma-1}}{\Gamma_L(N_{IT})} + \frac{\gamma_{IT}(N_{IT})^{\sigma-1}}{\Gamma_{IT}(N_{IT})}}\frac{1}{N_{IT}}\end{aligned}$$

A.1 Total Supply of Human Service Inputs

Consider that $h(z) = p_H^\sigma H\left(\frac{A_{IT}}{w_{IT}}\right)^\sigma \gamma_{IT}(z)^\sigma$ for $z \in [N-1, N_{IT}$, and $h(z) = p_H^\sigma H\left(\frac{A_L}{w_L}\right)^\sigma \gamma_L(z)^\sigma$ for $z \in [N_{IT}, N]$. Plugging this in Equation (4.4) generates an expression for the total value of H:

$$H = \left(\int_{N-1}^{N_{IT}} h(z)^{\frac{\sigma-1}{\sigma}}dz + \int_{N_{IT}}^{N} h(z)^{\frac{\sigma-1}{\sigma}}dz\right)^{\frac{\sigma}{\sigma-1}}$$

$$= \left(\int_{N-1}^{N_{IT}}\left(p_H^\sigma H\left(\frac{A_{IT}}{w_{IT}}\right)^\sigma\gamma_I(z)^\sigma\right)^{\frac{\sigma-1}{\sigma}}dz + \int_{N_{IT}}^{N}\left(p_H^\sigma H\left(\frac{A_L}{w_L}\right)^\sigma\gamma_L(z)^\sigma\right)^{\frac{\sigma-1}{\sigma}}dz\right)^{\frac{\sigma}{\sigma-1}}$$

With $w_{IT} = p_H\left(\frac{H}{B_{IT}}\right)^{\frac{1}{\sigma}}(A_{IT})^{\frac{\sigma-1}{\sigma}}\left(\int_{N-1}^{N_{IT}}\gamma_{IT}(z)^{\sigma-1}dz\right)^{\frac{1}{\sigma}}$, we can write the expression for H as

$$\begin{aligned}H = \Bigg(&\int_{N-1}^{N_{IT}}(\gamma_{IT}(z)^\sigma)^{\frac{\sigma-1}{\sigma}}dz\left(p_H^\sigma H\left(\frac{A_{IT}}{w_{IT}}\right)^\sigma\right)^{\frac{\sigma-1}{\sigma}} \\ &+ \int_{N_{IT}}^{N}(\gamma_L(z)^\sigma)^{\frac{\sigma-1}{\sigma}}dz\left(p_H^\sigma H\left(\frac{A_L}{w_L}\right)^\sigma\right)^{\frac{\sigma-1}{\sigma}}\Bigg)^{\frac{\sigma}{\sigma-1}} \\ = \Bigg(&\int_{N-1}^{N_{IT}}\gamma_{IT}(z)^{\sigma-1}dz p_H^{\sigma-1}H^{\frac{\sigma-1}{\sigma}}\left(\frac{A_{IT}}{w_{IT}}\right)^{\sigma-1} \\ &+ \int_{N_{IT}}^{N}\gamma_L(z)^{\sigma-1}dz p_H^{\sigma-1}H^{\frac{\sigma-1}{\sigma}}\left(\frac{A_L}{w_L}\right)^{\sigma-1}\Bigg)^{\frac{\sigma}{\sigma-1}}\end{aligned}$$

$$= \left(\begin{array}{l} \int_{N-1}^{N_{IT}} \gamma_{IT}(z)^{\sigma-1} dz p_H^{\sigma-1} H^{\frac{\sigma-1}{\sigma}} \left(\frac{A_{IT}}{p_H \left(\frac{H}{B_{IT}}\right)^{\frac{1}{\sigma}} (A_{IT})^{\frac{\sigma-1}{\sigma}} \left(\int_{N-1}^{N_{IT}} \gamma_{IT}(z)^{\sigma-1} dz\right)^{\frac{1}{\sigma}}} \right)^{\sigma-1} \\ + \int_{N_{IT}}^{N} \gamma_L(z)^{\sigma-1} dz p_H^{\sigma-1} H^{\frac{\sigma-1}{\sigma}} \left(\frac{A_L}{p_H \left(\frac{H}{L_L}\right)^{\frac{1}{\sigma}} (A_L)^{\frac{\sigma-1}{\sigma}} \left(\int_{N_{IT}}^{N} \gamma_L(z)^{\sigma-1} dz\right)^{\frac{1}{\sigma}}} \right)^{\sigma-1} \end{array} \right)^{\frac{\sigma}{\sigma-1}}$$

$$= \left(\begin{array}{l} \int_{N-1}^{N_{IT}} \gamma_{IT}(z)^{\sigma-1} dz p_H^{\sigma-1} H^{\frac{\sigma-1}{\sigma}} \left(\frac{p_H^{-1} H^{-\frac{1}{\sigma}} B_{IT}^{\frac{1}{\sigma}} A_{IT}^{\frac{1}{\sigma}}}{\left(\int_{N-1}^{N_{IT}} \gamma_{IT}(z)^{\sigma-1} dz\right)^{\frac{1}{\sigma}}} \right)^{\sigma-1} \\ + \int_{N_{IT}}^{N} \gamma_L(z)^{\sigma-1} dz p_H^{\sigma-1} H^{\frac{\sigma-1}{\sigma}} \left(\frac{p_H^{-1} H^{-\frac{1}{\sigma}} L_L^{\frac{1}{\sigma}} A_L^{\frac{1}{\sigma}}}{\left(\int_{N_{IT}}^{N} \gamma_L(z)^{\sigma-1} dz\right)^{\frac{1}{\sigma}}} \right)^{\sigma-1} \end{array} \right)^{\frac{\sigma}{\sigma-1}}$$

$$= \left(\begin{array}{l} \int_{N-1}^{N_{IT}} \gamma_{IT}(z)^{\sigma-1} dz p_H^{\sigma-1} H^{\frac{\sigma-1}{\sigma}} \frac{p_H^{-(\sigma-1)} H^{-\frac{\sigma-1}{\sigma}} (B_{IT} A_{IT})^{\frac{\sigma-1}{\sigma}}}{\left(\int_{N-1}^{N_{IT}} \gamma_{IT}(z)^{\sigma-1} dz\right)^{\frac{\sigma-1}{\sigma}}} \\ + \int_{N_{IT}}^{N} \gamma_L(z)^{\sigma-1} dz p_H^{\sigma-1} H^{\frac{\sigma-1}{\sigma}} \frac{p_H^{-(\sigma-1)} H^{-\frac{\sigma-1}{\sigma}} (L_L A_L)^{\frac{\sigma-1}{\sigma}}}{\left(\int_{N_{IT}}^{N} \gamma_L(z)^{\sigma-1} dz\right)^{\frac{\sigma-1}{\sigma}}} \end{array} \right)^{\frac{\sigma}{\sigma-1}}$$

$$= \left(\int_{N-1}^{N_{IT}} \gamma_{IT}(z)^{\sigma-1} dz \frac{(B_{IT} A_{IT})^{\frac{\sigma-1}{\sigma}}}{\left(\int_{N-1}^{N_{IT}} \gamma_{IT}(z)^{\sigma-1} dz\right)^{\frac{\sigma-1}{\sigma}}} \right.$$

$$\left. + \int_{N_{IT}}^{N} \gamma_L(z)^{\sigma-1} d \frac{(L_L A_L)^{\frac{\sigma-1}{\sigma}}}{\left(\int_{N_{IT}}^{N} \gamma_L(z)^{\sigma-1} dz\right)^{\frac{\sigma-1}{\sigma}}} \right)^{\frac{\sigma}{\sigma-1}}$$

$$H = \left(\left(\int_{N-1}^{N_{IT}} \gamma_{IT}(z)^{\sigma-1} dz \right)^{\frac{1}{\sigma}} (B_{IT} A_{IT})^{\frac{\sigma-1}{\sigma}} + \left(\int_{N_{IT}}^{N} \gamma_L(z)^{\sigma-1} dz \right)^{\frac{1}{\sigma}} (L_L A_L)^{\frac{\sigma-1}{\sigma}} \right)^{\frac{\sigma}{\sigma-1}}$$

B Labor Share of Income from Human Services

To determine the contribution of standard labor to total service production, one can start from the total amount of H:

$$H = \left(\int_{N-1}^{N_{IT}} h(z)^{\frac{\sigma-1}{\sigma}} dz + \int_{N_{IT}}^{N} h(z)^{\frac{\sigma-1}{\sigma}} dz \right)^{\frac{\sigma}{\sigma-1}}$$

$$= \left(\int_{N-1}^{N_{IT}} \left(p_H^{\sigma} H \left(\frac{A_{IT}}{w_{IT}} \right)^{\sigma} \gamma_I(z)^{\sigma} \right)^{\frac{\sigma-1}{\sigma}} dz + \int_{N_{IT}}^{N} \left(p_H^{\sigma} H \left(\frac{A_L}{w_L} \right)^{\sigma} \gamma_L(z)^{\sigma} \right)^{\frac{\sigma-1}{\sigma}} dz \right)^{\frac{\sigma}{\sigma-1}}.$$

Using $w_{IT} = p_H \left(\frac{H}{B_{IT}}\right)^{\frac{1}{\sigma}} (A_{IT})^{\frac{\sigma-1}{\sigma}} \left(\int_{N-1}^{N_{IT}} \gamma_{IT}(z)^{\sigma-1} dz\right)^{\frac{1}{\sigma}}$ results in

$$H = \left(\int_{N-1}^{N_{IT}} \left(\gamma_{IT}(z)^{\sigma}\right)^{\frac{\sigma-1}{\sigma}} dz \left(p_H^{\sigma} H \left(\frac{A_{IT}}{w_{IT}}\right)^{\sigma}\right)^{\frac{\sigma-1}{\sigma}} + \int_{N_{IT}}^{N} \left(\gamma_L(z)^{\sigma}\right)^{\frac{\sigma-1}{\sigma}} dz \left(p_H^{\sigma} H \left(\frac{A_L}{w_L}\right)^{\sigma}\right)^{\frac{\sigma-1}{\sigma}}\right)^{\frac{\sigma}{\sigma-1}}$$

$$H = \left(\int_{N-1}^{N_{IT}} \gamma_{IT}(z)^{\sigma-1} dz p_H^{\sigma-1} H^{\frac{\sigma-1}{\sigma}} \left(\frac{A_{IT}}{w_{IT}}\right)^{\sigma-1} + \int_{N_{IT}}^{N} \gamma_L(z)^{\sigma-1} dz p_H^{\sigma-1} H^{\frac{\sigma-1}{\sigma}} \left(\frac{A_L}{w_L}\right)^{\sigma-1}\right)^{\frac{\sigma}{\sigma-1}}$$

$$1 = \left(\int_{N-1}^{N_{IT}} \gamma_{IT}(z)^{\sigma-1} dz \left(\frac{A_{IT}}{w_{IT}}\right)^{\sigma-1} + \int_{N_{IT}}^{N} \gamma_L(z)^{\sigma-1} dz \left(\frac{A_L}{w_L}\right)^{\sigma-1}\right)^{\frac{\sigma}{\sigma-1}} p_H^{\sigma}$$

Plugging in definitions $\Gamma_L(N_{IT}, N) = \int_{N_{IT}}^{N} \gamma_L(z)^{\sigma-1} dz = \Gamma(N_{IT}, N)\,\Pi(N_{IT}, N)^{\sigma-1}$ and $\Gamma_{IT}(N_{IT}, N) = \int_{N-1}^{N_{IT}} \gamma_{IT}(z)^{\sigma-1} dz = (1 - \Gamma(N_{IT}, N))\,\Pi(N_{IT}, N)^{\sigma-1}$, we obtain

$$1 = \left(\Gamma_{IT}(N_{IT}, N) \left(\frac{A_{IT}}{w_{IT}}\right)^{\sigma-1} + \Gamma_L(N_{IT}, N) \left(\frac{A_L}{w_L}\right)^{\sigma-1}\right)^{\frac{\sigma}{\sigma-1}} p_H^{\sigma}$$

$$1 = \left(\frac{\Gamma_{IT}(N_{IT}, N)}{\Gamma_L(N_{IT}, N)} \frac{\left(\frac{A_{IT}}{w_{IT}}\right)^{\sigma-1}}{\left(\frac{A_L}{w_L}\right)^{\sigma-1}} + 1\right)^{\frac{\sigma}{\sigma-1}} \Gamma_L(N_{IT}, N)^{\frac{\sigma}{\sigma-1}} \left(\frac{A_L}{w_L}\right)^{\sigma} p_H^{\sigma}$$

Rearranging this equation gives:

$$1 = \left(\frac{\Gamma_{IT}(N_{IT}, N)}{\Gamma_L(N_{IT}, N)} \frac{\left(\frac{A_{IT}}{w_{IT}}\right)^{\sigma-1}}{\left(\frac{A_L}{w_L}\right)^{\sigma-1}} + 1\right)^{\frac{\sigma}{\sigma-1}} \Gamma_L(N_{IT}, N)^{\frac{\sigma}{\sigma-1}} \left(\frac{A_L}{w_L}\right)^{\sigma} p_H^{\sigma}$$

$$\left(\frac{A_L}{w_L}\right)^{-(\sigma-1)} p_H^{-(\sigma-1)} = \left(\frac{\Gamma_{IT}(N_{IT}, N)}{\Gamma_L(N_{IT}, N)} \frac{\left(\frac{A_{IT}}{w_{IT}}\right)^{\sigma-1}}{\left(\frac{A_L}{w_L}\right)^{\sigma-1}} + 1\right) \Gamma_L(N_{IT}, N)$$

$$\left(\frac{A_L}{w_L}\right)^{(\sigma-1)} p_H^{(\sigma-1)} = \frac{1}{\left(\frac{\Gamma_{IT}(N_{IT}, N)}{\Gamma_L(N_{IT}, N)} \frac{\left(\frac{A_{IT}}{w_{IT}}\right)^{\sigma-1}}{\left(\frac{A_L}{w_L}\right)^{\sigma-1}} + 1\right) \Gamma_L(N_{IT}, N)}$$

Further, the following expression can be derived:

$$L_L = \int_{N_{IT}}^{N} \frac{p_H^\sigma H}{(w_L)^\sigma} (A_L)^{\sigma-1} \gamma_L(z)^{\sigma-1} dz = \frac{p_H^\sigma H}{(w_L)^\sigma} (A_L)^{\sigma-1} \int_{N_{IT}}^{N} \gamma_L(z)^{\sigma-1} dz.$$

Using the definition of labor share of income that $\phi_L = \frac{w_L L}{p_H H}$

$$\frac{L_L w_L}{p_H H} = \frac{w_L}{p_H} \frac{1}{H} \frac{p_H^\sigma H}{(w_L)^\sigma} (A_L)^{\sigma-1} \int_{N_{IT}}^{N} \gamma_L(z)^{\sigma-1} dz$$

$$\frac{L_L w_L}{p_H H} = \left(\frac{w_L}{p_H}\right)^{1-\sigma} (A_L)^{\sigma-1} \Gamma_L(N_{IT}, N)$$

Combining this with the expression above gives labor's share of income as fully depending on relative labor rewards, $\frac{w_L}{w_{IT}}$

$$\begin{aligned} \frac{L_L w_L}{p_H H} &= \left(\frac{w_L}{p_H}\right)^{1-\sigma} (A_L)^{\sigma-1} \Gamma_L(N_{IT}, N) \\ &= \frac{\Gamma_L(N_{IT}, N)}{\left(\frac{\Gamma_{IT}(N_{IT}, N)}{\Gamma_L(N_{IT}, N)} \frac{\left(\frac{A_{IT}}{w_{IT}}\right)^{\sigma-1}}{\left(\frac{A_L}{w_L}\right)^{\sigma-1}} + 1\right) \Gamma_L(N_{IT}, N)} \\ &= \left(\frac{\Gamma_{IT}(N_{IT}, N)}{\Gamma_L(N_{IT}, N)} \left(\frac{A_{IT}}{A_L}\right)^{\sigma-1} \left(\frac{w_L}{w_{IT}}\right)^{\sigma-1} + 1\right)^{-1} \end{aligned}$$

Plugging in the relative factor rewards $\frac{w_L}{w_{IT}} = \left(\frac{B_{IT}}{L_L}\right)^{\frac{1}{\sigma}} \left(\frac{A_L}{A_{IT}}\right)^{\frac{\sigma-1}{\sigma}} \left(\frac{\Gamma_L(N_{IT}, N)}{\Gamma_{IT}(N_{IT}, N)}\right)^{\frac{1}{\sigma}}$ (see above) finally leads to:

$$\begin{aligned} \phi_L &= \left(1 + \frac{\Gamma_{IT}(N_{IT}, N)}{\Gamma_L(N_{IT}, N)} \left(\frac{A_{IT}}{A_L}\right)^{\sigma-1} \left(\left(\frac{B_{IT}}{L_L}\right)^{\frac{1}{\sigma}} \left(\frac{A_L}{A_{IT}}\right)^{\frac{\sigma-1}{\sigma}} \right.\right. \\ &\quad \left.\left. \times \left(\frac{\Gamma_L(N_{IT}, N)}{\Gamma_{IT}(N_{IT}, N)}\right)^{\frac{1}{\sigma}}\right)^{\sigma-1}\right)^{-1} \\ &= \left(1 + \frac{\Gamma_{IT}(N_{IT}, N)}{\Gamma_L(N_{IT}, N)} \left(\frac{\Gamma_{IT}(N_{IT}, N)}{\Gamma_L(N_{IT}, N)}\right)^{-\frac{\sigma-1}{\sigma}} \left(\left(\frac{B_{IT}}{L_L}\right)^{\frac{1}{\sigma}} \left(\frac{A_L}{A_{IT}}\right)^{\frac{\sigma-1}{\sigma}} \right.\right. \\ &\quad \left.\left. \times \left(\frac{A_{IT}}{A_L}\right)\right)^{\sigma-1}\right)^{-1} \\ &= \left(1 + \frac{\Gamma_{IT}(N_{IT}, N)^{\frac{1}{\sigma}}}{\Gamma_L(N_{IT}, N)} \left(\left(\frac{B_{IT}}{L_L}\right)^{\frac{1}{\sigma}} \left(\frac{A_L}{A_{IT}}\right)^{\frac{\sigma-1}{\sigma}} \left(\frac{A_L}{A_{IT}}\right)^{-\frac{\sigma}{\sigma}}\right)^{\sigma-1}\right)^{-1}, \end{aligned}$$

which results in the labor share of income from human services:

$$\phi_L = \frac{w_L L_L}{p_H H} = \left(1 + \frac{\Gamma_{IT}(N_{IT}, N)}{\Gamma_L(N_{IT}, N)}^{\frac{1}{\sigma}} \left(\frac{B_{IT}}{L_L}\frac{A_{IT}}{A_L}\right)^{\frac{\sigma-1}{\sigma}}\right)^{-1}$$

Derivative with respect to A_{IT}: We first take the derivatives of Γ_{IT} and Γ_L,

$$\Gamma_{IT}(N_{IT}, N) = \int_{N-1}^{N_{IT}} \gamma_{IT}(z)^{\sigma-1} dz, \frac{d\Gamma_{IT}}{dN_{IT}} = \gamma_{IT}(N_{IT})^{\sigma-1}$$

$$\Gamma_L(N_{IT}, N) = \int_{N_{IT}}^{N} \gamma_L(z)^{\sigma-1} dz, \frac{d\Gamma_L}{dN_{IT}} = -\gamma_L(N_{IT})^{\sigma-1}.$$

Taking the derivative for the labor share of income gives:

$$\frac{d\phi_L}{dA_{IT}} = -\frac{1}{(\ldots)^2}\left(\frac{B_{IT}}{L_L}\right)^{\frac{\sigma-1}{\sigma}}$$

$$\left[\begin{array}{r} \frac{\sigma-1}{\sigma}\left(\frac{\Gamma_{IT}(N_{IT},N)}{\Gamma_L(N_{IT},N)}\right)^{\frac{1}{\sigma}}\left(\frac{A_{IT}}{A_L}\right)^{-\frac{\sigma-1}{\sigma}-1}\frac{1}{A_L} \\ +\frac{1}{\sigma}\left(\frac{A_{IT}}{A_L}\right)^{\frac{\sigma-1}{\sigma}}\left(\frac{\Gamma_{IT}(N_{IT},N)}{\Gamma_L(N_{IT},N)}\right)^{\frac{1}{\sigma}-1}\left(\frac{\frac{d\Gamma_{IT}}{dN_{IT}}\frac{dN_{IT}}{dA_{IT}}}{\Gamma_L(N_{IT},N)} - \frac{\Gamma_{IT}(N_{IT},N)\frac{d\Gamma_L}{dN_{IT}}\frac{dN_{IT}}{dA_{IT}}}{\Gamma_L(N_{IT},N)^2}\right)\end{array}\right]$$

Which can be simplified to:

$$\eta_{\phi_L,A_{IT}} = \frac{d\phi_L}{dA_{IT}}\frac{A_{IT}}{\phi_L} = \frac{-1}{\sigma}\frac{(\sigma-1) + \left(\frac{\gamma_{IT}(N_{IT})^{\sigma-1}}{\Gamma_{IT}(N_{IT},N)} + \frac{\gamma_L(N_{IT})^{\sigma-1}}{\Gamma_L(N_{IT},N)}\right)N_{IT}\eta_{N_{IT},A_{IT}}}{1 + \left(\frac{A_L L_L}{A_{IT} B_{IT}}\right)^{\frac{\sigma-1}{\sigma}}\left(\frac{\Gamma_L(N_{IT},N)}{\Gamma_{IT}(N_{IT},N)}\right)^{\frac{1}{\sigma}}} < 0.$$

Thus, for $1 < \sigma$, the share will clearly decline, as $\eta_{\phi_L,A_{IT}} < 0$. If $1 > \sigma$, the share will not necessarily increase. Introducing more IT tasks $-\left(\frac{\gamma_{IT}(N_{IT})^{\sigma-1}}{\Gamma_{IT}(N_{IT},N)} + \frac{\gamma_L(N_{IT})^{\sigma-1}}{\Gamma_L(N_{IT},N)}\right)N_{IT}\eta_{N_{IT},A_{IT}} < 0$ will decrease the share of labor income and overcompensate the potentially positive effect from complementarity, $1 > \sigma$.

5 Artificial Intelligence, Growth, and Inequality

5.1 INTRODUCTION

In Chapter 2, we described economists' interest in AI's possible impact on macroeconomic outcomes such as jobs, economic and productivity growth, and inequality. In Chapter 4, we argued that to better understand the impact of AI on jobs, it may be useful to take into account the specific nature of disembodied, software-based automation from AI. We therefore proposed a modified task approach wherein we emphasized the abilities of AI, rather than modeling it as providing skills that can automate certain tasks.

In this chapter, we embed this ability-modified task approach into an endogenous model, which allows us to investigate the impact of AI on growth and inequality. In doing so, we address two shortcomings in the approach that economists have been following up until now. Specifically, the most advanced growth model with AI, the AR model of Acemoglu and Restrepo (2018b), has two shortcomings. The first is that the creation of new tasks and jobs due to the productivity gains enabled by AI (known as "reinstatement effects") will depend, over the long run, on the impact of AI automation on income distribution. If income inequality worsens, such as that the labor share in GDP declines, aggregate demand will decline. This would reduce the economy's actual and potential growth. Lower growth in turn would limit the reinstatement of new jobs.

The AR model cannot take this into account, as it is purely supply driven and hence lacks a mechanism to take into account the consequences of an increase in income inequality, as in all supply-driven growth models (Dutt, 2006). In a related paper, Acemoglu and

Restrepo (2019a, p. 228) recognize this shortcoming.[1] In this chapter, drawing on Gries (2020b) and Gries and Naudé (2020), we address this shortcoming by allowing for growth in our model to be demand constrained by replacing the typical assumption of a representative household by the assumption of two groups of households with different preferences. By allowing for growth in our model to be demand constrained, we can show why the expectation of Erdil and Besiroglu (2023) that AI will may lead to "explosive" economic growth[2] is unlikely to materialize: the increase in inequality and decline in consumption that will occur will act as a negative feedback effect, which will truncate the growth rate. AI progress may even be accompanied by negative growth.

The second shortcoming of the AR model, which is due to the task approach to labor markets on which it is based, has been discussed in detail in Chapter 4. There we argued that the task approach inadequately engages with the nature of AI and its technological feasibility. The task approach is concerned with tasks and skills but not with *abilities*, although as we argued in Chapter 4, abilities better characterize the nature of the services that AI provide. In this chapter, we incorporate AI as providing abilities within the growth model.

The rest of the chapter will proceed as follows. In Section 5.2, an endogenous growth model is introduced that includes constraints from the demand side via a goods market matching mechanism, and that modifies the naive task approach to labor markets. In Section 5.3, the model is solved, and in Section 5.4, the dynamics of the model in terms of the impact of AI on jobs, inequality, wages, labor productivity, and long-run GDP growth are explored. Section

[1] Other scholars who have identified aggregate demand as a crucial determinant of the effect of automation on jobs and growth include Bessen (2018) and Benzell et al. (2018) and Sachs et al. (2015).

[2] Erdil and Besiroglu (2023) discuss and reject several objections that have been made to the possibility that AI will generate explosive economic growth. The only objection they do not discuss is demand constraints.

5.5 considers the impact of AI with simultaneous demand shocks. Section 5.6 concludes.

5.2 A NEW THEORETICAL MODEL: LABOR TASKS, DEMAND, AND GROWTH

We start off (in Section 5.2.1) by describing the production of final consumption goods by profit-maximizing firms who use labor, intermediate goods, as well as artificial intelligence (AI). In Section 5.2.2 the nature of the relationship between AI and labor is set out, in Section 5.2.3 intermediate goods production is specified, and in Section 5.2.4, aggregate budget constraints, income, and its distribution are derived. After having dealt with aggregate supply, we then focus our attention on aggregate demand in Section 5.2.5. Here we introduce the novelty of this chapter, namely the substitution of the typical assumption in endogenous growth models of a representative household by the assumption of two groups of households with different preferences.

5.2.1 *Final Goods–Producing Firms*

Final goods for consumption are produced by firms using labor, AI services, and intermediate inputs. Actual sales of output may fall short of potential sales due to imperfect markets, such as market mismatch and imperfect information in final goods markets. To maximize profits, firms will incur marketing and product placement activities, buy labor and AI services in a competitive market, and purchase intermediate goods. The rest of this section elaborates this maximization problem.

5.2.1.1 *Output of Final Goods*

Let firm $i \in \mathcal{F}$ be a representative firm that produces final goods using labor, AI services, and intermediate inputs. The combination of labor and AI provides what we term ***human services***. We combine labor and AI into human services because AI is a software and information technology that is human-related in that it provides abilities to produce goods but requires the skills and experience and knowledge of humans to add value. Skills and experiences are not in the domain of AI (Tolan et al., 2020). We denote human service inputs by H_{Qi}.

In addition to human services, the firm sources $N_i(t)$ differentiated intermediate inputs $x_{ji}(t)$ which are offered by $N(t)$ intermediate input-producing firms.

Given human service inputs and intermediate inputs, $Q_i(t)$, the potential output of final goods by firm i, is

$$Q_i(t) = H_{Qi}^{1-\alpha} \sum_{j=1}^{N_i} x_{ij}^{\alpha}(t) = N_i(t) H_{Qi}^{1-\alpha} x_i^{\alpha}(t) \tag{5.1}$$

5.2.1.2 *Market Mismatch, Sales Promotion, and Expected Sales*

The market imperfection is assumed to be a stochastic market mismatch. Not all of a firm's potential output will be sold immediately. Suppose that firm i can sell instantly only quantity Φ, so that its effective sales ratio is $\phi_i(t) = \frac{\Phi_i(t)}{Q_i(t)} \leq 1$. Then, the firm's subjective interpretation of $\phi_i(t) \leq 1$ is that this shortfall is due to the fact that customers are insufficiently informed about products, prices, qualities, and general market conditions. The extent of this mismatch[3] between potential and actual sales is referred to as the mismatch ratio $\delta_i(t)$ that determines the effective sales ratio

$$\phi_i(t) = 1 - \delta_i(t). \tag{5.2}$$

As a response to an imperfect effective sales ratio, firms allocate human services $H_{\phi i}$ to promote sales so as to counter this mismatch (δ_i) and improve the likelihood of selling all potential output in the market. The match-improving mechanism can be formulated as $m_i = m_i(H_{\phi i})$, with $\frac{\partial m_i(t)}{\partial H_{\phi i}(t)} > 0$. Given that δ_i' denotes the stochastic market mismatch, which the firm perceives as exogenous, the total mismatch of potential and actual sales is

$$\delta_i(t) = \delta_i'(t) - m_i(H_{\phi i})$$

[3] The matching model with frictions that we draw on here is closely related to that of Gries (2020a).

Each individual firm i observes that the expected effective sales ratio $E[\phi_i]$ is monotonically increasing with $H_{\phi i}$, and decreasing with δ_i', such that

$$E[\phi_i] = E\left[\phi_i\left(\delta_i', H_{\phi i}\right)\right] \quad \text{with} \quad \frac{\partial E[\phi_i]}{\partial H_{\phi i}} > 0, \quad \frac{\partial E[\phi_i]}{\partial \delta_i'} < 0. \quad (5.3)$$

5.2.1.3 *Factor Demands*

Having described the firm's output and expected effective sales ratio in subsections 5.2.1.1 and 5.2.1.2, we can now derive the firm's factor demands from its profit maximization. We start by denoting the price of the human services factor as p_H, and the price of intermediate inputs x as p_x. The firm's profit maximization function then is:

$$\begin{aligned} \max_{H_{Qi}, H_{\phi i}, x_i} :E[\Pi_i(t)] = {} & Q_i(t)E[\phi_i(t)] - p_H(t)\left(H_{\phi i}(t) + H_{Qi}(t)\right) \\ & - N_i(t)p_x(t)x_i(t) \end{aligned} \quad (5.4)$$

To maximize profits, firms first have to organize an efficient sales process, and second, they need to determine optimal production.

First, consider the organization of an *efficient sales process.* Firm i allocates $H_{\phi i}$ to the search and information process and improves its effective sales. In order to sell all potential output, the firm increases $H_{\phi i}$ until all goods that have been produced and supplied can be expected to be absorbed by the market. The firm's total revenues $Q_i E[\phi_i]$ are determined by the production of even more goods Q_i and the expected success rate $E[\phi_i]$ of selling this produced output. As each element depends on the respective human service input, we assume that placing an already existing (but not yet demanded) output in the market can be more easily done than producing a new unit of output. That is, until the point when all production in fact finds a customer, the marginal revenue generated by human services in the matching process is greater than the marginal revenue of human service in production, and zero otherwise

$$\frac{\partial E[\phi_i]}{\partial H_{\phi i}} Q_i > E[\phi_i](1-\alpha)\frac{Q_i}{H_{Qi}} \quad \textit{for} \quad E[\phi_i] \leq 1. \quad (5.5)$$

As a result of this assumption, the firm will first increase $H_{\phi i}$ until the expected sales ratio becomes

$$E[\phi_i] = 1, \tag{5.6}$$

and thus no unsold output remains. The firm will be in a sales equilibrium. Any time when condition (5.6) holds, Equation (5.3) implicitly defines a function for the allocation of human services to each firm i's sales activities[4]

$$H^*_{\phi i} = H_{\phi i}\left(E\left[\delta'_i\right]\right), \quad \frac{\partial H_{\phi i}}{\partial E\left[\delta'_i\right]} > 0 \tag{5.7}$$

Second, under the condition that $E[\phi_i] = 1$, and hence an already identified $H^*_{\phi i}$, the firm needs to determine the other *optimal factor inputs*. A firm's profit (5.4) is

$$E[\Pi_{Qi}] = Q_i - N_i p_X x_i - p_H\left(H^*_{\phi i} + H_{Qi}\right)$$

As p_H is the price payable to human services (also in production), the first-order condition for the efficient use of labor in production gives

$$H_{Qi}(t) = (1-\alpha)\, Q_i(t) p_H(t)^{-1} \tag{5.8}$$

and the demand for intermediate goods can be derived as

$$x_i(t) = \left(\frac{\alpha}{p_X(t)}\right)^{\frac{1}{1-\alpha}} H_{Qi} \tag{5.9}$$

5.2.2 *Human Services: Labor and AI*

In this section, we elaborate on the human services input and clarify the relationship between labor and AI. We draw on Gries and Naudé (2021).

5.2.2.1 *The Production of Human Services*

Human services H_i, as already indicated, consist of labor and AI. It is produced following a task-based approach. As such, $H = H(L_L,\ A_L,\ A_{IT},\ L_{IT})$, where L_L is the number of workers each providing one unit of human experience, A_L is an index of general

[4] See Appendix A for the implicit function theorem.

knowledge, A_{IT} is the total number of machine learning (ML) abilities (e.g., software algorithms) in the economy, and L_{IT} is the IT labor providing IT skills. Hence, our approach enriches and extends the task approach by integrating human skills and experience with AI abilities, as per the arguments of Hernández-Orallo (2017) and Tolan et al. (2020). Furthermore, L_L and L_{IT} are different groups of labor, allowing us to have two separate segments in the labor market. The general function $H = H(\ldots)$ can be specified as

$$H = \left(\int_{N-1}^{N} h(z)^{\frac{\sigma-1}{\sigma}} dz \right)^{\frac{\sigma}{\sigma-1}} \tag{5.10}$$

where z denotes each task in a unit interval $[N-1, N]$ and $h(z)$ is the output of task z. As tasks range between $N-1$ and N, the total number of tasks is constant. While formally following the task approach, the more explicit specification of the nature of AI and its technological feasibility (reflected in A_{IT}) is a novel contribution.

Each task can either be produced only with labor, $l(z)$, or only with AI labor services, $l_{IT}(z)$, if the task can be automated. Therefore, there are two sets of tasks. Tasks $z \in [N-1, N_{IT}]$ can be produced by both labor and AI services and tasks $z \in (N_{IT}, N]$ can only be produced by labor. Thus, the output of a task can be generated in two ways, namely

$$h(z) = \begin{cases} A_L \gamma_L(z) l(z) + A_{IT} \gamma_{IT}(z) l_{IT}(z) & \text{if } z \in [N-1, N_{IT}] \\ A_L \gamma_L(z) l(z) & \text{if } z \in (N_{IT}, N] \end{cases} \tag{5.11}$$

Here $\gamma_L(x)$ is the classic productivity of labor of task z and A_L generally available knowledge, which is usable without rivalry and labor augmenting.

The AI service consists of three elements, which reflect the fact that modern AI affects the workplace through the combination and interaction between skills, knowledge, experience, and ML abilities. The first element is $l_{IT}(z)$, which is IT-specific labor – in other words, so-called IT skills. The task-related experience and expertise of these specialists is the second element and is given by $\gamma_{IT}(z)$. The third element or ingredient in AI services is ML abilities, denoted A_{IT}. A_{IT}

could, for instance, indicate the number or quality of software programs/algorithms available in the economy, reflecting for instance different ML techniques, see, for example, LeCun et al. (2015). As each software program has no rivalry in use, the same program can be applied in each task. Therefore, the property of a software technology (ML ability) is contained in A_{IT}.

For an existing stock of AI technology, the number and kind of tasks which are used and which fully substitute for labor (automation) will be endogenous. The relative factor prices and efficiency of these services will determine the extent of the use of automation technologies. Thus, the degree of automation in this model is endogenous. In Subsection 5.2.2.2, this process is described in detail.

For now, it can be noted that if a task z with prize $p_h(z)$ is produced with pure labor $h(z) = A_L \gamma_L(z) l(z)$ and labor rewards are calculated according to marginal productivity, then $p_h(z) A_L \gamma_L(z) = w_L$. Symmetrically, the same task could be produced with an AI technology so that $p_h(z) A_{IT} \gamma_{IT}(z) = w_{IT}$. Given these two conditions, and given wages in the market, for any particular task, the firm will choose the kind of production (automation or not) that results in the lowest unit labor costs. Thus, if the following condition holds, the task will be automated:

$$\frac{w_{IT}}{p_h(z) A_{IT} \gamma_{IT}(z)} < \frac{w_L}{p_h(z) A_L \gamma_L(z)}$$

This rule leads to condition (5.12) that identifies the switching point between automated (AI) tasks and labor tasks. If tasks are ordered in such a way that $\frac{A_L \gamma_L(z)}{A_{IT} \gamma_{IT}(z)}$ is increasing in z and the tasks with lower numbers $z \in [N-1, N_{IT}]$ are the automated tasks, task N_{IT} is the switching point from an automation task to a labor task. N_{IT} is the highest number in this order for which

$$\frac{A_L \gamma_L(N_{IT})}{A_{IT} \gamma_{IT}(N_{IT})} < \frac{w_L}{w_{IT}} \tag{5.12}$$

holds. Apart from these automated (AI) tasks $[N-1, N_{IT}]$, all other tasks $(N_{IT}, N]$ are produced with standard labor. Thus, the costs and respectively the price $p_h(z)$ for any task z are

$$p_h(z) = \begin{cases} \frac{w_{IT}}{A_{IT}\gamma_{IT}(z)} & \text{if } z \in [N-1, N_{IT}] \\ \frac{w_L}{A_L\gamma_L(z)} & \text{if } z \in (N_{IT}, N] \end{cases} \tag{5.13}$$

5.2.2.2 *Human Service Firm's Optimization*

Human services are produced by human service firms that take the price for human services, the price for each task, and the wages for various labor inputs, as given. It is assumed that these firms operate in competitive markets and that they will aim to maximize profits for a given price p_H subject to the production process in Equation (5.10), such that

$$\pi_H = p_H H - p_h(z)h(z) = p_H\left(\int_{N-1}^{N} h(z)^{\frac{\sigma-1}{\sigma}}dz\right)^{\frac{\sigma}{\sigma-1}} - p_h(z)h(z)$$

From which the demand for task z can be derived to be:

$$h(z) = \frac{p_H^{\sigma}H}{p_h(z)^{\sigma}} \tag{5.14}$$

Combining Equations (5.13) and (5.14), we can derive the demand for automation and labor tasks z as follows[5]

$$h(z) = \begin{cases} p_H^{\sigma}H\left(\frac{A_{IT}}{w_{IT}}\right)^{\sigma}\gamma_{IT}(z)^{\sigma} & \text{if } z \in [N-1, N_{IT}] \\ p_H^{\sigma}H\left(\frac{A_L}{w_L}\right)^{\sigma}\gamma_L(z)^{\sigma} & \text{if } z \in [N_{IT}, N] \end{cases} \tag{5.15}$$

Further, from Equations (5.15) and (5.11), we can obtain the optimal demand for IT labor:

$$l_{IT}(z) = \begin{cases} \frac{p_H^{\sigma}H}{(w_{IT})^{\sigma}}(A_{IT})^{\sigma-1}\gamma_{IT}(z)^{\sigma-1} & \text{if } z \in [N-1, N_{IT}] \\ 0 & \text{if } z \in [N_{IT}, N] \end{cases} \tag{5.16}$$

and standard labor:

$$l_L(z) = \begin{cases} 0 & \text{if } z \in [N-1, N_{IT}] \\ \frac{p_H^{\sigma}H}{(w_L)^{\sigma}}(A_L)^{\sigma-1}\gamma_L(z)^{\sigma-1} & \text{if } z \in (N_{IT}, N] \end{cases} \tag{5.17}$$

Relative labor productivity can be determined from factor abundance and technology- and productivity-related parameters. Assuming that all types of labor are fully used in the various tasks, labor in all tasks adds up to the given total labor in each labor market segment

[5] For details, see Appendix B.

$$L_{IT} = \int_{N-1}^{N_{IT}} l_{IT}(z)dz, \text{ and} \tag{5.18}$$

$$L_L = \int_{N_{IT}}^{N} l_L(z)dz \tag{5.19}$$

By using Equations (5.16), (5.17), (5.18), and (5.19), relative labor productivity is:

$$\frac{w_L}{w_{IT}} = \left(\frac{L_{IT}}{L_L}\right)^{\frac{1}{\sigma}} \left(\frac{A_L}{A_{IT}}\right)^{\frac{\sigma-1}{\sigma}} \left(\frac{\int_{N_{IT}}^{N} \gamma_L(z)^{\sigma-1}dz}{\int_{N-1}^{N_{IT}} \gamma_{IT}(z)^{\sigma-1}dz}\right)^{\frac{1}{\sigma}} \tag{5.20}$$

5.2.2.3 *Optimal Number of Automated Tasks*

Combining relative marginal productivity (5.20) with condition (5.12) and applying the *implicit function theorem* gives an expression for calculating the optimal number of automated tasks in the economy, which is endogenous[6]:

$$N_{IT} = N_{IT}\left(L_{IT}, L_L, A_{IT}, \ldots\right), \text{ with } \frac{dN_{IT}}{dL_{IT}} > 0, \quad \frac{dN_{IT}}{dL_L} < 0, \quad \frac{dN_{IT}}{dA_{IT}} > 0 \tag{5.21}$$

This equation indicates that the number of automated tasks crucially depends on the relative availability of the production factors as well as the availability of AI technologies. If IT labor is broadly available and hence its relative wage low, more tasks could be automated.

Similarly, if IT knowledge and AI algorithms are readily available, relative wages $\frac{w_L}{w_{IT}}$ increase and make standard labor tasks relatively more expensive. This results in a higher share of automated tasks. The clear implication is that if an economy is advanced in terms of IT technologies and IT labor, this economy will be more automated.

5.2.2.4 *Optimal Human Service Supply*

From the demands for the various tasks, total human service production can be derived. Aggregating automated tasks and labor, Equation (5.10) leads to

[6] For details, see Appendix, B at the end of this chapter.

$$H = \left(\int_{N-1}^{N_{IT}} h(z)^{\frac{\sigma-1}{\sigma}} dz + \int_{N_{IT}}^{N} h(z)^{\frac{\sigma-1}{\sigma}} dz \right)^{\frac{\sigma}{\sigma-1}}$$

Using Equation (5.15), (Equation 5.82 in the Appendix to this chapter) and (Equation 5.83 in the Appendix), respectively, and rearranging gives the expression for total production of human services as[7]:

$$H = \left(\left(\int_{N-1}^{N_{IT}} \gamma_{IT}(z)^{\sigma-1} dz \right)^{\frac{1}{\sigma}} (A_{IT}L_{IT})^{\frac{\sigma-1}{\sigma}} + \left(\int_{N_{IT}}^{N} \gamma_{L}(z)^{\sigma-1} dz \right)^{\frac{1}{\sigma}} (A_{L}L_{L})^{\frac{\sigma-1}{\sigma}} \right)^{\frac{\sigma}{\sigma-1}}$$

In order to simplify this equation, Acemoglu and Restrepo (2018a,b) and Acemoglu and Restrepo (2019b) propose two equations that allow for a more compact equation. With the equations

$$\Gamma(N_{IT}, N) = \frac{\int_{N_{IT}}^{N} \gamma_{L}(z)^{\sigma-1} dz}{\int_{N-1}^{N_{IT}} \gamma_{IT}(z)^{\sigma-1} dz + \int_{N_{IT}}^{N} \gamma_{L}(z)^{\sigma-1} dz} \tag{5.22}$$

and

$$\Pi(N_{IT}, N) = \left(\int_{N-1}^{N_{IT}} \gamma_{IT}(z)^{\sigma-1} dz + \int_{N_{IT}}^{N} \gamma_{L}(z)^{\sigma-1} dz \right)^{\frac{1}{\sigma-1}} \tag{5.23}$$

one may substitute $B_1\,(N_{IT}) = \int_{N-1}^{N_{IT}} \gamma_{IT}(z)^{\sigma-1} dz = (1 - \Gamma(N_{IT}, N))$ $\Pi(N_{IT}, N)^{\sigma-1}$ and $B_2\,(N_{IT}) = \int_{N_{IT}}^{N} \gamma_{L}(z)^{\sigma-1} dz = \Gamma(N_{IT}, N)\Pi(N_{IT}, N)^{\sigma-1}$ and thus rewrite the aggregate optimal human service production as

$$H = \Pi\,(N_{IT}, N) \Big[(1 - \Gamma\,(N_{IT}, N))^{\frac{1}{\sigma}} (A_{IT}L_{IT})^{\frac{\sigma-1}{\sigma}} + \Gamma\,(N_{IT}, N)^{\frac{1}{\sigma}} (A_{L}L_{L})^{\frac{\sigma-1}{\sigma}} \Big]^{\frac{\sigma}{\sigma-1}} \tag{5.24}$$

This equation is similar to the familiar constant elasticity of supply (CES) production function.

5.2.2.5 *Earning Shares of Laborers*

From Equation (5.24), the earning share of each group of L_L and L_{IT} can be deduced. After rearranging these, the earning share of standard

[7] For details, see Appendix, B at the end of this chapter.

labor from revenues earned by human services can be written as[8]:

$$\phi_L = \frac{w_L L_L}{p_H H} = \frac{1}{1 + \left(\frac{(1-\Gamma(N_{IT},N))}{\Gamma(N_{IT},N)}\right)^{\frac{1}{\sigma}} \left(\frac{L_{IT}}{L_L}\frac{A_{IT}}{A_L}\right)^{\frac{\sigma-1}{\sigma}}} \quad \text{(non-IT labor)},$$

$$\phi_{IT} = \frac{w_{IT} L_{IT}}{p_H H} = 1 - \phi_L \quad \text{(IT labor)} \tag{5.25}$$

5.2.3 *Intermediate Goods–Producing Firms*

In our model, we have final good-producing firms (whose final goods production under market mismatch was set out earlier in Section 5.2.1), as well as human service firms that produce human services, as described in Section 5.2.2. The third group of firms consists of firms producing intermediate goods that are used by final goods-producing firms. In this subsection, we describe these firms in greater detail.

5.2.3.1 *Market Entry of Intermediate Goods-Producing Firms*

The intermediate goods-supplying firms in our model are monopolists because they each sell a unique product, which is the outcome of entrepreneurial (product) innovation. The costs for the typical firm (denominated in units of final output) to produce one unit of x are c_X, and the profits this results in are $\pi_X = (p_X - c_X)\, x$.

Using the demand function (5.9) and plugging in $p_X = \alpha H_Q^{1-\alpha} x^{-(1-\alpha)}$ results in:

$$\pi_X(t) = \alpha H_Q^{1-\alpha} x(t)^{-(1-\alpha)} x(t) - c_X x(t) \tag{5.26}$$

From the first-order condition[9] and using Equations (5.9) and (5.28), the optimal price p_X and optimal production of intermediate goods $x(t)$ are, respectively:

$$p_X = \frac{c_X}{\alpha} \tag{5.27}$$

[8] For details, see Appendix B to this chapter.

[9] The first-order condition is $\frac{\partial \pi_x}{\partial x} = \alpha^2 (1 - \theta_i) H^{1-\alpha} x^{\alpha-1} - c_x = 0$, thus $c_x = \alpha^2 (1 - \theta_i) H^{1-\alpha} x^{\alpha-1} \Leftrightarrow x^{1-\alpha} = (c_x)^{-1} \alpha^2 (1 - \theta_i) L^{1-\alpha}$.

and

$$x(t) = \left(\frac{\alpha^2}{c_X}\right)^{\frac{1}{1-\alpha}} H_Q \tag{5.28}$$

Given Equations (5.28) and (5.27), maximum profits $\pi_X(t)$ are:

$$\pi_X(t) = \left(\frac{1}{\alpha} - 1\right) (c_X)^{\frac{-\alpha}{1-\alpha}} \alpha^{\frac{2}{1-\alpha}} H_Q \tag{5.29}$$

The present value of this future profit flow, discounted at the steady state interest rate r, is:

$$V_X(t) = \frac{1}{r}\pi_X(t) = \int_t^{\infty} \pi_X(t) e^{-r(v,t)(v-t)} dv \tag{5.30}$$

Here, $\frac{1}{r}\pi_X$ is the present value of profits per innovation and $\frac{1}{r}\pi_X \dot{N}$ are the total profits of the intermediate goods-producing firm introducing $\dot{N}(t)$ new goods. In addition to the cost of innovation, the new firm also has to cover the costs of market entry (e.g., commercialization costs) for the new intermediate good, which is ν. Thus, the total entry cost of the start-up with innovation rate $\dot{N}$ and thus total investment is

$$\dot{N}(t)\nu = I(t) \tag{5.31}$$

With competitive market entry, the net rents of a new good turn to zero and the net present value of the new goods just about covers its total start-up costs:

$$\frac{1}{r}\pi_X(t)\dot{N}(t) - I(t) = 0, \tag{5.32}$$

and the gross return of an innovation in the steady state is:

$$r = \frac{\pi_X(t)}{\nu} \tag{5.33}$$

5.2.3.2 *Supply of New Innovative Intermediate Products*

Innovation in the intermediate goods market is exogenously given as $\dot{A}(t) = \frac{dA(t)}{dt}$, which is the number of innovative intermediate products invented at t. These innovative intermediate products are not automatically successful in the market. The success or failure to find a buyer can be modeled as an *aggregate matching* process.[10]

In such a matching process, the number of new intermediate products successfully entering the market $\dot{N}$ is a function of two elements: (1) the given number of new, innovative intermediate products $\dot{A}(t)$ potentially ready for market entry, and (2) the number of opportunities for market entry that entrepreneurs (start-ups) discover. These opportunities are determined by the capacity of the market. Absorption capacity for intermediate goods is a function of total demand for intermediate goods in the economy $X^D(t)$.

Through an aggregate matching function, these two elements can be combined, and the resulting process of market entry can be described as $\dot{N} = f(\dot{A}, X^D)$. For simplicity, it is assumed here that the matching technology is subject to constant economies of scale, so that the number of new products in the market will be given by

$$\dot{N}(t) = \left(X^D(t)\right)^{\varphi} (\dot{A}(t))^{1-\varphi} \tag{5.34}$$

where φ is the contribution of market opportunities. Although the assumption of a macro-matching process is basic, it represents the main idea behind the mechanism. Given Equation (5.34), the growth of new products in the economy is a partially endogenous process because the number of new products $\dot{A}$ is exogenous but the number of new technologies implemented to establish intermediate products $\dot{N}$ is endogenous.[11]

5.2.4 *Aggregate Production and Income Distribution*

Having specified final goods and intermediate goods production, and in having showed how the task approach can be used to account for human service production in the preceding sections, this subsection

[10] For a microfoundation of this process, see Gries and Naudé (2011).

[11] The model is therefore a semi-endogenous growth model in terms of its very long-run dynamics and logic, in which the growth rate will adjust to the exogenous technology growth rate (not the population growth rate as usual) in the very long run. However, we want to work out that by then, the growth rate may also be affected by this market entry mechanism.

is concerned with the aggregate budget constraint and the distribution of income to the various agents in the economy, starting with labor income.

5.2.4.1 *Labor Income*

As we discussed in the preceding sections, human services H are allocated to two activities, namely production H_Q and sales promotion H_ϕ, $H = H_Q + H^*_\phi$. For the representative firm $H^*_{\phi i}$ has already been determined by conditions (5.6) and (5.7). Thus, the allocation of human services to production must be

$$H_Q = H - H_\phi \tag{5.35}$$

From Equation (5.8), we know that the price for human services in production is equal to its marginal productivity $p_H = \frac{(1-\alpha)Q}{H_Q}$. However, not only do firms have to pay human services used in physical production H_Q, they also need to pay human services used in sales promotion H_ϕ. As factor rewards are paid in physical output goods at an amount $(1 - \alpha)Q\left(H_Q\right)$, all human services need to be paid out of this amount. With a homogeneous H in a perfectly integrated human service market, only one reward is paid to H, irrespective of whether used in production or sales promotion. Thus, total or aggregate human service income is less than marginal human service activity in production $p_H H_Q = (1-\alpha)Q$.[12] However, we assume that H_ϕ is relatively small such that we approximate and simplify to

$$p_H(t) = (1-\alpha)\frac{Q(t)}{H}. \tag{5.36}$$

5.2.4.2 *Wealth Holders' Income*

$N(t)\pi_x(t)$ denotes total profit in the economy. All new products, results of innovation (R&D), are financed by issuing new debt, $\dot{N}(t)v = \dot{F}(t)$, which is taken up by a financial investor. Thus, profits

[12] Actually, it would be no problem to write down the full effect at this point, but that would mean unnecessary complexity and unnecessary calculations. Therefore, without loss of generality or change in qualitative results, we adopt this simplifying assumption.

accrue to the owner of this debt – the financiers – and generate their return

$$N(t)\pi_X(t) = r(t)F(t) \tag{5.37}$$

5.2.4.3 *Production and Income Constraints*

Effective output in the economy has to be divided among intermediate goods x, standard labor L_L, and the IT technology service provider L_{IT}. The budget constraint for effective output is therefore

$$Q(t) = N(t)H_Q^{1-\alpha}x^{\alpha}(t) = N(t)p_X(t)x(t) + w_L(t)L_L + w_{IT}(t)L_{IT} \tag{5.38}$$

Note that effective output is not the same as GDP or aggregate income. As x is produced by using c_X units of final goods, net final output and thus *income* are

$$Y(t) = Q(t) - N(t)x(t)c_X \tag{5.39}$$

Further, Equations (5.38) and (6.3) imply that $Q - Nxc_X = Np_Xx - Nxc_X + w_LL_L + w_{IT}L_{IT}$. With the definition of profits in the intermediate goods sector (5.26), the income constraint then becomes:

$$Y(t) = N(t)\pi_X(t) + w_L(t)L_L + w_{IT}(t)L_{IT} \tag{5.40}$$

According to Equation (5.40), total or aggregate income in the economy consists of profits, labor, and technology income. Further, from Equation (5.37), we obtain that the value added generated by innovative intermediate firms therefore turns into the income of financial asset owners $r(t)F(t) = N(t)\pi_X(t)$. The accumulation process is thus essentially a process of financial wealth accumulation through the financing of new products and (intermediate good-producing) new ventures. We call this a "Silicon Valley" model of growth.

Finally, using Equation (5.37) results in the familiar income decomposition of GDP:

$$Y(t) = rF(t) + w_L(t)L_L + w_{IT}(t)L_{IT} \tag{5.41}$$

In addition to the income of financial wealth owners, the value added generated by the human service input is distributed to labor ($w_L(t)L_L$) and the providers of AI technologies and services ($w_{IT}(t)L_{IT}$).

5.2.4.4 *Income Distribution*

To allow us to eventually trace the distributional consequences of progress in AI, the income shares of the three input and resource-providing agents in the model need to be derived. These are the income of standard labor $(w_L(t)L_L)$, the AI service providers $(w_{IT}(t)L_{IT})$, and the financial investors $(r(t)F(t))$.

Wages and income share of labor: Using the equation for factor demand (5.36) and (5.25), wages can be related to total income as follows:

$$w_L = \phi_L \frac{p_H H}{L_L} = \frac{\phi_L}{1+\alpha} \frac{Y(t)}{L_L} \tag{5.42}$$

Because ϕ_L is constant, w_L is the standard wage rate in the economy. The income share of standard labor can now be derived by using Equations (5.42), (5.28), and (6.3) as[13]:

$$\frac{w_L(t)L_L}{Y(t)} = \frac{\phi_L}{(1+\alpha)} < 1 \tag{5.43}$$

Wages and income share of the AI provider: The factor reward, or wage rate, of the economic agent that provides the AI at amount A_{IT} can be derived in a symmetrical manner as in Equation (5.42) and can thus be specified as:

$$w_{IT} = (1-\phi_L) \frac{p_H H}{L_{IT}} = \frac{1-\phi_L}{1+\alpha} \frac{Y(t)}{L_{IT}} \tag{5.44}$$

The income share of providers of the AI service is accordingly:

$$\frac{w_{IT}(t)L_{IT}}{Y(t)} = \frac{1-\phi_L}{1+\alpha} < 1 \tag{5.45}$$

Income share of financial investors: The income share of financial investors can be calculated using Equations (6.3), (5.37), and (5.26) as[14]

$$\frac{N(t)\pi_x(t)}{Y(t)} = \frac{\alpha}{1+\alpha} \tag{5.46}$$

[13] Note that $\frac{1-\alpha}{1-\alpha^2} = \frac{1}{(1+\alpha)}$. See also Appendix C.

[14] Details of the calculation are contained in Appendix C to this chapter. The fact that all income shares add up to one holds as $\frac{\alpha}{1+\alpha} + \frac{1-\phi_L}{1+\alpha} + \frac{\phi_L}{(1+\alpha)} = 1$ is true.

5.2.5 *Aggregate Expenditure and Income*

To understand and analyze the role of aggregate demand, it is necessary to specify the consumption and savings behavior of the agents in the economy. In standard endogenous growth models, aggregate demand is typically modeled assuming *representative* intertemporal choices based on a *representative* household's Euler equation.[15] This, however, is not adequate when asymmetries in factor rewards and potential changes in income distribution are key features of interest – as is the case when considering automation technology. The representative household assumption in standard endogenous growth models assumes away differences in the intertemporal decisions of wealthy and poor households and their respective effects on aggregate consumption and savings. In Appendix D to this chapter, examples are provided for specific intertemporal choices at the individual or group level. Moreover, if group preferences are heterogeneous, they may lead to heterogeneous consumption and savings behavior, which needs to be taken into consideration given that it specifies that effective aggregate supply and demand for intermediate inputs depend on aggregate demand.

The novel model proposed here does not assume away the idea of rational intertemporal choices. However, what it does reject is the idea of a simple aggregation rule like a representative household (Gries, 2020b). Instead, for present purposes, the Keynesian tradition is followed by assuming that some households only earn wage income $w_L L_L$ and another group of households earn only financial income from assets rF. A third group, providers of AI services, is also regarded as its own group. Each group has its own consumption preferences and patterns. Labor income accrues to poorer households, while financial wealth holders and AI service providers accrue income for richer households.

15 $\frac{\dot{C}}{C} = \frac{r_D - \rho}{\eta_U}$ with ρ denoting the representative agent's time preference rate and η_U the intertemporal elasticity of substitution.

5.2.5.1 *Consumption and Investment Expenditure*

We define group-specific intertemporal choices and assume plausible group-specific parameters for the choice problem. From Equation (5.43), we know the share of labor income is $\frac{w_L L_L}{Y} = \frac{\phi_L}{(1+\alpha)}$. Further, we assume that total wage income is fully consumed, and that labor income is the only source of consumption expenditure. The latter is a traditional assumption in Keynesian growth models (Gries, 2020b). In Appendix D to this chapter, we show that once we depart from the representative household approach, motivating this assumption by group-specific optimal intertemporal choices is not difficult. For labor income (poor household), we assume parameters for the Euler equation that imply no savings. For all other households with income from IT and financial services (wealthy household), we assume for the Euler equation that consumption growth is slow (less than innovation and income growth), such that in the long run, the consumption rate converges to zero. That is, these households still consume, but their consumption rate converges to zero and their savings rate converges to one. These values are used for our steady state estimates.

Further, in an economy with nonperfect matching, consumers also devote income to search and matching activities whenever their desired consumption cannot find a suitable output. Searching for appropriate consumption goods leads to the experience that using fraction θ_j of their income in the search and matching procedure would reduce the mismatch.[16] Therefore, aggregate consumption is:

$$C(t) = w_L(t) L_L (1-\theta) + \varepsilon = c(1-\theta) Y(t) + \varepsilon \tag{5.47}$$

$$\text{with} \quad c = \frac{\phi_L}{(1+\alpha)} \tag{5.48}$$

[16] In Section 5.3.2 when we introduce the aggregate *match-improvement function* (5.57), we will see how θ affects the matching process. This simple way of modeling the consumers' search activity implies that subtracting search costs θ from income is a kind of iceberg cost of this search.

Note here that c is the economy's marginal (and average) rate of consumption. ε denotes a randomness in consumption demand with an expected value $E[\varepsilon] = 0$.

As far as investment expenditure is concerned, in our model, innovation by intermediate goods-producing start-up ventures requires investment.[17] It is assumed that such investment ν is identical for each innovation. Thus, total start-up investments $I(t)$ are described by

$$I(t) = \nu \dot{N}(t) \tag{5.49}$$

5.2.5.2 *The Keynesian Income-Expenditure Equilibrium*

Income Y can be used for consumption C and investment I. Thus, demand for GDP is $Y^D \equiv C + I$. While the consumption rate is determined by Equation (5.47) and a constant fraction of total effective income, investments are driven only by the market entry of new goods (i.e., innovation), $\dot{N}$. With the consumption rate (5.48) being a constant, the Keynesian income-expenditure mechanism can be applied to determine effective total demand, Y^D. Therefore, in income-expenditure equilibrium, aggregate effective demand equals effective income

$$Y(t) \stackrel{!}{=} Y^D(t) \equiv C(t) + I(t), \tag{5.50}$$

and we obtain the Keynesian income-expenditure multiplier for the effective expected demand in the aggregate goods market

$$Y^D(t) = \frac{I(t) + \varepsilon(t)}{1 - c\,(1 - \theta)} \tag{5.51}$$

5.2.5.3 *Expected Aggregate Demand for Total Production*

To determine the total or aggregate demand for final output Q, we begin with the demand for GDP, $Y^D(t) \equiv C(t) + I(t)$. We also need to add the demand for input goods taken from final goods sector

[17] Note that the term investment stands for start-up expenditure on final output goods. It is not a capital formation that accumulates to a stock of real capital for production purposes.

$N(t)x(t)c_X$. The Keynesian income-expenditure mechanism tells us that effective aggregate demand for GDP is $\frac{\nu\dot{N}+\varepsilon}{1-c(1-\theta)}$, adding $N(t)x(t)c_X$ gives the effective demand for total output Q, namely

$$Q^D = \frac{\nu\dot{N}(t) + E\left[\varepsilon(t)\right]}{1 - c\left(1 - \theta\right)} + N(t)x(t)c_X$$

Demand is hence an endogenous value in which investment expenditures are independent from households' savings decisions. Further, to determine the expected excess demand ratio under current demand conditions, we need to divide by $Q(t)$. As a result, the aggregate effective demand ratio $\lambda(t)$ describes the ratio of effective aggregate demand to current output

$$\lambda(t) = \frac{Q^D(t)}{Q(t)}$$

and in expected values, we obtain the *ratio of expected aggregate demand*[18]

$$E\left[\lambda(t)\right] = \frac{\nu}{1 - c\left(1 - \theta\right)} \frac{1}{H_Q\left(\frac{\alpha^2}{c_X}\right)^{\frac{\alpha}{1-\alpha}}} g_N + \alpha^2 \qquad (5.52)$$

5.3 SOLVING THE MODEL

In this section, we depart from the perspective of individual firms and consumers and assume the perspective of an omniscient observer of the economy.

5.3.1 Solving for Technology Growth

We start to solve the model by determining the partially endogenous growth rate of new products that successfully enter and remain in the market $g_N(t) = \frac{\dot{N}(t)}{N(t)}$. From Equation (5.34), we know that the growth rate of implemented technologies depends on effective demand for intermediate goods and thus depends on labor in the effective production H_Q, and is

18 $\frac{E[Q^D]}{Q} = \frac{\nu}{1-c(1-\theta)} \frac{\dot{N}(t)}{Q(t)} + \alpha^2$ and using Equations (5.1) and (5.28), we obtain Equation (5.52).

$$g_N(t) = \frac{\dot{N}(t)}{N(t)} = \left(\left(\frac{\alpha^2}{c_X} \right)^{\frac{1}{1-\alpha}} H_Q \right)^{\varphi} (g_A)^{1-\varphi} \tag{5.53}$$

This process is partially endogenous, as the exogenous g_A is an essential driver of g_N. However, the extent to which the exogenous innovative process g_A becomes usable and implemented in the economy is endogenous.

5.3.2 *From Perceived Individual Frictions to Aggregate Market Mismatch*

In Section 5.2.1, we introduced the notion of a firm facing market mismatch in selling its potential output.[19] From the perspective of an individual firm i, we have discussed firm i's perception of market mismatch δ_i, which they relate to their individual market conditions and their counteractivities. They use human services $H_{\phi i}$ for placement and reduce their individual sales problems accordingly. Furthermore, in the preceding sections, we explained that it is not only firms that are affected by a market mismatch. In their search for the desired consumption goods, consumers also face a mismatch and hence devote a fraction θ_j of their income on this search.

These micro-level (idiosyncratic) problems in the market are not the only reason for firms' sales and customers' purchase problems. These problems are, in fact, also due to aggregate market conditions, even if individual decision-makers are not aware of this fact.

What are the reasons for firms' sales problems? From the perspective of firms, effective sales are determined by stochastic market mismatch δ_i, [$\phi_i(t) = 1 - \delta_i(t)$ see 5.2]. Thus, to answer this question, we need to find out more about the random variable $\delta_i(t)$. Furthermore, what is behind the firm's observed market mismatch $\delta_i'(t)$?

The mismatch is clearly determined by two components: (1) aggregate market conditions and (2) an idiosyncratic component for each individual firm.

[19] This section is closely related to the modeling in Gries (2020a).

The first component, the aggregate market condition, reflects a shortage of aggregate demand $\delta^D(t)$, which is the difference between total supply and effective aggregate demand $Q^D(t)$

$$\delta^D(t) = \frac{Q(t) - Q^D(t)}{Q(t)} = 1 - \lambda(t) \tag{5.54}$$

A second and additional component of the mismatch is the idiosyncratic component for each firm. These sales problems are firm-specific obstacles and are described by the random variable ε_{Fi}, with $1 > E[\varepsilon_{Fi}] > 0$. For given aggregate market conditions $\delta^D(t)$, ε_{Fi} is the element of the mismatch that is due to individual firm conditions. Therefore, the friction perceived by each firm i combines the aggregate market and idiosyncratic component and can be described as

$$\delta_i'(t) = \delta^D(t)\varepsilon_{Fi} \tag{5.55}$$

However, individual firms or consumers do not have this insight into the breakdown of the friction. An individual firm only perceives an expected sales ratio $E[\phi_i(t)] = 1 - E[\delta_i(t)]$, interpreting it as being caused by friction that can be addressed by allocating more labor toward the matching process $[\frac{\partial E[\phi_i(t)]}{\partial E[\delta_i']} < 0, \quad \frac{\partial E[\phi_i(t)]}{\partial H_{\phi i}(t)} > 0$; see Equation (5.3) in Section 5.2.1].

We have to aggregate to connect these individual activities with total and current market conditions to determine aggregate market equilibrium. Assuming that ε_{Fi} are independent and identically distributed (i.i.d) for $i \in \mathcal{I}$, we can aggregate $(\varepsilon_{Fi} = \varepsilon_F)$, and obtain as given mismatch $\delta'(t)$; and in expectations[20]

$$E\left[\delta'(t)\right] = \left(1 - E[\lambda]\right) E[\varepsilon_F] - cov(\lambda, \varepsilon_F), \quad \text{with} \quad cov(\lambda, \varepsilon_F) < 0 \tag{5.56}$$

We assume that $cov(\lambda, \varepsilon_F)$ is negative because a random increase in aggregate demand ε trickles down to each firm's market demand, reduces the tightness in each firm's market, and, as a result, also reduces the idiosyncratic mismatch. The aggregate market condition affects each idiosyncratic matching process. Thus, this random

[20] Note that firms observe the given mismatch but have no insight in its composition and mechanisms.

increase in aggregate demand is accompanied by a reduction in the firm's idiosyncratic difficulty of finding a customer ε_F, and we can assume that $cov(\lambda, \varepsilon_F)$ is negative and sufficiently large in absolute terms, such that $E[\delta'(t)]$ is always positive. However, we have not specified how countermeasures by firms and customers affect the mismatch. To do this, we define the aggregate match-improvement function $m(t)$ for the aggregate market. We assume that the matching of the two market sides is determined by the firms' allocation of human services to combat mismatch $H_{\phi i}(t)$ and the fraction $\theta(t)$ of consumers' income spent to find the desired consumption good, so the match improvement function is assumed to be

$$m = L_\phi(t)\left(1-\theta(t)\right)^{-1}, \quad \text{with } \frac{dm}{dH_\phi} > 0, \quad \frac{dm}{d\theta} > 0 \tag{5.57}$$

Thus, the rate of expected effective aggregate mismatch – after implementing countermeasures – is

$$E[\delta(t)] = E\left[\delta'(t)\right] - m \tag{5.58}$$

When the mismatch is completely eliminated, such that the aggregate expected mismatch becomes zero, we obtain a perfect matching

$$E[\delta(t)] = 0 \tag{5.59}$$

Thus, Equation (5.59) implies that firms expected effective sales ratio turns to one $[E[\phi(t)] = 1 - E[\delta(t)] = 1.]$, and consumers have fully eliminated the mismatch by devoting respective resources. Further, we simultaneously need to determine aggregate market equilibrium. For the aggregate market, we know that effective sales must be equal to effective aggregate demand, and in aggregate market equilibrium, both must equal aggregate supply $E\left[Q^D\right] = Q$. Thus, as the second equilibrium condition, we obtain

$$1 = \frac{E\left[Q^D\right]}{Q} = E[\lambda(t)] \tag{5.60}$$

5.3.3 *The Aggregate Model in Two Equations*

Using Equation (5.53) reduces the system to the following two simultaneous equations, namely Equations (5.59a) and (5.60a).

5.3.3.1 *Eliminating Mismatch*

From Equation (5.6) in Section 5.2.1, we know that a firm allocates human services in the market placement process until all output is sold. The aggregate Equation (5.58) tells us that producers and customers allocate resources to improving aggregate matching until mismatch is eliminated. Using the constraint for human service allocation Equation (5.35), we can now determine the allocation of H for a perfect match equilibrium for producers and consumers as[21]

$$H_Q = cov\,(\lambda, \varepsilon_F)\,(1-\theta) + H \tag{5.59a}$$

5.3.3.2 *Aggregate Market Equilibrium*

In Section 5.2.5, we specified aggregate demand and the aggregate effective demand ratio (see Equation (5.52)). Aggregate goods market equilibrium requires that demand equals production and supply, such that the effective demand ratio turns to one and plugging in Equations (5.60) and (5.53) gives[22]

$$H_Q = \left(\frac{\nu}{\left(1-\alpha^2\right)\left(1-c\,(1-\theta)\right)}\right)^{\frac{1}{(1-\varphi)}} \left(\frac{\alpha^2}{c_X}\right)^{\frac{\varphi-\alpha}{(1-\alpha)(1-\varphi)}} g_A \tag{5.60a}$$

Equations (5.59a) and (5.60a) hence remain to solve for the two endogenous variables, namely human services used in production H_Q and consumers' spending on search and matching θ.

5.3.4 *Current Market Equilibrium*

We can now solve for equilibrium. Combining Equations (5.59a), with (5.60a), we are left with only Equation (5.61) and one variable, H_Q

$$0 = F = H_Q^{(1-\varphi)} - \frac{\nu}{\left(1-\alpha^2\right)\left(1-c\frac{H-H_Q}{-cov(\lambda,\varepsilon_F)}\right)} \left(\frac{\alpha^2}{c_X}\right)^{\frac{\varphi-\alpha}{1-\alpha}} (g_A)^{1-\varphi} \tag{5.61}$$

[21] For details, see Appendix E at the end of this chapter. Note that assumption (5.5) makes sure that H_Q is allocated to production only, if before all mismatches have been eliminated.

[22] For details, see Appendix E at the end of this chapter.

As we cannot explicitly solve for H_Q, we apply the *implicit function theorem* to determine the equilibrium $\tilde{H}_Q$, and other interesting variables.

Current market equilibrium: Equation (5.61) implicitly defines a function for
(1) the equilibrium value of $\tilde{H}_Q$

$$\tilde{H}_Q = H_Q\left(\nu, g_A, c_X, A_{IT}, \ldots, cov\left(\lambda, \varepsilon_F\right)\right), \text{ with } \frac{d\tilde{H}_Q}{dg_A} > 0, \quad \frac{d\tilde{H}_Q}{d\nu} > 0 \tag{5.62}$$

Further, Equation (5.62) leads to
(2) the rate of consumers' devoting on improving the matching process

$$\tilde{\theta} = 1 - \frac{H - \tilde{H}_Q}{-cov\left(\lambda, \varepsilon_F\right)}, \quad \text{with} \quad cov\left(\lambda, \varepsilon_F\right) < 0 \tag{5.63}$$

(3) total production of the final good

$$\tilde{Q}(t) = N(t)\tilde{H}_Q\left(\frac{\alpha^2}{c_X}\right)^{\frac{\alpha}{1-\alpha}}, \tag{5.64}$$

(4) total income and hence the level of the growth path

$$\tilde{Y}(t) = N(t)\left(1 - \alpha^2\right)\tilde{H}_Q\left(\frac{\alpha^2}{c_X}\right)^{\frac{\alpha}{1-\alpha}}, \tag{5.65}$$

(5) the growth rate of income (GDP) gives

$$\tilde{g}_Y = \frac{\dot{Y}(t)}{Y(t)} = g_N = \frac{\dot{N}(t)}{N(t)} = \left(\frac{\alpha^2}{c_X}\right)^{\frac{\varphi}{1-\alpha}}\left(\tilde{H}_Q\right)^{\varphi}(g_A)^{1-\varphi}, \tag{5.66}$$

For proof, see Appendix F at the end of this chapter.

With $\tilde{H}_Q$ and $\tilde{H}_\phi$, we have determined a current market equilibrium at a level below potential output $\tilde{H}_Q < H$. Further, as $\tilde{H}_Q$ depends on demand-side parameters, for example, ν, the level of the income path and the growth rate depends on the demand side as well.[23]

[23] Some convergence processes are described in Appendix G at the end of this chapter.

5.3.5 *Stationarity of Equilibrium*

Although market equilibrium for each period is described in Section 5.3.4, two important questions remain. First, how can the equilibrium output steadily remain below potential output and represent a long-term stationary equilibrium? Second, how can aggregate demand become central and determine both the stationary level and the speed of the growth path? The rest of Section 3.5 provides answers.

These questions are worth asking because mainstream dynamic macroeconomics is based on the idea that the path of potential growth – often regarded as the outcome of some kind (variety) of neoclassical or endogenous growth model – is the only relevant process for economic growth. After a temporary deviation from this path, the economy returns to it and continues to grow, as described in the fundamental growth model. There is no permanent deviation. In contrast, the equilibrium we derived here can indeed become a permanent, stationary process. In other words, such a growth with a mismatch (path level and growth rate) is a stationary path. The economy will not necessarily return to the path of potential growth.

In this approach, we suggest a different concept for a stationary equilibrium[24] that is directly related to stochastic modeling. We describe stationary behavior from the perspective of individual decision-makers. We assume that a systematic difference of expectations and planning with the average outcome of a stochastic variable is perceived as an inconsistency of one's own behavior and reality that leads to an adjustment in behavior toward an experience of less inconsistency. For instance, if in a stochastic environment an individual plans and organizes a specific outcome – according to their subjective expectations – and their plans and outcome do not coincide with observed expected values, we refer to this difference as an *expectation error*. As a consequence, the individual learns from this

[24] This equilibrium concept draws on Gries (2020b).

error and changes their behavior by adjusting their plans. Individual behavior becomes stationary if the planned and realized outcome is indeed the observed expected outcome. This condition defines a behavioral equilibrium such that it implies no (need) for a change in behavior. Thus, we refer to this condition as the *no-expectation-error equilibrium* (n-e-ee). It is an equilibrium in terms of a stationary behavior.

In this approach, the general concept of a no-expectation-error equilibrium can be illustrated by looking at the matching procedure. The mismatch $E[\delta]$ defines the gap between planned production $Q_i(t)$ and the mean of effective sales $E[\Phi_i(t)] = (1 - E[\delta(t)])\, Q_i(t)$. Thus, as long as firms and customers do not counter the mismatch by devoting sufficient resources to the matching, they cannot expect the mismatch to disappear, and $E[\delta] = E[\delta'] - m\left(L_\phi, \theta\right) > 0$. Thus, individuals face an expectation error as their actions do not coincide with the observed expected values. In other words, there is an error in their planning as their subjective expectations are false (expectation error). Thus, they continue to adjust their plans until they correctly expect and plan their counteractivities, such that the expected mismatch is on average fully eliminated $0 = E[\delta] = E[\delta'] - m\left(L_\phi, \theta\right)$. As a result, there is no expectation error with respect to the final goods matching mechanism. Firms are in sales equilibrium ($E[\phi] = 1$). There is also no expectation error with respect to consumers and aggregate markets. In aggregate market equilibrium, consumers allocate income share θ to the search process and find a matching equilibrium, for all their income planned for consumption, such that we also obtain equilibrium in the aggregate goods market $E[\lambda(t)] = 1$.

5.4 THE DYNAMIC, LONG-RUN IMPACTS OF AI

Section 5.3 of this chapter presented an appropriate endogenous growth model to identify the labor market and the growth consequences of technological progress in AI. In this section, the model is used to analyze the long-run impacts of AI. For simplicity, we assume a once-and-for-all increase in the availability of AI technologies reflected by A_{IT}.

5.4.1 Impact on the Number of Automated Tasks

The first effect we consider is the impact of increasing AI availability $(\frac{dA_{IT}}{A_{IT}} > 0)$ on the number of automated tasks. Taking the derivative of Equation (5.21), we obtain[25]

$$\frac{dN_{IT}}{N_{IT}} = \eta_{N_{IT},A_{IT}} \frac{dA_{IT}}{A_{IT}} > 0 \tag{5.67}$$

with

$$\eta_{N_{IT},A_{IT}} = \frac{1}{\sigma \frac{\partial \gamma(N_{IT})}{\partial N_{IT}} \left(\frac{A_L L_L}{A_{IT} L_{IT}} \frac{B_1(N_{IT})}{B_2(N_{IT})} \right)^{\frac{1}{\sigma}} + \frac{\gamma_L(N_{IT})^{\sigma-1}}{B_2(N_{IT})} + \frac{\gamma_{IT}(N_{IT})^{\sigma-1}}{B_1(N_{IT})}} \frac{1}{N_{IT}} > 0. \tag{5.68}$$

Thus, with more AI, more tasks will be automated.

5.4.2 Impact on Human Service Production

Progress in AI $(\frac{dA_{IT}}{A_{IT}} > 0)$ will increase the supply of human services inputs H

$$\frac{dH}{H} = \eta_{H,A_{IT}} \frac{dA_{IT}}{A_{IT}} > 0, \quad \text{with} \quad \eta_{H,A_{IT}} > 0, \quad \text{for} \quad \sigma > 1 \tag{5.69}$$

given that[26]

$$1 > \eta_{H,A_{IT}} = \left[1 + \left(\frac{B_2(N_{IT})}{B_1(N_{IT})} \right)^{\frac{1}{\sigma}} \left(\frac{A_L L_L}{A_{IT} L_{IT}} \right)^{\frac{\sigma-1}{\sigma}} \right]^{-1} > 0 \tag{5.70}$$

Thus, the supply of human services inputs will increase at a rate slower than the rate of AI change $\frac{dA_{IT}}{A_{IT}}$. This is a similar result as in the standard constant elasticity of substitution (CES) approach, as in Gries and Naudé (2018).

[25] See Appendix B1 at the end of this chapter.

[26] For calculations, see Appendix H.

5.4.3 Impact on Inequality

To analyze the impact of AI ($\frac{dA_{IT}}{A_{IT}}$) on inequality, the changes it brings about in the income share of labor, the income share of technology providers, and the income share of financial wealth holders will be determined.

Income share of labor: The income share of labor was described in Equation (5.43). The derivative of Equation (5.25) shows how the income share of labor income changes as a result of new AI technologies:[27]

$$\frac{d\left(w_L L_L/Y\right)}{w_L L_L/Y} = \frac{d\phi_L}{\phi_L} = \eta_{\phi_L,A_{IT}} \frac{dA_{IT}}{A_{IT}} < 0, \text{ for } 1 < \sigma \tag{5.71}$$

$$\text{with } \eta_{\phi_L,A_{IT}} = \frac{1}{\sigma} \frac{-\left(\sigma-1\right) - \left(\frac{\gamma_{IT}\left(N_{IT}\right)^{\sigma-1}}{B_1\left(N_{IT}\right)} + \frac{\gamma_L\left(N_{IT}\right)^{\sigma-1}}{B_2\left(N_{IT}\right)}\right) N_{IT}\eta_{N_{IT},A_{IT}}}{1 + \left(\frac{A_L L_L}{A_{IT} L_{IT}}\right)^{\frac{\sigma-1}{\sigma}} \left(\frac{B_2\left(N_{IT}\right)}{B_1\left(N_{IT}\right)}\right)^{\frac{1}{\sigma}}} < 0 \tag{5.72}$$

For $1 < \sigma$ (high elasticity of substitution), the income share of labor will clearly decline since $-\left(\frac{\gamma_{IT}\left(N_{IT}\right)^{\sigma-1}}{B_1\left(N_{IT}\right)} + \frac{\gamma_L\left(N_{IT}\right)^{\sigma-1}}{B_2\left(N_{IT}\right)}\right)$ $N_{IT}\eta_{N_{IT},A_{IT}} < 0$. However, if $1 > \sigma$, the income share of labor will not necessarily increase, in contrast to what would be the case in a standard CES approach. This shows that the integration of the task-based approach in the model means that automation will likely decrease the share of labor income, even if σ is low. This is because $-\left(\frac{\gamma_{IT}\left(N_{IT}\right)^{\sigma-1}}{B_1\left(N_{IT}\right)} + \frac{\gamma_L\left(N_{IT}\right)^{\sigma-1}}{B_2\left(N_{IT}\right)}\right) N_{IT}\eta_{N_{IT},A_{IT}}$ is always negative and for not too large levels of σ, the negative effect still dominates. This effect is the same as that identified by Acemoglu and Restrepo (2019b, p. 9).

It can also be noted that A_{IT} progress will not only depress the income share that labor receives from providing human service inputs (for $1 < \sigma$), but that the share of labor income in the *total economy* will also decline.

[27] For calculations, see Appendix H at the end of this chapter.

Income share of technology providers: Departing from Equation (5.45) and taking the derivatives shows that the income share of the technology providers increases when there is high elasticity of substitution between AI and labor, as can be seen from:

$$\frac{d\left(w_{IT}L_{IT}/Y\right)}{dA_{IT}}\frac{1}{w_{IT}L_{IT}/Y} = -\frac{\eta_{\phi_L,A_{IT}}}{\left(\frac{1}{\phi_L}-1\right)}\frac{dA_{IT}}{A_{IT}} > 0$$

$$\text{with } \eta_{\phi_L,A_{IT}} < 0 \text{ for } 1 < \sigma \tag{5.73}$$

Income share of financial wealth holders: According to Equation (5.46), the income share of financial wealth holders is $\frac{\alpha}{(1+\alpha)}$. Hence, this income share will not change with the technology shock of AI progress, $dA_{IT} > 0$.

5.4.4 *Impact on Demand and Absorption*

Impact on consumption rate: From earlier, it is clear that a high elasticity of substitution leads to a shift in income distribution in favor of technology providers and financial wealth holders. Combining this insight with the result that consumption demand is determined by the labor share, the consumption rate c is affected by progress in AI (dA_{IT}) as follows[28]:

$$\frac{dc}{c} = \overset{(-)}{\eta}_{c,A_{IT}}\frac{dA_{IT}}{A_{IT}} < 0 \tag{5.74}$$

with $\eta_{c,A_{IT}} = \eta_{\phi_L,A_{IT}} < 0$, for $\sigma > 1$. This shows that AI unambiguously tightens the demand constraint when the elasticity of substitution between AI technologies and labor is high ($\sigma > 1$).

5.4.5 *Impact on Long-Term Efficiency*

How high current equilibrium output is to potential output is measured by the utilization or deployment rate[29] which is $\omega = \tilde{Y}/\tilde{Y}^p$. $1 - \omega$ is a of measure of (hidden) inefficiency. The economy is below its potential, but the various agents are not aware of it. Given current

[28] For a proof and the respective conditions, see Appendix H at the end of this chapter.

[29] As a reminder, $\tilde{\omega}$ is the result of optimal individual behavior in steady state.

equilibrium output (5.65) and potential output [maximum possible output ($\tilde{H}_Q = H$), $\tilde{Y}^P(t) = N(t)\left(1-\alpha^2\right)H\left(\frac{\alpha^2}{c_X}\right)^{\frac{\alpha}{1-\alpha}}$], the *deployment rate* is

$$\omega(t) = \frac{\tilde{Y}(t)}{\tilde{Y}^P(t)} = \frac{\tilde{H}_Q(t)}{H}. \tag{5.75}$$

AI progress dA_{IT} will affect $\omega(t)$ through the total availability of human services H and H_Q (see Equation (5.62)). As the effects on H and H_Q are different, the effect on the deployment rate, that is, $\frac{d\omega(t)}{\omega(t)} = \frac{dH_Q}{H_Q} - \frac{dH}{H}$ is not clear. While $\frac{dH}{H}$ is known from Equation (5.69), we need to determine the equilibrium change of human service in production, as a result of AI progress, which is given by[30]

$$\frac{d\tilde{H}_Q}{H_Q} = \eta_{H_Q,A_{IT}}\frac{dA_{IT}}{A_{IT}} > 0 \tag{5.76}$$

$$\eta_{H_Q,A_{IT}} = \frac{\frac{\phi_L}{(1+\alpha)}\left[\overset{<0}{\eta_{\phi_L,A_{IT}}}H_\phi + \overset{>0}{\eta_{H,A_{IT}}}H\right]}{\left[(2-\varphi)\,cH_Q + (1-\varphi)\left(-cov\left(\lambda,\varepsilon_F\right) - cH\right)\right]} > 0 \tag{5.77}$$

At first glance, the total effect $\frac{d\tilde{H}_Q}{H_Q}$ is ambiguous. There are two opposing forces. First, on the supply side, an increase in technology, which is quasi-factor augmenting, should lead to more factors available for production $\eta_{H,A_{IT}}$ in Equation (5.76). Second, the term $\eta_{\phi_L,A_{IT}} < 0$ in Equation (5.76) shows that the potential increase on the supply side is countered by a negative effect through income distribution and a reduction in absorption on the demand side. Higher inequality and a declining consumption rate restrict the total effect of AI on factor utilization for production, which otherwise had been solely $\eta_{H,A_{IT}}$ in Equation (5.76). The demand constraint can substantially reduce the supply-side expansion. However, the overall effect of progress in AI remains positive as long as we do not assume additional effects of AI, which may occur simultaneously and reduce demand further. We discuss these additional affects in Section 5.5.

[30] See appendix H at the end of this chapter.

After the identification of $\eta_{H_Q,A_{IT}}$, we can turn back to the deployment rate. If we plug in and rearrange, for the change of the deployment rate we obtain for a broad range of parameter values that

$$\frac{d\omega(t)}{\omega(t)} = \eta_{\omega,A_{IT}} \frac{dA_{IT}}{A_{IT}} < 0 \quad \text{for } \frac{(2-\varphi)}{(1-\varphi)} cH_{\phi} < -cov\,(\lambda, \varepsilon_F) \quad (5.78)$$

$$\eta_{\omega,A_{IT}} = \left[\frac{\frac{\phi_L}{(1+\alpha)} \left(\overset{<0}{\eta_{\phi_L,A_{IT}}} H_{\phi} + H \overset{>0}{\eta_{H,A_{IT}}} \right)}{(2-\varphi)\, cH_Q + (1-\varphi)\left(-cov\,(\lambda, \varepsilon_F) - cH\right)} - \overset{>0}{\eta_{H,A_{IT}}} \right] < 0 \quad (5.79)$$

If the covariance $cov\,(\lambda, \varepsilon_F)$ is sufficiently large in absolute terms, $\omega(t)$ decreases, such that an increase in A_{IT} increases the gap between the current equilibrium steady state and potential steady state output.[31] In this comparative static analysis, a once-and-for-all increase in AI technologies may generally lead to a positive or negative effect on the deployment rate $\omega(t)$. However, from Equations (5.72) and (5.74), we know that inequality increases and absorption declines if AI increases. As a consequence, with higher inequality and declining consumption, the deployment rate may decline and the economy will find itself on a long-term path of stagnating growth.

This path of stagnating growth has a simple intuitive explanation. If progress in AI technologies generates asymmetric benefits in favor of financial wealth holders and the owners of the AI technology, at the cost of the labor share of income and the consumption rate, the demand side will grow less than the supply side. Since our model has jettisoned Say's Law and market adjustments take place through search and sales promotion decisions, the demand side can become a constraint on growth. Resources that could be used for more production and absorption are increasingly used to achieve a match between supply and demand. The economy could produce more, but it has to deploy more and more resources to find the equilibrium.

[31] See Appendix H at the end of this chapter.

5.4.6 Impact on Wages and Labor Productivity

Changes in the expected ratio of market absorption $\frac{dc}{c}$ have implications for wages, labor productivity, and GDP growth. Because wages are equal to marginal labor productivity, the effects of AI on wage and labor productivity growth are:

$$\frac{dw_L(t)}{w_L(t)} = \left[\overset{(ii)\quad <0}{\eta_{\phi_L,A_{IT}}} + \overset{(i)\quad >0}{\eta_{H_Q,A_{IT}}}\right]\frac{dA_{IT}}{A_{IT}} \lesseqgtr 0 \tag{5.80}$$

The result in Equation (5.80) shows that there are again two effects of AI on labor productivity and wages. First, growth in human service input and more human services in production is driven by IT and AI growth and described by $\eta_{H_Q,A_{IT}}$ [see (i) in Equations (5.80) and (5.76)]. Second, if the elasticity of substitution is high $(\sigma > 1)$, labor share of income and the consumption rate decline, that is, $\eta_{\phi_L,A_{IT}} < 0$. This demand-constraining effect occurs because aggregate demand is not growing sufficiently to absorb all additional supply [see (ii) in Equation (5.80)]. Even more, if the covariance $cov(\lambda, \varepsilon_F)$ is sufficiently large in absolute terms, wage and labor productivity growth may stagnate or even decline.[32]

5.4.7 Impact on Long-Run GDP Growth

The implementation of IT and AI technologies affects not only wages and labor but also the GDP growth rate. The same mechanisms that were discussed in Section 5.4.5 are also responsible for a negative net impact on GDP growth. These mechanisms are again (1) a positive productivity effect and (2) a negative effect of a tightening demand constraint. Overall, however, the net impact is not unambiguous. From Equation (5.66), we know that the GDP growth rate is $\tilde{g}_Y = \left(\frac{\alpha^2}{c_x}\right)^{\frac{\varphi}{1-\alpha}}\left(\tilde{H}_Q\right)^{\varphi}(g_A)^{1-\varphi}$. Taking the derivative

$$\frac{d\tilde{g}_Y}{\tilde{g}_Y} = \varphi\eta_{H_Q,A_{IT}}\frac{dA_{IT}}{A_{IT}} > 0 \quad \text{with } \eta_{H_Q,A_{IT}} > 0 \text{ see Equation (5.76)} \tag{5.81}$$

32 See Appendix H at the end of this chapter.

we see that the direction and extent of this effect depend on $\eta_{H_Q,A_{IT}}$. As Section 5.4.5 provides an extensive discussion of Equation (5.76), we can conclude: if A_{IT} increases, the overall growth rate increases as well. However, demand side effects restrict the growth expansion to a lower than potential level. This means that the expectation by some that AI will lead to "explosive" economic growth is rather unlikely.

5.5 EFFECTS WITH SIMULTANEOUS AI-RELATED DEMAND SHOCKS

Simultaneous demand shock: As we pointed out in earlier chapters, AI progress is often modeled or described as essentially process innovations – innovations in how algorithms learn. In the model presented in this chapter, we have however AI progress showing up in *product innovations*, specifically in the form of new intermediate products which are brought to the market following start-up investments by entrepreneurs. These intermediate products could be seen as embodying ML – and being based on so-called foundational AI models (see Chapter 2). Think for instance of a chatbot that assists online shoppers or provides computer code. If AI progress changes the characteristics of such innovative intermediate goods and reduces start-up investment expenditures – as we found for IT and computer equipment – then v in Equation (5.49) declines, specifically, $\frac{dv}{dA_{IT}} < 0$. In this case, the impact of AI on the economy will be a combined, simultaneous shock on both the supply and demand sides. In terms of GDP growth ($\tilde{g}_Y$), we now have that

$$\frac{d\tilde{g}_Y}{\tilde{g}_Y} = \eta_{g_N,A_{IT}} \frac{dA_{IT}}{A_{IT}} \lesseqgtr 0 \quad \text{with}$$

$$\eta_{g_N,A_{IT}}$$

$$= \varphi \left[\frac{c\left[\eta_{c,A_{IT}} H_\phi + \eta_{H,A_{IT}} H\right] \frac{\dot{A}_{IT}}{A_{IT}} - \frac{cov(\lambda,\varepsilon_F)}{(1-\alpha^2)} v \left(\frac{\alpha^2}{c_x}\right)^{\frac{\varphi-\alpha}{1-\alpha}} \left(\frac{g_A}{H_Q}\right)^{1-\varphi} \eta_{v,A_{IT}}}{\left[(2-\varphi)\, cH_Q + (1-\varphi)\left(-cov\left(\lambda,\varepsilon_F\right) - cH\right)\right]} \right] < 0$$

for sufficiently large $|cov\,(\lambda, \varepsilon_F)|$, see Appendix I at the end of this chapter.

Total production and the overall growth rate can turn negative if in absolute terms $cov(\lambda, \varepsilon_F)$ is sufficiently large. This will be the case if a positive (but potentially weak) supply-side effect on process innovation is overcompensated by a simultaneous sufficiently large demand-side shock triggered by AI.

Simultaneous innovation shock: A second example illustrates, perhaps more forcefully, that progress in AI can lead to perverse innovation effects, particularly if it crowds out product innovations, for instance, innovations in the intermediate goods sector. If AI progress does not fall from heaven, but is subject to opportunity cost, then in our model, an increase in AI process innovations will lead to a reallocation of innovation away from the intermediate product sector. This effect could counter the positive AI resource shock. AI only becomes available through reallocation of resources and less intermediate innovation. Even if $dAI > 0$ is positive, the growth rate of innovation g_A may decline. With the simultaneous demand side effect of AI, total growth will be reduced as can be seen from the fact that

$$\frac{d\tilde{g}_Y}{\tilde{g}_Y} = \eta_{g_N, A_{IT}} \frac{dA_{IT}}{A_{IT}} \lesseqgtr 0 \quad \text{with}$$
$$\eta_{g_N, A_{IT}} = \left[\varphi \overset{<0}{\eta_{H_Q, A_{IT}}} + (1 - \varphi) \overset{<0}{\eta_{g_A, A_{IT}}} \right] < 0,$$

for sufficiently large $|cov(\lambda, \varepsilon_F)|$, see Appendix I at the end of this chapter.

This example describes a potential perverse innovation process where more resources are allocated toward process innovation and away from product innovation. As a result then of a simultaneous demand and supply shocks, income and growth could decline even in absolute terms. We can, again, conclude that expectations of "explosive" growth from AI will be rather unlikely.

5.6 CONCLUDING REMARKS

In this chapter, we provided a semi-endogenous growth model that addressed two shortcomings of the growth model proposed by Acemoglu and Restrepo (2018b) – the AR model. The first is that its reinstatement effects will depend, over the long run, on the impact of AI automation on income distribution. If income inequality worsens, such as that the labor share in GDP declines, aggregate demand will decline. This would reduce the economy's actual and potential growth. Lower growth in turn would limit the reinstatement of new jobs. Unfortunately, the AR model cannot take this into account, as it is supply driven. We addressed this shortcoming by allowing for growth in our model to be demand constrained by replacing the typical assumption of a representative household by the assumption of two groups of households with different preferences.

The second shortcoming of the AR model, which is also a more general shortcoming of the task approach on which it is based, is that it inadequately engages with the nature of AI and its technological feasibility. As we discussed in detail in Chapter 4, AI may perform tasks or help to perform tasks, but this depends on the abilities of AI and the abilities of labor. We addressed this shortcoming by incorporating the adjusted task approach as described in Chapter 4, modeling AI abilities as the outcome of a combination of IT-specific labor, IT-specific abilities, and ML algorithms.

By integrating the task approach with a more nuanced specification of the nature of AI and its technological feasibility in the form of abilities, we showed that AI automation can decrease the share of labor income even for a substitution between AI and labor below one, and increase the income share of financial wealth owners and the owners of the technology. We also showed that when the elasticity of substitution between AI technologies and labor is high, AI will unambiguously reduce the aggregate consumption rate and retard aggregate demand expansion. With higher inequality and a declining consumption rate, the economy will move toward a declining utilization (deployment) rate of production potential and increasing structural inefficiency.

Since our model has jettisoned the typical assumption of Say's Law – most often motivated by perfect price adjustments, and instead model market adjustments through search, sales promotion decisions, and matching mechanisms, the demand side can become a binding constraint on the supply side. Resources that could be used for more production and absorption are used to match supply and demand. As a result, the growth potential from AI is reduced. As such, our chapter perhaps throws cold water on the belief of some that AI – at least narrow AI -could lead to explosive growth.

On the contrary, while progress in AI technologies could generate additional growth, this growth may turn negative if innovation activities and resources for AI simultaneously reduce innovation in traditional, non-AI fields. In our model, progress in AI technologies amounts to process innovations, and traditional innovations are product innovations. If AI process-innovations displace traditional product innovations, economic growth may turn negative. Furthermore, wages will stagnate in line with slower GDP and productivity growth so as to maintain employment levels.

In sum, with the model presented in this chapter, we can explain why contemporary advanced countries experience the simultaneous existence of high employment with stagnating wages, productivity, and GDP, all despite AI progress.

The kind of AI that we modeled in this and Chapter 4 was narrow AI – such as applications of foundational models with particular abilities to specific domains. In Chapter 2, two we contrasted narrow AI with AGI, which has been described as an AI system that "can perform all human cognitive skills better than the smartest humans" (Suleyman, 2023, p. vii). Perhaps, once an AGI is invented, the economic growth impacts of AI may be more significant. Erdil and Besiroglu (2023), for instance, condition their expectations of explosive economic growth on an AGI. As we also discussed in Chapter 2, many believe that the advances made in recent years in LLMs have brought us close to an AGI and represent at least an *artificial capable intelligence* (ACI). Given the potential impacts of such an AGI on growth through its impact on innovation (see Chapter 2), and the potential winner-takes-all consequences it may bestow on whoever first invents it, it is clear why there would be a race for an AGI ongoing (see the discussion in Chapter 7 for more detail). In Chapter 6, therefore, we develop an extended real options model to study the investment in R&D decision of firms engaged in the race for an AGI.

Appendices

A Final Goods-Producing Firm

Implicit function theorem for optimal $H_{\phi i}$ Condition for applying the implicit function theorem hold: $0 = F = E\left[\phi_i\left(\delta_i, H_{\phi i}\right)\right] - 1$, and $\frac{dF}{dH_{\phi i}} = \frac{\partial E[\phi_i(t)]}{\partial H_{\phi i}(t)} > 0$. For the effect of $E[\delta_i]$, we suppose $\frac{dF}{dE[\delta_i]} = \frac{\partial E[\phi_i(t)]}{\partial E[\delta_i]} < 0$.

B The Task-Based Approach

B1 The Optimal Allocation of Tasks, and Task Production

Demand for tasks: Human service firms

$$\max : \pi_H = p_H H - p_h(z)h(z) = p_H \left(\int_{N-1}^{N} h(z)^{\frac{\sigma-1}{\sigma}} dz \right)^{\frac{\sigma}{\sigma-1}} - p_h(z)h(z).$$

F.O.C.

$$p_H \frac{\sigma}{\sigma-1} \left(\int_{N-1}^{N} h(z)^{\frac{\sigma-1}{\sigma}} dz \right)^{\frac{\sigma}{\sigma-1}-1} \frac{\sigma-1}{\sigma} h(z)^{\frac{\sigma-1}{\sigma}-1} - p_h(z) = 0$$

$$p_H \left(\int_{N-1}^{N} h(z)^{\frac{\sigma-1}{\sigma}} dz \right)^{\frac{\sigma}{\sigma-1}-1} h(z)^{\frac{\sigma-1}{\sigma}-1} = p_h(z)$$

$$p_H \left(\int_{N-1}^{N} h(z)^{\frac{\sigma-1}{\sigma}} dz \right)^{\frac{1}{\sigma-1}} h(z)^{-\frac{1}{\sigma}} = p_h(z)$$

$$p_H H^{\frac{1}{\sigma}} h(z)^{-\frac{1}{\sigma}} = p_h(z)$$

arriving at $h(z) = \frac{H}{p_h(z)^{\sigma}} p_H^{\sigma}$, see Equation (5.14).

Demand for task z: Using marginal production and productivity rules

$h(z_{IT}) = A_{IT}\gamma_{IT}(z)l_{IT}(z)$	production (5.11)	$h(z_L) = A_L\gamma_L(z)l_L(z)$
$p_h A_{IT}\gamma_{IT}(z)l_{IT}(z) = l_{IT}(z)w_{IT}$	marginal productivity and factor reward	$p_h A_L\gamma_L(z)l_L(z) = l_L(z)w_L$
$p_h(z_{IT}) = \frac{w_{IT}}{A_{IT}\gamma_{IT}(z_{IT})}$	price = unit labor costs	$p_h(z_L) = \frac{w_L}{A_L\gamma_L(z_L)}$

and plugging in gives Equation (5.15) as being the optimal demand for $h(z)$,

$$h(z) = \frac{H}{\left(\frac{w_{IT}}{A_{IT}\gamma_{IT}(z)}\right)^{\sigma}} p_H^{\sigma}, \qquad h(z) = \frac{H}{\left(\frac{w_L}{A_L\gamma_L(z)}\right)^{\sigma}} p_H^{\sigma},$$
$$h(z) = p_H^{\sigma} H \left(\frac{A_{IT}}{w_{IT}}\right)^{\sigma} \gamma_{IT}(z)^{\sigma}, \quad h(z) = p_H^{\sigma} H \left(\frac{A_L}{w_L}\right)^{\sigma} \gamma_L(z)^{\sigma}.$$

Demand for various kinds of labor: In order to determine the marginal productivity for each total labor input, the productivity for each kind of labor is derived from Equations (5.15) and (5.11), and we can obtain the optimal demand for IT labor:

$$h(z) = p_H^{\sigma} H \left(\frac{A_{IT}}{w_{IT}}\right)^{\sigma} \gamma_{IT}(z)^{\sigma}$$
$$A_{IT}\gamma_{IT}(z) l_{IT}(z) = p_H^{\sigma} H \left(\frac{A_{IT}}{w_{IT}}\right)^{\sigma} \gamma_{IT}(z)^{\sigma}$$
$$l_{IT}(z) = p_H^{\sigma} H \left(A_{IT}\right)^{\sigma-1} w_{IT}^{-\sigma} \gamma_{IT}(z)^{\sigma-1},$$

see Equation (5.16),

and standard labor:

$$l_L(z) = p_H^{\sigma} H \left(A_L\right)^{\sigma-1} w_L^{-\sigma} \gamma_L(z)^{\sigma-1}, \text{ see Equation (5.17).}$$

To determine wages for each kind of labor, we have to rearrange. As the following calculations are symmetric for each kind of labor, we present the details only for L_{IT}

$$l_{IT}(z) = p_H^{\sigma} H \left(A_{IT}\right)^{\sigma-1} w_{IT}^{-\sigma} \gamma_{IT}(z)^{\sigma-1}$$

Total IT labor is fully employed and allocated to all tasks using IT labor.

$$L_{IT} = \int_{N-1}^{N_{IT}} l_{IT}(z) dz.$$

With the integral in Equation (5.16) $[l_{IT}(z) = \frac{p_H^{\sigma}}{w_{IT}^{\sigma}} H \gamma_{IT}(z)^{\sigma-1} \left(A_{IT}\right)^{\sigma-1}]$, we obtain

$$\int_{N-1}^{N_{IT}} l_{IT}(z) dz = \int_{I}^{N_{IT}} \frac{p_H^{\sigma}}{w_{IT}^{\sigma}} H \gamma_{IT}(z)^{\sigma-1} \left(A_{IT}\right)^{\sigma-1} dz$$
$$L_{IT} = \frac{p_H^{\sigma}}{w_{IT}^{\sigma}} H \left(A_{IT}\right)^{\sigma-1} \int_{N-1}^{N_{IT}} \gamma_{IT}(z)^{\sigma-1} dz$$
$$w_{IT}^{\sigma} = p_H^{\sigma} \frac{H}{L_{IT}} \left(A_{IT}\right)^{\sigma-1} \int_{N-1}^{N_{IT}} \gamma_{IT}(z)^{\sigma-1} dz$$

such that with fully employed IT labor, we can determine their wages as

$$w_{IT} = p_H \left(\frac{H}{L_{IT}}\right)^{\frac{1}{\sigma}} (A_{IT})^{\frac{\sigma-1}{\sigma}} \left(\int_{N-1}^{N_{IT}} \gamma_{IT}(z)^{\sigma-1} dz\right)^{\frac{1}{\sigma}}, \tag{5.82}$$

and, in a symmetrical fashion, we obtain for standard labor

$$w_L = p_H \left(\frac{H}{L_L}\right)^{\frac{1}{\sigma}} (A_L)^{\frac{\sigma-1}{\sigma}} \left(\int_{N_{IT}}^{N} \gamma_L(z)^{\sigma-1} dz\right)^{\frac{1}{\sigma}}. \tag{5.83}$$

The resulting internal relative factor productivity for labor is:

$$\frac{w_L}{w_{IT}} = \frac{\left(\frac{p_H H}{L_L}\right)^{\frac{1}{\sigma}} (A_L)^{\frac{\sigma-1}{\sigma}} \left(\int_{N_{IT}}^{N} \gamma_L(z)^{\sigma-1} dz\right)^{\frac{1}{\sigma}}}{\left(\frac{p_H H}{L_{IT}}\right)^{\frac{1}{\sigma}} (A_{IT})^{\frac{\sigma-1}{\sigma}} \left(\int_{N-1}^{N_{IT}} \gamma_{IT}(z)^{\sigma-1} dz\right)^{\frac{1}{\sigma}}}$$

$$\frac{w_L}{w_{IT}} = \left(\frac{L_{IT}}{L_L}\right)^{\frac{1}{\sigma}} \left(\frac{A_L}{A_{IT}}\right)^{\frac{\sigma-1}{\sigma}} \left(\frac{\int_{N_{IT}}^{N} \gamma_L(z)^{\sigma-1} dz}{\int_{N-1}^{N_{IT}} \gamma_{IT}(z)^{\sigma-1} dz}\right)^{\frac{1}{\sigma}}$$

Endogenously automated tasks N_{IT}: From the discussion of Equation (5.12), it is known that tasks are ordered such that $\gamma(z) = \frac{\gamma_L(z)}{\gamma_{IT}(z)}$, and $\frac{\partial \gamma(z)}{\partial z} > 0$. If it is assumed that task N_{IT} is the task that exactly separates the production mode, and if tasks are continued, the condition (5.12) can be rewritten as follows:

$$\frac{A_L \gamma_L(N_{IT})}{A_{IT} \gamma_{IT}(N_{IT})} < \frac{w_L}{w_{IT}} = \left(\frac{L_{IT}}{L_L}\right)^{\frac{1}{\sigma}} \left(\frac{A_L}{A_{IT}}\right)^{\frac{\sigma-1}{\sigma}} \left(\frac{\int_{N_{IT}}^{N} \gamma_L(z)^{\sigma-1} dz}{\int_{N-1}^{N_{IT}} \gamma_{IT}(z)^{\sigma-1} dz}\right)^{\frac{1}{\sigma}}$$

$$0 = G = \gamma(N_{IT}) - \left(\frac{A_{IT} L_{IT}}{A_L L_L}\right)^{\frac{1}{\sigma}} \left(\frac{\int_{N_{IT}}^{N} \gamma_L(z)^{\sigma-1} dz}{\int_{N-1}^{N_{IT}} \gamma_{IT}(z)^{\sigma-1} dz}\right)^{\frac{1}{\sigma}} \tag{5.84}$$

If $\frac{dG}{dN_{IT}} \neq 0$, G implicitly defines a function $N_{IT} = N_{IT}(L_{IT}, L_L, A_{IT}, \ldots)$. Thus, we need to calculate the respective interesting derivatives.

$$\frac{dG}{dN_{IT}} = \frac{\partial \gamma(N_{IT})}{\partial N_{IT}} + \left[\begin{array}{c} \frac{1}{\sigma}\left(\frac{A_{IT} L_{IT}}{A_L L_L}\right)^{\frac{1}{\sigma}} \left(\frac{\int_{N_{IT}}^{N} \gamma_L(z)^{\sigma-1} dz}{\int_{N-1}^{I} \gamma_{IT}(z)^{\sigma-1} dz}\right)^{\frac{1}{\sigma}} \\ \left[\frac{\gamma_L(N_{IT})^{\sigma-1}}{\int_{N_{IT}}^{N} \gamma_L(N_{IT})^{\sigma-1} dz} + \frac{\gamma_{IT}(N_{IT})^{\sigma-1}}{\int_{N-1}^{N_{IT}} \gamma_{IT}(N_{IT})^{\sigma-1} dz}\right] \end{array}\right] > 0$$

and defining $B_1(N_{IT}) = \int_{N-1}^{N_{IT}} \gamma_{IT}(z)^{\sigma-1} dz = (1 - \Gamma(N_{IT}, N))\Pi(N_{IT}, N)^{\sigma-1}$, $\frac{dB_1}{dN_{IT}} = \gamma_{IT}(N_{IT})^{\sigma-1}$; and $B_2(N_{IT}) = \int_{N_{IT}}^{N} \gamma_L(z)^{\sigma-1} dz = \Gamma(N_{IT}, N)\Pi(N_{IT}, N)^{\sigma-1}$, $\frac{dB_2}{dN_{IT}} = -\gamma_L(N_{IT})^{\sigma-1}$, we obtain

$$\frac{\partial G}{\partial N_{IT}} = \frac{\partial \gamma\,(N_{IT})}{\partial N_{IT}} + \frac{1}{\sigma}\left(\frac{A_{IT}L_{IT}}{A_L L_L}\right)^{\frac{1}{\sigma}}\left(\frac{B_2\,(N_{IT})}{B_1\,(N_{IT})}\right)^{\frac{1}{\sigma}}$$
$$\left[\frac{\gamma_L(N_{IT})^{\sigma-1}}{B_2\,(N_{IT})} + \frac{\gamma_{IT}(N_{IT})^{\sigma-1}}{B_1\,(N_{IT})}\right] > 0$$

$$\frac{\partial G}{\partial A_{IT}} = -\frac{1}{\sigma}\left(\frac{A_{IT}L_{IT}}{A_L L_L}\right)^{\frac{1}{\sigma}-1}\left(\frac{B_2\,(N_{IT})}{B_1\,(N_{IT})}\right)^{\frac{1}{\sigma}}\frac{L_{IT}}{A_L L_L} < 0$$

and the derivative of the implicit function $N_{IT} = N_{IT}\,(A_{IT})$ is

$$\frac{dN_{IT}}{dA_{IT}} = -\frac{\frac{\partial G}{\partial A_{IT}}}{\frac{\partial G}{\partial N_{IT}}} > 0$$

More specifically:

$$\frac{dN_{IT}}{dA_{IT}} = \frac{\frac{1}{\sigma}\left(\frac{A_{IT}L_{IT}}{A_L L_L}\right)^{\frac{1}{\sigma}}\left(\frac{B_2(N_{IT})}{B_1(N_{IT})}\right)^{\frac{1}{\sigma}}\frac{1}{A_{IT}}}{\frac{\partial\gamma(N_{IT})}{\partial N_{IT}} + \frac{1}{\sigma}\left(\frac{A_{IT}L_{IT}}{A_L L_L}\right)^{\frac{1}{\sigma}}\left(\frac{B_2(N_{IT})}{B_1(N_{IT})}\right)^{\frac{1}{\sigma}}\left[\frac{\gamma_L(N_{IT})^{\sigma-1}}{B_2(N_{IT})} + \frac{\gamma_{IT}(N_{IT})^{\sigma-1}}{B_1(N_{IT})}\right]}$$

$$\eta_{N_{IT},A_{IT}} = \frac{dN_{IT}}{dA_{IT}}\frac{A_{IT}}{N_{IT}}$$
$$= \frac{1}{\sigma\frac{\partial\gamma(N_{IT})}{\partial N_{IT}}\left(\frac{A_L L_L}{A_{IT}L_{IT}}\frac{B_1(N_{IT})}{B_2(N_{IT})}\right)^{\frac{1}{\sigma}} + \frac{\gamma_L(N_{IT})^{\sigma-1}}{B_2(N_{IT})} + \frac{\gamma_{IT}(N_{IT})^{\sigma-1}}{B_1(N_{IT})}}\frac{1}{N_{IT}}$$

B2 Total Supply of Human Service Inputs

From Equation (5.15), it is known that $h(z) = p_H^{\sigma}H\left(\frac{A_{IT}}{w_{IT}}\right)^{\sigma}\gamma_{IT}(z)^{\sigma}$ for $z \in [N-1, N_{IT}$, and $h(z) = p_H^{\sigma}H\left(\frac{A_L}{w_L}\right)^{\sigma}\gamma_L(z)^{\sigma}$ for $z \in [N_{IT}, N]$. Plugging this in Equation (5.10) generates an equation for the total value of H:

$$H = \left(\int_{N-1}^{N_{IT}} h(z)^{\frac{\sigma-1}{\sigma}}dz + \int_{N_{IT}}^{N} h(z)^{\frac{\sigma-1}{\sigma}}dz\right)^{\frac{\sigma}{\sigma-1}}$$
$$= \left(\int_{N-1}^{N_{IT}}\left(p_H^{\sigma}H\left(\frac{A_{IT}}{w_{IT}}\right)^{\sigma}\gamma_I(z)^{\sigma}\right)^{\frac{\sigma-1}{\sigma}}dz\right.$$
$$\left.+\int_{N_{IT}}^{N}\left(p_H^{\sigma}H\left(\frac{A_L}{w_L}\right)^{\sigma}\gamma_L(z)^{\sigma}\right)^{\frac{\sigma-1}{\sigma}}dz\right)^{\frac{\sigma}{\sigma-1}}.$$

Using Equations (5.82) and (5.83) results in: $w_{IT} = p_H\left(\frac{H}{L_{IT}}\right)^{\frac{1}{\sigma}}(A_{IT})^{\frac{\sigma-1}{\sigma}}\left(\int_{N-1}^{N_{IT}}\gamma_{IT}(z)^{\sigma-1}dz\right)^{\frac{1}{\sigma}}$

$$H=\left(\int_{N-1}^{N_{IT}}\left(\gamma_{IT}(z)^{\sigma}\right)^{\frac{\sigma-1}{\sigma}}dz\left(p_H^{\sigma}H\left(\frac{A_{IT}}{w_{IT}}\right)^{\sigma}\right)^{\frac{\sigma-1}{\sigma}}\right.$$

$$\left.+\int_{N_{IT}}^{N}\left(\gamma_{L}(z)^{\sigma}\right)^{\frac{\sigma-1}{\sigma}}dz\left(p_H^{\sigma}H\left(\frac{A_{L}}{w_{L}}\right)^{\sigma}\right)^{\frac{\sigma-1}{\sigma}}\right)^{\frac{\sigma}{\sigma-1}} \tag{5.85}$$

$$=\left(\int_{N-1}^{N_{IT}}\gamma_{IT}(z)^{\sigma-1}dzp_H^{\sigma-1}H^{\frac{\sigma-1}{\sigma}}\left(\frac{A_{IT}}{w_{IT}}\right)^{\sigma-1}\right.$$

$$\left.+\int_{N_{IT}}^{N}\gamma_{L}(z)^{\sigma-1}dzp_H^{\sigma-1}H^{\frac{\sigma-1}{\sigma}}\left(\frac{A_{L}}{w_{L}}\right)^{\sigma-1}\right)^{\frac{\sigma}{\sigma-1}}$$

$$=\left(\begin{array}{l}\int_{N-1}^{N_{IT}}\gamma_{IT}(z)^{\sigma-1}dzp_H^{\sigma-1}H^{\frac{\sigma-1}{\sigma}}\left(\frac{A_{IT}}{p_H\left(\frac{H}{L_{IT}}\right)^{\frac{1}{\sigma}}(A_{IT})^{\frac{\sigma-1}{\sigma}}\left(\int_{N-1}^{N_{IT}}\gamma_{IT}(z)^{\sigma-1}dz\right)^{\frac{1}{\sigma}}}\right)^{\sigma-1}\\ +\int_{N_{IT}}^{N}\gamma_{L}(z)^{\sigma-1}dzp_H^{\sigma-1}H^{\frac{\sigma-1}{\sigma}}\left(\frac{A_{L}}{p_H\left(\frac{H}{L_{L}}\right)^{\frac{1}{\sigma}}(A_{L})^{\frac{\sigma-1}{\sigma}}\left(\int_{N_{IT}}^{N}\gamma_{L}(z)^{\sigma-1}dz\right)^{\frac{1}{\sigma}}}\right)^{\sigma-1}\end{array}\right)^{\frac{\sigma}{\sigma-1}}$$

$$=\left(\begin{array}{l}\int_{N-1}^{N_{IT}}\gamma_{IT}(z)^{\sigma-1}dzp_H^{\sigma-1}H^{\frac{\sigma-1}{\sigma}}\left(\frac{p_H^{-1}H^{-\frac{1}{\sigma}}L_{IT}^{\frac{1}{\sigma}}A_{IT}^{\frac{1}{\sigma}}}{\left(\int_{N-1}^{N_{IT}}\gamma_{IT}(z)^{\sigma-1}dz\right)^{\frac{1}{\sigma}}}\right)^{\sigma-1}\\ +\int_{N_{IT}}^{N}\gamma_{L}(z)^{\sigma-1}dzp_H^{\sigma-1}H^{\frac{\sigma-1}{\sigma}}\left(\frac{p_H^{-1}H^{-\frac{1}{\sigma}}L_{L}^{\frac{1}{\sigma}}A_{L}^{\frac{1}{\sigma}}}{\left(\int_{N_{IT}}^{N}\gamma_{L}(z)^{\sigma-1}dz\right)^{\frac{1}{\sigma}}}\right)^{\sigma-1}\end{array}\right)^{\frac{\sigma}{\sigma-1}}$$

$$=\left(\begin{array}{l}\int_{N-1}^{N_{IT}}\gamma_{IT}(z)^{\sigma-1}dzp_H^{\sigma-1}H^{\frac{\sigma-1}{\sigma}}\frac{p_H^{-(\sigma-1)}H^{-\frac{\sigma-1}{\sigma}}(L_{IT}A_{IT})^{\frac{\sigma-1}{\sigma}}}{\left(\int_{N-1}^{N_{IT}}\gamma_{IT}(z)^{\sigma-1}dz\right)^{\frac{\sigma-1}{\sigma}}}\\ +\int_{N_{IT}}^{N}\gamma_{L}(z)^{\sigma-1}dzp_H^{\sigma-1}H^{\frac{\sigma-1}{\sigma}}\frac{p_H^{-(\sigma-1)}H^{-\frac{\sigma-1}{\sigma}}(L_{L}A_{L})^{\frac{\sigma-1}{\sigma}}}{\left(\int_{N_{IT}}^{N}\gamma_{L}(z)^{\sigma-1}dz\right)^{\frac{\sigma-1}{\sigma}}}\end{array}\right)^{\frac{\sigma}{\sigma-1}}$$

$$=\left(\int_{N-1}^{N_{IT}}\gamma_{IT}(z)^{\sigma-1}dz\frac{(L_{IT}A_{IT})^{\frac{\sigma-1}{\sigma}}}{\left(\int_{N-1}^{N_{IT}}\gamma_{IT}(z)^{\sigma-1}dz\right)^{\frac{\sigma-1}{\sigma}}}\right.$$

$$\left.+\int_{N_{IT}}^{N}\gamma_{L}(z)^{\sigma-1}d\frac{(L_{L}A_{L})^{\frac{\sigma-1}{\sigma}}}{\left(\int_{N_{IT}}^{N}\gamma_{L}(z)^{\sigma-1}dz\right)^{\frac{\sigma-1}{\sigma}}}\right)^{\frac{\sigma}{\sigma-1}}$$

$$H = \left(\left(\int_{N-1}^{N_{IT}} \gamma_{IT}(z)^{\sigma-1} dz \right)^{\frac{1}{\sigma}} (L_{IT} A_{IT})^{\frac{\sigma-1}{\sigma}} + \left(\int_{N_{IT}}^{N} \gamma_L(z)^{\sigma-1} dz \right)^{\frac{1}{\sigma}} (L_L A_L)^{\frac{\sigma-1}{\sigma}} \right)^{\frac{\sigma}{\sigma-1}}$$

B2.1 Earning Shares

To determine the contribution of standard labor to total service production, one can start from Equation (5.85)

$$H = \left(\int_{N-1}^{N_{IT}} \gamma_{IT}(z)^{\sigma-1} dz p_H^{\sigma-1} H^{\frac{\sigma-1}{\sigma}} \left(\frac{A_{IT}}{w_{IT}} \right)^{\sigma-1} + \int_{N_{IT}}^{N} \gamma_L(z)^{\sigma-1} dz p_H^{\sigma-1} H^{\frac{\sigma-1}{\sigma}} \left(\frac{A_L}{w_L} \right)^{\sigma-1} \right)^{\frac{\sigma}{\sigma-1}}$$

$$1 = \left(\int_{N-1}^{N_{IT}} \gamma_{IT}(z)^{\sigma-1} dz \left(\frac{A_{IT}}{w_{IT}} \right)^{\sigma-1} + \int_{N_{IT}}^{N} \gamma_L(z)^{\sigma-1} dz \left(\frac{A_L}{w_L} \right)^{\sigma-1} \right)^{\frac{\sigma}{\sigma-1}} p_H^{\sigma}$$

$$1 = \left((1 - \Gamma(N_{IT}, N)) \Pi(N_{IT}, N)^{\sigma-1} \left(\frac{A_{IT}}{w_{IT}} \right)^{\sigma-1} + \Gamma(N_{IT}, N) \Pi(N_{IT}, N)^{\sigma-1} \left(\frac{A_L}{w_L} \right)^{\sigma-1} \right)^{\frac{\sigma}{\sigma-1}} p_H^{\sigma}$$

Plugging in Equations (5.23) and (5.22), $\int_{N_{IT}}^{N} \gamma_L(z)^{\sigma-1} dz = \Gamma(N_{IT}, N) \Pi(N_{IT}, N)^{\sigma-1}$, $\int_{N-1}^{N_{IT}} \gamma_{IT}(z)^{\sigma-1} dz = (1 - \Gamma(N_{IT}, N)) \Pi(N_{IT}, N)^{\sigma-1}$, we obtain

$$1 = \left(\frac{(1 - \Gamma(N_{IT}, N))}{\Gamma(N_{IT}, N)} \frac{\left(\frac{A_{IT}}{w_{IT}} \right)^{\sigma-1}}{\left(\frac{A_L}{w_L} \right)^{\sigma-1}} + 1 \right)^{\frac{\sigma}{\sigma-1}} \Gamma(N_{IT}, N) \Pi(N_{IT}, N)^{\sigma} \left(\frac{A_L}{w_L} \right)^{\sigma} p_H^{\sigma}$$

$$1 = \left(1 + \frac{(1 - \Gamma(N_{IT}, N))}{\Gamma(N_{IT}, N)} \left(\frac{w_L}{w_{IT}} \frac{A_{IT}}{A_L} \right)^{\sigma-1} \right)^{\frac{\sigma}{\sigma-1}} \times \Gamma(N_{IT}, N)^{\frac{\sigma}{\sigma-1}} \Pi(N_{IT}, N)^{\sigma} \left(\frac{A_L}{w_L} \right)^{\sigma} p_H^{\sigma}$$

Rearranging this equation gives:

$$\Gamma(N_{IT},N)^{-\frac{\sigma}{\sigma-1}}\Pi(N_{IT},N)^{-\sigma}=\left(1+\frac{(1-\Gamma(N_{IT},N))}{\Gamma(N_{IT},N)}\left(\frac{w_L}{w_{IT}}\frac{A_{IT}}{A_L}\right)^{\sigma-1}\right)^{\frac{\sigma}{\sigma-1}}\left(\frac{A_L}{w_L}\right)^{\sigma}p_H^{\sigma}$$

$$\Pi(N_{IT},N)^{\sigma-1}\Gamma(N_{IT},N)=\left(1+\frac{(1-\Gamma(N_{IT},N))}{\Gamma(N_{IT},N)}\left(\frac{w_L}{w_{IT}}\frac{A_{IT}}{A_L}\right)^{\sigma-1}\right)^{-1}$$

$$\times\,(A_L)^{-(\sigma-1)}\left(\frac{p_H}{w_L}\right)^{-(\sigma-1)} \tag{5.86}$$

$$(A_L)^{(\sigma-1)}\left(\frac{p_H}{w_L}\right)^{(\sigma-1)}=\frac{1}{\left(1+\frac{(1-\Gamma(N_{IT},N))}{\Gamma(N_{IT},N)}\left(\frac{w_L}{w_{IT}}\frac{A_{IT}}{A_L}\right)^{\sigma-1}\right)\Pi(N_{IT},N)^{\sigma-1}\Gamma(N_{IT},N)}$$

Further, from Equations (5.19) and (5.17), the following equation can be derived:

$$L_L=\int_{N_{IT}}^{N}\frac{p_H^{\sigma}H}{(w_L)^{\sigma}}(A_L)^{\sigma-1}\gamma_L(z)^{\sigma-1}dz=\frac{p_H^{\sigma}H}{(w_L)^{\sigma}}(A_L)^{\sigma-1}\int_{N_{IT}}^{N}\gamma_L(z)^{\sigma-1}dz$$

using the equation of labor share of income $\phi_L=\frac{w_L L}{p_H H}$ and using the equations (5.23) and (5.22), $\int_{N_{IT}}^{N}\gamma_L(z)^{\sigma-1}dz=\Gamma(N_{IT},N)\Pi(N_{IT},N)^{\sigma-1}$ results in:

$$\frac{L_L w_L}{p_H H}=\frac{w_L}{p_H}\frac{1}{H}\frac{p_H^{\sigma}H}{(w_L)^{\sigma}}(A_L)^{\sigma-1}\int_{N_{IT}}^{N}\gamma_L(z)^{\sigma-1}dz$$

$$\frac{L_L w_L}{p_H H}=\left(\frac{w_L}{p_H}\right)^{1-\sigma}(A_L)^{\sigma-1}\Gamma(N_{IT},N)\Pi(N_{IT},N)^{\sigma-1}$$

Combining these with Equation (5.86) gives labor's share of income as fully depending on relative labor rewards $\frac{w_L}{w_{IT}}$

$$\phi_L=\frac{\Gamma(N_{IT},N)\Pi(N_{IT},N)^{\sigma-1}}{\left(1+\frac{(1-\Gamma(N_{IT},N))}{\Gamma(N_{IT},N)}\left(\frac{w_L}{w_{IT}}\frac{A_{IT}}{A_L}\right)^{\sigma-1}\right)\Pi(N_{IT},N)^{\sigma-1}\Gamma(N_{IT},N)}$$

$$\phi_L=\left(1+\frac{(1-\Gamma(N_{IT},N))}{\Gamma(N_{IT},N)}\left(\frac{w_L}{w_{IT}}\frac{A_{IT}}{A_L}\right)^{\sigma-1}\right)^{-1}$$

labor's share of income in the human service sector is determined by relative factor abundance and productivity parameters. Thus, plugging in the relative factor rewards, Equation (5.20) finally results in:

$$\phi_L = \left(1 + \frac{(1-\Gamma(N_{IT},N))}{\Gamma(N_{IT},N)} \left(\left[\left(\frac{L_{IT}}{L_L}\right)^{\frac{1}{\sigma}} \left(\frac{A_L}{A_{IT}}\right)^{\frac{\sigma-1}{\sigma}} \left(\frac{\Gamma(N_{IT},N)}{(1-\Gamma(N_{IT},N))}\right)^{\frac{1}{\sigma}} \right] \frac{A_{IT}}{A_L} \right)^{\sigma-1} \right)^{-1}$$

$$= \left(1 + \frac{(1-\Gamma(N_{IT},N))}{\Gamma(N_{IT},N)} \left(\left(\frac{L_{IT}}{L_L}\right)^{\frac{1}{\sigma}} \left(\frac{A_{IT}}{A_L}\right)^{\frac{1}{\sigma}} \left(\frac{(1-\Gamma(N_{IT},N))}{\Gamma(N_{IT},N)}\right)^{-\frac{1}{\sigma}} \right)^{\sigma-1} \right)^{-1}$$

$$= \left(1 + \frac{(1-\Gamma(N_{IT},N))}{\Gamma(N_{IT},N)} \left(\frac{A_{IT}}{A_L}\frac{L_{IT}}{L_L}\right)^{\frac{\sigma-1}{\sigma}} \left(\frac{(1-\Gamma(N_{IT},N))}{\Gamma(N_{IT},N)}\right)^{-\frac{\sigma-1}{\sigma}} \right)^{-1}$$

$$= \left(1 + \frac{(1-\Gamma(N_{IT},N))}{\Gamma(N_{IT},N)} \left(\frac{(1-\Gamma(N_{IT},N))}{\Gamma(N_{IT},N)}\right)^{-\frac{\sigma-1}{\sigma}} \left(\frac{A_{IT}}{A_L}\frac{L_{IT}}{L_L}\right)^{\frac{\sigma-1}{\sigma}} \right)^{-1}$$

$$= \left(1 + \left(\frac{(1-\Gamma(N_{IT},N))}{\Gamma(N_{IT},N)}\right)^{\frac{1}{\sigma}} \left(\frac{A_{IT}}{A_L}\frac{L_{IT}}{L_L}\right)^{\frac{\sigma-1}{\sigma}} \right)^{-1}$$

which results in Equation (5.25).

C Income Distribution

***Income** Y **(GDP) and total production** Q.* Before determining the income shares, it is necessary to determine the relation between income Y (GDP) and total production Q. Since

$$Y(t) = Q(t) - N(t)x(t)c_X = \left(1 - \frac{Nxc_X}{Q}\right) Q(t).$$

Applying Equation (5.28) gives

$$\frac{Nxc_X}{Q} = \frac{Nc_X}{NH_Q^{1-\alpha}\alpha^{\frac{-(1-\alpha)2}{1-\alpha}} c_X^{-\frac{-(1-\alpha)}{1-\alpha}} H_Q^{-(1-\alpha)}} = \frac{c_X}{\alpha^{-2}c_X} = \alpha^2, \quad (5.87)$$

and using Equations (5.1) and (5.28), the result for $Y(t)$ is:

$$Y(t) = \left(1-\alpha^2\right) Q(t) = \left(1-\alpha^2\right) N(t)\alpha^{\frac{2\alpha}{1-\alpha}} c_X^{-\frac{\alpha}{1-\alpha}} H_Q \quad (5.88)$$

Income share of labor: From Equation (5.42), we know

$$w_L = \phi_L \frac{p_H H}{L_L} = \frac{\phi_L}{1+\alpha}\frac{Y}{L_L}$$

and directly obtain

$$\frac{w_L L_L}{Y} = \frac{(1-\alpha)\,\phi_L}{1-\alpha^2} = \frac{\phi_L}{1+\alpha}$$

Wages and income share of IT providers:

$$\frac{w_{IT}(t) L_{IT}}{Y(t)} = \frac{(1-\alpha)\,(1-\phi_L)}{1-\alpha^2} = \frac{1-\phi_L}{1+\alpha}$$

Income share of financial wealth owners: From Equations (5.26), (5.28), and (6.3), it can be seen that:

$$\begin{aligned}
\frac{N(t)\pi_x(t)}{Y(t)} &= \frac{N\left(\frac{1}{\alpha}-1\right)(c_X)\left[\alpha^{\frac{2}{1-\alpha}} c_X^{-\frac{1}{1-\alpha}} H_Q\right]}{NH_Q^{1-\alpha}x^{\alpha} - Nxc_X} \\
&= \frac{\left(\frac{1}{\alpha}-1\right) Nc_X x}{NH_Q^{1-\alpha}x^{\alpha} - Nxc_X} \\
&= \frac{N\left(\frac{1}{\alpha}-1\right) c_X x}{\left(1-\frac{Nxc_X}{Q}\right) NH_Q^{1-\alpha}x^{\alpha}}
\end{aligned}$$

Using Equation (5.87) $\frac{Nxc_X}{Q} = \alpha^2$ results in:

$$\frac{N(t)\pi_x(t)}{Y(t)} = \frac{(1-\alpha)\,\frac{1}{\alpha}\alpha^2}{\left(1-\alpha^2\right)} = \frac{\left(\alpha-\alpha^2\right)}{\left(1-\alpha^2\right)} = \frac{\alpha}{(1+\alpha)}.$$

D Intertemporal Choices for Labor and Capital Owners

In standard endogenous growth models, aggregate consumption expenditure and savings are determined by a representative household conducting an optimal intertemporal choice according to the Euler equation

$$\frac{\dot{C}}{C} = \frac{r-\rho}{\eta_U}.$$

However, this assumption of a *representative household* is rather restrictive and is introduced more for the sake of simplification. Therefore, in the model proposed in this chapter, this assumption is replaced by assuming two groups of households differing with respect to their income, their income sources, and their intertemporal choice behavior. Both ρ and η_U vary across low- and high-income households, such that households in each group make their own intertemporal choices. The result of these differing intertemporal choices will lead to our assumptions that workers with wage income represent the low-income group, which only consumes. The second group, the owners of financial assets F, and IT labor represents the high-income group. For wealth owners, returns on their financial wealth r_F are the only source of income. They will consume and save. However, in the long term, their intertemporal choices (parameter values of ρ and η_U) will lead to a consumption growth lower than income growth, such that the consumption rate converges to zero and the savings rate converges toward one. That is, they still consume, but compared to their high income, the consumption is small, and the ratio converges toward zero. In more detail:

(a) *Low-income, wage-earning households*: if it is assumed that the time preference rate of low-income households is high, for example, $\rho_L \geq r$, and if household debt is not allowed or possible, then the Euler equation $\frac{\dot{C}_L}{C_L} = \frac{r-\rho_L}{\eta_{U_L}}$ implies that these households do not intend to shift consumption into future periods, such that they simply consume what they earn from wage income.

(b) *High-income households*: high-income households obtain their total income from returns on financial assets $F(t)r$. and from IT wages.

As a representative of a high-income household, we consider a financial asset owner. The budget constraint requires that savings cannot be larger than his financial income minus consumption

$$S(t) \leq F(t)r(t) - C_F(t).$$

The savings rate is one minus the consumption rate, $s(t) = 1 - c(t)$, and the consumption rate is

$$c(t) = \frac{C_F(t)}{F(t)r(t)}.$$

For a stationary interest rate, we can determine the change of the consumption rate over time as

$$\dot{c}(t) = \frac{\dot{C}_F(t)}{F(t)r(t)} \frac{C_F(t)}{C_F(t)} - \frac{C_F(t)}{F(t)r(t)} \frac{\dot{F}(t)}{F(t)}$$

$$\frac{\dot{c}(t)}{c(t)} = \frac{\dot{C}_F(t)}{C_F(t)} - \frac{\dot{F}(t)}{F(t)}$$

If the desired growth rate of consumption (parameters in the Ramsey rule: $\frac{\dot{C}_F}{C_F} = \frac{r-\rho_F}{\eta_{U_F}}$) is less than the total accumulation rate of financial wealth, the consumption rate will fall steadily and eventually approach zero.

$$\frac{\dot{c}(t)}{c(t)} = \frac{r^* - \rho}{\eta_U} - \frac{\dot{F}(t)}{F(t)}.$$

In steady state $r(t) = r^*$, and financial wealth cannot grow faster than real income which is growing at rate $g_N = \frac{\dot{N}(t)}{N(t)}$,

$$\frac{\dot{F}(t)}{F(t)} \leq \frac{\dot{N}(t)}{N(t)}.$$

Further, as we assume parameter values, such that $(g_N - 1)\,\eta_U + \rho \leq r^* \leq g_N \eta_U + \rho$, we obtain $-1 < \frac{r^*-\rho}{\eta_U} - g_N \leq 0$, and hence

$$-1 < \frac{\dot{c}(t)}{c(t)} \leq 0 \qquad \text{(A1)}$$

Thus, we obtain in the long term

$$\lim_{t\to\infty} c(t) = 0.$$

This is our assumption that financial investors consume, but with their growing income and a desired consumption growth that is below income growth, the consumption rate c of this income group turns to zero and the savings rate $s(t)$ turns to one in the long run, $\lim_{t\to\infty} s(t) = 1$. Figure 5.1 describes this process.

E Calculations to Solve the Model

Determine the growth rate g_N: From Equations (5.34) and (5.28), we obtain $X^D = Nx = N\alpha^{\frac{2}{1-\alpha}} c_X^{-\frac{1}{1-\alpha}} H_Q$ and $\dot{N} = \left(\alpha^{\frac{2}{1-\alpha}} c_X^{-\frac{1}{1-\alpha}} H_Q\right)^{\varphi} N^{\varphi} (\dot{A}))^{1-\varphi}$.

Rearranging gives $\frac{\dot{N}(t)}{N(t)} = \left(\alpha^{\frac{2}{1-\alpha}} c_X^{-\frac{1}{1-\alpha}} H_Q\right)^{\varphi} \left(\frac{\dot{A}(t)}{A(t)}\right)^{1-\varphi}$ for $N(t) = A(t)$.

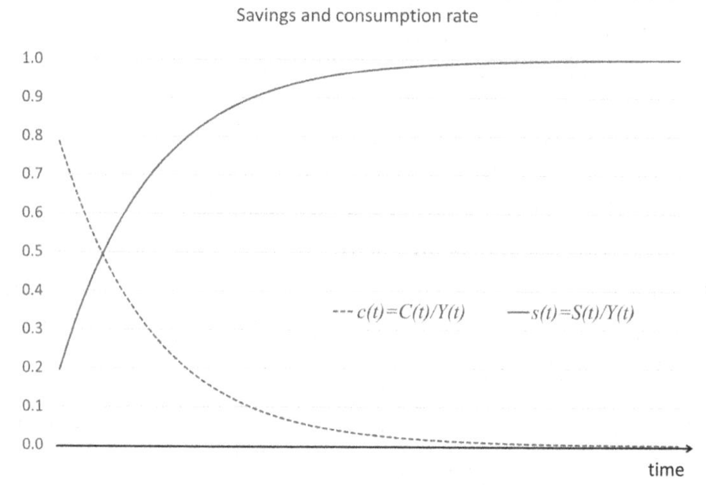

FIGURE 5.1 Convergence of $c(t)$ and $s(t)$ in steady state
Source: Authors' compilation.

Eliminating mismatch: Combining Equations (5.59) with (5.58) for the aggregate economy we require for the elimination of mismatch $0 \stackrel{!}{=} \delta(t) = \delta'(t) - m$. With the equation of the given mismatch $\delta'(t) = (1-\lambda)\,\varepsilon_F$, and taking expectations leads to

$$0 \stackrel{!}{=} E\left[\varepsilon_F\right] - E\left[\lambda\right] E\left[\varepsilon_F\right] - \operatorname{cov}\left(\lambda, \varepsilon_F\right) - H_\phi \left(1-\theta\right)^{-1},$$

and thus

$$H_\phi \left(1-\theta\right)^{-1} = E\left[\varepsilon_F\right] - E\left[\lambda\right] E\left[\varepsilon_F\right] - \operatorname{cov}\left(\lambda, \varepsilon_F\right).$$

Using Equations (5.35) and (5.60), we obtain Equation (5.59a)

Determine current aggregate market equilibrium: According to Equation (5.60), market equilibrium requires $1 = E[\lambda(t)]$. With Equation (5.52)

$$1 = E\left[\lambda(t)\right] = \frac{\nu}{1-c\left(1-\theta\right)} \frac{1}{H_Q \left(\frac{\alpha^2}{c_x}\right)^{\frac{\alpha}{1-\alpha}}} g_N + \alpha^2,$$

and using Equation (5.53) leads to

$$1 = \frac{\nu}{1-c(1-\theta)} \frac{1}{H_Q \left(\frac{\alpha^2}{c_X}\right)^{\frac{\alpha}{1-\alpha}}} \left(\left(\frac{\alpha^2}{c_X}\right)^{\frac{1}{1-\alpha}} H_Q \right)^{\varphi} (g_A)^{1-\varphi} + \alpha^2.$$

and Equation (5.60a)

F Proof of Proposition 5.3.4

Implicit function theorem: Function F can be derived by:

$$\begin{aligned} H_\phi (1-\theta)^{-1} &= -cov(\lambda, \varepsilon_F). \\ (1-\theta) &= \frac{H - H_Q}{-cov(\lambda, \varepsilon_F)} \end{aligned}$$

and

$$= \frac{\nu}{(1-\alpha^2)(1-c(1-\theta))} \frac{1}{H_Q^{1-\varphi} \left(\frac{\alpha^2}{c_X}\right)^{\frac{\alpha}{1-\alpha}}} \left(\frac{\alpha^2}{c_X}\right)^{\frac{1}{1-\alpha}\varphi} (g_A)^{1-\varphi} (1-\theta)$$

$$= -\frac{\nu}{c(1-\alpha^2)} \frac{1}{H_Q^{1-\varphi} \left(\frac{\alpha^2}{c_X}\right)^{\frac{\alpha}{1-\alpha}}} \left(\frac{\alpha^2}{c_X}\right)^{\frac{1}{1-\alpha}\varphi} (g_A)^{1-\varphi} + \frac{1}{c}$$

plugging in gives

$$\frac{H - H_Q}{-cov(\lambda, \varepsilon_F)} = -\frac{\nu}{c(1-\alpha^2)} \frac{1}{H_Q^{1-\varphi}} \left(\frac{\alpha^2}{c_X}\right)^{\frac{\varphi-\alpha}{1-\alpha}} (g_A)^{1-\varphi} + \frac{1}{c}$$

$$(H - H_Q) H_Q^{1-\varphi} - \frac{-cov(\lambda, \varepsilon_F) H_Q^{1-\varphi}}{c} = -\frac{-cov(\lambda, \varepsilon_F)\nu}{c(1-\alpha^2)} \left(\frac{\alpha^2}{c_X}\right)^{\frac{\varphi-\alpha}{1-\alpha}} (g_A)^{1-\varphi}$$

$$\begin{aligned} 0 = F = &-c(H - H_Q) H_Q^{1-\varphi} - cov(\lambda, \varepsilon_F) H_Q^{1-\varphi} \\ &+ \frac{-cov(\lambda, \varepsilon_F)\nu}{c(1-\alpha^2)} \left(\frac{\alpha^2}{c_X}\right)^{\frac{\varphi-\alpha}{1-\alpha}} (g_A)^{1-\varphi} \end{aligned}$$

$$\begin{aligned} F = &-cHH_Q^{1-\varphi} + cH_Q^{2-\varphi} - cov(\lambda, \varepsilon_F) H_Q^{1-\varphi} \\ &- \frac{-cov(\lambda, \varepsilon_F)\nu}{(1-\alpha^2)} \left(\frac{\alpha^2}{c_X}\right)^{\frac{\varphi-\alpha}{1-\alpha}} (g_A)^{1-\varphi} \\ = &\ cH_Q^{2-\varphi} + (-cov(\lambda, \varepsilon_F) - cH) H_Q^{1-\varphi} - \frac{-cov(\lambda, \varepsilon_F)\nu}{(1-\alpha^2)} \left(\frac{\alpha^2}{c_X}\right)^{\frac{\varphi-\alpha}{1-\alpha}} (g_A)^{1-\varphi} \end{aligned}$$

To apply the implicit function theorem $\frac{dF}{dH_Q} \neq 0$:

$\frac{dF}{dH_Q}$:

$$\frac{dF}{dH_Q} = (2-\varphi)\,cH_Q^{1-\varphi} + (1-\varphi)\,(-cov\,(\lambda,\varepsilon_F) - cH)\,H_Q^{-\varphi}$$
$$= [(2-\varphi)\,cH_Q + (1-\varphi)\,(-cov\,(\lambda,\varepsilon_F) - cH)]\,H_Q^{-\varphi} > 0$$
$$\text{for}: H_Q/H > (1-\varphi)\,/\,(2-\varphi)$$

proof:

$$(2-\varphi)\,cH_Q - cov\,(\lambda,\varepsilon_F)\,(1-\varphi) - (1-\varphi)\,cH > 0$$
$$-cov\,(\lambda,\varepsilon_F) > c\left(H - \frac{(2-\varphi)}{(1-\varphi)}H_Q\right)$$
$$\text{sufficient}: \frac{(2-\varphi)\,H_Q}{(1-\varphi)} > H$$
$$\frac{H_Q}{H} > \frac{(1-\varphi)}{(2-\varphi)}$$

$\frac{dF}{dA_{IT}}$:

$$\frac{dF}{dA_{IT}} = -\frac{dc}{dA_{IT}}\left(HH_Q^{1-\varphi} - H_Q^{2-\varphi}\right) - c\frac{dH}{dA_{IT}}H_Q^{1-\varphi}$$
$$= \left[-\frac{dc}{dA_{IT}}\,(H - H_Q) - c\frac{dH}{dA_{IT}}\right]H_Q^{1-\varphi}$$
$$= \left[-\frac{dc}{dA_{IT}}\frac{A_{IT}}{c}\frac{dA_{IT}}{A_{IT}}c\,(H - H_Q) - c\frac{dH}{dA_{IT}}\frac{A_{IT}}{H}H\frac{1}{A_{IT}}\right]H_Q^{1-\varphi}$$
$$= -c\left[\frac{dc}{dA_{IT}}\frac{A_{IT}}{c}\,(H - H_Q) + \frac{dH}{dA_{IT}}\frac{A_{IT}}{H}H\right]\frac{1}{A_{IT}}H_Q^{1-\varphi}$$

Further derivatives:

$\frac{dH_Q}{dA_{IT}}$:

$$\frac{dH_Q}{dA_{IT}} = -\frac{\frac{\partial F}{\partial A_{IT}}}{\frac{\partial F}{\partial \tilde{H}_Q}} = -\frac{-c\left[\overset{<0}{\eta_{c,A_{IT}}}H_\phi + H\overset{>0}{\eta_{H,A_{IT}}}\right]\frac{1}{A_{IT}}H_Q^{1-\varphi}}{[(2-\varphi)\,cH_Q + (1-\varphi)\,(-cov\,(\lambda,\varepsilon_F) - cH)]\,H_Q^{-\varphi}}$$

$\frac{dH_Q}{dg_A}$:

$$\frac{dF}{dg_A} = (1-\varphi)\,\frac{cov\,(\lambda,\varepsilon_F)\,\nu}{(1-\alpha^2)}\left(\frac{\alpha^2}{c_x}\right)^{\frac{\varphi-\alpha}{1-\alpha}}(g_A)^{-\varphi} < 0$$

$$\frac{dH_Q}{dg_A} = -\frac{(1-\varphi)\,cov\,(\lambda,\varepsilon_F)\,\nu\left(\frac{\alpha^2}{c_X}\right)^{\frac{\varphi-\alpha}{1-\alpha}}(g_A)^{-\varphi}}{(1-\alpha^2)\,[(2-\varphi)\,cH_Q+(1-\varphi)\,(-cov\,(\lambda,\varepsilon_F)-cH)]\,H_Q^{-\varphi}} > 0$$

$\frac{dH_Q}{dv}$:

$$\frac{dF}{dv} = cov\,(\lambda,\varepsilon_F)\left(\frac{\alpha^2}{c_X}\right)^{\frac{\varphi-\alpha}{1-\alpha}}(g_A)^{1-\varphi}$$

$$\frac{dH_Q}{dv} = -\frac{cov\,(\lambda,\varepsilon_F)\left(\frac{\alpha^2}{c_X}\right)^{\frac{\varphi-\alpha}{1-\alpha}}(g_A)^{1-\varphi}}{(1-\alpha^2)\,[(2-\varphi)\,cH_Q+(1-\varphi)\,(-cov\,(\lambda,\varepsilon_F)-cH)]\,H_Q^{-\varphi}} > 0$$

With $cov\,(\lambda,\varepsilon_F) < 0$, the derivative $\frac{dF}{dH_Q} < 0$ and the implicit function theorem (requiring $\frac{dF}{dL_Q} \neq 0$) can be applied.

q.e.d.

Other equilibrium values: From Equations (5.59a) and (5.62), we directly obtain Equation (5.63). From production function (5.1) and the optimal intermediate goods input (5.28) ($x(t) = \left(\frac{\alpha^2}{c_X}\right)^{\frac{1}{1-\alpha}} H_Q$), we obtain Equation (5.64). Using Equation (5.88) in Equation (5.6), we obtain the Y. Combining with Equation (5.64) gives Equation (5.88). Taking the time derivative of Equation (5.65) in equilibrium, we obtain $\dot{Y}(t) = \dot{N}(t)\,(1-\alpha^2)\,H_Q\left(\frac{\alpha^2}{c_X}\right)^{\frac{\alpha}{1-\alpha}}$ and thus $g_Y = \frac{\dot{Y}(t)}{Y(t)} = \frac{\dot{N}(t)}{N(t)}$, and using Equation (5.53), we arrive at Equation (5.66). According to Equation (5.49), investments are $I(t) = \dot{N}(t)\nu$.

G Dynamic Consistency and Steady State Convergence

As investments and savings are independently determined, we must make sure that the aggregate budget constraint holds. Investments are restricted to $I(t) = \dot{N}(t)\nu$ and savings are determined by the two wealthy groups, which in a steady state have a savings rate of one. Since investments have to be financed by issuing a financial asset $F(t)$, the financial asset is traded in an asset market at price $p_F(t)$. This price is the result of the demand and supply of such assets in the financial market. This means that for investors, the expenditure for purchasing newly issued financial assets that finance $\dot{N}(t)$ innovation is $\dot{N}(t)\nu p_F(t)$, where $\dot{F}(t) = \dot{N}(t)\nu$. Further, if $\nu p_F(t)$ is the expenditure for an asset financing one innovation with profit $\pi_X(t)$, financial investor's return on this financial investment is $r_F(t) = \frac{\pi_X(t)}{\nu P_F(t)}$. Thus, the value of financial wealth is $F(t)p_F(t)$, and income from this financial wealth is

$$Y_F(t) = F(t)p_F(t)r_F(t),$$

and savings of this group are

$$S_F(t) = F(t)p_F(t)r_F(t) - C_F(t),$$

so that financial investment increase by this savings

$$\dot{F}(t)p_F(t) = F(t)p_F(t)r_F(t) - C_F(t).$$

While up to this point we have only considered financial wealth holders, we now want to add wealthy IT labor which also accumulates financial wealth. Thus,

$$\begin{aligned}
\dot{N}(t)\nu p_F(t) &= p_F(t)\nu N(t)\frac{\pi_X(t)}{\nu p_F(t)} + w_{IT}(t)L_{IT} - C_{F+IT}(t)\\
&= N(t)\pi_X(t) + w_{IT}(t)L_{IT} - C_{F+IT}(t)\\
\frac{\dot{N}(t)}{N(t)}\nu p_F(t) &= \pi_X(t) + \frac{w_{IT}(t)}{N(t)}L_{IT} - \frac{C_{F+IT}(t)}{N(t)}.
\end{aligned}$$

From Equation (5.44), we know

$$w_{IT}(t) = (1-\phi_L)\frac{p_H H}{L_{IT}} = \frac{1-\phi_L}{1+\alpha}\frac{Y(t)}{L_{IT}}$$

and from Equation (5.65), we obtain in steady state $\tilde{Y}(t) = N(t)\left(1-\alpha^2\right)\tilde{H}_Q\left(\frac{\alpha^2}{c_X}\right)^{\frac{\alpha}{1-\alpha}}$. Plugging in gives

$$w_{IT}(t) = \frac{1-\phi_L}{1+\alpha}\frac{\left(1-\alpha^2\right)\tilde{H}_Q\left(\frac{\alpha^2}{c_X}\right)^{\frac{\alpha}{1-\alpha}}}{L_{IT}}N(t),$$

and defining $B_3 = \frac{1-\phi_L}{1+\alpha}\frac{\left(1-\alpha^2\right)\tilde{H}_Q\left(\frac{\alpha^2}{c_X}\right)^{\frac{\alpha}{1-\alpha}}}{L_{IT}}$, we can write

$$w_{IT}(t) = B_3 N(t)$$

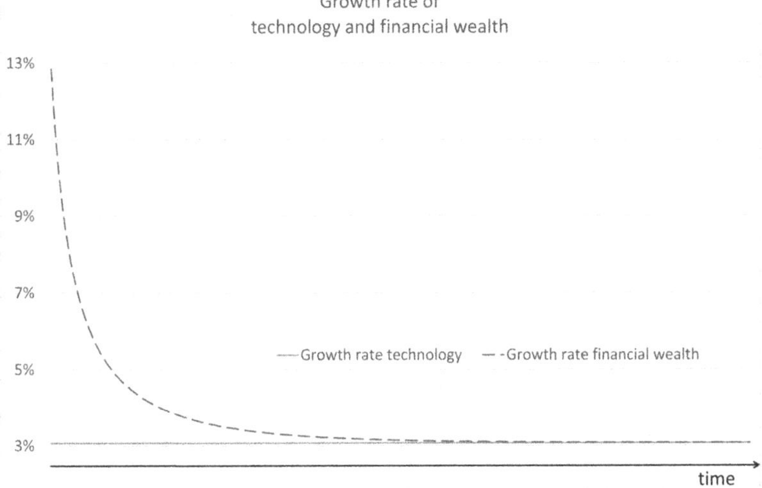

FIGURE 5.2 Convergence of the asset price toward its steady state value
Source: Authors' compilation.

As a result, we obtain

$$\frac{\dot{N}(t)}{N(t)}\nu p_F(t) = \pi_X + B_3 L_{IT} - \frac{C_{F+IT}(t)}{N(t)}$$
$$p_F(t) = \left[\pi_X + B_3 L_{IT} - \frac{C_{F+IT}(t)}{N(t)}\right]\frac{1}{\nu g_N}$$

As we assumed that $C_{F+IT}(t)$ grows at a lower rate than $N(t)$ (see Appendix D), $\frac{C_{F+IT}(t)}{N(t)}$ turns to zero and the asset price converges to its long-run value

$$\lim_{t\to\infty} p_F(t) = \frac{\tilde{\pi}_X + B_3 L_{IT}}{\nu \tilde{g}_N}.$$

Figure 5.2 describes the converging of wealth growth toward technology growth and Figure 5.3 describes the adjustment of the asset price toward its steady state value.

H Effects of Automation

Effects on human service *H*: Departing from Equation (5.24) $H = \Pi\left(N_{IT}, N\right)\left[\left(1-\Gamma\left(N_{IT}, N\right)\right)^{\frac{1}{\sigma}}\left(A_{IT}L_{IT}\right)^{\frac{\sigma-1}{\sigma}} + \Gamma\left(N_{IT}, N\right)^{\frac{1}{\sigma}}\left(A_L L_L\right)^{\frac{\sigma-1}{\sigma}}\right]^{\frac{\sigma}{\sigma-1}}$ and thus

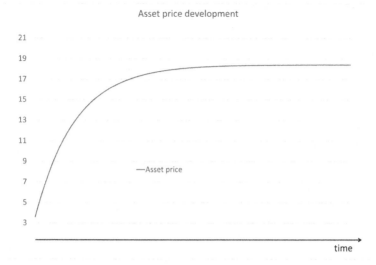

FIGURE 5.3 Adjustment of the asset price toward its steady state value
Source: Authors' compilation.

$$H = \left[\left((1 - \Gamma(N_{IT}, N)) \Pi(N_{IT}, N)^{\sigma-1} \right)^{\frac{1}{\sigma}} (A_{IT} L_{IT})^{\frac{\sigma-1}{\sigma}} \right.$$
$$\left. + \left(\Gamma(N_{IT}, N) \Pi(N_{IT}, N)^{\sigma-1} \right)^{\frac{1}{\sigma}} (A_L L_L)^{\frac{\sigma-1}{\sigma}} \right]^{\frac{\sigma}{\sigma-1}},$$

and using the equations, $B_1(N_{IT}) = \int_{N-1}^{N_{IT}} \gamma_{IT}(z)^{\sigma-1} dz = (1 - \Gamma(N_{IT}, N))\Pi(N_{IT}, N)^{\sigma-1}$, $\frac{dB_1}{dN_{IT}} = \gamma_{IT}(N_{IT})^{\sigma-1}$, and $B_2(N_{IT}) = \int_{N_{IT}}^{N} \gamma_L(z)^{\sigma-1} dz = \Gamma(N_{IT}, N)\Pi(N_{IT}, N)^{\sigma-1}$, $\frac{dB_2}{dN_{IT}} = -\gamma_L(N_{IT})^{\sigma-1}$, we rewrite H as

$$H = \left[\left(\int_{N-1}^{N_{IT}} \gamma_{IT}(z)^{\sigma-1} dz \right)^{\frac{1}{\sigma}} (A_{IT} L_{IT})^{\frac{\sigma-1}{\sigma}} + \left[\int_{N_{IT}}^{N} \gamma_L(z)^{\sigma-1} dz \right]^{\frac{1}{\sigma}} (A_L L_L)^{\frac{\sigma-1}{\sigma}} \right]^{\frac{\sigma}{\sigma-1}}$$
$$= \left[(B_1(N_{IT}))^{\frac{1}{\sigma}} (A_{IT} L_{IT})^{\frac{\sigma-1}{\sigma}} + [B_2(N_{IT})]^{\frac{1}{\sigma}} (A_L L_L)^{\frac{\sigma-1}{\sigma}} \right]^{\frac{\sigma}{\sigma-1}}$$

Taking the derivative with respect to A_{IT} gives

$$\frac{dH}{dA_{IT}} = \frac{\sigma}{\sigma-1} \left[\begin{array}{c} (B_1(N_{IT}))^{\frac{1}{\sigma}} (A_{IT} L_{IT})^{\frac{\sigma-1}{\sigma}} \\ + (B_2(N_{IT}))^{\frac{1}{\sigma}} (A_L L_L)^{\frac{\sigma-1}{\sigma}} \end{array} \right]^{\frac{\sigma}{\sigma-1}-1}$$
$$\times \frac{1}{\sigma} (A_{IT} L_{IT})^{\frac{\sigma-1}{\sigma}} (B_1(N_{IT}))^{\frac{1}{\sigma}-1} \frac{dB_1}{dN_{IT}} \frac{dN_{IT}}{dA_{IT}}$$

$$+\frac{\sigma}{\sigma-1}\left[\begin{array}{c}(B_1(N_{IT}))^{\frac{1}{\sigma}}(A_{IT}L_{IT})^{\frac{\sigma-1}{\sigma}}\\+(B_2(N_{IT}))^{\frac{1}{\sigma}}(A_LL_L)^{\frac{\sigma-1}{\sigma}}\end{array}\right]^{\frac{\sigma}{\sigma-1}-1}$$

$$\times(B_1(N_{IT}))^{\frac{1}{\sigma}}\frac{\sigma-1}{\sigma}(A_{IT}L_{IT})^{\frac{\sigma-1}{\sigma}-1}L_{IT}\dot{A}_{IT}$$

$$+\frac{\sigma}{\sigma-1}\left[\begin{array}{c}(B_1(N_{IT}))^{\frac{1}{\sigma}}(A_{IT}L_{IT})^{\frac{\sigma-1}{\sigma}}\\+(B_2(N_{IT}))^{\frac{1}{\sigma}}(A_LL_L)^{\frac{\sigma-1}{\sigma}}\end{array}\right]^{\frac{\sigma}{\sigma-1}-1}$$

$$\times\frac{1}{\sigma}(A_LL_L)^{\frac{\sigma-1}{\sigma}}(B_2(N_{IT}))^{\frac{1}{\sigma}-1}\frac{dB_2}{dN_{IT}}\frac{dN_{IT}}{dA_{IT}}$$

$$=\left[\begin{array}{c}(B_1(N_{IT}))^{\frac{1}{\sigma}}(A_{IT}L_{IT})^{\frac{\sigma-1}{\sigma}}\\+[B_2(N_{IT})]^{\frac{1}{\sigma}}(A_LL_L)^{\frac{\sigma-1}{\sigma}}\end{array}\right]^{\frac{\sigma}{\sigma-1}-1}(\sigma-1)^{-1}(A_{IT}L_{IT})^{\frac{\sigma-1}{\sigma}}$$

$$\times(B_1(N_{IT}))^{\frac{1}{\sigma}-1}\frac{dB_1}{dN_{IT}}\frac{dN_{IT}}{dA_{IT}}$$

$$+\left[\begin{array}{c}(B_1(N_{IT}))^{\frac{1}{\sigma}}(A_{IT}L_{IT})^{\frac{\sigma-1}{\sigma}}\\+[B_2(N_{IT})]^{\frac{1}{\sigma}}(A_LL_L)^{\frac{\sigma-1}{\sigma}}\end{array}\right]^{\frac{\sigma}{\sigma-1}-1}(B_1(N_{IT}))^{\frac{1}{\sigma}}(A_{IT}L_{IT})^{\frac{\sigma-1}{\sigma}-1}L_{IT}$$

$$+\left[\begin{array}{c}(B_1(N_{IT}))^{\frac{1}{\sigma}}(A_{IT}L_{IT})^{\frac{\sigma-1}{\sigma}}\\+[B_2(N_{IT})]^{\frac{1}{\sigma}}(A_LL_L)^{\frac{\sigma-1}{\sigma}}\end{array}\right]^{\frac{\sigma}{\sigma-1}-1}(\sigma-1)^{-1}$$

$$\times(A_LL_L)^{\frac{\sigma-1}{\sigma}}(B_2(N_{IT}))^{\frac{1}{\sigma}-1}\frac{dB_2}{dN_{IT}}\frac{dN_{IT}}{dA_{IT}}$$

$$=\frac{H\left[\begin{array}{c}(A_{IT}L_{IT})^{\frac{\sigma-1}{\sigma}}(B_1(N_{IT}))^{\frac{1}{\sigma}-1}\frac{dB_1}{dN_{IT}}\frac{dN_{IT}}{dA_{IT}}\\+(\sigma-1)(B_1(N_{IT}))^{\frac{1}{\sigma}}(A_{IT}L_{IT})^{\frac{\sigma-1}{\sigma}-1}L_{IT}\\+(A_LL_L)^{\frac{\sigma-1}{\sigma}}(B_2(N_{IT}))^{\frac{1}{\sigma}-1}\frac{dB_2}{dN_{IT}}\frac{dN_{IT}}{dA_{IT}}\end{array}\right]}{\left[\begin{array}{c}(B_1(N_{IT}))^{\frac{1}{\sigma}}(A_{IT}L_{IT})^{\frac{\sigma-1}{\sigma}}\\+[B_2(N_{IT})]^{\frac{1}{\sigma}}(A_LL_L)^{\frac{\sigma-1}{\sigma}}\end{array}\right](\sigma-1)}$$

$$=H\frac{\left(\begin{array}{l}(A_{IT}L_{IT})^{\frac{\sigma-1}{\sigma}}(B_1(N_{IT}))^{\frac{1}{\sigma}-1}\frac{dB_1}{dN_{IT}}\\+(A_LL_L)^{\frac{\sigma-1}{\sigma}}(B_2(N_{IT}))^{\frac{1}{\sigma}-1}\frac{dB_2}{dN_{IT}}\end{array}\right)\frac{dN_{IT}}{dA_{IT}}+(\sigma-1)(B_1(N_{IT}))^{\frac{1}{\sigma}}(A_{IT}L_{IT})^{\frac{\sigma-1}{\sigma}-1}L_{IT}}{(\sigma-1)\left[(B_1(N_{IT}))^{\frac{1}{\sigma}}(A_{IT}L_{IT})^{\frac{\sigma-1}{\sigma}}+[B_2(N_{IT})]^{\frac{1}{\sigma}}(A_LL_L)^{\frac{\sigma-1}{\sigma}}\right]}$$

$$=H\frac{\begin{array}{c}\left(\begin{array}{c}(A_{IT}L_{IT})^{\frac{\sigma-1}{\sigma}}(B_1(N_{IT}))^{\frac{1}{\sigma}-1}\gamma_{IT}(N_{IT})^{\sigma-1}\\+(A_LL_L)^{\frac{\sigma-1}{\sigma}}(B_2(N_{IT}))^{\frac{1}{\sigma}-1}(-)\gamma_L(N_{IT})^{\sigma-1}\end{array}\right)\frac{dN_{IT}}{dA_{IT}}\\+(\sigma-1)(B_1(N_{IT}))^{\frac{1}{\sigma}}(A_{IT}L_{IT})^{\frac{\sigma-1}{\sigma}-1}L_{IT}\end{array}}{(\sigma-1)\left[(B_1(N_{IT}))^{\frac{1}{\sigma}}(A_{IT}L_{IT})^{\frac{\sigma-1}{\sigma}}+[B_2(N_{IT})]^{\frac{1}{\sigma}}(A_LL_L)^{\frac{\sigma-1}{\sigma}}\right]}$$

$$=\frac{\frac{H}{A_{IT}}\left[\begin{array}{c}\left(1-\frac{(A_LL_L)^{\frac{\sigma-1}{\sigma}}(B_2(N_{IT}))^{\frac{1}{\sigma}-1}\gamma_L(N_{IT})^{\sigma-1}}{(A_{IT}L_{IT})^{\frac{\sigma-1}{\sigma}}(B_1(N_{IT}))^{\frac{1}{\sigma}-1}\gamma_{IT}(N_{IT})^{\sigma-1}}\right)\\\frac{dN_{IT}}{dA_{IT}}\frac{A_{IT}}{N_{IT}}N_{IT}(A_{IT}L_{IT})^{\frac{\sigma-1}{\sigma}}(B_1(N_{IT}))^{\frac{1}{\sigma}-1}\gamma_{IT}(N_{IT})^{\sigma-1}\\+(\sigma-1)(B_1(N_{IT}))^{\frac{1}{\sigma}}(A_{IT}L_{IT})^{\frac{\sigma-1}{\sigma}}\end{array}\right]}{(\sigma-1)\left[(B_1(N_{IT}))^{\frac{1}{\sigma}}(A_{IT}L_{IT})^{\frac{\sigma-1}{\sigma}}+[B_2(N_{IT})]^{\frac{1}{\sigma}}(A_LL_L)^{\frac{\sigma-1}{\sigma}}\right]}$$

$$= \frac{\frac{H}{A_{IT}}\left[\begin{array}{c}\left(1-\left(\frac{(A_L L_L)}{(A_{IT}L_{IT})}\frac{B_1(N_{IT})}{B_2(N_{IT})}\right)^{\frac{\sigma-1}{\sigma}}\left(\frac{\gamma_L(N_{IT})}{\gamma_{IT}(N_{IT})}\right)^{\sigma-1}\right)\\ \frac{dN_{IT}}{dA_{IT}}\frac{A_{IT}}{N_{IT}}N_{IT}\left(B_1\left(N_{IT}\right)\right)^{-1}\gamma_{IT}(N_{IT})^{\sigma-1}\\ +(\sigma-1)\end{array}\right](A_{IT}L_{IT})^{\frac{\sigma-1}{\sigma}}\left(B_1\left(N_{IT}\right)\right)^{\frac{1}{\sigma}}}{(\sigma-1)\left[\left(B_1\left(N_{IT}\right)\right)^{\frac{1}{\sigma}}(A_{IT}L_{IT})^{\frac{\sigma-1}{\sigma}}+\left[B_2\left(N_{IT}\right)\right]^{\frac{1}{\sigma}}(A_L L_L)^{\frac{\sigma-1}{\sigma}}\right]}$$

Using the switching condition (5.84), $\frac{\gamma_L(N_{IT})}{\gamma_{IT}(N_{IT})}=\left(\frac{A_{IT}L_{IT}}{A_L L_L}\right)^{\frac{1}{\sigma}}\left(\frac{B_2(N_{IT})}{B_1(N_{IT})}\right)^{\frac{1}{\sigma}}$, we obtain

$$0=\frac{\gamma_L(N_{IT})}{\gamma_{IT}(N_{IT})}-\left(\frac{A_{IT}L_{IT}}{A_L L_L}\right)^{\frac{1}{\sigma}}\left(\frac{B_2\left(N_{IT}\right)}{B_1\left(N_{IT}\right)}\right)^{\frac{1}{\sigma}}$$

$$\frac{\gamma_L(N_{IT})}{\gamma_{IT}(N_{IT})}=\left(\frac{A_{IT}L_{IT}}{A_L L_L}\right)^{\frac{1}{\sigma}}\left(\frac{B_2\left(N_{IT}\right)}{B_1\left(N_{IT}\right)}\right)^{\frac{1}{\sigma}}$$

$$0=1-\left(\frac{(A_L L_L)}{(A_{IT}L_{IT})}\frac{B_1\left(N_{IT}\right)}{B_2\left(N_{IT}\right)}\right)^{\frac{\sigma-1}{\sigma}}\left(\frac{A_{IT}L_{IT}}{A_L L_L}\right)^{\frac{\sigma-1}{\sigma}}\left(\frac{B_2\left(N_{IT}\right)}{B_1\left(N_{IT}\right)}\right)^{\frac{\sigma-1}{\sigma}}$$

$1-\left(\frac{(A_L L_L)}{(A_{IT}L_{IT})}\frac{B_1(N_{IT})}{B_2(N_{IT})}\right)^{\frac{\sigma-1}{\sigma}}\left(\frac{\gamma_L(N_{IT})}{\gamma_{IT}(N_{IT})}\right)^{\sigma-1}=0$, and thus we can write

$$=H\frac{(\sigma-1)\,(A_{IT}L_{IT})^{\frac{\sigma-1}{\sigma}}\left(B_1\left(N_{IT}\right)\right)^{\frac{1}{\sigma}}}{(\sigma-1)\left[\left(B_1\left(N_{IT}\right)\right)^{\frac{1}{\sigma}}(A_{IT}L_{IT})^{\frac{\sigma-1}{\sigma}}+\left[B_2\left(N_{IT}\right)\right]^{\frac{1}{\sigma}}(A_L L_L)^{\frac{\sigma-1}{\sigma}}\right]}\frac{1}{A_{IT}}$$

$$1>\eta_{H,A_{IT}}=\left[1+\frac{\left[B_2\left(N_{IT}\right)\right]^{\frac{1}{\sigma}}(A_L L_L)^{\frac{\sigma-1}{\sigma}}}{\left[B_1\left(N_{IT}\right)\right]^{\frac{1}{\sigma}}(A_{IT}L_{IT})^{\frac{\sigma-1}{\sigma}}}\right]^{-1}>0$$

Effects on the income share of labor in the service sector and total economy: $\phi_L, \frac{w_L L_L}{Y(t)}$

Effects on labor share of income in service sector: ϕ_L Departing from Equation (5.25) with $\phi_L=\left(1+\left(\frac{(1-\Gamma(N_{IT},N))}{\Gamma(N_{IT},N)}\right)^{\frac{1}{\sigma}}\left(\frac{A_{IT}}{A_L}\frac{L_{IT}}{L_L}\right)^{\frac{\sigma-1}{\sigma}}\right)^{-1}$ and using the equations, $B_1\left(N_{IT}\right)=\int_{N-1}^{N_{IT}}\gamma_{IT}(z)^{\sigma-1}dz=(1-\Gamma(N_{IT},N))\Pi(N_{IT},N)^{\sigma-1}$, $\frac{dB_1}{dN_{IT}}=\gamma_{IT}(N_{IT})^{\sigma-1}$, and $B_2\left(N_{IT}\right)=\int_{N_{IT}}^{N}\gamma_L(z)^{\sigma-1}dz=\Gamma(N_{IT},N)\Pi(N_{IT},N)^{\sigma-1}$, $\frac{dB_2}{dN_{IT}}=-\gamma_L(N_{IT})^{\sigma-1}$, we rewrite ϕ_L as

$$\phi_L=\frac{1}{\left(\frac{L_{IT}}{L_L}\frac{A_{IT}}{A_L}\right)^{\frac{\sigma-1}{\sigma}}\left(\frac{B_1(N_{IT})}{B_2(N_{IT})}\right)^{\frac{1}{\sigma}}+1}.$$

Taking the derivative gives:

$$\frac{d\phi_L}{dA_{IT}} = -\frac{1}{(\ldots)^2}\left(\frac{L_{IT}}{L_L}\right)^{\frac{\sigma-1}{\sigma}}$$
$$\times\left[\begin{array}{c} \frac{\sigma-1}{\sigma}\left(\frac{B_1(N_{IT})}{B_2(N_{IT})}\right)^{\frac{1}{\sigma}}\left(\frac{A_{IT}}{A_L}\right)^{-\frac{\sigma-1}{\sigma}-1}\frac{1}{A_L} \\ +\frac{1}{\sigma}\left(\frac{A_{IT}}{A_L}\right)^{\frac{\sigma-1}{\sigma}}\left(\frac{B_1(N_{IT})}{B_2(N_{IT})}\right)^{\frac{1}{\sigma}-1}\left(\frac{\frac{dB1}{dN_{IT}}\frac{dN_{IT}}{dA_{IT}}}{B_2(N_{IT})}-\frac{B_1(N_{IT})\frac{dB_2}{dN_{IT}}\frac{dN_{IT}}{dA_{IT}}}{B_2(N_{IT})^2}\right)\end{array}\right]$$

$$\frac{d\phi_L}{dA_{IT}}\frac{1}{\phi_L} = -\frac{\left(\frac{L_{IT}}{L_L}\right)^{\frac{\sigma-1}{\sigma}}}{(\ldots)\sigma}$$
$$\times\left[\begin{array}{c} (\sigma-1)\left(\frac{B_1(N_{IT})}{B_2(N_{IT})}\right)^{\frac{1}{\sigma}}\left(\frac{A_{IT}}{A_L}\right)^{-\frac{\sigma-1}{\sigma}-1}\frac{1}{A_L} \\ +\left(\frac{A_{IT}}{A_L}\right)^{\frac{\sigma-1}{\sigma}}\left(\frac{B_1(N_{IT})}{B_2(N_{IT})}\right)^{\frac{1}{\sigma}-1}\frac{B_1(N_{IT})}{B_2(N_{IT})}\left(\frac{dB_1}{dN_{IT}}\frac{1}{B_1(N_{IT})}\frac{dN_{IT}}{dA_{IT}}-\frac{dB_2}{dN_{IT}}\frac{1}{B_2(N_{IT})}\frac{dN_{IT}}{dA_{IT}}\right)\end{array}\right]$$

$$\frac{d\phi_L}{dA_{IT}}\frac{1}{\phi_L} = \frac{-\left(\frac{L_{IT}}{L_L}\right)^{\frac{\sigma-1}{\sigma}}\left(\frac{B_1(N_{IT})}{B_2(N_{IT})}\right)^{\frac{1}{\sigma}}\left(\frac{A_{IT}}{A_L}\right)^{\frac{\sigma-1}{\sigma}}}{(\ldots)\sigma}$$
$$\times\left[(\sigma-1)\frac{1}{A_{IT}}+\left(\begin{array}{c}\frac{dB_1}{dN_{IT}}\frac{N_{IT}}{B_1(N_{IT})}\frac{dN_{IT}}{dA_{IT}}\frac{A_{IT}}{N_{IT}} \\ -\frac{dB_2}{dN_{IT}}\frac{N_{IT}}{B_2(N_{IT})}\frac{dN_{IT}}{dA_{IT}}\frac{A_{IT}}{N_{IT}}\end{array}\right)\frac{1}{A_{IT}}\right]$$

$$\frac{d\phi_L}{dA_{IT}}\frac{1}{\phi_L} = \frac{-\left(\frac{L_{IT}}{L_L}\right)^{\frac{\sigma-1}{\sigma}}\left(\frac{B_1(N_{IT})}{B_2(N_{IT})}\right)^{\frac{1}{\sigma}}\left(\frac{A_{IT}}{A_L}\right)^{\frac{\sigma-1}{\sigma}}}{\left(\left(\frac{L_{IT}}{L_L}\right)^{\frac{\sigma-1}{\sigma}}\left(\frac{A_{IT}}{A_L}\right)^{\frac{\sigma-1}{\sigma}}\left(\frac{B_1(N_{IT})z}{B_2(N_{IT})}\right)^{\frac{1}{\sigma}}+1\right)\sigma}$$
$$\times\left[(\sigma-1)+\left(\begin{array}{c}\frac{\gamma_{IT}(N_{IT})^{\sigma-1}}{B_1(N_{IT})} \\ +\frac{\gamma_L(N_{IT})^{\sigma-1}}{B_2(N_{IT})}\end{array}\right)N_{IT}\eta_{N_{IT},A_{IT}}\right]\frac{1}{A_{IT}}$$

$$\begin{aligned}\eta_{\phi_L,A_{IT}} &= \frac{d\phi_L}{dA_{IT}}\frac{A_{IT}}{\phi_L} \\ &= \frac{-1}{\sigma}\frac{(\sigma-1)+\left(\frac{\gamma_{IT}(N_{IT})^{\sigma-1}}{B_1(N_{IT})}+\frac{\gamma_L(N_{IT})^{\sigma-1}}{B_2(N_{IT})}\right)N_{IT}\eta_{N_{IT},A_{IT}}}{1+\left(\frac{A_L L_L}{A_{IT}L_{IT}}\right)^{\frac{\sigma-1}{\sigma}}\left(\frac{B_2(N_{IT})}{B_1(N_{IT})}\right)^{\frac{1}{\sigma}}} < 0.\end{aligned}$$

For $1 < \sigma$, the share will clearly decline, $\eta_{\phi_L,A_{IT}} < 0$. If $1 > \sigma$, the share will not necessarily increase. Introducing more IT tasks $-\left(\frac{\gamma_{IT}(N_{IT})^{\sigma-1}}{B_1(N_{IT})}+\frac{\gamma_L(N_{IT})^{\sigma-1}}{B_2(N_{IT})}\right)N_{IT}\eta_{N_{IT},A_{IT}} < 0$ will decrease the share of labor income and overcompensate the potentially positive effect from complementarity, $1 > \sigma$.

Effects on labor share of income in the total economy: $\frac{w_L L_L}{Y}$.

$$\frac{w_L L_L}{Y} = \frac{\phi_L}{(1+\alpha)}, \quad \frac{\frac{dw_L L_L/Y}{dA_{IT}}}{w_L L_L/Y} = \frac{d\phi_L}{\phi_L} = \eta_{\phi_L,A_{IT}}\frac{dA_{IT}}{A_{IT}} < 0$$

Effect on income share of technology providers $\frac{w_{it}l_{it}}{Y}$

$$\frac{w_{IT}(t)L_{IT}}{Y(t)} = \frac{1-\phi_L}{1+\alpha}$$

$$\frac{d\frac{w_{IT}(t)L_{IT}}{Y(t)}}{\frac{w_{IT}(t)L_{IT}}{Y(t)}} = \frac{-1}{1+\alpha}\frac{1+\alpha}{1-\phi_L}\frac{\partial\phi_L}{\partial A_{IT}}\frac{dA_{IT}}{A_{IT}}A_{IT}$$

$$= \frac{-1}{\frac{1}{\phi_L}-1}\frac{\partial\phi_L}{\partial A_{IT}}\frac{A_{IT}}{\phi_L}\frac{dA_{IT}}{A_{IT}}$$

If A_{IT} is repeatedly increasing, the limit is:

$$\lim_{A_{IT}\to\infty}\frac{w_{IT}(t)L_{IT}}{Y(t)} = \frac{1-\phi_L}{1+\alpha} = \frac{1}{1+\alpha} - 0.$$

Effects on consumption rate: *c*

$$c = \frac{\phi_L}{(1+\alpha)}, \quad dc = \frac{\phi_L}{(1+\alpha)}\frac{\partial\phi_L}{\partial A_{IT}}\frac{dA_{IT}}{A_{IT}}\frac{A_{IT}}{\phi_L}$$

$$\frac{dc}{c}\frac{A_{IT}}{dA_{IT}} = \frac{\partial\phi_L}{\partial A_{IT}}\frac{A_{IT}}{\phi_L} = \eta_{c,A_{IT}} = \eta_{\phi_L,A_{IT}}$$

Effects of human service in production: H_Q We reconsider the discussion of the implicit function $\tilde{H}_Q$ and restate the effect of a change of A_{IT} on H_Q as we have derived in Section F of this chapter's Appendix.

$$\frac{dH_Q}{dA_{IT}} = -\frac{\frac{\partial F}{\partial A_{IT}}}{\frac{\partial F}{\partial \tilde{H}_Q}} = -\frac{-c\left[\overset{<0}{\eta_{c,A_{IT}}}H_\phi + H\overset{>0}{\eta_{H,A_{IT}}}\right]\frac{1}{A_{IT}}H_Q^{1-\varphi}}{\left[(2-\varphi)\,cH_Q + (1-\varphi)\left(-cov\left(\lambda,\varepsilon_F\right) - cH\right)\right]H_Q^{-\varphi}}$$

$$\eta_{H_Q,A_{IT}} = \frac{dH_Q}{H_Q}\frac{A_{IT}}{dA_{IT}} = \frac{\frac{\phi_L}{(1+\alpha)}\left[\overset{<0}{\eta_{\phi_L,A_{IT}}}H_\phi + \overset{>0}{\eta_{H,A_{IT}}}H\right]}{\left[(2-\varphi)\,cH_Q + (1-\varphi)\left(-cov\left(\lambda,\varepsilon_F\right) - cH\right)\right]} > 0$$

Effects on deployment rate: ω

$$\omega(t) = \frac{\tilde{Y}(t)}{\tilde{Y}^P(t)} = \frac{\tilde{H}_Q(t)}{H}$$

$$d\omega = \left[\eta_{H_Q,A_{IT}} - \eta_{H,A_{IT}}\right]\frac{dA_{IT}}{A_{IT}} = \left(\frac{d\tilde{H}_Q(t)}{dA_{IT}}\frac{A_{IT}}{\tilde{H}_Q} - \frac{dH}{dA_{IT}}\frac{A_{IT}}{H}\right)\frac{\tilde{H}_Q}{H}\frac{dA_{IT}}{A_{IT}} =$$

$$\frac{d\omega}{\omega} = \left[\frac{c\left(\eta_{\phi_L,A_{IT}}H_\phi + H\eta_{H,A_{IT}}\right)}{(2-\varphi)\,cH_Q + (1-\varphi)\left(-cov\left(\lambda,\varepsilon_F\right) - cH\right)} - \eta_{H,A_{IT}}\right]\frac{dA_{IT}}{A_{IT}}$$

In order to have a negative deployment effect, we want to show that

$$\frac{\frac{\phi_L}{(1+\alpha)}\left[\eta_{\phi_L,A_{IT}} H_\phi + H\eta_{H,A_{IT}}\right]}{\left[(2-\varphi)\,cH_Q + (1-\varphi)\,(-cov\,(\lambda,\varepsilon_F) - cH)\right]} - \eta_{H,A_{IT}} < 0$$

$$c\left[\eta_{\phi_L,A_{IT}} H_\phi + H\eta_{H,A_{IT}}\right] < \eta_{H,A_{IT}}\left[(2-\varphi)\,cH_Q - (1-\varphi)\,cov\,(\lambda,\varepsilon_F) - (1-\varphi)\,cH\right]$$

$$c\frac{\eta_{\phi_L,A_{IT}}}{\eta_{H,A_{IT}}}H_\phi + cH < (2-\varphi)\,cH_Q - (1-\varphi)\,cov\,(\lambda,\varepsilon_F) - (1-\varphi)\,cH$$

$$c\frac{\eta_{\phi_L,A_{IT}}}{\eta_{H,A_{IT}}}H_\phi < (2-\varphi)\,cH_Q - (1-\varphi)\,cov\,(\lambda,\varepsilon_F) - 2cH + \varphi cH$$

$$c\frac{\eta_{\phi_L,A_{IT}}}{\eta_{H,A_{IT}}}H_\phi < (2-\varphi)\,cH_Q - (2-\varphi)\,cH - (1-\varphi)\,cov\,(\lambda,\varepsilon_F)$$

$$c\frac{\overset{<0}{\eta}_{\phi_L,A_{IT}}}{\eta_{H,A_{IT}}}H_\phi < -(2-\varphi)\,c\left[H - H_Q\right] - (1-\varphi)\,cov\,(\lambda,\varepsilon_F)$$

A sufficient condition for this suggestion is

$$0 < -(2-\varphi)\,c\left[H - H_Q\right] - (1-\varphi)\,cov\,(\lambda,\varepsilon_F)$$

$$\frac{(2-\varphi)}{(1-\varphi)}cH_\phi < -cov\,(\lambda,\varepsilon_F)$$

and this condition holds if $cov\,(\lambda,\varepsilon_F)$ is sufficiently negative, and thus, for a large variety of parameters.

Effects on wages: $w_L(t)$ Detailed calculations are available from the authors on request.

$$\frac{dw_L(t)}{w_L(t)} = \left[\overset{(ii)\;<0}{\eta_{C,A_{IT}}} + \overset{>0}{\eta_{H_Q,H}}\overset{(i)\;>0}{\eta_{H,A_{IT}}}\right]\frac{dA_{IT}}{A_{IT}} \lessgtr 0$$

$$w_L = \phi_L\frac{p_H H}{L_L}, \quad p_H(t) = (1-\alpha)\frac{Q(t)}{H}$$

$$w_L = \phi_L(1-\alpha)\frac{Q}{H}\frac{H}{L_L} = \phi_L(1-\alpha)\frac{Q}{L_L}$$

$$\frac{dw_L}{dA_{IT}} = \frac{d\phi_L}{dA_{IT}}(1-\alpha)\frac{Q}{L_L} + \phi_L(1-\alpha)\frac{1}{L_L}\frac{dQ}{dA_{IT}}$$

$$\frac{dQ}{dA_{IT}} = N_i(t)H_{Qi}^{1-\alpha}x_i^\alpha(t)\frac{dH_Q}{dA_{IT}}\frac{1}{H_Q} = Q\frac{dH_Q}{dA_{IT}}\frac{1}{H_Q}$$

$$\frac{dw_L}{dA_{IT}} = \frac{d\phi_L}{dA_{IT}}\frac{A_{IT}}{\phi_L}\phi_L(1-\alpha)\frac{Q}{L_L} + \phi_L(1-\alpha)\frac{Q}{L_L}\frac{dH_Q}{dA_{IT}}\frac{A_{IT}}{H_Q}$$

$$\frac{dw_L}{dA_{IT}}\frac{A_{IT}}{w_L} = \frac{d\phi_L}{dA_{IT}}\frac{A_{IT}}{\phi_L} + \frac{dH_Q}{dA_{IT}}\frac{A_{IT}}{H_Q} = \overset{<0}{\eta}_{\phi_L,A_{IT}} + \overset{>0}{\eta}_{H_Q,A_{IT}}$$

$$\eta_{\phi_L,A_{IT}} = \frac{d\phi_L}{dA_{IT}}\frac{A_{IT}}{\phi_L} = \frac{1}{\sigma}\frac{-(\sigma-1)-\left(\frac{\gamma_{IT}(N_{IT})^{\sigma-1}}{B_1(N_{IT})}+\frac{\gamma_L(N_{IT})^{\sigma-1}}{B_2(N_{IT})}\right)N_{IT}\eta_{N_{IT},A_{IT}}}{1+\left(\frac{A_L L_L}{A_{IT}L_{IT}}\right)^{\frac{\sigma-1}{\sigma}}\left(\frac{B_2(N_{IT})}{B_1(N_{IT})}\right)^{\frac{1}{\sigma}}} < 0$$

$$\eta_{H_Q,A_{IT}} = \frac{dH_Q}{H_Q}\frac{A_{IT}}{dA_{IT}} = \frac{\frac{\phi_L}{(1+\alpha)}\left[\overset{<0}{\eta_{\phi_L,A_{IT}}}H_\phi + \overset{>0}{\eta_{H,A_{IT}}}H\right]}{[(2-\varphi)\,cH_Q + (1-\varphi)\,(-cov\,(\lambda,\varepsilon_F) - cH)]} > 0$$

$$\eta_{w_L,A_{IT}} = \eta_{\phi_L,A_{IT}} + \frac{\frac{\phi_L}{(1+\alpha)}\left[\overset{<0}{\eta_{\phi_L,A_{IT}}}H_\phi + \overset{>0}{\eta_{H,A_{IT}}}H\right]}{(2-\varphi)\,cH_Q + (1-\varphi)\,(-cov\,(\lambda,\varepsilon_F) - cH)} < 0$$

$$= \frac{\left[\begin{array}{c}\eta_{\phi_L,A_{IT}}\left[(2-\varphi)\,cH_Q + (1-\varphi)\,(-cov\,(\lambda,\varepsilon_F) - cH)\right] \\ +c\left[\eta_{\phi_L,A_{IT}}H_\phi + \eta_{H,A_{IT}}H\right]\end{array}\right]}{(2-\varphi)\,cH_Q + (1-\varphi)\,(-cov\,(\lambda,\varepsilon_F) - cH)}$$

$$= \frac{\left[\begin{array}{c}\eta_{\phi_L,A_{IT}}\,(2-\varphi)\,cH_Q + c\eta_{\phi_L,A_{IT}}H_\phi \\ +\eta_{\phi_L,A_{IT}}\,(1-\varphi)\,(-cov\,(\lambda,\varepsilon_F) - cH) + c\eta_{H,A_{IT}}H\end{array}\right]}{(2-\varphi)\,cH_Q + (1-\varphi)\,(-cov\,(\lambda,\varepsilon_F) - cH)}$$

$$= \frac{\left[\begin{array}{c}\eta_{\phi_L,A_{IT}}\,(1-\varphi)\,cH_Q + \eta_{\phi_L,A_{IT}}cH \\ +\eta_{\phi_L,A_{IT}}\,(1-\varphi)\,(-cov\,(\lambda,\varepsilon_F) - cH) + c\eta_{H,A_{IT}}H\end{array}\right]}{(2-\varphi)\,cH_Q\,(1-\varphi)\,(-cov\,(\lambda,\varepsilon_F) - cH)}$$

$$= \frac{\left[\begin{array}{c}\eta_{\phi_L,A_{IT}}\,(1-\varphi)\,cH_Q + \eta_{\phi_L,A_{IT}}cH - cov\,(\lambda,\varepsilon_F)\,\eta_{\phi_L,A_{IT}}\,(1-\varphi) \\ -\eta_{\phi_L,A_{IT}}cH\,(1-\varphi) + c\eta_{H,A_{IT}}H\end{array}\right]}{(2-\varphi)\,cH_Q + (1-\varphi)\,(-cov\,(\lambda,\varepsilon_F) - cH)}$$

$$= \frac{\left[\begin{array}{c}\eta_{\phi_L,A_{IT}}\,(1-\varphi)\,cH_Q + \eta_{\phi_L,A_{IT}}cH - cov\,(\lambda,\varepsilon_F)\,\eta_{\phi_L,A_{IT}}\,(1-\varphi) \\ -\eta_{\phi_L,A_{IT}}cH + \eta_{\phi_L,A_{IT}}c\varphi H + c\eta_{H,A_{IT}}H\end{array}\right]}{(2-\varphi)\,cH_Q + (1-\varphi)\,(-cov\,(\lambda,\varepsilon_F) - cH)}$$

$$= \frac{\left[\begin{array}{c}\eta_{\phi_L,A_{IT}}\,(1-\varphi)\,cH_Q - cov\,(\lambda,\varepsilon_F)\,\eta_{\phi_L,A_{IT}}\,(1-\varphi) \\ +\eta_{\phi_L,A_{IT}}c\varphi H + c\eta_{H,A_{IT}}H\end{array}\right]}{(2-\varphi)\,cH_Q + (1-\varphi)\,(-cov\,(\lambda,\varepsilon_F) - cH)}$$

$$0 < \eta_{\phi_L,A_{IT}}\,(1-\varphi)\,cH_Q - cov\,(\lambda,\varepsilon_F)\,\eta_{\phi_L,A_{IT}}\,(1-\varphi) + \eta_{\phi_L,A_{IT}}c\varphi H + c\eta_{H,A_{IT}}H < 0$$

$$-c\frac{\eta_{H,A_{IT}}}{\eta_{\phi_L,A_{IT}}}H < (1-\varphi)\,cH_Q - \operatorname{cov}(\lambda,\varepsilon_F)(1-\varphi) + c\varphi H$$

$$-\operatorname{cov}(\lambda,\varepsilon_F)(1-\varphi) > -c\left(\left(\frac{\eta_{H,A_{IT}}}{\eta_{\phi_L,A_{IT}}}-\varphi\right)H-(1-\varphi)\,H_Q\right)$$

$$\operatorname{cov}(\lambda,\varepsilon_F) < c\left(\left(\frac{\eta_{H,A_{IT}}}{\eta_{\phi_L,A_{IT}}}-\varphi\right)\frac{H}{(1-\varphi)}-H_Q\right)$$

Effects on the growth rate $\frac{d\tilde{g}_Y}{\tilde{g}_Y}$: From Equation (5.53), we know

$$g_N = \left(\left(\frac{\alpha^2}{c_X}\right)^{\frac{1}{1-\alpha}}H_Q\right)^{\varphi}(g_A)^{1-\varphi}.$$

Taking the derivative gives

$$\frac{dg_N}{dA_{IT}} = \varphi\left(\left(\frac{\alpha^2}{c_X}\right)^{\frac{1}{1-\alpha}}H_Q\right)^{\varphi-1}(g_A)^{1-\varphi}\left(\frac{\alpha^2}{c_X}\right)^{\frac{1}{1-\alpha}}\frac{dH_Q}{dA_{IT}}$$

$$\eta_{g_N,A_{IT}} = \frac{dg_N}{dA_{IT}}\frac{A_{IT}}{g_N} = \varphi\eta_{H_Q,A_{IT}} = \varphi\frac{dH_Q}{dA_{IT}}\frac{A_{IT}}{H_Q} > 0$$

I Simultaneous Demand Shocks

Simultaneous demand shock: We depart from Equation (5.53)

$$\frac{dg_N}{dA_{IT}} = \varphi g_N\frac{1}{H_Q}\frac{dH_Q^{\text{total}}}{dA_{IT}}.$$

In addition to the pure supply-side mechanism which we derived in Equation (5.76), we now consider a simultaneous demand shock with $\frac{dv}{dA_{IT}} < 0$. Thus, labor in production is now determined by

$$\frac{dH_Q^{\text{total}}}{dA_{IT}}\frac{A_{IT}}{H_Q} = \frac{\partial H_Q^{\text{supply}}}{\partial A_{IT}}\frac{A_{IT}}{H_Q} + \frac{\partial H_Q^{\text{demand}}}{\partial A_{IT}}\frac{A_{IT}}{H_Q}$$

$$\eta_{H_Q,A_{IT}}^{\text{total}} = \eta_{H_Q,A_{IT}}^{\text{supply}} + \eta_{H_Q,A_{IT}}^{\text{demand}}$$

While $\frac{\partial H_Q^{\text{supply}}}{\partial A_{IT}} > 0$ is the effect derived in Equation (5.76), we need to determine $\frac{\partial H_Q^{\text{demand}}}{\partial A_{IT}} = \frac{dH_Q}{dv}\frac{dv}{dA_{IT}}$. With $\frac{dH_Q}{dv} = -\frac{\frac{\operatorname{cov}(\lambda,\varepsilon_F)}{(1-\alpha^2)}\left(\frac{\alpha^2}{c_X}\right)^{\frac{\varphi-\alpha}{1-\alpha}}(g_A)^{1-\varphi}}{[(2-\varphi)cH_Q+(1-\varphi)(-\operatorname{cov}(\lambda,\varepsilon_F)-cH)]H_Q^{-\varphi}} > 0$ (see Appendix F and Equation (5.62))

$$\frac{\partial H_Q^{\text{supply}}}{\partial A_{IT}} = -\frac{-c\left[\overset{<0}{\eta_{c,A_{IT}}} H_\phi + H \overset{>0}{\eta_{H,A_{IT}}}\right] \frac{1}{A_{IT}} H_Q^{1-\varphi}}{\left[(2-\varphi)\, cH_Q + (1-\varphi)\left(-cov\left(\lambda, \varepsilon_F\right) - cH\right)\right] H_Q^{-\varphi}}$$

$$\eta_{H_Q,A_{IT}}^{\text{supply}} = \frac{\partial H_Q^{\text{supply}}}{\partial A_{IT}} \frac{A_{IT}}{H_Q} = \frac{c\left[\overset{<0}{\eta_{c,A_{IT}}} H_\phi + H \overset{>0}{\eta_{H,A_{IT}}}\right]}{\left[(2-\varphi)\, cH_Q + (1-\varphi)\left(-cov\left(\lambda, \varepsilon_F\right) - cH\right)\right]}$$

$$\frac{\partial H_Q^{\text{demand}}}{\partial A_{IT}} = -\frac{\frac{cov(\lambda,\varepsilon_F)}{(1-\alpha^2)} \left(\frac{\alpha^2}{c_x}\right)^{\frac{\varphi-\alpha}{1-\alpha}} \left(g_A\right)^{1-\varphi}}{\left[(2-\varphi)\, cH_Q + (1-\varphi)\left(-cov\left(\lambda, \varepsilon_F\right) - cH\right)\right] H_Q^{-\varphi}} \times \frac{dv}{dA_{IT}} < 0$$

$$\eta_{H_Q,A_{IT}}^{\text{demand}} = \frac{\partial H_Q^{\text{demand}}}{\partial A_{IT}} \frac{A_{IT}}{H_Q}$$

$$= -\frac{\frac{cov(\lambda,\varepsilon_F)}{(1-\alpha^2)} v \left(\frac{\alpha^2}{c_x}\right)^{\frac{\varphi-\alpha}{1-\alpha}} \left(g_A\right)^{1-\varphi}}{\left[(2-\varphi)\, cH_Q + (1-\varphi)\left(-cov\left(\lambda, \varepsilon_F\right) - cH\right)\right] H_Q^{1-\varphi}} \frac{A_{IT}}{v} \frac{dv}{dA_{IT}} < 0.$$

Combining both elements gives

$$\frac{dH_Q^{\text{total}}}{dA_{IT}} = \frac{c\left[\overbrace{\overset{<0}{\eta_{c,A_{IT}}} H_\phi + H \overset{>0}{\eta_{H,A_{IT}}}}^{>0}\right] \frac{1}{A_{IT}} H_Q^{1-\varphi} - \frac{cov(\lambda,\varepsilon_F)}{(1-\alpha^2)} \left(\frac{\alpha^2}{c_x}\right)^{\frac{\varphi-\alpha}{1-\alpha}} \left(g_A\right)^{1-\varphi} \frac{dv}{dA_{IT}}}{\left[(2-\varphi)\, cH_Q + (1-\varphi)\left(-cov\left(\lambda, \varepsilon_F\right) - cH\right)\right] H_Q^{-\varphi}} < 0$$

$$0 > c\left[\overset{<0}{\eta_{c,A_{IT}}} H_\phi + H \overset{>0}{\eta_{H,A_{IT}}}\right] \frac{1}{A_{IT}} H_Q^{1-\varphi} - \frac{cov\left(\lambda, \varepsilon_F\right)}{\left(1-\alpha^2\right)} \left(\frac{\alpha^2}{c_x}\right)^{\frac{\varphi-\alpha}{1-\alpha}} \left(g_A\right)^{1-\varphi} \frac{dv}{dA_{IT}}$$

$$c\left[\overset{<0}{\eta_{c,A_{IT}}} H_\phi + H \overset{>0}{\eta_{H,A_{IT}}}\right] \frac{1}{A_{IT}} H_Q^{1-\varphi} < \frac{cov\left(\lambda, \varepsilon_F\right)}{\left(1-\alpha^2\right)} \left(\frac{\alpha^2}{c_x}\right)^{\frac{\varphi-\alpha}{1-\alpha}} \left(g_A\right)^{1-\varphi} \frac{dv}{dA_{IT}}$$

$$\frac{c\left(1-\alpha^2\right) \overbrace{\left[\eta_{c,A_{IT}} H_\phi + \eta_{H,A_{IT}} H\right]}^{>0}}{v \left(\frac{\alpha^2}{c_x}\right)^{\frac{\varphi-\alpha}{1-\alpha}}} \frac{\left(\frac{H_Q}{g_A}\right)^{1-\varphi}}{\underset{<0}{\eta_{v,A_{IT}}}} > \overset{<0}{cov\left(\lambda, \varepsilon_F\right)}$$

This holds if in absolute terms $cov(\lambda, \varepsilon_F)$ is sufficiently large.

$$\eta_{g_N,A_{IT}} = \frac{dg_N}{dA_{IT}}\frac{A_{IT}}{g_N} = \varphi\left[\frac{c\left[\eta_{c,A_{IT}}H_\phi + \eta_{H,A_{IT}}H\right]}{\left[(2-\varphi)\,cH_Q + (1-\varphi)\,(-cov\,(\lambda,\varepsilon_F) - cH)\right]}\right]$$

$$- \frac{\frac{cov(\lambda,\varepsilon_F)}{(1-\alpha^2)}v\left(\frac{\alpha^2}{c_x}\right)^{\frac{\varphi-\alpha}{1-\alpha}}\left(\frac{g_A}{H_Q}\right)^{1-\varphi}\eta_{v,A_{IT}}}{\left[(2-\varphi)\,cH_Q + (1-\varphi)\,(-cov\,(\lambda,\varepsilon_F) - cH)\right]} < 0$$

Simultaneous innovation shock: The effect on the growth rate

$$\frac{dg_N}{dA_{IT}} = \varphi\left(\left(\frac{\alpha^2}{c_x}\right)^{\frac{1}{1-\alpha}}H_Q\right)^{\varphi-1}(g_A)^{1-\varphi}\left(\frac{\alpha^2}{c_x}\right)^{\frac{1}{1-\alpha}}\frac{dH_Q}{dA_{IT}}$$

$$+ (1-\varphi)\left(\left(\frac{\alpha^2}{c_x}\right)^{\frac{1}{1-\alpha}}H_Q\right)^{\varphi}(g_A)^{-\varphi}\frac{dg_A}{dA_{IT}}$$

$$= \varphi g_N\frac{1}{H_Q}\frac{dH_Q}{dA_{IT}} + (1-\varphi)\,g_N\frac{1}{g_A}\frac{dg_A}{dA_{IT}}$$

$$\eta_{g_N,A_{IT}} = \frac{dg_N}{dA_{IT}}\frac{A_{IT}}{g_N} = \varphi\eta_{H_Q,A_{IT}} + (1-\varphi)\,\eta_{g_A,\,A_{IT}}$$

As in Section H of this Appendix, we depart from

$$\eta^{total}_{H_Q,A_{IT}} = \eta^{supply}_{H_Q,A_{IT}} + \eta^{demand}_{H_Q,A_{IT}}.$$

While the supply effect $\frac{\partial H_Q^{supply}}{\partial A_{IT}} > 0$ is known [see Equation (5.76)], we need to determine $\frac{\partial H_Q^{demand}}{\partial A_{IT}} = \frac{dH_Q}{dg_A}\frac{dg_A}{dA_{IT}}$, the effect related to the demand side. And we follow the idea that an increase in AI leads to a shift in resources that simultaneously reduces the product innovations rate g_A, with $\frac{dg_A}{dA_{IT}} < 0$. Thus, labor in production is now determined (see Appendix F and Equation (5.62)) by

$$\frac{\partial H_Q^{supply}}{\partial A_{IT}} = \frac{c\left[\overset{<0}{\eta_{c,A_{IT}}}H_\phi + H\overset{>0}{\eta_{H,A_{IT}}}\right]\frac{1}{A_{IT}}H_Q^{1-\varphi}}{\left[(2-\varphi)\,cH_Q + (1-\varphi)\,(-cov\,(\lambda,\varepsilon_F) - cH)\right]H_Q^{-\varphi}}$$

$$\eta_{H_Q,A_{IT}}^{\text{supply}} = \frac{c\left[\overset{<0}{\eta_{c,A_{IT}}} H_\phi + H\overset{>0}{\eta_{H,A_{IT}}}\right]}{\left[(2-\varphi)\,cH_Q + (1-\varphi)\left(-cov\left(\lambda,\varepsilon_F\right) - cH\right)\right]}$$

$$\frac{\partial H_Q^{\text{demand}}}{\partial A_{IT}} = -\frac{\frac{(1-\varphi)cov(\lambda,\varepsilon_F)\nu}{(1-\alpha^2)}\left(\frac{\alpha^2}{c_x}\right)^{\frac{\varphi-\alpha}{1-\alpha}}(g_A)^{-\varphi}}{\left[(2-\varphi)\,cH_Q + (1-\varphi)\left(-cov\left(\lambda,\varepsilon_F\right) - cH\right)\right]H_Q^{-\varphi}}\frac{dg_A}{dA_{IT}} > 0$$

$$\eta_{H_Q,A_{IT}}^{\text{demand}} = \frac{-\frac{(1-\varphi)cov(\lambda,\varepsilon_F)\nu}{(1-\alpha^2)}\left(\frac{\alpha^2}{c_x}\right)^{\frac{\varphi-\alpha}{1-\alpha}}\left(\frac{g_A}{H_Q}\right)^{1-\varphi}}{\left[(2-\varphi)\,cH_Q + (1-\varphi)\left(-cov\left(\lambda,\varepsilon_F\right) - cH\right)\right]}\frac{A_{IT}}{g_A}\frac{dg_A}{dA_{IT}}$$

The overall effect on H_Q is $\eta_{H_Q,A_{IT}}^{\text{total}} = \eta_{H_Q,A_{IT}}^{\text{supply}} + \eta_{H_Q,A_{IT}}^{\text{demand}}$, which is negative if

$$\frac{dH_Q^{\text{total}}}{dA_{IT}} = c\left[\overset{<0}{\eta_{c,A_{IT}}} H_\phi + H\overset{>0}{\eta_{H,A_{IT}}}\right]\frac{1}{A_{IT}}H_Q^{1-\varphi} - \frac{(1-\varphi)\,cov\left(\lambda,\varepsilon_F\right)\nu}{\left(1-\alpha^2\right)}\left(\frac{\alpha^2}{c_x}\right)^{\frac{\varphi-\alpha}{1-\alpha}}(g_A)^{-\varphi}\frac{dg_A}{dA_{IT}} < 0$$

$$c\left[\overset{<0}{\eta_{c,A_{IT}}} H_\phi + H\overset{>0}{\eta_{H,A_{IT}}}\right]\frac{1}{A_{IT}}H_Q^{1-\varphi} < \frac{(1-\varphi)\,cov\left(\lambda,\varepsilon_F\right)\nu}{\left(1-\alpha^2\right)}\left(\frac{\alpha^2}{c_x}\right)^{\frac{\varphi-\alpha}{1-\alpha}} \times (g_A)^{-\varphi}\frac{dg_A}{dA_{IT}}$$

$$\frac{c\left(1-\alpha^2\right)}{v\left(1-\varphi\right)}\frac{\left[\overset{<0}{\eta_{c,A_{IT}}} H_\phi + H\overset{>0}{\eta_{H,A_{IT}}}\right]}{\left(\frac{\alpha^2}{c_x}\right)^{\frac{\varphi-\alpha}{1-\alpha}}}\frac{\left(\frac{H_Q}{g_A}\right)^{1-\varphi}}{\underset{<0}{\eta_{g_A,A_{IT}}}} > cov\left(\lambda,\varepsilon_F\right)$$

and thus,

$$\eta_{H_Q,A_{IT}}^{\text{total}} < 0$$

With this effect on H_Q and the assumption $\frac{dg_A}{dA_{IT}} < 0$, we can now determine the overall effect on the growth rate [from $g_N = \left(\left(\frac{\alpha^2}{c_x}\right)^{\frac{1}{1-\alpha}} H_Q\right)^{\varphi}(g_A)^{1-\varphi}$] and obtain

$$\eta_{g_N,A_{IT}} = \varphi\overset{<0}{\eta_{H_Q,A_{IT}}} + (1-\varphi)\overset{<0}{\eta_{g_A,A_{IT}}} < 0.$$

6 Investing in Artificial Intelligence

Breakthroughs and Backlashes

6.1 INTRODUCTION

Although an artificial general intelligence (AGI) does not yet exist, some anticipate that it would be only a matter of time before breakthrough innovations would render it possible. In Chapter 2, we discussed that the development of the transformer architecture on which LLMs such as GPT-4 are based has raised concern (and hope) in many circles that AI is getting closer to being an AGI. These LLMs have been referred to as artificial capable intelligence (ACI), "a fast-approaching point between AI and AGI" (Suleyman, 2023, p. vii), and according to Bubeck et al. (2023, p. 1), "Given the breadth and depth of GPT-4's capabilities, we believe that it could reasonably be viewed as an early (yet still incomplete) version of an artificial general intelligence (AGI) system." Nor surprisingly then that many AI experts expect an AGI to become a reality before 2060.[1]

An AGI would be a truly radical innovation, so radical that it could perhaps even be humans' last invention (Good, 1965). Whether it would be desirable, however, is hotly contested. Some hope that it will catapult innovation into exponential growth, culminating in a *Singularity* (Kurzweil, 2005), while others have warned that it could wipe humanity out or be misused by whoever invents it first, given its winner-takes-all consequences (Armstrong et al., 2016; Bostrom, 2014; Russel et al., 2015; Yudkowsky, 2023).

Whether an AGI will become a reality before 2060 depends on the extent and sustainability of investment into the broad R&D

[1] See, for cxample, https://research.aimultiple.com/artificial-general-intelligence-singularity-timing/ and https://aiimpacts.org/ai-timeline-surveys/

effort that it requires. So far, as we discussed in Chapter 2, developments in AI have traced a cyclical pattern of optimism followed by despair, breakthroughs followed by eventual backlashes. Historical accounts of the development of AI describe both these breakthroughs and backlashes, labeling the latter as "AI winters" and identifying such winters in the 1970s, 1980s, and 1990s (Floridi, 2020). These winters or backlashes were marked by a reduction in investment in R&D and a decline in venture capital (Liu et al., 2017) – see also the historical timeline of AI as discussed in Chapter 2. In 1973, for example, the Lighthill Report in the UK brought to an end a phase of investment in AI when it concluded that "in no part of the field have discoveries made so far produced the major impact that was then promised" (Hendler, 2008, p. 2). Thus, the failure of scientists to come up with a viable technology resulted in a backlash.

Conversely, as we pointed out in Chapter 2, the most recent AI winter gave way to a "spring" around 2006 following technological breakthroughs in deep learning by Hinton et al. (2006) and Hinton and Salakhutdinov (2006). Since 2012, there has been a boom in AI R&D and venture capital investments (Naudé, 2021). This has fueled hopes that this investment in AI R&D will ultimately lead to the development of an AGI. For instance, Joshi (2019) expects that "the rapid rate at which AI is developing new capabilities means that we might be get close to the inflection point when the AI research community surprises us with the development of artificial general intelligence."

The sensitivity of investment in a radical technology such as AI to either breakthroughs or backlashes is characteristic of most investments that are subject to substantial uncertainty, especially when coupled with winner-take-all outcomes and possible adverse social consequences. So far, however, there has been little consideration of this in the literature dealing with the possible realization of an AGI. Rather, the literature has dealt with the technical considerations, for instance, debating whether the ML approach will be able to lead to an AGI or whether a completely different tack is needed, outlining how an AGI can be made safe, or discussing the possibility and nature of an arms race for an AGI and how this could be influenced by AI governance (Armstrong et al., 2016; Bostrom, 2017; Naudé and Dimitri, 2020). The AGI literature has been more concerned about aligning the behavior of an AGI in its postinvention period, rather than on what determines investment in R&D in the preinvention period.

In this chapter, we use an extended real options model, proposed by Bilkic et al. (2013), that incorporates a stochastic compound Poisson process, to study the preinvention period in AI R&D. From this, we conclude that the investment effort for an AGI may ultimately be too time-consuming, and too expensive, to be feasible for most private firms. This has implications for the governance of AI and AI arms races, as it suggests that it will be largely government-funded agencies or state-owned enterprises efforts (e.g., by the USA or Chinese governments) and/or a few large corporations (such as Google or Alibaba) that will invent an AGI, if ever.

The chapter is structured as follows. Section 6.2 provides an overview of the relevant literature pertaining to investment in AI and real option modeling. Section 6.3 sets out our extended real options model. In Section 6.4, the model is used to analyze the duration and extent of R&D investment toward an AGI. Section 6.5 concludes.

6.2 RELEVANT LITERATURE

6.2.1 *Breakthroughs, Backlashes, and the Uncertainty of Investment in AI*

We begin by stressing the difference between incremental and radical innovations. Incremental innovations are "relatively minor changes in technology and provide relatively low incremental customer benefits per dollar," while radical innovations "involve substantially new technology and provide substantially greater customer benefits" (Chandy and Tellis, 1998, p. 476). Radical innovations tend to be disruptive (O'Connor and McDermott, 2004). Given that an AGI is a general-purpose technology that could be very disruptive, by leading to either a Singularity and/or an Apocalypse, it clearly counts as a "radical" innovation.

Investing in R&D for a radical innovation such as an AGI involves a great degree of uncertainty – much more so than the uncertainty characterizing investment for an incremental innovation. It requires that the firm or agency undertaking the R&D investments be prepared to make possibly very large investments in R&D over a sustained period, even if it does not deliver immediate results, with the hope that a breakthrough may eventually occur which would make all of the investment worthwhile. As we have mentioned in the introduction, research into AI actively started in the 1950s – and although many advances have been booked, more than seventy years later, the development of an AGI has not yet been achieved.

Indeed, during these seventy years, there have been several major events, which can be described as "jumps," that have either been negative or positive for the development of an AGI. For example, the year 1973 sent a major signal to investors that progress in AI was at a dead end, after which investment in AI collapsed (Hendler, 2008; Liu et al., 2017). Between the 1980s and 1987, there was again a boom in AI development, inspired by breakthroughs in the technology of expert systems (Durkin, 1996). By the end of the 1980s, a backlash again set in, mainly because the application of expert systems turned out to be too expensive and not profitable. Hundreds of AI-based firms went bankrupt (Newquist, 1994). And since 2006, the boom in AI has been fueled by technological breakthroughs in the technique of deep learning by Hinton et al. (2006) and Hinton and Salakhutdinov (2006). It is feared by some that this boom will come to an end soon, perhaps due to a backlash against "awful AI"[2] or due to a slowdown in advances in computing power (Moore's law) (Floridi, 2020; Hao, 2019; Naudé and Dimitri, 2021).

[2] See for instance the GitHub site devoted to Awful AI, at https://github.com/daviddao/awful-ai

Thus, both positive events such as breakthroughs (e.g., deep learning) and negative major events such as backlashes due to fears about Awful AI and/or high costs of adoption, growing government regulation of data, or even unmet expectations may cause the expected value of R&D going into AGI to exhibit major stochastic "jumps." These stochastic jumps take place against the fact that any investment aiming at a radical innovation would already be characterized by high costs, as a result of the costs of creating complementary inputs or markets to exploit radical innovations, because such R&D investment projects are complex to manage, and require patience and a long-term focus (Freeman, 1994; Marvel and Lumpkin, 2007; Golder et al., 2009). The high costs and uncertainty of generating radical innovation explain why it is most often the outcome of large firms' efforts, often with the support of (mission-oriented) governments (Ahuja and Lampert, 2001; Azoulay et al., 2018b; Hill and Rothaermel, 2003; Mazzucato, 2015, 2018).

The upshot is that a breakthrough that will lead to an AGI is not guaranteed. In particular, since the current state of scientific knowledge about intelligence, the human brain, and related aspects such as consciousness may still be too rudimentary to allow a breakthrough AGI innovation – see, for instance, the arguments in Meese (2018), Allen and Greaves (2011), and Koch (2012).

6.2.2 *Real Option Models*

Real option models are well-established tools to inform intertemporal optimization choices in the face of irreversible cost in investment, where deferring a decision has value (Dixit, 1989, 1993). It therefore seems well suited to study the question of how much and for how long to invest in R&D for an AGI.[3]

Examples of studies using real option theory to study the optimal timing and investment in technology invention and adoption include Farzin et al. (1998), Whalley (2011), Sarkar (2000), Jorgensen

[3] In this section we draw on Bilkic et al. (2013).

et al. (2006), and Doraszelski (2001). For instance, Doraszelski (2001) found that uncertainty about when a new technology will arrive and how disruptive it may be may lead firms to postpone innovations or technology adoptions. Sarkar (2000) considered circumstances when an increase in uncertainty may cause firms to accelerate investments in R&D.

These studies, typical of the literature on real option models, model the stochastic process either by a Brownian motion or a simple Poisson process. This may not be appropriate when dealing with significant random jumps associated with breakthroughs and backlashes in AI as described in Subsection 6.2.1. Particularly, one needs to allow for uncertainty about the time of occurrence of a jump (breakthrough or backlash) as well as about its magnitude. As pointed out by Bilkic et al. (2013), the innovation literature has neglected the decision on how long to sustain investment in R&D for a radical innovation, particularly in the face of nontrivial stochastic jumps.

Such nontrivial stochastic jumps have been studied in the fields of financial economics, business cycle theory, and natural hazards. Merton (1976) introduced jump processes into financial economics to deal with "rare" events that lead to sudden large changes in the values of financial assets. Studies on natural hazards have modeled these as sudden (downward) jumps and jump diffusion processes in certain measurements (Cox and Pedersen, 2000; Cox et al., 2004; Yang and Zhang, 2005; Jang, 2007). A discussion of general "jump diffusion processes" and their characteristics is contained in Kou (2002), Kou and Wang (2003), Cai and Kou (2011), and Pham (1997).

In Section 6.3, we use the real option model extended by Bilkic et al. (2013) to include stochastic jumps, which we then deploy to analyze the magnitude and duration of investment in R&D for an AGI.

6.3 THE MODEL

Before deriving our model mathematically, we provide an intuitive description.

6.3.1 Intuitive Description

When a firm or government scientific agency invests in R&D for a radical innovation such as an AGI, it has to overcome challenges. The first to achieve technical success by developing a workable AGI (as in this case). The second challenge is to successfully commercialize the new technology. In the case of commercialization, it may not be automatic to assume that an AGI will be profitable: it may be nationalized or restricted through regulations and/or a competing AGI.

The period before invention and commercialization, which is wherein the world is at the moment of writing, is characterized by ongoing investments in technological innovation – for example, in expanding and improving deep learning algorithms, gathering and improving the quality of data, and boosting computer power further. It is expensive and may take a very long time – currently, the AI R&D stage is already exceeding eighty years!

The firm or agency constantly evaluates whether, and if so when, the AGI is ready to be launched and commercialized. Therefore, at any moment, this evaluation could lead the firm or agency to (1) enter the market with the new invention; (2) postpone market entry to the future and continue investment in R&D; or (3) realize that eventual commercialization will be unprofitable – perhaps due to determining in its evaluation that the technology that they have been working on is a dead end and/or that a consumer and regulatory backlash is eminent.

In the case of (2), the firm or agency postpones market entry in order to invest further in R&D. Further investments may improve the technology. Also, by in effect exercising the option of waiting with market entry, the firm may benefit from changes in the market, such as new complementary technologies and favorable changes in attitudes and regulations on AGI.

The questions that our model helps to answer in this regard are what criteria should the optimizing firm be using when evaluating whether and when to enter the market, or instead to exercise the option of waiting and investing more? or to stop pursuing investment toward the radical innovation altogether?

In the rest of this section, we describe how our model helps to answer these questions by focusing on four key decisions: (1) how much accumulated investments to make toward an AGI?; (2) how to evaluate the potential profit at market entry?; (3) how to model the expected profit flow subsequent to commercialization?; and (4) whether to consider the option value of postponing commercialization and continuing with R&D investment toward an AGI.

6.3.2 *How Much to Invest in an AGI*

The time at which a firm or agency commences its R&D investment project aimed at investing in an AGI is $t = 0$. This could be at the beginning of a new AI boom phase. The current AI boom phase started roughly around 2007, due to the availability of data and ICT connectivity (see, e.g., Friedman, 2016). How much and for how long to maintain this R&D investment project is, as we discussed in Section 5.2, of unknown duration.

The R&D cost is denoted by C. These costs, which we assume are constant, will differ among firms and agencies depending on firm-specific innovation capabilities. Total R&D investment is denoted by $I(T)$, which consists of the sum C incurred during the R&D period. Thus, at time T, when the AGI is launched, the total value investment in R&D will amount to

$$I(T) = \int_0^T Ce^{r(T-t)}dt, \tag{6.1}$$

Here, r denotes the risk-free interest rate.

6.3.3 *Potential Profit at Market Entry*

While undertaking R&D, progress in the technological sophistication of the AGI will at each moment in time be associated with a particular level of profit (Y) that can be realized if it should be placed on the market then. This reflects the fact that an AGI invention will be at various states of sophistication – some AGIs can be better then others in terms of quality, safety, and other features (Bostrom, 2017; Armstrong et al., 2016). However, at any period, the profit associated with the state of the AGI, even if positive, may not be adequate. As we mentioned, the profitability of an eventual AGI for the firm or agency developing it will depend on factors such as whether it may be nationalized or restricted through regulations and/or face a competing AGI.

Hence, the firm or agency may just continue its R&D efforts, perhaps to comply with or by-pass regulations, improve the alignment of the AGI with human interest, or improve the quality and safety to an extent that it will outperform a potential rival's AGI. Each additional period that the firm abstains from market entry, it benefits from the possibility of further technical progress or favorable changes in market conditions. Hence, postponing market entry could potentially be profitable – however, it also does not need to be. For instance, while further R&D could produce a breakthrough in terms of the technology that will enable the AGI, it could also fail, run up against a deep technological problem, or encounter stricter legislation and regulations. The breakthrough would represent an upward jump in the economic value that will be realized from R&D, and the backlash would represent a downward jump.

Jump processes are needed to model these potential breakthroughs or backlashes/failures in R&D that will cause significant stochastic shocks to the profit (Y) from the AGI. Therefore, the development of potential profits ($\tilde{Y}$) from market entry during any R&D period can be specified an *compound Poisson process*:

$$d\tilde{Y} = \tilde{Y} \int_{U_1} u N_1(t, du) \quad \textit{for} \quad 0 < t < T. \tag{6.2}$$

Here the stochastic "jump" is the integral $\int_{U_1} z N_1(t, dz)$ where $N_1(t, dz)$ a Poisson process that has an intensity of λ_1 and U_1 is the step height at which nontrivial stochastic jumps accumulate. It is a Borel set (Λ) in $\mathbb{R}$ such that $0 \notin \Lambda$.

The essence of Equation (2) is to specify the accumulation of stochastic jumps with the implication that the occurrence of breakthroughs and backlashes in this model is unpredictable.

6.3.4 *Profit Flow after Market Entry*

When a firm or agency has decided to commercialize its current form of AGI, its profits depend on market conditions – which are highly uncertain. The conditions may either be good or bad for profits. For example, if the market contains some other technological invention or resource that is complementary to their AGI technology, it will be good for profits. However, market conditions may be characterized by a consumer backlash against an AGI, with governments restricting its free use, which would be bad for profits. It could also be that potential profitability is negatively affected by a macroeconomic recession, perhaps due to an unexpected crisis, such as posed by a global pandemic or global financial crisis.

Based on these considerations, profit flow after the market can be described as following a second compound Poisson process:

$$dY = Y \int_{U_2} z N_2(t, dz) \quad \text{for} \quad T < t. \tag{6.3}$$

In Equation (3), the accumulation of stochastic jumps associated with good or bad macroeconomic prospects for profits is denoted by the integral $\int_{U_2} z N_2(t, dz)$. The term $N_2(t, dz)$ describes a Poisson process with λ_2 intensity. As previously, the stochastic jumps have an uncertain step height of U_2, which is a Borel set (Λ) in $\mathbb{R}$ such that $0 \notin \Lambda$. It indicates that stochastic jumps are random – and can be positive as well as negative.

Once the AGI is launched, the profit stream will evolve according to this random process. If we assume a risk-neutral firm or agent, the market value of its R&D V^{gross} is given by the expected present value of the profit stream:

$$V^{gross} = \frac{Y(T)}{\left(r - \int\limits_{f^{-1}(U_2)} z\upsilon_2(dz) - \int\limits_{U_2} [\ln(1+z) - z]\,\upsilon_2(dz)\right)}; \tag{6.4}$$

$$r > \int\limits_{f^{-1}(U_2)} z\upsilon_2(dz) + \int\limits_{U_2} [\ln(1+z) - z]\,\upsilon_2(dz),$$

with r the risk-free interest rate. f is the function $f(z) = ln(1 + z)$ and υ_2 the Lévy measure of the Poisson process N_2, which describes the expected number of jumps. The firm or agent undertaking the investment is assumed to have an infinite life.

The expected net value from launching the AGI is calculated as the expected gross value (6.4) minus the costs of innovation $I(T)$:

$$V = V^{gross} - I(T).$$

6.3.5 *Option Value of Innovation*

Although market entry may be profitable at a particular point in time, it may still be better to defer it and continue investment in R&D – deferral may have an option value as we discussed, and which we now denote by F. Taking this into account in the compound Poisson process (6.2) results in the Hamilton–Jacobi–Bellman equation:

$$rFdt = E(dF). \tag{6.5}$$

This indicates that the expected return on investment in R&D is equal to the expected rate of capital appreciation, over the period dt.

6.4 MODEL ANALYTICS

The model described in Section 6.3 can now be used to derive the duration and amount of R&D to be invested in an AGI. First, we derive the duration and implied amount of investment, where after we consider the determinants of the duration.

6.4.1 *Expected Time of Market Entry*

The firm or agent investing in R&D aiming at an AGI will constantly evaluate (V) against the option value (F) of continued R&D investment (Bilkic et al., 2009).

F is obtained by solving (see Bilkic et al., 2013):

$$\max\left\{V^{\text{gross}}(T) - I(T), F(T)\right\}. \tag{6.6}$$

This shows that the expected time of market entry results from first determining the level of profits (the threshold Y^*) that will trigger such entry. When this threshold is reached, the value of current R&D exceeds (F) (Bilkic et al., 2009). Consequently, market entry is indicated.

The expected time at which market entry will occur will secondarily be determined by whether the premarket entry value $\tilde{Y}$ is equal to or greater than this threshold value or not.

This leads us to recall proposition 1 from Bilkic et al. (2013):

For the costs of innovation I, a premarket entry value of current profits (6.2), and future profit streams after market entry as per Equation (6.3), we can determine the threshold Y^* that would trigger the commercialization of the AGI invention

$$Y^* = \frac{\beta}{\beta - 1}\left[r - \int\limits_{f^{-1}(U_2)} z\upsilon_2(dz) - \int\limits_{U_2} [\ln(1+z) - z]\,\upsilon_2(dz)\right] I(T) \tag{6.7}$$

$$\text{with } r > \int\limits_{f^{-1}(U_2)} z\upsilon_2(dz) + \int\limits_{U_2} [\ln(1+z) - z]\,\upsilon_2(dz)$$

β is an implicit function resulting from the differential equation $rFdt = E(dF)$ with solution $F = B\tilde{Y}^{\beta}$.

Proof: see Appendix A at the end of this chapter. □

In determining the expected time at which the premarket entry value ($\tilde{Y}$) will reach the threshold (6.7) and trigger market entry, we use the double exponential distribution of Kou and Wang (2003) as for this an analytical solution is possible in the event that overshooting occurs. It can be written as

$$h(z) = p\eta_1 e^{-\eta_1 z} 1_{\{z \geq 0\}} + q\eta_2 e^{\eta_2 z} 1_{\{z<0\}},$$

where p is the probability of a *breakthrough* and q is the probability of a *backlash*. It is the case that $p + q = 1$. $\frac{1}{\eta_1}$ and $\frac{1}{\eta_2}$ are the means of the two exponential distributions. These are distributions of deferment of entry, given breakthroughs or backlashes.

In order to analytically determine the expected time at which the premarket entry value $(\tilde{Y})$ is expected to reach the threshold, we allow for a nonlinear development of the threshold. As in Bilkic et al. (2009) and Bilkic et al. (2013) for the random process ($\tilde{Y}$ see Equation (6.2)), we derive the expected time of first realizing or overshooting a certain market entry profit $\tilde{Y}_i$ (given the existing value $\tilde{Y}_0$). By calling on the Girsanov theorem, we can derive a probability density function for $\tilde{T}_i$. Given that we can determine the expected time of first realizing or overshooting of each value of the strictly monotonic increasing sequence $\tilde{Y}_i \in \left\{\tilde{Y}_1, \tilde{Y}_2, \ldots, \tilde{Y}_n\right\}$ with $0 = \tilde{Y}_1 \leq \tilde{Y}_2 \leq \cdots \leq \tilde{Y}_n$ and $\tilde{Y}_1 > \tilde{Y}_0$, we can write the expected first realization or overshooting time as a function of $\tilde{Y}_i$ and of the overall drift of the jump process $\bar{u} = \lambda_1 \left(\frac{p}{\eta_1} - \frac{q}{\eta_2}\right)$.

Using the compound Poisson process (6.2), we can derive the expected time of first realization or overshooting $E\tilde{T}$ of each market profit $\tilde{Y}_i \in \left\{\tilde{Y}_1, \tilde{Y}_2, \ldots, \tilde{Y}_n\right\}$ with $0 = \tilde{Y}_1 \leq \tilde{Y}_2 \leq \cdots \leq \tilde{Y}_n$ and $\tilde{Y}_1 > \tilde{Y}_0$ as a function of $\tilde{Y}_i$, and hence determine the expected time until any market entry profit $\tilde{Y}$ is reached for the first time as:

$$E(\tilde{T}) = \frac{1}{\bar{u}} \left[\tilde{Y}_i + \frac{\mu_2^* - \eta_1}{\eta_1 \mu_2^*}(1 - e^{-Y^* \mu_2^*})\right]. \tag{6.8}$$

$\bar{u}$ refers to the overall drift $\bar{u} = \lambda_1 \left(\frac{p}{\eta_1} - \frac{q}{\eta_2}\right)$ of the jump process, and μ_2^* is a constant derived in the technical note, for which $0 < \eta_1 < \mu_2^* < \infty$ holds.

Proof: see Appendix A at the end of this chapter. □

To determine the expected time at which the premarket entry value $(\tilde{Y})$ is expected to reach the threshold T^*, we have to compare all points $(\tilde{Y}_i, E(\tilde{T}, \tilde{Y}_i))$ and (Y_i, T) from the sets of the threshold as well as from the ET_i set and choose the point that is included in both sets.

The resulting T^* determines the expected time at which the premarket entry value $(\tilde{Y})$ is expected to attain the threshold. As the image set of ET_i is a sequence, there may be no exact match with the threshold. In this case, we choose the first point in time for which the threshold exceeds ET_i, that is, $T(Y) > E(\tilde{T}, \tilde{Y}_i)$. The next proposition provides conditions for the existence of a solution to the expected time at which the premarket entry value $(\tilde{Y})$ is expected to cross the threshold.

With the threshold $Y^*(T)$ (see Equation (6.9)), the expected first-time realization of initial market profit $E\tilde{T}$ (see Equation (6.8)), and conditions (6.10) and (6.11), there exists an expected time to enter the market $T^* = E(T) > 0$. T^* is the first time point for which the following conditions hold:

$$T^*(Y) \geq E(\tilde{T}, \tilde{Y}_i). \tag{6.9}$$

$$\frac{1}{r}\ln\frac{\tilde{Y}_1 + KC}{KC} < \frac{1}{\bar{u}}\left[\tilde{Y}_1 + \frac{\mu_2^* - \eta_1}{\eta_1\mu_2^*}(1 - e^{-\tilde{Y}_1\mu_2^*})\right], \tag{6.10}$$

$$\frac{1}{r}\ln\frac{\left(\tilde{Y}_t + KC\right)\left(\tilde{Y}_i + KC\right)}{\left(\tilde{Y}_s + KC\right)\left(\tilde{Y}_j + KC\right)} < \frac{1}{\bar{u}}\left[\begin{array}{c}\tilde{Y}_t + \tilde{Y}_i - \tilde{Y}_s - \tilde{Y}_j \\ +\frac{\mu_2^*-\eta_1}{\eta_1\mu_2^*}(e^{-\tilde{Y}_s\mu_2^*} + e^{-\tilde{Y}_j\mu_2^*} \\ -e^{-\tilde{Y}_t\mu_2^*} - e^{-\tilde{Y}_i\mu_2^*})\end{array}\right] \tag{6.11}$$

with $K = \frac{\beta}{\beta-1}(r - \int_{f^{-1}(U_2)} z\upsilon_2(dz) - \int_{U_2} [\ln(1+z) - z]\,\upsilon_2(dz) - \alpha)$.

Proof: see Appendix A at the end of this chapter. □

The existence of T^* means that at any period, a firm or agency could consider deferring entry and continue to invest in the R&D project. Because the threshold is higher than the expected market profit means that innovation costs during the R&D phase (preceding T^*) and the option value to enter the market are not yet compensated by the current value of R&D.

In addition, condition (6.10) is important to understand the logic of the decision problem.[4] The decision in favor of initiating a research process for a certain time will only be positive if the minimum profit is sufficiently small compared to the R&D costs at the beginning, and that the time path of the research value can

[4] Both conditions are required for the existence of a solution to the problem.

be expected to hit the profit threshold as the result of the research activity.

Further, T^* indicates the expected duration of research under the present conditions. T^* is the answer to the question of how long a firm or agency may invest in R&D. Second, with T^*, the firm or agency aiming for an AGI can also determine their expected total investment volume $I(T^*)$.

6.4.2 Determinants of Expected Time of Market Entry

In the previous sections (Sections 6.3 and 6.4.1), we showed that high uncertainty or stochastic shocks and irreversibility are important ingredients of a radical innovation process such as that for an AGI. In this section, we provide a closer examination of the effects of such stochastic shocks. In particular, we consider the frequency of jumps and the effect of the jump size during the innovation period, where we can already identify a market entry but when the firm has not yet decided to commercialize its available AGI.

An increase in the frequency of sudden breakthroughs or backlashes during the R&D period is generally ambiguous. However, an increase in λ_1 may lead to an earlier market entry ET^* if $\frac{p}{\eta_1} - \frac{q}{\eta_2} > 0, 1 < \frac{\mu_2^* - \eta_1}{\eta_1} e^{-Y^* \mu_2^*}$ and the sum of upward jumps is sufficiently large to outweigh the sum of negative jumps so that $\frac{\partial \beta}{\partial \lambda_1} < 0$.

$$
\begin{aligned}
\frac{\partial E(T^*)}{\partial \lambda_1} = & -\frac{\left(\frac{p}{\eta_1} - \frac{q}{\eta_2}\right)}{\left[\lambda_1 \left(\frac{p}{\eta_1} - \frac{q}{\eta_2}\right)\right]^2} \left[Y^* + \frac{\mu_2^* - \eta_1}{\eta_1 \mu_2^*} (1 - e^{-Y^* \mu_2^*}) \right] \\
& + \frac{1}{\lambda_1 \left(\frac{p}{\eta_1} - \frac{q}{\eta_2}\right)} \left[\begin{array}{c} -\frac{\frac{\partial \beta}{\partial \lambda_1}}{(\beta - 1)^2} (r - \int\limits_{f^{-1}(U_2)} z v(dz) \\ - \int\limits_{U_2} [\ln (1 + z)] \, v_2(dz)) \end{array} \right] \\
& \cdot (1 - \frac{\mu_2^* - \eta_1}{\eta_1} e^{-Y^* \mu_2^*}) < 0.
\end{aligned}
$$

Proof: see Appendix B at the end of this chapter. □

The conditions $\frac{p}{\eta_1} - \frac{q}{\eta_2} > 0$ and $1 < \frac{\mu_2^* - \eta_1}{\eta_1} e^{-Y^* \mu_2^*}$ are connected to the probabilities of sudden breakthroughs or backlashes and the mean waiting times until an event occurs. The decision whether to enter the market if the frequency of jumps increases strongly depends on the direction of those jumps and therefore whether a sudden breakthrough or a backlash happens. In general, an increase in λ_1 implies that more fundamental events are occurring that imply non-marginal changes in the expected path of technical findings and the associated profits. Hence, sudden positive discoveries become more frequent and the increase in the value of research results accelerates.

An increase in the magnitude of breakthroughs or backlashes during the R&D period is generally ambiguous. However, an increase in u leads to an earlier market entry if $\frac{p}{\eta_1} - \frac{q}{\eta_2} > 0$, $1 < \frac{\mu_2^* - \eta_1}{\eta_1} e^{-Y^* \mu_2^*}$ and the sum of upward jumps is sufficiently large to outweigh the sum of downward jumps so that $\frac{\partial \beta}{\partial u} < 0$.

$$\frac{\partial E(T^*)}{\partial u} = \frac{\left(1 - \frac{\mu_2^* - \eta_1}{\eta_1} e^{-Y^* \mu_2^*}\right)}{\lambda_1 \left(\frac{p}{\eta_1} - \frac{q}{\eta_2}\right)} \cdot \left[\frac{-\frac{\partial \beta}{\partial u}}{(\beta - 1)^2} \begin{pmatrix} r - \int\limits_{f^{-1}(U_2)} z v(dz) \\ - \int\limits_{U_2} [\ln(1+z) - z] \, v_2(dz) \end{pmatrix} I(T) \right] < 0.$$

Proof: see Appendix B at the end of this chapter. □

An increase in u means that breakthroughs become more beneficial and threats less disastrous. Larger upward jumps suggest that research steps are larger up to a sudden immediate breakthrough and hence a successful market entry can be expected earlier. Hence, discoveries become more important and have a larger impact, with just one new research result potentially producing the final invention needed to successfully enter the market.

While the above two effects consider large uncertain events during the phase of research, the following two effects look at large uncertain events after market entry and reflect the impact of these high market uncertainties on the investment decision.

An increase in the frequency of sudden breakthroughs or backlashes after market entry is generally ambiguous. However, an increase in λ_2 may lead to an earlier market entry ET^* if $\frac{p}{\eta_1} - \frac{q}{\eta_2} > 0$, $\frac{\mu_2^* - \eta_1}{\eta_1} e^{-Y^* \mu_2^*} > 1$, and the sum of upward jumps is sufficiently large to outweigh the sum of negative jumps.

$$\frac{\partial E(T^*)}{\partial \lambda_2} = \frac{1}{\lambda_1\left(\frac{p}{\eta_1} - \frac{q}{\eta_2}\right)} \left[\frac{\beta}{\beta - 1} \left(\begin{array}{c} -\int\limits_{f^{-1}(U_2)} zh(dz) \\ -\int\limits_{U_2} [\ln(1+z) - z]\, h(dz) \end{array} \right) I(T) \right] \times \left(1 - \frac{\mu_2^* - \eta_1}{\eta_1} e^{-Y^*\mu_2^*}\right) > 0.$$

Proof: see Appendix B at the end of this chapter. □

As we discuss in Appendix B at the end of this chapter, the sign of the derivative according to λ_2 is ambiguous. However, we assume that breakthroughs are frequent and large enough to outweigh the sum of backlashes such that a fast market entry will be preferred. More positive jumps indicate that more breakthroughs than threats and losses can be expected after market entry. Having invented an AGI and launched it on the market, new information may reveal additional and unexpected applications for the AGI. Upon market entry, information about the new product will spread, enabling the firm to expand the uptake of the AGI. This will make market entry more attractive, so the firm or agency may then want to try and enter the market with its first viable AGI prototype.

An increase in the magnitude of breakthroughs and backlashes after market entry is ambiguous. However, an increase in z leads to an earlier market entry if $\frac{p}{\eta_1} - \frac{q}{\eta_2} > 0$, $\frac{\mu_2^* - \eta_1}{\eta_1} e^{-Y^*\mu_2^*} > 1$ and the sum of upward jumps is sufficiently large to outweigh the sum of downward jumps.

$$\frac{\partial E(T^*)}{\partial z} = \frac{1}{\lambda\left(\frac{p}{\eta_1} - \frac{q}{\eta_2}\right)} \left[\begin{array}{l} -\underbrace{\frac{\beta}{\beta-1}}_{>0}\Big(\int\limits_{f^{-1}(U_2)} 1\upsilon_2(dz) \\ +\int\limits_{U_2} \left[\frac{1}{(1+z)} - 1\right] \upsilon_2(dz)\Big) \underbrace{I(T)}_{>0} \end{array} \right] \left(1 - \frac{\mu_2^* - \eta_1}{\eta_1} e^{-Y^*\mu_2^*}\right) < 0$$

Proof: see Appendix B at the end of this chapter. □

An increase in z indicates that opportunities become more beneficial and threats less disastrous. Larger upward jumps imply that the benefits from opportunities provided by market entry increase. At the same time, smaller downward jumps reduce the loss in profits generated by threats. Hence, opportunities are more beneficial than threats, so that market entry is expected to have a greater payoff. We observe that further R&D becomes less attractive because the existing AGI prototype, even if not perfect, and perhaps subject to safety risks, promises such commercialization success that an earlier market entry is preferred.

From the model analytics described in this section, we can conclude that stochastic shocks have a determining impact on the decision to invest in R&D for an AGI. The extent of R&D may be prolonged or terminated, potentially affecting the safety of an AGI, depending on such stochastic events.

6.5 CONCLUDING REMARKS

The firms or agents that invest in R&D in search of an AGI, which can potentially yield winner-take-all-benefits, need to take strategic decisions with respect to the possibility of the occurrence (or not) of stochastic events such as breakthroughs and backlashes. The key strategic decisions for a firm or agent that wishes to be a successful developer and provider of an AGI are (1) how much to invest in R&D; and (2) when to bring the AGI prototype innovation to market.

In this chapter, we used an extended real options model to derive the optimal entry timing and show that stochastic jumps such as breakthroughs and backlashes affect both the investment amount and market entry decisions of firms and agents that aim to develop an AGI. The novelty is twofold: first, we considered the economic dimensions of developing an AGI – in contrast to most of the literature where considerations of technical and ethical feasibility dominate; and second, by using a novel extended real options theory that includes non-marginal stochastic jump processes, we discussed the effects of such large uncertain events on the AGI investment decision.

From our model analytics, we determined that the average magnitude of sudden events as well as the direction (up or down) and frequency of the associated jumps are the most important parameters in this highly uncertain decision process. These stochastic shocks imply that investment in an AGI will be too time-consuming and expensive for most private entrepreneurs. Hence, if ever an AGI will be realized, it will most likely be either through the investment efforts of a government, such as the USA or Chinese governments, or the efforts of a very large private firm with deep pockets and other resources for innovation in the AI field, such as Google or Alibaba.

The downside of this is that whether or not an AGI will ever be invented will depend on only a few efforts, and may suggest that a Singularity or "explosive growth" as envisaged by Erdil and Besiroglu (2023) will not occur any time soon. The upside however is that an arms race for an AGI, which may result in an inferior and unsafe AGI being pushed into the market, may be easier to avoid, as the coordination and collaboration possibilities are easier with fewer players in the markets, and governments may threaten the postcommercialization profits of such firms and agencies to put pressure on them to postpone launching the AGI to a later date when a better quality can be ensured. It may also be easier to govern and check the process of development of the AGI if the appropriate regulatory and transparency measures can be agreed on at a global level.

In Chapter 7, we delve deeper into how governments may regulate the arms race for an AGI. We do so through a game-theoretic lens. Our point of departure is Armstrong et al. (2016) who established that the likelihood of avoiding an AI disaster and getting a "friendlier" AGI depends crucially on reducing the number of competing teams (which we showed in this chapter not to be very large due to the nature of the innovation process). They also established that with better AI development capabilities, research teams will be less inclined to take risks in compromising on safety and alignment. The unanswered questions in Armstrong et al. (2016) are however: "precisely how government can steer the number of competing teams? How can government policy reduce competition in the race for an AGI and raise the importance of capability? Should AI be taxed and/or nationalized?" (Naudé and Dimitri, 2020, p. 369).

Chapter 7 answers these questions and shows that the danger of an unfriendly AGI can in principle be reduced by taxing AI and by using public procurement.

Appendices

Appendix A: Expected Time of Market Entry

Proof of Proposition 1. Apply the boundary conditions

$$F(0) = 0$$

$$F(Y^*) = V^{\text{gross}}(Y^*) - I \qquad \textit{value matching condition,}$$

$$\frac{dF(Y^*)}{dY} = \frac{d(V^{\text{gross}}(Y^*) - I)}{dY} \qquad \textit{smooth pasting condition.}$$

and solve the equation system for Y^*. □

Proof of Proposition 2. The problem of determining the expected time at which the premarket entry value $(\tilde{Y})$ is expected to reach the threshold T^* can be solved analytically if we assume an explicit distribution of the jump sizes. Following Kou and Wang (2003), we assume the double exponential distribution

$$h(z) = p\eta_1 e^{-\eta_1 z} 1_{\{z \geq 0\}} + q\eta_2 e^{\eta_2 z} 1_{\{z<0\}},$$

where p is the probability of a positive jump (a breakthrough) and q for a negative jump (backlash), respectively. $\frac{1}{\eta_1}$ and $\frac{1}{\eta_2}$ are the means of the two exponential distributions. The moment generating function for $\tilde{Y}(t)$ with $\theta \in (-\eta_2, \eta_1)$ is

$$\phi(\theta, t) := E(e^{\theta \tilde{Y}(t)}) = \exp(G(\theta)t)$$

where the function G is defined as

$$G(x) := \lambda_1 \left(\frac{p\eta_1}{\eta_1 - x} + \frac{p\eta_2}{\eta_2 + x} - 1 \right).$$

To determine the expected time at which the premarket entry value $(\tilde{Y})$ is expected to reach the threshold T^* times, one has to consider the exact hit of a constant boundary, as well as overshooting. Accordingly, two cases can be distinguished. The Laplace transformation of the first hitting time, which is when $\tilde{Y}(t)$ hits the boundary Y^* exactly, is:

$$E(e^{-\varepsilon \tilde{T}_i} 1_{\{\tilde{Y}(\tilde{T}_i)=Y^*\}}) = \frac{\eta_1 - \beta_{1,\varepsilon}}{\beta_{2,\varepsilon} - \beta_{1,\varepsilon}} e^{-Y^*\beta_{1,\varepsilon}} + \frac{\beta_{2,\varepsilon} - \eta_1}{\beta_{2,\varepsilon} - \beta_{1,\varepsilon}} e^{-Y^*\beta_{2,\varepsilon}}$$

with $\mu_{1,\varepsilon}$ and $\mu_{2,\varepsilon}$ being the only positive roots of $G(\beta) = \varepsilon$ and $0 < \beta_{1,\varepsilon} < \eta_1 < \beta_{2,\varepsilon} < \infty$. For every overshoot $\tilde{Y}(\tilde{T}) - Y^*$, the Laplace transformation is

$$E(e^{-\varepsilon \tilde{T}} 1_{\{\tilde{Y}(\tilde{T}_i)-Y^*>y\}}) = e^{-\eta_1 y} \frac{(\eta_1 - \mu_{1,\varepsilon})(\mu_{2,\varepsilon} - \eta_1)}{\eta_1(\mu_{2,\varepsilon} - \mu_{1,\varepsilon})} \left(e^{-Y^*\mu_{1,\varepsilon}} - e^{-Y^*\mu_{2,\varepsilon}}\right)$$

$$\text{for all } y \geq 0.$$

The expectation of the expected time at which the premarket entry value $(\tilde{Y})$ is expected to reach the threshold T^* is finite, that is, $E(T^*) < \infty$, if and only if the overall drift of the jump process is positive. Hence,

$$E(T^*) < \infty \Leftrightarrow \bar{u} = \lambda_1 \left(\frac{p}{\eta_1} - \frac{q}{\eta_2}\right) > 0.$$

Now for $\bar{u} > 0$, we determine the expected time at which the premarket entry value $(\tilde{Y})$ is expected to reach the threshold T^* as

$$E(T^*) = \frac{1}{\bar{u}} \left[Y^* + \frac{\mu_2^* - \eta_1}{\eta_1 \mu_2^*} (1 - e^{-Y^*\mu_2^*}) \right] \tag{6.12}$$

where μ_2^* is defined as the unique root of $G(\mu_2^*) = 0$ with $0 < \eta_1 < \mu_2^* < \infty$. □

Proof of Proposition 3. For each $\tilde{Y}_i$, we can determine the corresponding expected time $E(\tilde{T}_i)$ when this market entry profit $\tilde{Y}_i$ is reached for the first time. In order to find the expected time of market entry, we have to consider all combinations of profit levels $\tilde{Y}_i$ (and, Y_i respectively) and the required time to reach this level $E(\tilde{T}_i)$ (T_i, respectively) from the expected time at which the premarket entry value $(\tilde{Y})$ is expected to reach the threshold T^* and the threshold function. That is, we compare the image sets of those functions and choose the point in time, which refers to the exact hit or overshoot of the threshold as the expected time of market entry. The proof for the existence of this point is as follows.

Assume that $\tilde{Y}_i$ is an element of the strictly monotonic increasing sequence $\left\{\tilde{Y}_0, \tilde{Y}_1, \ldots, \tilde{Y}_n\right\}$ with $0 = \tilde{Y}_0 \leq \tilde{Y}_1 \leq \cdots \leq \tilde{Y}_n$, so that $E(\tilde{T})$ can be written as a function of any $\tilde{Y}_i$. In this case, $E(\tilde{T}, \tilde{Y}_i)$ is a strictly monotonic increasing sequence as well, and all pairs of values $(\tilde{Y}_i, E(\tilde{T}, \tilde{Y}_i))$ form its image set. In order to derive the expected time before market entry, which is the time at which $\tilde{Y}$ reaches the time-dependent threshold Y^* for the first time, we have to prove that there exists a point $(\tilde{Y}_i, E(\tilde{T}, \tilde{Y}_i))$ which is also in the image set of the function $T(Y)$. $T(Y)$ is determined by the threshold curve

$$Y^*(T) = \underbrace{\frac{\beta}{\beta - 1}\left(r - \int_{f^{-1}(U_2)} z\upsilon_2(dz) - \int_{U_2} [\ln(1+z) - z]\,\upsilon_2(dz) - \alpha\right)C}_{=:K}\left(e^{rT} - 1\right)$$

$$= KC\left(e^{rT} - 1\right) = KCe^{rT} - KC$$

$$\Rightarrow T^*(Y) = \frac{1}{r}\ln\frac{Y + KC}{KC}.$$

The proof is as follows. We analyze the functions $E(\tilde{T}, \tilde{Y}_i)$ and $T(Y)$ near the origin and show that one function lies above the other. Next, we can show that although both curves increase, the increasing rate of one function decreases faster, leading to an image point that may be in both image sets. Hence, we consider the two functions in 0.

$$T(0) = \frac{1}{r}\ln\frac{0 + KC}{KC} = 0$$

and

$$E(\tilde{T}, 0) = \frac{1}{\bar{u}}\left[0 + \frac{\mu_2^* - \eta_1}{\eta_1\mu_2^*}\left(1 - e^{-0\mu_2^*}\right)\right] = 0.$$

As both functions start in 0, we consider their increment of growth between 0 and $\tilde{Y}_1$.

$$\frac{\frac{1}{r}\ln\frac{\tilde{Y}_1 + KC}{KC} - \frac{1}{r}\ln\frac{0 + KC}{KC}}{\tilde{Y}_1}$$

$$= \frac{\frac{1}{r}\ln\frac{\tilde{Y}_1 + KC}{KC}}{\tilde{Y}_1}$$

$$\frac{\frac{1}{\bar{u}}\left[\tilde{Y}_1+\frac{\mu_2^*-\eta_1}{\eta_1\mu_2^*}(1-e^{-\tilde{Y}_1\mu_2^*})\right]-\frac{1}{\bar{u}}\left[\tilde{Y}_1+\frac{\mu_2^*-\eta_1}{\eta_1\mu_2^*}(1-e^{-\tilde{Y}_1\mu_2^*})\right]}{\tilde{Y}_1}$$

$$=\frac{\frac{1}{\bar{u}}\left[\tilde{Y}_1+\frac{\mu_2^*-\eta_1}{\eta_1\mu_2^*}(1-e^{-\tilde{Y}_1\mu_2^*})\right]}{\tilde{Y}_1}.$$

The increment of growth of $T(Y)$ is smaller than the increment of growth of $E(\tilde{T},Y)$ for

$$\frac{1}{r}\ln\frac{\tilde{Y}_1+KC}{KC}<\frac{1}{\bar{u}}\left[\tilde{Y}_1+\frac{\mu_2^*-\eta_1}{\eta_1\mu_2^*}(1-e^{-\tilde{Y}_1\mu_2^*})\right].$$

Furthermore, we analyze the change in the increments of growth with the second difference quotient. For any $\tilde{Y}_i, \tilde{Y}_j, \tilde{Y}_s, \tilde{Y}_t$ with $\tilde{Y}_i<\tilde{Y}_j<\tilde{Y}_s<\tilde{Y}_t$ and $\tilde{Y}_i\neq 0$, the second difference quotient is

$$\frac{\frac{1}{r}\ln\frac{\tilde{Y}_t+KC}{KC}-\frac{1}{r}\ln\frac{\tilde{Y}_s+KC}{KC}-\frac{1}{r}\ln\frac{\tilde{Y}_j+KC}{KC}+\frac{1}{r}\ln\frac{\tilde{Y}_i+KC}{KC}}{\tilde{Y}_t-\tilde{Y}_i}$$

$$=\frac{\frac{1}{r}\ln\frac{\tilde{Y}_t+KC}{\tilde{Y}_s+KC}-\frac{1}{r}\ln\frac{\tilde{Y}_j+KC}{\tilde{Y}_i+KC}}{\tilde{Y}_t-\tilde{Y}_i}$$

$$=\frac{\frac{1}{r}\ln\frac{\left(\tilde{Y}_t+KC\right)\left(\tilde{Y}_i+KC\right)}{\left(\tilde{Y}_s+KC\right)\left(\tilde{Y}_j+KC\right)}}{\tilde{Y}_t-\tilde{Y}_i}$$

and

$$\frac{\begin{array}{c}\frac{1}{\bar{u}}\left[\tilde{Y}_t+\frac{\mu_2^*-\eta_1}{\eta_1\mu_2^*}(1-e^{-\tilde{Y}_t\mu_2^*})\right]-\frac{1}{\bar{u}}\left[\tilde{Y}_s+\frac{\mu_2^*-\eta_1}{\eta_1\mu_2^*}(1-e^{-\tilde{Y}_s\mu_2^*})\right]\\-\frac{1}{\bar{u}}\left[\tilde{Y}_j+\frac{\mu_2^*-\eta_1}{\eta_1\mu_2^*}(1-e^{-\tilde{Y}_j\mu_2^*})\right]-\frac{1}{\bar{u}}\left[\tilde{Y}_i+\frac{\mu_2^*-\eta_1}{\eta_1\mu_2^*}(1-e^{-\tilde{Y}_i\mu_2^*})\right]\end{array}}{\tilde{Y}_t-\tilde{Y}_i}$$

$$=\frac{\frac{1}{\bar{u}}\left[\tilde{Y}_t-\tilde{Y}_s+\frac{\mu_2^*-\eta_1}{\eta_1\mu_2^*}(e^{-\tilde{Y}_s\mu_2^*}-e^{-\tilde{Y}_t\mu_2^*})\right]-\frac{1}{\bar{u}}\left[\tilde{Y}_j-\tilde{Y}_i+\frac{\mu_2^*-\eta_1}{\eta_1\mu_2^*}(e^{-\tilde{Y}_i\mu_2^*}-e^{-\tilde{Y}_j\mu_2^*})\right]}{\tilde{Y}_t-\tilde{Y}_i}$$

$$=\frac{\frac{1}{\bar{u}}\left[\tilde{Y}_t+\tilde{Y}_i-\tilde{Y}_s-\tilde{Y}_j+\frac{\mu_2^*-\eta_1}{\eta_1\mu_2^*}(e^{-\tilde{Y}_s\mu_2^*}+e^{-\tilde{Y}_j\mu_2^*}-e^{-\tilde{Y}_t\mu_2^*}-e^{-\tilde{Y}_i\mu_2^*})\right]}{\tilde{Y}_t-\tilde{Y}_i}.$$

The function T increases more slowly than the sequence of E(T) for

$$\frac{1}{r}\ln\frac{\left(\tilde{Y}_t+KC\right)\left(\tilde{Y}_i+KC\right)}{\left(\tilde{Y}_s+KC\right)\left(\tilde{Y}_j+KC\right)}<\frac{1}{\bar{u}}\left[\tilde{Y}_t+\tilde{Y}_i-\tilde{Y}_s-\tilde{Y}_j+\frac{\mu_2^*-\eta_1}{\eta_1\mu_2^*}\times(e^{-\tilde{Y}_s\mu_2^*}+e^{-\tilde{Y}_j\mu_2^*}-e^{-\tilde{Y}_t\mu_2^*}-e^{-\tilde{Y}_i\mu_2^*})\right].$$

□

Appendix B: Derivatives of the Expected First Realization of Market Entry Profit Level:

Proof of Proposition 4.

$$\frac{\partial E(T^*)}{\partial \lambda_1} = -\underbrace{\frac{\left(\frac{p}{\eta_1} - \frac{q}{\eta_2}\right)}{\left[\lambda_1\left(\frac{p}{\eta_1} - \frac{q}{\eta_2}\right)\right]^2}}_{(1)} \underbrace{\left[Y^* + \frac{\mu_2^* - \eta_1}{\eta_1 \mu_2^*}(1 - e^{-Y^*\mu_2^*})\right]}_{(2)}$$

$$+\underbrace{\frac{1}{\lambda_1\left(\frac{p}{\eta_1} - \frac{q}{\eta_2}\right)}}_{(3)} \underbrace{\left[\begin{array}{c} -\frac{\frac{\partial \beta}{\partial \lambda_1}}{(\beta-1)^2}(r - \int\limits_{f^{-1}(U_2)} zv(dz) \\ -\int\limits_{U_2} [\ln(1+z) - z]\, v_2(dz))I(T) \end{array}\right]}_{(4)} \underbrace{(1 - \frac{\mu_2^* - \eta_1}{\eta_1} e^{-Y^*\mu_2^*})}_{(5)}$$

For the first term (1), we obtain

$$\frac{\left(\frac{p}{\eta_1} - \frac{q}{\eta_2}\right)}{\left[\delta + \lambda_1\left(\frac{p}{\eta_1} - \frac{q}{\eta_2}\right)\right]^2} > 0 \Leftrightarrow \frac{p}{\eta_1} - \frac{q}{\eta_2} > 0 \text{ with } q = 1 - p.$$

With the same condition, we obtain a positive sign also for term (3)

$$\frac{1}{\delta + \lambda_1\left(\frac{p}{\eta_1} - \frac{q}{\eta_2}\right)} > 0.$$

For the second term (2), it holds that

$$\underbrace{Y^*}_{>0} + \underbrace{\frac{\mu_2^* - \eta_1}{\eta_1 \mu_2^*}}_{>0} \underbrace{(1 - e^{-Y^*\mu_2^*})}_{\geq 0} > 0.$$

The sign of the fourth term (4) depends on whether $\frac{\partial \beta}{\partial \lambda_1}$ is positive or negative. Assuming $\frac{\partial \beta}{\partial \lambda_1} < 0$, then term (4) becomes

$$-\frac{\frac{\partial \beta}{\partial \lambda_1}}{(\beta - 1)^2} \underbrace{(r - \int\limits_{f^{-1}(U_2)} zv(dz) - \int\limits_{U_2} [\ln(1+z) - z]\, v_2(dz))}_{>0} \underbrace{I(T)}_{>0} > 0$$

The last term (5)

$$1 - \frac{\mu_2^* - \eta_1}{\eta_1} e^{-Y^*\mu_2^*}$$

is negative if

$$1 < \frac{\mu_2^* - \eta_1}{\eta_1} e^{-Y^*\mu_2^*}.$$

Summarizing all conditions leads to $\frac{\partial E(T^*)}{\partial \lambda_1} < 0$. □

Proof of Proposition 5.

$$\frac{\partial E(T^*)}{\partial u} = \underbrace{\frac{1}{\lambda\left(\frac{p}{\eta_1} - \frac{q}{\eta_2}\right)}}_{(1)} \underbrace{\left[\begin{array}{c} -\frac{\frac{\partial\beta}{\partial u}}{(\beta-1)^2}\left(r - \int\limits_{f^{-1}(U_2)} z\upsilon(dz)\right. \\ \left. - \int\limits_{U_2} [\ln(1+z) - z]\,\upsilon_2(dz)\right) I(T) \end{array}\right]}_{(2)}$$

$$\times \underbrace{\left(1 - \frac{\mu_2^* - \eta_1}{\eta_1} e^{-Y^*\mu_2^*}\right)}_{(3)}.$$

As before, the term (1) is positive. Accordingly, the last component (3) is negative for $1 < \frac{\mu_2^* - \eta_1}{\eta_1} e^{-Y^*\mu_2^*}$. The sign of (2) depends on whether $\frac{\partial\beta}{\partial u} \gtrless 0$. Assuming that $\frac{\partial\beta}{\partial u} < 0$, it follows that $\frac{\partial E(\tilde{T})}{\partial u} < 0$. □

Proof of Proposition 6.

$$\frac{\partial E(T^*)}{\partial \lambda_2} = \underbrace{\frac{1}{\lambda_1\left(\frac{p}{\eta_1} - \frac{q}{\eta_2}\right)}}_{(1)} \underbrace{\left[\underbrace{\frac{\beta}{\beta-1}}_{>0} \left(\begin{array}{c} - \int\limits_{f^{-1}(U_2)} zh(dz) \\ - \int\limits_{U_2} [\ln(1+z) - z]\,h(dz) \end{array}\right) \underbrace{I(T)}_{>0}\right]}_{(2)}$$

$$\times \underbrace{\left(1 - \frac{\mu_2^* - \eta_1}{\eta_1} e^{-Y^*\mu_2^*}\right)}_{(3)}.$$

From the conditions above, (1) is positive and (3) is negative. Hence, the sign of $\frac{\partial E(T^*)}{\partial \lambda_2}$ depends on the second term and especially on the sign of $- \int\limits_{f^{-1}(U_2)} zh(dz) - \int\limits_{U_2} [\ln(1+z) - z]\,h(dz)$. Assuming more negative than positive jumps leads to a positive sign. □

Proof of Proposition 7.

$$\frac{\partial E(T^*)}{\partial z} = \underbrace{\frac{1}{\lambda\left(\frac{p}{\eta_1} - \frac{q}{\eta_2}\right)}}_{(>0)} \underbrace{\left[\begin{array}{c} -\underbrace{\frac{\beta}{\beta-1}}_{>0}\left(\int\limits_{f^{-1}(U_2)} 1\upsilon_2(dz)\right. \\ \left. + \int\limits_{U_2} \left[\frac{1}{(1+z)} - 1\right] \upsilon_2(dz)\right) \underbrace{I(T)}_{>0} \end{array}\right]}_{(2)} \underbrace{\left(1 - \frac{\mu_2^* - \eta_1}{\eta_1} e^{-Y^*\mu_2^*}\right)}_{(<0)}$$

According to the above assumptions, (1) is positive and (3) is negative. The second term again depends on the jump part. However, even if there are more negative than positive jumps, the effect on the jump part is not so large as to result in a negative sign. Therefore, the sign of the overall derivative is negative. □

7 Artificial Intelligence Arms Races as Innovation Contests*

7.1 INTRODUCTION

In Chapter 2, we explained the distinction between narrow AI and an artificial general intelligence (AGI). That section and Chapters 2 and 3 stressed that an AGI did not exist at the time of the writing of this book – although many have expressed concerns and hopes that the advances made in Large Language Models (LLMs) since around 2017 have brought the world much closer to an AGI (Bubeck et al., 2023). As we mentioned in Chapter 6, LLMs have been referred to as artificial capable intelligence (ACI), "a fast-approaching point between AI and AGI" (Suleyman, 2023, p. vii), and according to Bubeck et al. (2023, p. 1), "Given the breadth and depth of GPT-4's capabilities, we believe that it could reasonably be viewed as an early (yet still incomplete) version of an artificial general intelligence (AGI) system." With AGI seemingly within reach, one may reasonably expect the arms race for an AGI, that is, to say the contest between various teams (firms, government labs, inventors) to invent the first AGI to accelerate (Naudé and Dimitri, 2020; Armstrong et al., 2016).

The winner of such an AI arms race may have at its disposal an AGI technology that may allow it to dominate the world. In Chapter 10, we speculate on how such a world with a dominant AGI could look like, and describe Alexander's (2016a) notion of *"Ascended Corporations."* These are AGI-based corporations that have succeeded in the AI-invention process as described in Chapter 6,

* This chapter is based on, updates and extends, Naudé and Dimitri (2018) and Naudé and Dimitri (2020). The latter has been published under a Creative Commons License.

and have evolved into the ultimate decentralized autonomous organizations (DAO), which are organizations that are "managed entirely through protocols that are encoded and enforced via smart contracts rather than human managers" (Murray et al., 2021, p. 2021). Such ascended corporations will eventually result in an economy that features only "robot companies with robot workers owned by robot capitalists" and with humans not even needed to be the proximate owners of businesses and investment funds. An economy filled with ascended corporations may eventually end up with one large corporation coordinating and running the entire economy – because an AGI will overcome the coordination and transaction costs and information problems that limit human-run cooperations from growing past a certain scale. Countries may end up deciding to nationalize all their resources and placing them under the command of a central AGI, generating thereby significant efficiency gains and scale economies (Dai, 2019). It could forever lock humanity into a technological autocracy – perhaps the ultimate tech dystopia.

Apart from this ultimate tech dystopia, the winners of an AI arms race may end up with an AGI that is of poor quality, more particularly unaligned with human goals and values (see the discussion in Chapter 3 on the AI alignment problem). This is because during the AI race, in their haste to be the first across the goal line, competing firms may cut corners and compromise on the safety standards in AGI (Armstrong et al., 2016). An unaligned, "unfriendly" AI could turn out to be, as Stephen Hawking warned, the "worst mistake in history" (Ford, 2016, p. 225). It could, as in the visions of AI-Doomerism, wipe out all humans, on purpose or through neglect, or it may be misused by some humans against others, or benefit only the tech elite (AI Impacts, 2016).

In 2016, Armstrong et al. (2016) modeled an arm for an AGI. They established that the likelihood of avoiding an AI disaster and getting a "friendlier" AGI depends crucially on reducing the number of competing teams. They also established that with better

AI development capabilities, research teams will be less inclined to take risks in compromising on safety and alignment. As Naudé and Dimitri (2020) pointed out, Armstrong et al. (2016) left several questions unanswered, namely: precisely how government can steer the number of competing teams? How can government policy reduce competition in the race for an AGI and raise the importance of capability? Should AI be taxed and/or nationalized?

In this chapter, we answer these questions by providing a strategic analysis, from an economics perspective, on how government policies can influence the nature of AI. We develop an *All-Pay Contest* model of an AGI race and illustrate the following results. First, in a winner-takes-all race, where players must invest in R&D, only the most competitive teams will participate. Thus, given the difficulty of AGI, the number of competing teams is unlikely ever to be very large. This reduces the AI-alignment problem introduced in Chapter 3. Second, the intention of teams competing in an AGI race as well as the possibility of an intermediate outcome (prize) is important. The possibility of an intermediate prize will improve the probability that an AGI will be created and hence make public control even more urgent. In sum, the contribution of this chapter is to illustrate that the danger of an unfriendly AGI can in principle be reduced by taxing AI and by using public procurement. This would reduce the pay-off of contestants, raise the amount of R&D needed to compete, and coordinate and incentivize cooperation. All of these effects will help alleviate the AI alignment problem.

The chapter is structured as follows. Section 7.2 provides an overview of the current literature and underscores the importance of the development of a friendly AI and the fundamental challenges in this respect, consisting of a *control* (or alignment) problem and a *political* problem. In Section 7.3, an *All-Pay Contest* model of an AGI race is developed wherein the key mechanisms and public policy instruments to reduce an unfavorable outcome are identified. Section 7.4 discusses various policy implications. Section 7.5 concludes.

7.2 RELEVANT LITERATURE

It is recognized that there is an AI race between high-tech giants such as *Meta, Google, Amazon, Alibaba,* and *Tencent* among others. Governments are not neutral in this: the Chinese government is providing much direct support for the development of AI,[1] aiming explicitly to be the world's AI leader by 2030 (Mubayi et al., 2017); in 2016, the USA government[2] released its "National Artificial Intelligence Research and Development Strategic Plan;" and in 2018, the UK's Select Committee on Artificial Intelligence, appointed by the House of Lords, released their report on a strategic vision for AI in the UK, arguing that "the UK is in a strong position to be among the world leaders in the development of artificial intelligence during the twenty-first century" (House of Lords, 2018, p. 5). By 2018, at least twenty-two countries around the world, and also the EU, had launched grand national strategies for becoming leaders in AI. As mentioned, the EU documented more than 350 AI policy initiatives in individual EU member states between 2016 and 2020.[3]

The races or contests in AI development are largely in the narrow domains of AI. These pose, at present, no existential threat, although relative lesser threats and problems in the design and application of these narrow AI have been the subject of increased scrutiny. Naudé (2023a) discusses several "digital dystopias" wherein AI systems play a role. These include digital platform capitalism, tech exceptionalism, the surveillance state, the digital poorhouse, digital divides, the loss of sense-making (including fake news), digital addiction, digital depression, and cybercrime. In addition, there has been an extensive debate on the potential for AI to automate jobs and raise unemployment, see, for example, Acemoglu and Restrepo

[1] One of the world's largest AI start-ups in recent years is a Chinese company, *SenseTime,* which raised more than US$ 1.2 billion in start-up capital over the past three years. The company provides facial-recognition technology that is used in camera surveillance (Bloomberg, 2018).

[2] See the National Science and Technology Council (2016).

[3] See the EU Agency for Fundamental Rights' project on artificial intelligence (AI), big data, and fundamental rights.

(2017), Bessen (2018), Brynjolfsson and McAfee (2015), Eloundou et al. (2023), Frey and Osborne (2017), and Ford (2016).

Given the huge incentives for inventing an AGI, it is precautionary to assume that such a race is part of the general AI race described earlier. As was mentioned in the introduction, whichever firm or government lab succeeds in inventing the first AGI will obtain a potentially world-dominating technology – they will enjoy winner-takes-all profits. The problem with this is not only the potential to lock-in humanity for all time into a world dominated by Ascended Corporations – or a single Ascended Corporation – but also that even if the winner designs an AGI that appears to be friendly, it may still have compromised on ensuring that this is the case and leave it open that the AGI will not necessarily serve the interests of humans. In this latter case, the challenge has been described as the "Fallacy of the Giant Cheesecake." As put by Yudkowsky (2008, p. 314–315):

> A superintelligence could build enormous cheesecakes – cheesecakes the size of cities – by golly, the future will be full of giant cheesecakes! The question is whether the superintelligence wants to build giant cheesecakes. The vision leaps directly from capability to actuality, without considering the necessary intermediate of motive.

There is no guarantee that an AGI will have the motive, or reason, to help humans. In fact, it may even, deliberately or accidentally, wipe out humanity, or make it easier for humans to wipe themselves out.[4] This uncertainty is what many see as perhaps the most dangerous aspect of current investments into developing an AGI, because no cost-benefit analysis can be made, and risks cannot be quantified (Yudkowsky, 2008).

[4] Hence "Moore's Law of Mad Science: Every 18 months, the minimum IQ necessary to destroy the world drops by one point" (Yudkowsky, 2008, p. 338).

Thus, it seems that there is a strong prudential case to be made for steering the development of all AI, but especially so for an AGI, where the risks are potentially existential. Another reason for steering the development of an AGI is that a competitive race for an AGI is sub-optimal from the point of view of the nature of an AGI as a public good (AI Impacts, 2016). An AGI would be a "single best effort public good," which is the kind of global public good that can be supplied "unilaterally or multilaterally" that is, it requires a deliberate effort of one country or a coalition of countries to be generated but will benefit all countries in the world once it is available (Barrett, 2007, p. 3).

To steer the development of AGI, and specifically through ameliorating the dangers of a race for an AGI, the literature has identified two generic problems: the alignment problem (see also Chapter 3) and the political problem (Bostrom, 2014, 2017).

The alignment problem is defined by Bostrom (2014, p. v), as "the problem of how to control what the superintelligence would do," in other words, the challenge to "design AI systems such that they do what their designers intend" (Bostrom, 2017, p. 5). In Chapter 3, it was discussed why the alignment problem is a very hard problem. Among other difficulties, whatever utility function that the AGI tries to optimize, the harm to humans may be unintentional. As Gallagher (2018) put it, the difficulty of aligning AI is that "a misaligned AI doesn't need to be malicious to do us harm."

The *political problem* in AI research refers to the challenge of "how to achieve a situation in which individuals or institutions empowered by such AI use it in ways that promote the common good" (Bostrom, 2017, p. 5). For instance, promoting the common good would lead society to try and prevent that any self-interested group monopolizes the benefits of an AGI for itself (Bostrom, 2017).

Both the alignment problem and the political problem may be made worse if a race for an AGI starts. This is illustrated by Armstrong et al. (2016). In their model, there are various competing teams all racing to develop the first AGI. They are spurned on by the incentive of reaping winner-takes-all effects and will do so if they can by "skimping" on safety precautions (including alignment) (Armstrong et al., 2016, p. 201). As winners, they can monopolize the benefits of AGI and during the race, they are less concerned about alignment. The outcome could therefore be of the worst kind.

The model of Armstrong et al. (2016) shows that the likelihood of avoiding an AI disaster and getting a "friendlier" AGI depends crucially on reducing the number of competing teams. They also show that with better AI development capabilities, research teams will be less inclined to take risks in compromising on safety and alignment. As these are the core results from which the modeling in Section 7.3 of this chapter proceeds, it is worthwhile to provide a short summary of the Armstrong et al. (2016) model in this respect.

They model n different teams, each with an ability c, and with choice s of "safety precautions" (which can also be taken to stand for degree of alignment more broadly) where $0 \leq s \leq 1$ with $s = 0$ when there is no alignment and $s = 1$ when there is perfect alignment. They award each team a score of $(c - s)$ and the team with the highest score wins by creating the first AGI. Whether or not the AGI is friendly depends on the degree of alignment (s) of the winning team. They assume that teams do not have a choice of c, which is randomly assigned as given by the exogenous state of technology, and then show that the Nash equilibrium depends on the information that the teams have about their own c and the c of other teams. They can have either no information, only information about their own c, or full public information about every team's c.

Under each Nash equilibrium, Armstrong et al. (2016) then calculate the probability of an AI disaster with either two or five teams competing. Their results show that "competition might spur a race to the bottom if there are too many teams. . . " (p. 205) and that "increasing the importance of capability must decrease overall risk. One is less inclined to skimp on safety precautions if one can only get a small advantage from doing so" (p. 204).

As Naudé and Dimitri (2020) pointed out, Armstrong et al. (2016) left several questions unanswered, namely: precisely how government can steer the number of competing teams? How can government policy reduce competition in the race for an AGI and raise the importance of capability? Should AI be taxed and/or nationalized?

In Section 7.3, an *All-Pay Contest* model is used to answer the above questions. All-Pay Contests model is a class of games where various participants compete for a prize, or more than one prize. Their distinguishing feature is that everyone pays for participation, and so losers will also have to pay. Moreover, since Tullock (1980), contests have been conceived as probabilistic competitions where despite the effort made victory is not certain, and with the winning probability being positively related to one's investment and negatively related to the opponent's investment. They have been applied to a variety of socioeconomic situations (Konrad, 2009; Kydd, 2015; Vojnovic, 2015). An important aspect of contests is individuals' asymmetries (Siegel, 2009), which could determine if, and how much, effort would be exerted in the competition.

It is appropriate to study an AGI arms race as an all-pay contest given that, as Armstrong et al. (2016) also stress, the differing ability (c in their model) of competing teams (and their information about this c) is a determining factor in the race. Indeed, *All-Pay Contest* models have been used in the literature to study very similar problems, such as, for instance, R&D competitions (Dasgupta, 1986).

7.3 THEORETICAL MODEL

Assuming the AGI arms race to be a winner-takes-all type of competition, it can be modeled as an *All-Pay Contest*, where only the winning team gets a prize, the invention of the AGI, but every team has to invest resources to enter the race, and so everyone pays. With no major loss of generality, for an initial illustration of the model, consider the following static framework in Section 3.1.

7.3.1 Setup and Decision to Enter the Race

The decision to enter an AGI race will depend on a team's perceptions of the factors that will most critically affect its chance to win the race: (1) its own current technology, (2) the effort made by competing teams; and (3) the unit cost of a team's own effort.

Suppose $i = 1, 2$ denotes two teams. Each team participates in the race for developing an AGI, which will dominate all previous AI applications and confer a definitive advantage over the other team. The final outcome of such an investment is normalized to 1, in case the AGI race is won, and to 0 if the AGI race is lost. Later, this assumption of only one prize to the winner is relaxed, and an intermediate possibility, akin to a second prize, will be considered given that there may still be commercial value in the investments that the losing firm has undertaken.

If x_i is the amount invested by team i in the race and $0 \leq a_i \leq 1$, then the probability for team i to win the AGI race is given by Equation (7.1)

$$p_i = a_i \left(\frac{x_i}{b_i + x_i + x_j} \right) \tag{7.1}$$

with $i \neq j = 1, 2$

Equation (7.1) is a specification of the so-called contest function (Konrad, 2009; Vojnovic, 2015), which defines the winning probability in a competition.

The parameter a_i is the maximum probability that team i will invent the dominating AGI application. In this sense, it can be interpreted as what team i can innovate since, based on the team's technology and knowledge and innovation capability, it could not achieve a higher likelihood of success.

The number $b_i \geq 0$ reflects how team i can find the AGI-dominant application. This is because even if the opponent does not invest, $x_j = 0$, team i may still fail to obtain the highest successful probability a_i since for $b_i > 0$, it is

$$a_i \left(\frac{x_i}{b_i + x_i} \right) < a_i \tag{7.2}$$

If in this case $b_i = 0$, then team i could achieve a_i with an arbitrarily small investment $x_i > 0$, which means that the only obstacle preventing i to obtain the highest possible success probability is the opposing team.

Success in the race depends on how much the opponents invest as well as on the technological difficulty associated to the R&D process. For this reason, it may be that even with very high levels of investment, success may not be guaranteed since technological difficulties could be insurmountable given the current level of knowledge, see, for example, Marcus (2015).

Parameters a_i and b_i formalize the intrinsic difficulty for team i of the AI R&D activity: the higher the a_i, the higher potential has i's technology, while the higher is b_i, the more difficult the R&D. Based on Equation (7.1), it follows that the total probability that one of the two teams will find the dominating AGI application is:

$$a_1\left(\frac{x_1}{b_1+x_1+x_2}\right)+a_2\left(\frac{x_2}{b_2+x_1+x_2}\right)\leq 1 \tag{7.3}$$

where Equation (7.3) is satisfied with equality only if $a_i = 1$ and $b_i = 0$ for both $i = 1, 2$. When (7.3) is satisfied as a strict inequality, there is a positive probability that no team would succeed in winning the race due to the difficulty of the R&D process, given that AGI is a "hard" challenge (Van de Gevel and Noussair, 2013b).

For both teams, it is assumed that the winning probability is the objective function and that its maximization is their goal, subject to the (economic) constraint that the expected profit should be non-negative. Moreover, if c_i is the unit cost for team i, then the firm's profit is a random variable defined as: $\Pi_i = 1 - c_i x_i$ with probability $a_i\left(\frac{x_i}{b_i+x_i+x_j}\right)$ and $\Pi_i = -c_i x_i$ with probability $1 - a_i\left(\frac{x_i}{b_i+x_i+x_j}\right)$.

This means that the team's expected profit is given by:

$$E\Pi_i = a_i\left(\frac{x_i}{b_i+x_i+x_j}\right)-c_i x_i \tag{7.4}$$

so that $E\Pi_i \geq 0$ defines the self-sustainability of the R&D process, which represents the constraint in the probability maximization problem. Hence, team i's problem, in the AGI race, can be formulated as $\text{Max}_{x_i} a_i \left(\frac{x_i}{b_i+x_i+x_j}\right)$ such that $E\Pi_i = a_i\left(\frac{x_i}{b_i+x_i+x_j}\right) - c_i x_i \geq 0$ and $x_i \geq 0$

Defining $\rho_i = \frac{a_i}{c_i} - b_i$, it is possible to find the best response correspondences $x_1 = B_1(x_2)$ and $x_2 = B_2(x_1)$ for the two teams as follows:

$$x_1 = B_1(x_2) = \begin{cases} 0 & \text{if } \rho_1 \leq x_2 \\ \rho_1 - x_2 & \text{otherwise} \end{cases} \quad (7.5)$$

and

$$x_2 = B_2(x_1) = \begin{cases} 0 & \text{if } \rho_2 \leq x_1 \\ \rho_2 - x_1 & \text{otherwise} \end{cases} \quad (7.6)$$

The coefficient ρ_i is a summary of the relevant economic and technological parameters playing a role in the AGI arms race, including, as was discussed in Section 6.2, the state of technology, the capability of teams, the openness of information, and the potential size of the winner-takes-all effccts. For this reason, ρ_i is the competition coefficient of player *i*.

The following first result can now be formulated as proposition 1:

Proposition 1: Suppose $\rho_1 > \max(0, \rho_2)$: then the unique Nash equilibrium of the AGI race is the pair of strategies $(x_1 = \rho_1;\ x_2 = 0)$, while if $\max(\rho_1, \rho_2) \leq 0$, the unique Nash equilibrium of the game is $(x_1 = 0;\ x_2 = 0)$. If $\rho_2 > \max(0, \rho_1)$, then the unique Nash equilibrium of the game is the pair of strategies $(x_1 = 0;\ x_2 = \rho_2)$. Finally, if $\rho_1 = \rho = \rho_2$, then any pair $(x_1 = x;\ x_2 = \rho - x)$ with $0 \leq x \leq \rho$ is a Nash equilibrium of the game.

Proof: see Appendix A at the end of this chapter.

The above result provides some early, interesting insights. Generally, in such a winner-takes-all race, only the team with the best competition coefficient will participate in the race, while the other(s) will not enter the race. If teams have the same coefficient, they both participate (unless $\rho = 0$), in which case, there is a multiplicity of Nash equilibria.

When the Nash equilibrium is defined by $(x_i = \frac{a_i}{c_i} - b_i; x_j = 0)$, the winning probability (1) for team i is:

$$p_i = a_i \left(\frac{\frac{a_i}{c_i} - b_i}{\frac{a_i}{c_i}} \right) = a_i - c_i b_i \tag{7.7}$$

In other words, the winning probability is equal to the maximum probability of success a_i minus a term that is increasing in the unit cost and the technological parameter b_i. The smaller are these last two quantities, the closer to its maximum is team i's winning probability.

The above result can be generalized to any number $n > 1$ of teams as follows.

Corollary 1: Suppose $\rho_1 = \rho_2 = \cdots = \rho_k = \rho > \rho_{k+1} \geq \cdots \geq \rho_n$, with $1 \leq k \leq n$ the competition coefficients of the n teams. Then any profile $(x_1, x_2, \ldots, x_k, x_{k+1} = 0, x_{k+2} = 0, \ldots, x_n = 0)$ with $x_i \geq 0$ for all $i = 1, 2, \ldots, n$ and $\Sigma x_i = \rho$ is a Nash equilibrium, since for each $i = 1, 2, \ldots, n$, the best reply correspondence is defined as $x_i = B_i(x_{-i}) = 0$ if $\rho_i \leq x_{-i}$ and $x_i = B_i(x_{-i}) = \rho_i - x_{-i}$, if otherwise.

Proof: see Appendix B at the end of this chapter.

It is easy to see that any of the above profiles is a Nash equilibrium by simply checking that each component is the best reply against the remaining ones.

To summarize, in a winner-takes-all race for developing an AGI, where players must invest in R&D effort in order to maximize success probability, only the most competitive teams will participate, while the others would prefer not to. This suggests that, given the hard challenge that AGI poses, the degree of competition in the race, as reflected by the number of competing teams, is unlikely to be very large, thus potentially signaling that the alignment problem is not as arduous as may be assumed. Armstrong et al. (2016) are, for instance, concerned about the number of teams competing for AI. The conclusion that the number of competing teams for a AGI will never be very large seems, at least at present, to be borne out by the fact that most of the competitive research into AI, as reflected by USA patent applications in for example machine learning, is by far dominated by a handful of firms: Microsoft, Google, IBM, and Amazon. In Chapter 6, we showed why this would be the case.

7.3.2 *Goals of Competing Teams*

The pool of participating teams may change if teams would pursue alternative goals. To see this, consider again two teams, $i = 1, 2$ with $\rho_1 \geq \rho_2$, but now suppose that team 1 rather than maximizing success probability would pursue expected profit maximization. That is, it would solve the following problem:

$$\text{Max}_{x_1} = \text{Max}\left(0, E\Pi_1 = a_1\left(\frac{x_1}{b_1 + x_1 + x_2}\right) - c_1 x_1\right) \text{ such that } x_1 \geq 0. \tag{7.8}$$

From the first-order conditions for team 1, one can derive :

$$x_1 = B_1(x_2) = \sqrt{\frac{a_1}{c_1}(b_1 + x_2)} - (b_1 + x_2) \tag{7.9}$$

Because when $\rho_1 > 0$ at $x_2 = 0$, it is $0 < B_1(0) = \sqrt{\frac{a_1}{c_1} b_1} - b_1 < \rho_1$ and since (11) is concave in x_2, with $B_1(x_2) = 0$ at $x_2 = -b_1$ and $x_2 = \rho_1$, the following holds:

Proposition 2: Suppose $\rho_1 > 0$. If $\sqrt{\frac{a_1}{c_1} b_1} - b_1 \geq \text{Max}(0, \rho_2)$, then the unique Nash equilibrium of the game is the pair of strategies $(x_1 = \sqrt{\frac{a_1}{c_1} b_1} - b_1;\ x_2 = 0)$. If $0 < \sqrt{\frac{a_1}{c_1} b_1} - b_1 \leq \rho_2$ then $(x_1 = \rho_2 - x_2;\ x_2 = \frac{(\rho_2 + b_1)^2 c_1}{a_1} - b_1)$ is the unique Nash equilibrium.

Proof: see Appendix C at the end of this chapter.

Proposition 2 illustrates conditions for which both teams could participate in the AGI race but pursue different goals. The intuition is the following. If the more competitive team maximizes profit, then in general it would invest less to try to win the race than when aiming to maximize the probability of winning. As a result, the less competitive team would not be discouraged by an opponent who invests a high amount and, in turn, takes part in the race.

7.4 COMPARATIVE STATICS AND POLICY IMPLICATIONS

This section explores how the teams' behavior can be affected by changing some of the elements in the race. In Subsection 7.4.1, the set of possible race outcomes is enlarged.

7.4.1 *Offering a Second Prize*

Consider again the previous two team models but suppose that the set of outcomes rather than being 0 or 1, that is, either the dominant AGI application is found, or nothing is found, there is a possible third result of $0 < \alpha < 1$. This is to model the idea that some intermediate outcome, between dominance and failure, could be obtained even when the most desirable AGI application is not achieved. This is akin to a "second prize."

The interest here is in exploring how such a partial success (failure) could impact the investment decisions of participating teams. Moreover, introducing a third outcome (or second prize) can provide insights on the possible role of the public sector in steering the AGI race.

In what follows, it is assumed that achieving the dominant AGI application implies also obtaining the intermediate outcome, but that in this case only the dominant application will matter. Moreover, to keep things sufficiently simple, team i's probability of obtaining only the intermediate outcome is given by $d_i\left(\frac{x_i}{b_i+x_i+x_j}\right)$, with $0 < a_i \leq d_i < 1$, modeling the idea that the technology for obtaining such an AGI application is the same as for the dominant application, except for a higher upper bound in the success probability.

For this reason, assuming $0 \leq (\alpha_i + d_i) \leq 1$, team i's profit function can take on three values:

$$\Pi_i(x_i) = \begin{cases} 1 - c_i x_i & \text{with probability } a_i\left(\frac{x_i}{b_i+x_i+x_j}\right) \\ \alpha - c_i x_i & \text{with probability } d_i\left(\frac{x_i}{b_i+x_i+x_j}\right) \\ -c_i x_i & \text{with probability } 1 - (a_i + d_i)\left(\frac{x_i}{b_i+x_i+x_j}\right) \end{cases} \tag{7.10}$$

and its expected profit is given by:

$$E\Pi_i = (a_i + \alpha d_i) \left(\frac{x_i}{b_i + x_i + x_j} \right) - c_i x_i \qquad (7.11)$$

that is as if the race was still with two outcomes, 0 and 1, but with success probability now given by $(a_i + \alpha d_i) \left(\frac{x_i}{b_i + x_i + x_j} \right)$ rather than only by $a_i \left(\frac{x_i}{b_i + x_i + x_j} \right)$.

Note that (12) to (14) imply that, unlike the dominant winner-takes-all AGI application, α could also be obtained by both teams and not by one of them only.

Therefore, defining $\acute{a}_i = (a_i + \alpha d_i)$ and defining the modified competition coefficient as $\acute{\rho}_i = \frac{\acute{a}_i}{c_i} - b_i$, the following is an immediate consequence of Proposition 1:

Corollary 2: Suppose $\acute{\rho}_1 > \max(0, \acute{\rho}_2)$, then the unique Nash equilibrium of the AGI race is the pair of strategies $(x_1 = \acute{\rho}_1; x_2 = 0)$, while if $\max(\acute{\rho}_1, \acute{\rho}_2) \leq 0$, the unique Nash equilibrium of the game is $(x_1 = 0; x_2 = 0)$. If $\acute{\rho}_2 > \max(0, \acute{\rho}_1)$, then the unique Nash equilibrium of the game is the pair of strategies $(x_1 = 0; x_2 = \acute{\rho}_2)$. Finally, if $\acute{\rho}_1 = \rho = \acute{\rho}_2$, then any pair $(x_1 = x; x_2 = \acute{\rho} - x)$ with $0 \leq x \leq \acute{\rho}$ is a Nash equilibrium of the game.

The implication from this extension is as follows. Since $\acute{a}_i > a_i$, then $\acute{\rho}_i > \rho_i$: therefore, when a second prize is possible, teams in the race will tend to invest more than without such a possibility. Therefore, the presence of such an intermediate result or second prize serves as an incentive to strengthen team efforts, increasing both the probability of finding the dominant AGI application and the nondominant one. The outcome α reduces the risk of complete failure and in so doing induces higher investments than in a pure winner-takes-all race.

In this case, it is easy to see that outcome 1 would be obtained with probability:

$$\acute{p}_i = \acute{a}_i - c_i b_i \qquad (7.12)$$

and outcome α with probability:

$$q_i = d_i \left(\frac{\frac{\acute{a}_i}{c_i} - b_i}{\frac{\acute{a}_i}{c_i}} \right) = \frac{d_i \left(\acute{a}_i - c_i b_i \right)}{\acute{a}_i} = \frac{d_i \acute{p}_i}{\acute{a}_i} \tag{7.13}$$

with $q_i < \acute{p}_i$ if $a_i < d_i < \frac{a_i}{(1-\alpha)}$, that is if d_i is small enough.

7.4.2 *Policy Implications*

In Section 7.2, we concluded that the avoidance of an AGI race would require the government to influence AGI R&D in a manner that will reduce the returns to teams from taking risks.

In this regard, the model results set out in the preceding sections suggest a number of policy implications to steer the race for an AGI.

To see this, first consider the above winner-takes-all race with no intermediate outcome (no second prize) and assume that the dominant AGI application, if found, would be considered by a public authority undesirable (unfriendly) perhaps due to the fact that the winning team took too many risks and "skimped" on safety regulations.

What could the public sector do to decrease the likelihood of such an unfriendly discovery?

In the following subsections, four public policy initiatives that emanate from the model are discussed: (1) introducing an intermediate prize, (2) using public procurement of innovation, (3) taxing an AGI, and (4) addressing patenting by AI.

7.4.2.1 *Introducing an Intermediate Prize*

One drastic measure would be to prohibit altogether teams (firms) to work toward an AGI, declaring the existential risk to humanity (as was discussed in Section 7.2) to be the overriding constraint. This seems however not to be feasible.

The alternative is then not to prohibit the race but to restrict the number of teams that compete in the race and to incentivize these teams to invest more in pursuing a quality, friendly AGI. Given the difficult challenge that AGI poses, Chapter 6 has shown that in any case only the most competitive teams will compete: at present, in the world, there may perhaps be only half a dozen or so teams that could seriously compete for an AGI.

By keeping this competitive, and even raising the bar and incentivizing such teams to invest more in finding a dominant AGI, the public sector could introduce second prizes, that is, prizes for intermediate results (i.e., advanced, but not dominating AIs). According to the model presented in this chapter, this will increase the amount of resources invested to maximize success probability p. In doing so, it will either reduce the number of teams that could afford to participate and/or increase the amount of investment. This will help reduce the control and political problems characterizing AI.

7.4.2.2 *Public Procurement of Innovation*

How could the public sector in practice introduce an intermediate prize? It is proposed here that the public procurement of innovation can be a useful instrument in this regard, and moreover, one that has so far been neglected in the control or alignment of AI. Public procurement of innovation could attempt to steer AGI in a friendly direction by requiring that certain constraints be engineered into the AI.

Chalmers (2010, p. 31) discusses two types of constraints that will be important: internal and external constraints. Internal constraints come from the program of the AGI, wherein its ethical values can be encoded – for instance, in giving it reduced autonomy or prohibiting it from having its own goals. External constraints come from limitations on the relationship between humans and AGI – for instance, in disincentivizing the development of AGI that replaces human labor and incentivizing the development of AGI that enhances human labor, and in trying to first create an AGI in a virtual world without direct contact with the real world (although Chalmers (2010) concludes that this may be very difficult and perhaps even impossible to ensure).

Chalmers (2010) suggests that the internal constraints on an AGI could be fashioned through, among others, the method by which humans build an AGI. If an AGI is based on whole brain emulations

(WBEs) (see Chapter 10), rather than nonhuman data learning systems, as is primary the case, it may end up with different values, perhaps more akin to human values. Also, if values are established through allowing the AGI to learn and evolve, then initial conditions as well as the punishment/reward system for learning would be important to get right at the start. Care should be taken however to remove human biases from AGI, especially when they learn from data created by biased humans. Concerns have already been raised about AI reinforcing stereotypes (Cockburn et al., 2017).

In this regard, a further policy implication that emanates from the model in this chapter is that it may be important to promote complementary inventions in AI. This could also be done through public procurement of innovation, where the needed coordination could be better fostered. For instance, other complementary innovations to stimulate may be in technologies that enhance human intelligence and integrate human and artificial intelligence over the longer term. Chalmers (2010) speculates that once humans live in an AGI world, the options will be either extinction, isolation, inferiority, or integration of humans and AGIs.

A second role for public procurement of innovation, in addition to helping with the engineering of constraints into AI, is to help generate complementary innovations. This can be done for instance by stimulating research into how ICT can enhance human biology, and perhaps even dispense with it completely, for instance in genetic engineering and nanotechnology. In particular, projects that study the challenges in and consequences of uploading brains and/or consciousness onto computers (WBEs), or implanting computer chips and neural pathways into brains, have been gaining traction in the literature and popular media, and form the core agenda of *transhumanism* (O'Connell, 2017). In Chapter 10, we will return to this topic.

A strong argument for public procurement rests on its ability to coordinate the search for an AGI, and thus avoid excess competition, as suggested, for example, by the EU legal provisions on "pre-commercial procurement of innovation" (European Commission, 2007), as well as on the EU's "innovation partnership" (European Commission, 2014). In particular, the innovation partnership explicitly encourages a collaborative agreement between contracting authorities and the firms selected to develop an innovative solution.

The case for public procurement of AGI innovation is made stronger by the fact that because an AGI is a public good of the single-best effort type, a government coalition, such as the EU, should drive the development, rather than risk it being developed by the private tech-industry. In essence, this would boil down to the nationalization of AGI with the added advantage that the danger of the misuse of AGI technology may be reduced, see, for example, Floridi (2018) and Nordhaus (2015). It may also prevent private monopolies to capture all the rents from AGI innovations (Korinek and Stiglitz, 2017).

In Chapter 8, we delve deeper into the use of public procurement of innovation to steer AI. There we provide a simple theoretical model to show that such procurement of innovative AI solutions, underpinned by ethical considerations, can provide both the tools and audit trails and the financial incentives to incentivize friendly AI. We discuss three dimensions of the relationship between public procurement and innovation in Chapter 8: *public procurement for innovation* (PPfI), which deals with the question, how can public procurement drive innovation?; *public procurement of innovation* (PPoI), which deals with the question, how can public services be innovated?; and *innovative public procurement* (IPP), which deals with the question, how can public institutions procure innovatively?

7.4.2.3 *Taxation*

A third policy proposal from the model presented in this section is that the government announce the introduction of a tax rate $0 < t < 1$, on the team that would find the dominant AGI, with t depending on the extent to which the AGI is unfriendly. The taxation policy would thus be calibrated by the government in such a way that for a friendly AGI, the tax rate t is low and higher for an unfriendly AGI.

For example, if $t = 1$ for the most unfriendly solution, then in general the tax rate could be defined as:

$$t(f) = 1 - f$$

where $0 \leq f \leq 1$ is a numerical indicator set by the government to measure the friendliness of the AGI solution, with $f = 0$ indicating the most undesirable solution and $f = 1$ the most desirable one. In this case, for team i, the expected profit is:

$$E\Pi_i = (1 - t)a_i \left(\frac{x_i}{b_i + x_i + x_j} \right) - c_i x_i \tag{7.14}$$

with the competition coefficient becoming $\delta_i = \frac{(1-t)a_i}{c_i} - b_i < \rho_i$, so that the amount of resources invested and, accordingly, the success probability of the AGI dominant application would decrease. Notice that $\delta_i > 0$ if:

$$t < 1 - \frac{b_i c_i}{a_i} \tag{7.15}$$

This implies that for a large enough tax rate, teams could be completely discouraged to pursue investing in finding such an AGI-dominant application. The introduction of a tax rate is equivalent to an intermediate outcome defined now as $\alpha = -t(\frac{a_i}{d_i})$. In this case, α can be interpreted as an additional (random) component of the cost, which can only take place probabilistically.

With a high enough tax rate, the effect could be seen as equivalent to nationalizing AGI. A combination of a high tax rate on an unfriendly AGI, together with the public procurement of a friendly AGI that aims to establish a (government-led) coalition to drive the development of AGI, may be the more pertinent policy recommendation to emerge from our analysis, given that much R&D in AI currently tends to be open (and may be given further impetus through the public procurement process) (Bostrom, 2017). With more information about the capabilities of teams, including their source codes, data, and organizational intent known, the "more the danger [of an unfriendly AGI] increases" (Armstrong et al., 2016, p. 201).

7.4.2.4 *Addressing Patenting by AI*

A final policy recommendation that can be derived from the model presented in this chapter is that patent law and the legal status of AGI inventions will need to be amended to reduce the riskiness of AGI races. In this respect, the World Economic Forum (WEF, 2018) has warned that because an AGI will be able to generate its own innovations and patents, the firm that comes up with the first AGI will have a huge first-mover advantage, particularly if it enjoys patent protection – in essence, it will have patent rights over the inventor of future patents. Others, such as Jankel (2015), have been more dismissive of the potential of AI generating truly original and disruptive innovations. The debate is however far from settled.

In terms of the model presented, patent protection may raise the returns from investing in a dramatic fashion and will raise the number of teams competing. This is a topic that however needs more research and more careful modeling and is left for future research.

7.5 CONCLUDING REMARKS

We started this chapter by mentioning that with an AGI seemingly within reach given progress in LLMs, one may reasonably expect the arms race for an AGI to accelerate, and that the winner of such an AI arms race may have at its disposal an AGI technology that may allow it to dominate the world. To avoid this potentially dystopian outcome, we used an All-Pay Contest model in this chapter to provide some guidance on how public policy could steer the development of an AGI toward a friendly AI. In other words, this chapter was concerned about government directing the alignment problem that was outlined in Chapter 3.

Our model showed that in a winner-takes-all race where players must invest in R&D, only the most competitive teams will participate. This conclusion reinforces the conclusion that we already made in Chapter 6, where we used an extended real options model to investigate the investment in R&D decision to invent an AGI. This suggests that the number of competing teams in the AGI race is unlikely ever to be very large. This seems to be reflected in current reality, as the current number of feasible teams able to compete in an AGI race is quite low at around half a dozen or so. This is a positive conclusion given that the alignment problem becomes more vexing the more teams compete. Instead of pausing the development of LLMs, as more than 30,000 signatories demanded in 2023 through an open letter, it may be more sensible to restrict the ability of more teams to enter into the AGI race.

It was also shown that the intention (or goals) of teams competing in an AGI race, as well as the possibility of an intermediate outcome (second prize) may be important. Crucially, there will be more competitors in the race if the most competitive firm has as its objective the probability of profit maximization rather than success, and if some intermediate result (or second prize) is possible, rather than only one dominant prize. Moreover, the possibility of an intermediate prize is shown to raise the quality of R&D but also the probability of finding the dominant AGI application, and hence will give more urgency to public policy addressing the alignment problems.

Given that it is likely infeasible to ban (or pause) the AGI race, it was shown in this chapter that the danger of an unfriendly AGI can be reduced through a number of public policies. Specifically, by taxing AI and by publicly procuring an AGI, the public sector could reduce the pay-off from an AGI, raise the amount of R&D that firms need to invest in AGI development, and coordinate and incentivize cooperation.

In Chapter 8, we delve deeper into the use of public procurement of innovation to steer AI. There we provide a simple theoretical model to show that such procurement of innovative AI solutions, underpinned by ethical considerations, can provide both the tools and audit trails and the financial incentives to incentivize friendly AI.

Appendices

Appendix A

With two teams, it is possible to suggest a proof that could be graphically visualized. Suppose $\rho_1 < \max(0, \rho_2)$. It follows that team 1's best response is $x_1 = B_1(x_2) = 0$ if $\rho_1 \le x_2$ and $x_1 = B_1(x_2) = \rho_1 - x_2$, if otherwise.

when $\rho_1 > x_2$ can be written as $x_2 = \rho_1 - x_1$. Then, it follows immediately that team 2's best response is $x_2 = B_2(x_1) = 0$ if $\rho_2 \le x_1 \rho_2 - x_1$, and $x_2 = B_2(x_1) = \rho_2 - x_1$, if otherwise. This response can meet team 1's best response only at $x_1 = \rho_1$ and $x_2 = 0$.

Analogously, if $\rho_2 > \max(0, \rho_1)$, then the two best replies meet only at $x_1 = 0$ and $x_2 = \rho_2$. Finally, if $\rho_1 = \rho = \rho_2$ the two best replies overlap along the segment $x_2 = \rho - x_1$ and so any pair $(x_1 = x; x_2 = \rho - x)$ with $0 \le x \le \rho$ is a Nash equilibrium of the game.

Appendix B

Suppose $\rho_1 = \rho_2 = .. = \rho_k = \rho > \rho_{k+1} \ge .. \ge \rho_n$, with $1 \le k \le n$ are the competition coefficients of the n teams, and consider profile

$(x_1, x_2, .., x_k, x_{k+1} = 0, x_{k+2} = 0.., x_n = 0)$

with $x_i \ge 0$ for all $i = 1, 2, .., n$ and $\Sigma_i x_i = \rho$.

It is easy to see that the profile is a Nash equilibrium by simply checking that each component is the best reply against the others. Indeed, consider team 1, and notice that the argument will be identical for any team i with $1 < i \le k$. If $\Sigma_{i=2}^{k} x_i < \rho$ and $x_{k+1} = 0, x_{k+2} = 0.., x_n = 0$ then $x_{-1} = \Sigma_{i=2}^{n} x_i < \rho$ and its best reply would be $x_1 = \rho - x_{-1}$ so that $\Sigma_{i=1}^{k} x_i = \rho = \Sigma_{i=1}^{n} x_i$.

Consider now any team $i = k + 1$; the same argument will hold for all $i > k + 1$. In this case, $x_{-(k+1)} = \Sigma_{i \neq (k+1)}^{n} = \rho > \rho_{(k+1)}$ and so team $(k + 1)$'s best response would be $x_{k+1} = 0$, which proves the result.

Appendix C

Suppose team 1's best response is

$$x_1 = B_1(x_2) = \sqrt{\frac{a_1}{c_1}(b_1 + x_2)} - (b_1 + x_2)$$

Because when $\rho_1 > 0$ at $x_2 = 0$, it is $0 < B_1(0) = \sqrt{\frac{a_1}{c_1}b_1} - b_1$, and since

$$\frac{d^2 B_1(x_2)}{dx_2^2} = -\frac{1}{4}\left(\frac{a_1}{b_1}\right)^2\left(\frac{a_1}{b_1}\right)(b_1 + x_2)^{\frac{-3}{2}} < 0$$

then $B_1(x_2)$ is concave in x_2 with $B_1(x_2) = 0$ at $x_2 = -b_1$ and $x_2 = \rho_1$. Therefore, if $\sqrt{\frac{a_1}{c_1}b_1} - b_1 \geq \max(0, \rho_2)$, it follows immediately that team 2's best response is

$x_2 = B_2(x_1) = 0$ if $\rho_2 \leq x_1$, and $x_2 = B_2(x_1) = \rho_2 - x_1$, if otherwise.

This will match $B_1(x_2)$ only at $(x_1 = \sqrt{\frac{a_1}{c_1}b_1} - b_1; x_2 = 0)$, which is the unique Nash equilibrium pair of investments. However, if $0 < \sqrt{\frac{a_1}{c_1}b_1} - b_1 < \rho_2$, then the two best responses meet at the unique point $\left(x_1 = \rho_2 - x_2;\ x_2 = \left(\frac{(\rho_2+b_1)^2 c_1}{a_1}\right) - b_1\right)$, which is the only Nash equilibrium.

8 Directing Artificial Intelligence Innovation and Diffusion

8.1 INTRODUCTION

In Chapter 1, we mentioned that there are high expectations, and also fears, of AI. These are reflected not only in the declarations of scientists and government officials but also in the growing investments and research in the field of AI specifically, and data science more generally. With these expectations, however, have also come warnings and concerns about the possible existential threats of AI (Bostrom, 2014; Yudkowsky, 2023) as well as the shorter-term negative consequences. These include the dangerous possibility that large language models (LLMs) may make bioterrorism much easier (Soice et al., 2023) or may lead soon to an AGI being invented with possibly dystopian outcomes as we discussed in Section 7.2 of Chapter 7. As we mentioned in Chapter 7, the GitHub site "Awful AI" contains a repository of some of the negative consequences that AI already has.

These existing and possible future negative consequences of AI have given rise to calls for AI governance to ensure that AI-based applications are safe and that the development and diffusion of AI do not suffer from improper use and misuse (Dafoe, 2018). "The field of AI governance studies how humanity can best navigate the transition to advanced AI systems, focusing on the political, economic, military, governance, and ethical dimensions" (Dafoe, 2018, p. 5). In 2015, an open letter[1] by an eminent group of scientists ignited the field of AI governance by calling for "expanded research aimed at ensuring

[1] In 2023, an open letter would again be used, this time to call for a pause in the development of LLMs.

that increasingly capable AI systems are robust and beneficial: our AI systems must do what we want them to do" – see https://futureoflife.org/ai-open-letter/.

What would count as improper use and misuse, and safety risks such as those that could be caused by accidents or unintended consequences of AI systems, would within AI governance be determined by the extent to which AI systems are human-centered. Human-centered AI (HCAI) draws on ethical principles and puts forth actionable guidelines for reducing the risks mentioned (Shneiderman, 2020). As such, HCAI is concerned with *Ethical AI* and *Responsible AI*.

Ethical AI is also sometimes referred to as "Machine Ethics," which has been defined as being "concerned with ensuring that the behavior of machines toward human users, and perhaps other machines as well, is ethically acceptable" (Anderson and Anderson, 2007, p. 15). *Responsible AI* has been described as AI systems that "have an acceptably low risk of harming their users or society and, ideally, to increase their likelihood of being socially beneficial" (Askell et al., 2019, p. 2).

In recent years, there have been a growing number of initiatives to elaborate on ethical and responsible AI, see, for example, Boddington (2017), Etzioni and Etzioni (2017), Floridi (2018), and Yu et al. (2018). These include the Asilomar AI Principles of the Future of Life Institute[2] (2017), the European Union's (EU) April 2019 Ethics Guidelines for Trustworthy AI (EC, 2019), the OECD's May 2019 Principles on Artificial Intelligence (OECD, 2019), the G-20's June 2019 Human-Centered AI Principles (G-20, 2019), and the Institute of Electrical and Electronics Engineers' Ethically Aligned Design Principles (IEEE, 2019).

In 2021, the UN adopted UNESCO's *Recommendation on Ethics in AI*, the "first-ever global standard on AI ethics." It contains ten principles that AI systems should adhere to, namely: (1)

[2] See https://futureoflife.org/ai-principles/

proportionality and do no harm, (2) safety and security, (3) fairness and nondiscrimination, (4) sustainability, (5) right to privacy and data protection, (6) human oversight and determination, (7) transparency and explainability, (8) responsibility and accountability, (9) awareness and literacy, and (10) multi-stakeholder and adaptive governance and collaboration (UNESCO, 2022). In addition to these cross-country and multinational initiatives, the European Union Agency for Fundamental Rights (FRA) has documented more than 350 AI policy initiatives in individual EU Member States between 2016 and 2020.

A shortcoming of these is that they tend to lack strong incentives for developers and users of AI to adhere to them (Askell et al., 2019; Calo, 2017; Hagendorff, 2020). To incentivize the ethics for HCAI, Eitel-Porter (2020, p. 1) argues for "strong, mandated governance controls including tools for managing processes and creating associated audit trails." Floridi et al. (2018, p. 704) argues that governments should "incentivise financially the inclusion of ethical, legal and social considerations in AI research projects."

In this chapter, we contribute to the debate on HCAI by arguing that public procurement and innovation are potentially relevant tools with which to incentivize HCAI. We provide a simple theoretical model to show that such procurement of innovative AI solutions underpinned by ethical considerations can provide both the tools and audit trails and the financial incentives that scholars such as Eitel-Porter (2020) and Floridi et al. (2018) have called for.

With the concept of *public procurement and innovation* (PPaI), we encompass three dimensions of the relationship between PPaI (see Obwegeser and Müller, 2018, p. 5). The first is *public procurement for innovation* (PPfI), which deals with the question, how can public procurement drive innovation? The second is *public procurement of innovation* (PPoI), which deals with the question, how can public services be innovated? And the third is *innovative public procurement* (IPP), which deals with the question, how can public institutions procure innovatively?

This chapter is relevant for all three of these dimensions of innovation and public procurement, although we will lay more stress on the first, namely PPfI, and in particular one of its relatively new tools in the EU, the precommercial procurement of innovation (PCP).

Our argument in favor of PPaI to advance HCAI is also an argument for the more innovative use of public procurement. Most often in the past, public procurement has been used *ex post* to support new innovations by creating a demand for the product (being a customer for new products). This is also the way in which Lin (2020, p. 26) conceives of the relationship between PPfI support. However, this is a rather restricted view: we argue in this chapter that through PPfI, governments can also *ex ante* support research and development of goods and services that do not yet exist. This potential instrument for steering HCAI has been neglected in both the AI and innovation literature.[3] Miller and Lehoux (2020, p. 2), quoting from Uyarra et al. (2017, p. 828), confirm that the underlying mechanisms of how PPoI can shape the incentives of private agents in innovation are still "under-theorized." This chapter addresses this neglect.

Furthermore, our argument for PPaI as a policy toward HCAI is consistent with the calls for mission-oriented and challenge-led innovation policies, as made for instance by Mazzucato (2018). Mazzucato (2020, p. 101) describes challenge-led policies as "policies that use investment and innovation to solve difficult problems." Certainly, the issue of HCAI is a challenge and a difficult problem. It is preeminently a challenge facing humanity and requires challenge-led innovation policies. PPfI and PPoI can fulfill this purpose, as they "use public procurement strategically to address a need which cannot be met by conventional solutions" (Lenderink et al., 2019, p. 7).

Finally, this chapter also contributes to the emerging literature on public entrepreneurship (see, e.g., Hayter et al., 2018), in that the

[3] For instance, Bloom et al. (2019) provide an innovation policy toolkit, discussing eight policy tools: direct R&D grants, R&D tax credits, patent boxes, skilled immigration, supporting universities' research, competition policy, intellectual property rights, and mission-oriented policies. They do not discuss the role of PPoI.

use of PPoI for HCAI is an example of public entrepreneurship as it entails innovation, aims to contribute toward transformation of society, and is subject to uncertainty. These three elements – innovation, transformation, and uncertainty – are according to Hayter et al. (2018, p. 676) what characterizes public entrepreneurship.

The rest of the chapter will proceed as follows. In Sections 8.2 and 8.3, we review the relevant literature dealing respectively with HCAI and innovation policy. In Section 8.4, we provide a simple theoretical model wherein we show how PPoI can incentivize the development of HCAI. Section 8.5 concludes.

8.2 HUMAN-CENTERED ARTIFICIAL INTELLIGENCE

We start by reviewing the state of the literature on HCAI, in particular the role of ethical principles and actionable guidelines. This literature is part of the broader emerging literature on AI governance.

The downsides of AI, some of which were mentioned in the introduction, include intrusive surveillance and erosion of privacy, AI weapons, cybercrime, fake news and misinformation, job losses and tax losses due to automation, higher inequality, discrimination, and biased policymaking (Smith and Neupane, 2018). These are due to the misuse, accidents as well as systemic risks attached to the use of AI. It is clear that these downsides or risks posed by AI are of both an intentional nature (as in cybercrime, fake news, and AI weapons) and an unintentional nature (as in discrimination, inequality, and accidents). In this chapter, we are largely concerned with the unintentional harm that AI can cause, and which can be more broadly analyzed as being a "systemic" or "accidental" AI risk (Dafoe, 2018).

Systemic AI risk refers to "the risks of undesired outcomes – some of which may be very traditional – that can emerge from a system of competing and cooperating agents and can be amplified by novel forms of AI. For example, AI could increase the risk of inadvertent nuclear war, not because of an accident or misuse, but because of how AI could rapidly shift crucial strategic parameters, before we are able to build up compensating understandings, norms, and institutions" (Dafoe, 2018, p. 28).

One aspect of systemic risk is that AI models can unintentionally result in biased decisions and recommendations due to being based on biased data (or data with gaps and absences) as well as design bias, where the values of the designer influence the model design and functioning. AI models also suffer, due to the nature of ML from a lack of transparency and accountability resulting in the problem that decisions and outcomes from AI models very often cannot be easily explained. This is also known as the "black-box problem" (Castelvecchi, 2016; Nguyen et al., 2014). With bias and a lack of explainability, "inequality in application" is a consequence: AI does not benefit everyone equally or fairly (Calo, 2017). Moreover, these shortcomings "disproportionately affect groups that are already disadvantaged by factors such as race, gender and socio-economic back-ground" (Crawford and Calo, 2016, p. 312).

As far as accident risks are concerned, an AI accident occurs if "a human designer had in mind a certain (perhaps informally specified) objective or task, but the system that was designed and deployed for that task produced harmful and unexpected results" (Amodei et al., 2016, p. 2). "Normal" accidents from AI should be expected. According to Maas (2018, p. 4), it even "appears plausible that many AI applications may be even more susceptible to normal accidents than past 'textbook' case technologies such as nuclear power or aviation." There are at least three remedies for systemic and accident risks due to AI that have been given attention in the literature, and that forms part of the challenge of establishing a HCAI.

A first remedy is regulations and laws – to outlaw and police misuse – such as for instance through data privacy laws, combating cybercrime, and other clearly malicious uses of AI – but also to lay down regulations for improving the safety of AI and limiting accidents. This remedy may be necessary but not sufficient. As Askell et al. (2019, p. 7) remark, the difficulties are that "AI regulation seems particularly tricky to get right, as it would require a detailed understanding of the technology on the part of regulators" and that "regulation that is reactive and slow may also be insufficient to deal with the challenges raised by AI systems."

A second remedy is to improve the safety of AI and hence limit accidents and unintentional consequences, through, for instance, addressing technical issues in design, monitoring, and operation (Maas, 2018; Leike et al., 2017) and by subjecting AI systems to regular monitoring and redesign (van de Poel, 2020). The problem is that issues of AI technical safety are complex,[4] and moreover, as Leike et al. (2017, p. 1) pointed out, "This nascent field of AI safety still lacks a general consensus on its research problems."

Third, AI risks – both system and accident risks – can be addressed through the adoption and adherence to ethical principles and guidelines for the development and use of AI – for ethical and responsible AI. Such principles are needed for combating the misuse and under-use of AI, for instance, by making clear when the use of AI would constitute fair or unfair usage, as well as for informing the technical safety of AI, for instance, in identifying questions or problems that the design of an AI should incorporate.[5] The requirement of fairness has led to the concept of "Fair AI," a subset of Ethical AI, which refers to "systems that both quantify bias and mitigate discrimination against subgroups" (Feuerriegel et al., 2020, p. 379). HCAI extends beyond merely reducing misuse and negative side-effects and ensuring fairness. HCAI needs to be able to contribute to "a more diverse, fair, and equitable society" (AI and Inclusion Symposium, 2017, p. 2) and encourage and foster the diffusion and actual use of AI for the promotion of societal development (Vinuesa et al., 2020). Thus, ethical AI will increase trust, and increase the use of AI.

[4] Everitt et al. (2018) consider the safety challenges involved over the long term in the case of an AGI. In this chapter we are only concerned with the shorter and medium risks arising from narrow AI.

[5] Leike et al. (2017) pose eight questions or problems that need to be answered during the design of AI to ensure that it will be safe for humans, for example "How do we ensure that an agent behaves robustly when its test environment differs from the training environment?"

Safe and ethical AI will also help firms[6] to avoid costly mistakes and facilitate the uptake and diffusion of AI (Baker-Brunnbauer, 2020). Thus, HCAI approaches aim to establish the societal and commercial requisites for the greater use of AI (Floridi et al., 2018).

Eitel-Porter (2020, p. 3) argues that most proposals for HCAI have similar pillars, namely fairness,[7] accountability, transparency, explainability, and privacy. And according to Floridi et al. (2018, p. 689), the ethical principles[8] proposed by the *AI4People* initiative are of beneficence, nonmaleficence, autonomy, justice, and explicability. In June 2019, the *G-20* proposed five *Human-centered AI Principles* (G-20, 2019). These principles require AI to be consistent with (1) inclusive growth, sustainable development, and well-being, (2) human-centered values and fairness, (3) transparency and explainability, (4) robustness, security, and safety, and (5) accountability (G-20, 2019, p. 4).

Although the establishment of widely accepted and agreed-on pillars and principles for ethical and responsible AI is a necessary and important milestone for the development and use of HCAI, it has a problem. The problem with this third remedy is, as we already stated in the introduction, that these principles and ethical guidelines lack strong incentives for developers and users of AI to adhere to them (Askell et al., 2019; Calo, 2017; Hagendorff, 2020). According to Hagendorff (2020, p. 99), "Do those ethical guidelines have an actual impact on human decision-making in the field of AI and machine learning (ML)? The short answer is: No, most often not." He concludes, from a review of the field of AI ethics, that AI ethics, "lacks mechanisms to reinforce its own normative claims."

[6] It is no surprise that a growing number of multinational firms have been coming up with their own ethical AI principles. For example, Baker-Brunnbauer (2020) relates the case of German automotive company *Continental* who in June 2020 "announced its intention to develop a code of ethics for its internal development and usage of AI that is based on the EC Trustworthy AI guideline."

[7] See Feuerriegel et al. (2020, pp. 381–382) for a discussion of mathematical notions of fairness in AI.

[8] These are similar, with the exception of explicability, to principles of bioethics (Floridi et al., 2018).

Calo (2017, pp. 6–7) concurred with this assessment, noting that "... even assuming moral consensus, ethics lacks a hard enforcement mechanism. A handful of companies dominate the emerging AI industry. They are going to prefer ethical standards over binding rules for the obvious reason that no tangible penalties attach to changing or disregarding ethics should the necessity arise." In fact, AI developers and users may under highly competitive conditions face the incentive to "underinvest in ensuring their systems are safe" (Askell et al., 2019, p. 1). They may "skimp" on AI ethics also when lured by the potential winner-takes-all effects of eventually inventing an AGI, as Armstrong et al. (2016) emphasized.

To incentivize the ethics for HCAI, Eitel-Porter (2020, p. 1) argues for a strong, mandated governance controls including tools for managing processes and creating "associated audit trails." Floridi et al. (2018, p. 704) argue that governments should "incentivise financially the inclusion of ethical, legal and social considerations in AI research projects." This, then, is a key challenge facing HCAI: how to incentivize adherence to ethical principles? In the rest of the chapter, we argue that the nature of this challenge is such that PPaI are very relevant.

In Section 8.3, we argue that the literature on innovation policy suggests that public procurement can make an important contribution toward steering society toward its goals, in this case, the goal of a HCAI.

8.3 INNOVATION POLICY AND ARTIFICIAL INTELLIGENCE

In Section 8.2, we came to the conclusion that it is unlikely that HCAI will be forthcoming automatically from the market. This requires government intervention, and in particular, through steering the incentives for the private sector to develop and disseminate AI models that conform to the ethical and responsibility requirements of HCAI. For this, an innovation policy will be required. In this section, we discuss how directional innovation policies may be appropriate and effective, what the contribution of one specific innovation policy – innovation procurement – may be, and finally how PPaI, and specifically PPfI may be utilized.

8.3.1 *Directional Innovation Policies and AI*

According to Edler and Fagerberg (2017, p. 4), "Innovation is understood as the introduction of new solutions in response to problems, challenges, or opportunities that arise in the social and/or economic environment." According to Bloom et al. (2019, pp. 167–168), the empirical evidence from the literature suggests that social returns to innovation "are much higher than private returns, which provides a justification for government-supported innovation policy." More generally, an innovation such as AI generates both positive and negative externalities and markets do not adequately capture these in market prices. As such, there is, as Korinek (2019, p. 4) points out, "no theoretical reason to believe that the free market will direct innovative efforts to the most socially desirable innovations ... the market may thus guide innovation in the wrong direction." AI innovation will thus not automatically result in HCAI.

The implication is that HCAI is a challenge for innovation policies. Innovation policies are "public interventions to support the generation and diffusion of innovation, whereby an innovation is understood as the transformation of an invention into marketable products and services, the development of new business processes and methods of organization, and the absorption, adaptation and dissemination of novel technologies and know-how" (WTO, 2020b, p. 24).

There are many innovation policy tools aimed at the "generation and diffusion of innovation," from both the supply side and demand side.[9] Tools such as R&D subsidies and tax credits have typically been described as supply-side tools (Edler and Fagerberg, 2017),

[9] See, for example, Edler and Fagerberg (2017) who present and discuss fifteen major innovation policy instruments.

while regulations and public procurement have been described as demand-side tools (Aschhoff and Sofka, 2009). In recent years, there has been a subtle shift toward the increasing use of demand-side tools, in particular as these are seen as being potentially useful for industrial policy purposes and to facilitate economic restructuring (Crespi and Guarascio, 2019; Edler and Fagerberg, 2017). This growing use is part of what is termed the "directional turn" in innovation policy – not to encourage innovation for the sake of innovation but for addressing a pressing societal need or challenge (Miller and Lehoux, 2020).

Present concerns with directional innovation and industrial policies are based on the recognition that government intervention was in the past important for the development of important technologies, such as "jet engines, radar, nuclear power, the Global Positioning System (GPS), and the internet" (Bloom et al., 2019, p. 166). Clemens and Rogers (2020) studied how government procurement influenced innovation in prosthetics during the US Civil War and World War I, and concluded that the nature of government procurement can influence significantly whether innovation will be on costs or quality – which is a finding with much relevance for the challenge of HCAI, which is primarily a challenge relating to the quality of the technology. Another oft-quoted example of government steering the development of new technologies is the USA's efforts during World War II, which started with the creation of the National Defense Research Committee (NDRC) in 1940.

As we already mentioned in Chapter 2, these efforts resulted in many impactful new technologies and their diffusion during and after the war, including radar, mass-produced penicillin, radio communications, and pesticides such as Dichlorodiphenyltrichloroethane (DDT) (Gross and Sampat, 2020). After the World War II, three notable innovations where government incentives were important included the creation of the internet through the USA's DARPA program,[10] the creation of modern biomedical research through funding grants in the UK, and the creation of Google's search engine algorithm by a government grant (Lenderink et al., 2019). Interesting discussions of the specific role of government procurement in the establishment of the computer industry, the semiconductor industry, and the US commercial aircraft industry are contained in Geroski (1990).

Azoulay et al. (2018a, pp. 69–70) discuss the USA's DARPA program as a catalyst for many modern-day technologies, not only the internet but also personal computers, lasers, and Microsoft Windows. DARPA's approach may be argued to be eminently suitable to the challenge facing the development and diffusion of HCAI. Fouse et al. (2020) discuss how DARPA, through its various initiatives, had an "outsized" influence on the development of AI and continues to do so. For instance, DARPA is at the time of writing reported to be "investing more than US $2 billion in AI through its initiative, AI Next" (Fouse et al., 2020, p. 4).

As discussed by Azoulay et al. (2018a), DARPA's projects typically are focused on generating new technological solutions where three characteristics of the technology and markets overlap, namely: (1) there has to be a societal challenge; (2) the technology must be new and on the beginning of the technology *S-curve*; and (3) there are significant frictions in the markets for ideas and technology that will hinder a spontaneous market solution. In the case of HCAI, all three of these conditions are present, as it presents a significant societal challenge, the technology is new (in particular the alignment with human values), and the high degree to which the technology, being data-based, is subject to knowledge spillover and data network effects. These three conditions are also amenable to be influenced through public procurement for and of innovation as we will discuss

[10] Recall that DARPA is the acronym for the USA's Department of Defense's "Defense Advanced Research Projects Agency" which was launched in 1958 and created the Advanced Research Projects Agency Network (ARPANET) (Azoulay et al., 2018a).

in greater detail in Subsection 8.3.2. For instance, public procurement can effectively stimulate from the demand side the production of socially desirable technologies (Miller and Lehoux, 2020); it is better suited to technologies that are still early in the product-life cycle (such as AI) (Geroski, 1990); and it overcomes knowledge spillover externalities by creating new markets and networks.

In Subsection 8.3.2, we discuss the emerging literature on PPaI.

8.3.2 Public Procurement and Innovation

Public procurement refers to "the direct purchase of goods and services by the public sector" (Crespi and Guarascio, 2019, p. 783). The potential impact of public procurement is enormous. Gerdon and Molinari (2020) document for instance that there are more than 250,000 public authorities in the EU alone, who spend more than EUR 2 trillion annually on procurement.

Public procurement in general has long since been a tool to promote innovation (and industrialization). Most often in the past, it has been used *ex post* to support new innovations by creating a demand for the product (being a customer for new products). This is also the way in which Lin (2020, p. 26) conceives of the relationship between PPfI support. However, this is a rather restricted view: through the more targeted approaches of public procurement for and of innovation, governments can also *ex ante* support research and development of goods and services that do not yet exist – for present purposes, HCAI solutions. In this government can fulfill the function of a lead user role in innovation, as for instance argued by von Hippel (1976), and it can also create new networks and assist in the diffusion of innovations for instance by helping small and medium enterprises (SMEs) to adopt and use AI[11] (Czarnitzki et al., 2020). There has been a growing interest in recent years by governments to support innovation through public procurement – the WTO (2020a,

[11] In the case where the public sector procures a new innovation for its own use, it is termed *intrinsic procurement* and when it is procured for use outside of the government, it is termed *extrinsic procurement* (Czarnitzki et al., 2020).

p. 67) documents that 81 percent of Organization of Economic Cooperation and Development (OECD) countries have adopted initiatives to stimulate innovation through public procurement.

PPaI is, as we explained in the introduction, a term encompassing three modes of innovation from the perspective of public procurement. As discussed by Obwegeser and Müller (2018, p. 5), the first is PPfI, which deals with the question, how can public procurement drive innovation? This refers broadly to all public procurement initiatives aimed at innovation. There are many types and modalities of PPfI depending on focus, use, output, and interaction with suppliers (see Lenderink et al., 2019). A full discussion of the perturbations and typologies of procurement of and for innovation falls outside the scope of this chapter – the reader is referred to Lenderink et al. (2019) for an extensive overview.

For present purposes, though, PPfI includes the procurement of products and services that do not yet exist. In the EU, the explicit use of public procurement in order to procure such products or services is relatively recent (Czarnitzki et al., 2020). Edler and Georghiou (2007) relate how the PPfI, after having been neglected in the EU, got onto the EU's agenda around 2003. This eventually resulted in the European Commission's (EC) *Handbook on Public Procurement for Innovation* in 2007. One of the innovations in public procurement that the EU introduced herein was the legal instrument of *Precommercial Procurement (PCP) of innovation*. PCP "concerns the procurement of R&D services prior to commercialisation, where new solutions for a specific social need or challenge are developed in competition with risk-benefit sharing between the public organisation and potential suppliers" (Lenderink et al., 2019, p. 8). PCP is "a competitive and selective" instrument, as firms have to compete and come up with the best solution on their own (Aschhoff and Sofka, 2009, p. 1236), and it "emphasizes the need for new development of a solution to solve a specific requirement" (Obwegeser and Müller, 2018, p. 11).

The second mode of innovation from the perspective of public procurement is PPoI. This deals with the question, how can public services be innovated? For instance, government departments such as health, education, and energy, to name but a few, could increase efficiency through adopting AI solutions, for instance, AI diagnostic tools for hospitals and energy monitoring systems for reducing emissions from government buildings.

A third mode of innovation from the perspective of public procurement is IPP. It deals with the question, how can public institutions procure innovatively? The demands of steering societal outcomes through public procurement, including to steer advanced technologies such as AI, will require that public procurement itself be conducted in a more advanced manner – that the public sector innovate itself in how it procures innovation. This is not least due to the complexity of AI and the need for government agencies to understand the technology, but also due to the need to continually monitor and upgrade AI technologies, which are never static, a result of AI models constantly learning and changing behavior as they get exposed to more data.

PPaI has been shown to be an effective tool to steer innovation.[12] Czarnitzki et al. (2020) study the case of Germany, where the government has already since 2009 allowed for PPoI. They find from an analysis of 3,410 cases, between 2010 and 2012, that the use of this instrument by the German government "increased turnover with new products and services in the German business sector by EUR 13 billion in 2012, which represents 0.37% of GDP. Standard procurement tenders without innovation-related components, by contrast, show no detectable relationship" (Czarnitzki et al., 2020, p. 2). Moreover, based on calculations from German public procurement and R&D spending, they conclude that "the quantitative potential of

[12] Geroski (1990, p. 189) argues that PPI can be even better than R&D subsidies and tax credits to steer innovation, because "procurement programmes link the production of innovations to their use" while "subsidies focus only on the production of innovations."

public procurement of innovation is about ten times larger than the amount of public R&D subsidies distributed to the business sector" (Czarnitzki et al., 2020, p. 3). Other interesting studies of PPaI include Miller and Lehoux (2020), who study the use of PPoI in the Canadian healthcare sector.

We can also report examples of how government procurement is already having an impact on the development and diffusion of AI. Simonite (2020) reports that in the USA, the Centers for Medicare and Medicaid Services (CMS) will facilitate the dissemination of particular AI models for use in medical diagnostics in US hospitals. Through this, the government is paying the health service to use particular AI algorithms. Beraja et al. (2020) study the case of facial recognition AI in China and note the significant role that the government's steering of the technology played. They argue from this that because data is central to AI and furthermore that "the state is a key collector of data" as well as that there are economies of scope from sharing data across firms, that government is well positioned to stimulate AI innovation. Specifically, they find that "following the receipt of a government contract to supply AI software, firms produce more software both for government and commercial purposes when the contract provides access to more government data" (Beraja et al., 2020, p. 1).

Finally, Stojčić et al. (2020) argue that public procurement of and for innovation (PPoI, PPfI) can help build innovation capability, unlike R&D grants and tax credits, which depend on existing innovation capability. In the novel case of AI ethical embeddedness, innovation capability may not be broadly present among firms. Therefore, the suitability for PPoI and PPfI in the context of steering HCAI is particularly appropriate.

8.3.3 How Can Public Procurement and Innovation Steer AI?

We have noted on a few occasions in this chapter why PPoI and PPfI can be relevant and appropriate for the steering of AI toward HCAI.

Having established the why of public procurement for and of innovation, we will deal in the rest of this section with the how. We will in particular focus on the use of PCP.

For ordering the discussion, it is useful to start with the salient features of PCP, and then indicate what elements the contracting authority (CA) should emphasize in the case of steering toward HCAI, where after we will note some additional requirements – innovations in procurement – that may be particularly useful for the success of PCP with respect to HCAI.

8.3.3.1 Precommercial Procurement of Innovation

First, we discuss the salient features of PCP as a tool to steer HCAI. PCP for innovation is the very first EU legal provision, available to the public sector, to steer and procure innovative solutions that are not available in the market and that require R&D activity. As such, it is very relevant to steer innovation toward HCAI. The 2007 PCP Communication was followed by additional, clarifying documents released to specify its correct interpretation and for its implementation. Yet the main message has been clear from the very beginning, namely that PCP can be used to procure R&D services only, needed to develop an innovative solution that is unavailable in the market. More specifically, PCP can be used to develop prototypes, up to a few units of the final product, to make sure the solution is as desired by the procurer. However, PCP cannot be used by a CA to procure the needed quantity of the final product. Indeed, to do so, at the end of PCP, the CA should follow up with a commercial procurement, opening a competitive tendering, or some type of negotiated procedure within the legal framework defined by the 2014 EU Public Procurement Directive (EC, 2014). In such procurement, any eligible firm could compete for the commercial contract, and not just those that participated to the PCP.

The underlying idea, behind the separation of the R&D phase from the commercial procurement phase, is that the EC did not want to restrict the commercial procurement of potential innovative solutions only to PCP participants. As a matter of fact, if, while a PCP procedure is taking place, other firms in the market develop interesting new solutions, they should be allowed to participate in the commercial procurement of the final product. This would be compliant with the principle of fair treatment with respect to potential participants, with the principle of open competition, in the best interest of CA and of the entire society.

After more than a dozen years from its introduction, PCP is gradually diffusing across EU countries, and AI-based solutions are naturally being proposed within such purchasing procedures. A distinguishing feature of PCP is that the initial need is formulated directly by the public authorities, as much as the US Department of Defence (DoD) does it with DARPA, which implies that the solutions must satisfy technical but also ethical requirements, in compliance with the mission of the state. For this reason, AI-based solutions originated within the PCP would avoid innovations that are potentially harmful for the society.

The 2007 Communication elaborates on the fact that PCP should be founded on a risk-sharing principle, between companies and CA, concerning the possibility of project failure. Furthermore, EC suggests that as an incentive to participate in the PCP, the intellectual property rights (IPR) behind the new solutions should be left with the companies invited by CA, rather than being appropriated by CA. Though the reason behind the suggestion is clear, with some AI-based innovative solutions contracting authorities may consider keeping the IPR, in exchange of a compensation to the companies. This could take place when the CA wants to have under its own control the diffusion and continuous updating of the new product, which in the case of ethical and responsible AI solutions that it wants to disseminate to SMEs and update over time (as was shown to be necessary in Section 2.1) would be necessary.

In Article 31 of the 2014 Public Procurement Directive, the EC introduced an additional legal provision for procuring innovative solutions, the so-called Innovation Partnership (IP). Unlike PCP in the IP, the CA may not unbundle the procurement of the R&D phase from the commercial phase, that is, the procurement of the desired quantity of the final product. As a result, currently, public officers in the EU have two alternative legal instruments to procure innovative solutions, which have not been developed yet and require R&D activity: PCP and IP.

8.3.3.2 Using PCP to Steer Innovation toward HCAI

In what follows, we discuss some of the main elements of PCP and case studies to articulate how public procurement can steer AI solutions in the EU public sector. In the 2007 Communication, the EC suggests a model procedure for PCP composed of three phases to implement the PCP. CAs are by no means mandated to follow such a model, but it can certainly be a very helpful benchmark for them. A PCP is typically preceded by one, or more, sessions of market consultation. These sessions are publicly announced and organized by CA to inform all the potentially interested subjects of its needs and of the problem – for example, the need for an AI solution that is consistent with certain ethical principles – that will be the object of the PCP.

Then a call for manifestation of interest to participate in a PCP for an ethical AI solution is openly announced. After having received the initial manifestation of interest, CA can opt to invite a restricted number of companies for the first phase. In such a phase, CA asks the invited companies to propose an initial draft of the would-be final solution. Once received the proposals, a subset of them will be selected for the second phase where a prototype of the solution will be presented. Then, a subset of firms that submitted a prototype will be invited to the third phase, where the selected companies are asked by CA to produce a few units of the final solution, to check if it works as desired. To prevent the emergence of dominant/unique solutions, the 2007 Communication suggests that at least two companies should be invited to the third phase.

As said, if the solution is satisfactory, and the CA is interested in procuring a solution such as the one that emerged from the PCP, then after the conclusion of the PCP, the CA will have to open a follow-up procurement procedure, for products that no longer require R&D. For this reason, such a procedure would fall under the 2014 Public Procurement Directive, and the CA will now be able to describe precisely in the tender documentation what it wishes to purchase. Of course, in this case, those companies that were able to reach the third phase of the PCP will have some advantage, but no certainty to obtain the contract. Still, in this case, since the procured solution would be innovative, according to the EC terminology, it will be called PPI, that is, public procurement of an innovative solution, which however does not require R&D activity. It is still considered innovation procurement because it purchases an object which was not in the market yet.

The earlier short description should clarify how AI-based innovative solutions could be driven in the desired direction by the public sector, in all the PCP phases. From the original formulation of the problem, to the gradual screening and selection of proposals taking place across the three phases, until PCP ends, CA can navigate the whole process toward solutions that are beneficial for the society. In this navigation process, a number of elements are particularly relevant for HCAI solutions – and some of them may require innovation in public procurement.

The first is that the CA should from the outset approach the use of PCP for an ethical, HCAI solution with the intention to foster cooperation between firms and research organizations, as well as multidisciplinary cooperation. According to Askell et al. (2019, p. 1), "competition between AI companies could decrease the incentives of each company to develop responsibly by increasing their incentives to develop faster. As a result, if AI companies would prefer to develop AI systems with risk levels that are closer to what is socially optimal – as we believe many do – responsible AI development can be seen as a collective action problem." As said, the PCP benchmark is based on a procedure with a sequential selection of companies, hence in principle competitive. Yet, despite this, in using PCP, the CA can design calls for HCAI solutions that require and facilitate such cooperation. Askell et al. (2019) discuss various ways in which this can be incentivized, for instance, by creating high shared gains from cooperation and penalizing noncooperation. Finally, if the PCP model turns out to be unsuitable for convincingly establish cooperative behavior among invited firms, then the IP could be used instead as a legal instrument.

The second is that the CA should insist on ethical design approaches be followed through all the stages of the procurement process. In this respect, Crawford and Calo (2016) proposed two broad approaches to the ethical design of AI, which may also be applied by a CA using PCP. The first is to require developers of AI solutions to use frameworks such as value-sensitive design and responsible innovation, and the second is to require a social-systems approach to building AI, which would entail consideration of "the social and political history of the data" (Crawford and Calo, 2016, p. 313). The latter approach would be in line with the need for data justice.

The third is that the CA should promote greater openness in AI development – for instance by requiring open scrutiny of solutions that it purchases and requiring certain degrees of openness and outside participation in and evaluation of the solutions developed as part of the procurement action. Bostrom (2017) concludes that over the medium term, greater openness in AI development would be unambiguously positive by speeding up the development and diffusion of AI.

According to Bostrom (2017, p. 137), "openness would improve static efficiency, by making products available at marginal cost (e.g., in the form of open-source software) and allowing a given level of state-of-the-art technical capability to diffuse more quickly through the economy." He is more concerned that over the long run, the openness would discourage innovation to the extent that the effort may be motivated by having a monopoly in the market from a proprietary innovation. However, through PPI, this long-run disincentive effect of openness may be compensated for by the government not only by reducing the costs and risks of developing a new AI solution, but also by offering a firm the chance to build its capacity for developing and using AI, and even for a company to benefit in complementary areas to the AI being procured (Bostrom, 2017).

Fourth, and related to the need for openness, is the requirement that the PCP call specifically take care of the reliance of AI models on large datasets. Beraja et al. (2020), for instance, distinguish between "data-rich versus data-scarce government contracts." We want to argue that PCP contracts for HCAI should be of the data-rich variety. A data-rich PCP contract should in particular address the *data parity problem* (Calo, 2017), which refers to the fact that "a few large firms have disproportionate access to big data (BD) necessary to train AI models. Mostly, small businesses do not have the scale and scope and resources to gather data and benefit from data network economies. This could mean that ML applications will bend systematically toward the goals of profit-driven companies and not society at large" (Calo, 2017, p. 19).

The data parity problem is mirrored in society as a digital divide, with data gaps, and data absences creating and perpetuating inequality in access to the use and knowledge of AI, and in benefiting from AI. In recent times, the imperative of addressing these as a requirement for HCAI has resulted in the notion of data justice, which goes beyond data gaps and data absences to the recognition of structural inequalities. According to Dencik et al. (2019, p. 874), "The framework of data justice broadens the terms of the debate in a way that accounts for a host of issues that are compounded in the datafied society, as evidenced in recent scholarship relating to democratic procedures, the entrenchment and introduction of inequalities, discrimination and exclusion of certain groups, deteriorating working conditions, or the dehumanisation of decision-making and interaction around sensitive issues. These discussions suggest a need to position data in a way that engages more explicitly with questions of power, politics, inclusion and interests, as well as established notions of ethics, autonomy, trust, accountability, governance and citizenship." The discussion of data justice and the relevance of societal concerns about fairness, diversity, and equity in the application of potential general-purpose technologies such as AI reflects the fact that ultimately, AI is sociotechnical in that the value that it offers "depends on not only technical hardware but also human behavior and social institutions for their proper functioning" (van de Poel, 2020, p. 7).

Fifth, the CA should make sure that all documentation[13] and audits are captured, as it "is important to provide an audit trail in case of subsequent issues with the model" (Eitel-Porter, 2020, p. 4). This is relevant not only for adjudicating the quality of the solution offered but also to support efforts to continually review the solution so as to ensure that "ethical parameters are not breached over time" (Eitel-Porter, 2020, p. 5). This is not so much due to the ethical norms changing, but because of the nature of ML, which adapts and changes as it learns more (gathers more data). The important point is that ethical AI solutions may not automatically remain ethical given the possibility of learning, due to AI essentially being an intelligent agent (Riedl, 2019). Anderson and Anderson (2007) refer to this feature of AI to argue that the ultimate challenge is to create explicit ethical machines, which are able to learn and formulate "their own ethical choices based on their own set of principles."

Having ensured that the above five elements are followed, the CA purchasing an AI solution would finally need to be able to verify that the prototype solution offered during stage 3 of the PCP process conforms to the specifications set out in the call – in other words, the technical AI solution needed as well as the requirement that ethical principles are observed. In this regard, it is important to set up adequate measures for verification. As Brundage et al. (2020, p. 1) stress, "The capacity to verify claims made by developers, on its own, would be insufficient to ensure responsible AI development. Not all

[13] This should include all documentation including AI impact assessments (Gerdon and Molinari, 2020).

important claims admit verification, and there is also a need for oversight agencies such as governments and standards organizations to align developers' incentives with the public interest." Values[14] in AI models need to be "intended, embodied, and realized values" (van de Poel, 2020, p. 5). For present purposes, drawing on van de Poel (2020, p. 9), we can state that for a procured AI solution to embody a particular value, denoted by *V*, it should be the case that at least two conditions be met: first, the AI must be designed for *V*, and second, that in using the AI solution, the values of *V* would be promoted. Thus, AI models need to be designed in order to meet a particular value, for instance, human health, and second, utilizing the AI model should then indeed promote that value, for example, human health.

What measures can be used for verification and assessing whether desired values are intended, embodied, and realized? Brundage et al. (2020) discuss third-party auditing, red teaming exercises, the piloting of bias and safety bounties, and the sharing of information about AI accidents. In all of these actions, governments can benefit from having independent oversight bodies track the work of contractors, and subject them to risk analyses and public scrutiny. Tzachor et al. (2020) advocate the use of "red teaming" by oversight bodies to stress test any AI solutions that contractors may come up with, where "red teaming is a way of challenging the blind spots of a team by explicitly looking for flaws from an outsider or adversarial perspective" (Tzachor et al., 2020, p. 366). According to Tzachor et al. (2020), one legacy of the COVID-19 pandemic is the realization that circumstances can require the application of new AI solutions under extremely short time horizons and with urgency, and that "doing ethics with urgency" becomes important. Such doing ethics with urgency will require according to the authors that the government should be able to "rapidly conduct robust testing and verification of systems" (ibid., p. 366).

[14] See the discussion in van de Poel (2020) on the meaning of values and how to assess whether the desired values are indeed intended, embodied and realized.

Even if these various measures and methods for verification and assessment are successful in finding that the conditions for the AI solution to embody human-centered values are met, a further problem is that as was mentioned, AI models may have unintended results. Moreover, values may change over time. To deal with such unintended results and changes in values, it requires continuous involvement and monitoring by the CA. According to van de Poel (2020), the design of technologies can never remain static, and they may need to be redesigned at some future stage in light of possible unintended effects as well as possible shifts in values.

At this stage, once the CA is satisfied with the final prototype of the HCAI solution from the PCP process, it will have to ensure that the public sector more broadly has in place complementary mechanisms for dealing with the remaining safety risks posed by AI. As we mentioned, normal accidents are one of the salient risks posed by AI. It is unfortunately the case that the risks of accidents "cannot simply be 'designed out' of the technology – at least not without giving up on many of their benefits" (Maas, 2018, p. 5). Maas (2018) concludes that this requires two complementary approaches: first, that governments ensure that disaster and accident insurance schemes are appropriate to cover AI risks, and second, that more research be encouraged into AI safety and AI ethics – see also Anderson and Anderson (2007).

Finally, for the PCP process to be ultimately successful in contributing to innovations in the field of AI, the government and its contracting authorities will need to upgrade and continually invest in their own AI expertise (Calo, 2017). With this, they could even use data science and AI techniques within the public sector to explore and test the ethical consequences of AI. For example, Yu et al. (2018) survey various technical solutions to support the evaluation of ethical concerns in AI. These include useful resources and initiatives on which the public sector's scientists and advisors could draw, such as the *GenEth* ethical dilemma analyzer that can be used to explore ethical dilemmas; the *MoralDM* tool helping to resolve ethical dilemmas through first-principles reasoning and analogical reasoning; and crowdsourcing of self-reported preferences such as through the *Moral Machine* project.[15]

8.4 A MODEL OF PUBLIC PROCUREMENT AND RESPONSIBLE AI INNOVATION

As we outlined in Section 8.3, a CA in the EU could use the provisions of the EU's PCP instrument to procure an AI solution that conforms to high standards of ethical and responsible AI, as was identified in Section 7.2.1. By issuing an explicit call for such a solution and offering to fund the R&D costs of the successful company, the public sector could incentivize the development and diffusion of HCAI. This incentive is important, in the absence of which companies may skimp on adequate ethical and safety standards, as we argued in the introduction and Section 8.2.1.

We can now formalize these ideas. First, we can note that in the absence of the public sector's financial incentives, companies may not take the risks to provide the socially optimal AI solution. Let us suppose that a company X is willing, and has the competence, to develop an AI solution that could result in a socially desirable, HCAI system. The project requires resources to be invested and success in its development process is intrinsically uncertain. More specifically, if $C > 0$ is the amount of money invested in the project by company X and $\pi(C)$ is the success probability, with $\pi'(C) \geq 0$ and $\pi''(C) \leq 0$, then typically $0 \leq \pi(C) < 1$ for any level of C. That is, no matter how large the company's effort, success will remain uncertain.

Here $\pi(C)$ formalizes the technology available to develop the project and exhibit nonincreasing returns of scale.[16] Suppose now that, if development is successful and the project is commercialized,

[15] See www.moralmachine.net.

[16] In reality, several technologies exhibit increasing returns of scale, at least for some investment levels. However, to keep the exposition simple, with no major loss of generality, in what follows we do not consider this possibility.

that the company's revenue would be R. Therefore, its profit would be a random variable defined as:

$$\Pi(C,R) = \begin{cases} R - C & \text{with probability } \pi(C) \\ -C & \text{with probability } 1 - \pi(C) \end{cases} \tag{8.1}$$

and the related expected profit is

$$E\Pi(C,R) = R\pi(C) - C \tag{8.2}$$

If the company maximizes (8.2), then the first-order condition is

$$R\pi'(C) - 1 = 0 \tag{8.3}$$

and the optimal investment level C^* given by

$$\pi'(C^*) = \frac{1}{R} \tag{8.4}$$

as long as $E\Pi(C^*, R)$ is non-negative. Equation (8.4) suggests that, due to the concavity of the success probability, the larger the revenue, the higher is C^*. However, there is no guarantee that, regardless of the value of R, that the company would invest at all. Indeed, a non-negative expected profit requires that

$$\pi'(0) > \frac{1}{R} \tag{8.5}$$

which, if not satisfied, would discourage the company to undertake any investment.

For example, suppose $\pi(C) = a\left(1 - e^{-bC}\right)$ with $0 < a < 1$ and $b > 0$. It is immediate to see that the larger are both, a and b, the higher is $\pi(C)$, and so the less challenging is the development process of the AI project. Interestingly, the parameters a and b play two different roles. Indeed, while $a = \lim_{C\to\infty} \pi(C)$, that is, it defines the maximum level that success probability can take, b only defines how $\pi(C)$ changes as C changes. This can be seen by considering for example the elasticity of the function $\pi(C)$, namely the percentage change in $\pi(C)$ due to 1 percent change in C, which is given by

$$\frac{\pi'(C)C}{\pi(C)} = \frac{be^{-bC}C}{(1 - e^{-bC})} \tag{8.6}$$

that is independent of a. In this case (8.5) would become

$$ab > \frac{1}{R} \tag{8.7}$$

which suggests that the company decides to invest if the project is sufficiently rewarding, or technically, not too difficult, or both. In this case, the optimal level of investment C^* would be

$$C^* > \frac{log(abR)}{b} \tag{8.8}$$

which, consistently with Equation (8.7), is positive for $abR > 1$.

However, suppose now that Equation (8.7) is not satisfied and the company decides not to invest. Failure to develop the AI project may damage the society and so A could consider supporting the company, however, only if the ethical level of the solution is sufficiently high. Broadly speaking, suppose that company X has to compete for funding with other companies as per the EU's PCP, and that the ethical level of the solution under development, summarized by the indicator $e \geq 0$, is positively related to the probability $\theta(e)$ of being funded by A. We assume $\theta(e = 0) = 0$ if differentiable, $\theta'(e) > 0$, and that $\lim_{e \to \infty} \theta(e) = 1$. Finally, we now assume that the R&D total costs for the company are given by $C + ce$, where ce is the total cost due to reaching the ethical level e and $c > 0$ is the marginal cost for doing so. Under these assumptions, in the analysis conducted so far, X undertook no, or very low, investment to take care of the ethical features of the solution under development. Therefore, company X needs to decide the level of both C and e, and meticulously document e as per the CA's requirements.

For this, suppose A and X agree to write the following contract: "if the AI project is funded by A, with probability $\theta(e)$, and successfully developed then A pays to X the sum p while if the project fails to be developed then A pays to X the sum of q, with $p > q$. Moreover, the intellectual property rights will remain with X, which will still enjoy reward R." As we shall see later, such admittedly simple contract will induce the company to try developing a solution that contains consideration of the ethical requirements.

Before proceeding, it is worth noticing that conditional on A funding X, the above contract operates as a mixture of pull $(p - q)$ and push (q) incentives. That is, although we assume A will only pay at the end of the project, as it may be with the EU's PCP, q are guaranteed to X and it is as if they would be paid upfront, hence as a push incentive. For this reason, we could also imagine that should X lack resources for engaging in the process, then A may indeed pay upfront the sum q. Nonetheless, the additional sum $p - q$ will be paid only conditionally upon the success of the project, hence as a pull incentive.

Then the company's profit $\Pi(C, R, p, q, c, e)$ is defined as the following random variable:

$$\Pi(C, R, p, q, c, e) = \begin{cases} (p+R) - C - ce & \text{with probability } \theta(e)\pi(C + ce) \\ q - C - ce & \text{with probability } \theta(e)(1 - \pi(C+ce)) \\ 0 & \text{with probability} 1 - \theta(e) \end{cases} \tag{8.9}$$

Therefore, its expected profit will be

$$E\Pi(C, R, p, q, c, e) = \begin{cases} \theta(e)\pi(C+ce)(p+R-q) + \theta(e)(q - C - ce) & \text{if } e > 0 \\ 0 & \text{if } e = 0 \end{cases} \tag{8.10}$$

and the optimal level of investment C^{**} chosen by the firm would now be such that

$$\pi'(C^{**} + ce) = \frac{1}{(R + p - q)} \tag{8.11}$$

Condition (8.11) looks like Condition (8.4) except that the right-hand side now has the additional term $p - q > 0$ at the denominator. This basically increases X's expected revenues providing a stronger incentive for the company to invest resources and engage in developing a solution, provided it is ethically acceptable to A. This will now take place if

$$\lim_{(C+ce)\to 0} \pi'(C + ce) = ab > \frac{1}{R + p - q} \tag{8.12}$$

Condition (8.12) indicates that A could always find a large enough amount $p - q$ such that Condition (8.5) is satisfied. Moreover, notice that on the left-hand side of Condition (8.12) we are taking $\lim_{(C+ce)\to 0} \pi'(C + ce)$ because expression (10) is equal to 0 for $e = 0$, and so $\pi'(0)$ would not even be defined. Moreover, with an acceptable estimation of $\pi(C)$, authority A, from Condition (8.11), could also determine the effort $(C^{**} + ce)$ of X.

Considering again the previous example $\pi(C) = a(1 - e^{-bC})$, the optimal investment level for X would now be

$$C^{**} + ce = \frac{log(ab(R + p - q))}{b} \tag{8.13}$$

The element $p - q$ will work as a co-funding term for X to engage in the AI project. To summarize, what is important for A to motivate X to invest more in R&D activities are not the values of p and q separately, but rather only their difference. Indeed, this is true even if $q = 0$, as long as p is large enough.

It is worth stressing that the optimal level of R&D investment obtained from Condition (8.13) must include the component $ce > 0$, needed by X to receive funding from A, which represents the expenditure undertaken by X to introduce ethical features into the solution. The desirable level of the indicator e resolves a trade-off between increasing the probability of being funded by A, as well as of finding the innovative solution, and of increasing the costs. It would be found by maximizing Condition (8.10) also with respect to e.

To summarize, the above equations describe a simple framework where public procurement can induce HCAI solutions, by conditioning the funding of a company to the presence of ethical features, for example, in the outcome of a PCP as well as of IP procedures. This use of public procurement to promote HCAI, as we modeled it here, is complementary to the approach described in Chapter 7 of this book, where we modeled the use of public procurement to reduce the likelihood of arms races for AI.

The mechanism that we outlined earlier for incentivizing R&D for HCAI is relevant not only for addressing the general reluctance of companies to invest in HCAI but also more generally for the fact that concerns about technologies such as AI's have led to increasing calls in recent years to make "technology impact assessments" (TIAs) obligatory for entrepreneurs before implementing and investing in new technologies (Korinek, 2019). This could have negative effects, however, on innovation, over and above the impact of the risks already illustrated here. It may be worth pointing out that one reason why innovation in the digital economy has not been declining as innovation elsewhere is due to the fact that until now, such innovation has been relatively unencumbered by bureaucratic influence, that is, it has been rather more "permissionless." Rather than risk disincentivizing innovation, we want to argue that PCP, organized for example within a framework such as the one described here, can obtain the same results, but through rewarding entrepreneurs who do perform TIAs. In other words, PCP may reduce the fixed costs that a requirement such as TIA can cause, by requesting the solution to incorporate the requested features, possibly cofunding the engaged companies for this.

Finally, given the potential of PCP to steer HCAI as this simple model shows, we can conclude this section by pointing out that although PPfI as an instrument to steer AI is still relatively neglected, there are already a small sample of PCP AI-based initiatives undertaken in the EU since 2007 when PCP was launched. It is useful to briefly mention these projects, and to recommend further research to document the lessons learned from them.

A first example is that during the years 2015–2016, a consortium of five hospitals, in different European countries implemented an EU-funded PCP project to develop a highly interoperable, AI-based, telemedicine system for the cockpit of intensive care units in hospitals. The project, called *THALEA*, was successfully completed and as a result the Dutch company called *NewCompliance*, which developed its solution for the operating room cockpit, was able to attract venture capital and sell the solutions to several hospitals in the EU and in the US. Moreover, it established partnerships with some major companies in the field to improve the solution, scaling up its business volume and size.

Among the PCP AI projects that have not been funded by the EU, a very timely and successful project is the PCP sponsored by the Danish Market Development Fund for self-driving robots, based on ultraviolet light, to disinfect hospitals. The project was initially promoted in 2014, and completed in 2017, by a group of Danish hospitals, hence much earlier than 2020, when the COVID-19 pandemic hit the world. As a result of the PCP project, the Danish company *Blue Ocean Robotics* attracted millions of dollars in venture capital, and sold its robots across several countries, to be used in hospitals across the world to help disinfecting hospitals during the COVID-19 pandemic.

Another interesting example of a non-EU-funded PCP is an AI-based smart mobility PCP project developed in the period 2014–2016 and promoted by the Dutch Province of North-Brabant, to try solving shock-wave traffic jam problems in the area. Traffic jams often occur when a vehicle suddenly stops, inducing also the following vehicles to suddenly use their breaks even more strongly, originating traffic jams. As the outcome of PCP, the company *Be-Mobile* produced an application merging and analyzing real-time data on traffic, reported by various sources, data on vehicles' speed, and to advise drivers on which roads/lanes to take. This innovative solution has been so successful that *Be-Mobile* was able to meaningfully scale up in terms of employers and raise funds.

8.5 CONCLUDING REMARKS

In recent years, there have been a growing number of proposals for ethical and responsible AI. A shortcoming of these is that they lack strong incentives for developers and users of AI to adhere to them. In this chapter, we make the case that PPaI is a potentially relevant tool with which to incentivize HCAI. Indeed, if the governance of AI deals with "how decisions are made about AI," and what "institutions and arrangements could help in this decision-making" (Dafoe, 2018, 2020), then PPaI as presented in this chapter is a key element of AI governance – however, an element that we argued is still neglected.

We provided a simple theoretical model to show that the procurement for an innovative AI solution, underpinned by ethical considerations, can provide both the tools and audit trails and the financial incentives necessary to steer AI toward HCAI. Additionally, we highlighted five elements that the EU's PCP instrument should specifically take into account when aiming to steer HCAI, as well as complementary initiatives, such as supporting more multidisciplinary research into ethics and making ethics computable. This could inform further innovations in public procurement itself.

In Chapter 9, we apply some of the thinking in this chapter to the specific case of BD. In Chapter 2, we defined BD as the "explosion in the quantity (and sometimes, quality) of available and potentially relevant data, largely the result of recent and unprecedented advancements in data recording and storage technology" (Diebold, 2012; cited in Favaretto et al., 2020, p. 1). We quoted *The Economist Magazine* which declared in 2017 that "the world's most valuable resource is no longer oil, but data" and pointed out that larger firms have an advantage in the data economy – hence shortcomings in how BD is gathered, used, and owned can hinder the diffusion of AI and exacerbate digital divides. In light of the potential for government policy to steer AI R&D, we explore in Chapter 9 how a key ingredient of AI – BD – may be steered and, moreover, improve policymaking in the public sector. Hence, we consider the general relation between BD, AI, and public policy.

9 Artificial Intelligence, Big Data, and Public Policy

9.1 INTRODUCTION

The digital revolution has made possible the collection and storage of data of unprecedented size. Consumption and lifestyle habits, people and objects' geolocation, people's attitude and behavior as recorded by cameras, traffic intensity and volume, fiscal and economic variables, and many other socioeconomic and geographic phenomena produce massive amounts of data that can now be recorded, stored, and analyzed. As per our overview in Chapter 2, the availability of data went parallel with the development of computational power, artificial intelligence (AI), and machine learning (ML) techniques, which in fact allowed for an extensive use of such data. There is a bidirectional relation between AI and big data (BD): while AI techniques make widespread use of BD, large data sets can only be analyzed through AI and ML-based methods.

In a variety of situations, collection of large data sets could be appropriately planned, and data storage well organized and structured for the current, and subsequent, analysis. This is when data are gathered with one, or more, specific purposes in mind from the very beginning of a project. For example, data on tax payments are carefully collected by the public sector, as a way to be informed on tax revenues, but also to monitor and estimate tax evasion and/or avoidance. However, in other cases, data can become available, and stored, as the side product of some activity but less well organized, if at all, because initially there is no specific plan to use them. For example, cameras positioned for security purposes at the entrance of a building could also record data on vehicles traffic in the relevant area. However, if measuring traffic intensity was not the main purpose for those cameras, then traffic-related data may not be collected in a structured way.

The definition of BD that we gave in Chapter 2 includes both of the above cases. Moreover, there seems to be an agreement that besides an unprecedented volume, BD are also characterized by velocity, variety, and complexity (Souza and Jacob, 2017). Defining what is a BD and how to merge large data sets with each other, as well as with other available data, is a fundamental starting point, discussed by Emani et al. (2015), Lane (2016), Yiu (2012), Chen and Zhang (2014), Margetts and Sutcliffe (2013), Michael and Miller (2013), Lazer et al. (2014), Kim et al. (2014), Schintler and Kulkarni (2014), and Mergel et al. (2016). Souza and Jacob (2017) and Sivarajah et al. (2017) address challenges and opportunities for policy makers related to the advent of the internet and the availability of BD.

Kim et al. (2014) observe how data collection, often unstructured, from many sources such as video, social communications, and sensors, can serve citizens by improving health care, traffic, and many other services. Cook (2014), Washington (2014), Clarke (2015), and Jarmin and O'Hara (2016) pose the issue of individual privacy and security associated to the reuse of US public data in BD projects, while Stough and McBride (2014) discuss methods on how to eliminate personal references for such reuse. Lavertu (2014) focuses on the consistency between publicly released data and public administration goals. In particular, due to BD availability, he points out how the public could mismeasure the performance of public administrations unless their goal is well specified and made public. Hilbert (2016) discusses how the availability of BD can create a digital divide in developing countries, between those who can inform their public policy with BD, and those who cannot.

Public procurement, which in Organization for Economic Development and Organization (OECD) countries counts for about 18 percent of the GDP, could also benefit from BD. In particular, Fazekas et al. (2016) show how one of its main challenges, the risk of corruption in the public sector, could be tackled by constructing indicators based on BD. The private sector too can take advantage of BD and its analytics in supply chain management (Wang et al., 2016).

In this chapter, we focus on the general relation between BD, AI, and public policy. More specifically, we discuss under what conditions the availability of large data sets can support and enhance public policy effectiveness – including in the use of AI – along two main directions. We first analyze how BD can help existing policy measures to improve their effectiveness and, second, we discuss how the availability of BD can suggest new, not yet implemented, policy solutions that can improve upon existing ones. In doing so, we assume that data represent a fundamental element in policymaking. Both points are discussed within a very simple model, which, despite its simplicity, may provide some interesting early insights on the issues. Our findings suggest that the desirability of BD to enhance policymaking depends on the goal of the public authority as well as on a variety of additional elements such as the cost of data collection and storage and the complexity and importance of the policy issue.

The chapter is structured as follows. In Section 9.2, we introduce the basics of the model and discuss conditions under which BD can improve the effectiveness of already existing policy solutions. In Section 9.3, we develop the model to investigate if and how BD can help suggesting new measures for solving policy issues, not yet implemented, while Section 9.4 concludes.

9.2 IMPROVING PUBLIC POLICY WITH BIG DATA

In the introduction, we mentioned several reasons why BD could be beneficial for the public sector. In this section, and in the next, we summarize some of them considering the following two general functions of BD in policymaking. The first one is that BD can help increase the effectiveness of policy measures already adopted by the public sector and, second, BD can help conceiving, implementing, new desirable policy solutions.

The former function takes place, for example, when BD can help increase the precision of a given measure on a policy target and, in so doing, improve the citizens' satisfaction and well-being. Policies related to public procurement contracts could represent a good example for this. Suppose the public sector is able to collect complete and detailed data on important procurement-related variables. For instance, procurement contracts costs and duration, overruns, bids of invited firms, size of the firms competing for the contract, market structure of the relevant firms, degree of compliance between the quality promised by the contractor when bidding and the quality effectively delivered during the contract execution, etc. Then contracting authorities could certainly design and conduct more effective procurement than when such data are unavailable, both in the selection phase of the contractor and when monitoring the execution phase. In a sense, BD in this case could be seen as a production factor to enhance the quality of existing policy measures.

The latter function takes place when data availability may help implementing policy measures that otherwise could not be undertaken, or even thought of. In this sense, BD could be seen as a factor producing new policy measures altogether. For example, a real-time road traffic control system could be used to distribute vehicles along available routes to prevent congestion. This could be done by closing, or rationing traffic, in certain roads when selected numerical indicators (for example, the number and size of vehicles per unit of time) reach some early warning value. Even if routes could be opened or closed in a flexible way, these actions may effectively be taken if decision-makers are well informed by data. Possibly, in some circumstances, it is precisely the availability of such detailed data that could suggest this policy measure altogether.

A general, though very stylized, framework to discuss these two issues may be the following. Suppose I is a set of public policy issues to be solved, somewhat related with each other, with $i \in I$ the generic open issue. Further, define as d the available data set that may be used for solving i. Moreover, assume S is the set of feasible policy solutions that can be adopted to tackle $i \in I$, where $s \in S$ stands for a generic solution.

Therefore, in general terms, policymaking activity of the public authority can be represented by a policy function p defined as follows:

$$p : I \times D \rightarrow S \tag{9.1}$$

where D is the set of feasible data sets, with $d \in D$ the generic data set. The interpretation of s is standard: $s = p(i, d)$ stands for the solution selected by the public authority to solve issue i with data d.

Though not necessary, to simplify the exposition and related analysis, we assume that i, d, and s could all be unambiguously represented by numerical indicators. In particular, we assume that higher values of i indicate more complex, demanding, policy issues, while larger values of d stand for bigger data sets. Moreover, in such a simple framework, $d < d'$ will also mean that the data set d is included in the data set d'. That is, for present purposes, we assume that D is a completely ordered set of feasible data sets. This is because they all concern a set of related policy issues, and for this reason also, the relevant data are related.

9.2.1 *Welfare Maximization as Goal*

Solving a policy issue requires choosing a policy measure, whose effectiveness depends on the data set. Which solution to take depends on the goal of the public authority and how it is affected by the policy issue. Therefore, to study the relation between data and public policy, we first need to specify the goal of the public authority.

Based on the above assumptions, a possible, general, way to formalize the public authority's benefit function could be as follows:

$$b(i, d) = b(\alpha(i)i - p(i, d)) \tag{9.2}$$

where $\alpha(i) \geq 0$, which we assume nondecreasing in i, is a function expressing the importance assigned by the authority to the policy issue i. The higher the $\alpha(i)$, the more important is the issue. The benefit function is defined in monetary terms and is interpretable as the monetary equivalent, for the public authority, of a certain level of well-being for the relevant community.

The intuition underlying Equation (9.2) is immediate. Because the authority is a public institution, its benefits are defined as a function of the difference, distance, between the targeted issue and the policy measure adopted for solving it. In general, we would expect b to be decreasing in the argument $|\alpha(i)i - p(i,d)|$, to formalize the idea that the policy measure must solve the open issue, and the wider the gap between the targeted issue and the solution, the lower the citizens' well-being. Notice however that definition (8.2) may not satisfy the above condition, for both positive and negative values of the function argument. For example, as we shall also discuss later, the function

$$b(i,d) = \frac{1}{(\alpha(i)i - p(i,d))} \tag{9.3}$$

being discontinuous at $\alpha(i)i - p(i,d) = 0$, hence decreasing and positive for $\alpha(i)i - p(i,d) > 0$ and decreasing, but negative, for $\alpha(i)i - p(i,d) < 0$, would not decrease with $|\alpha(i)i - p(i,d)|$.

For this reason, still assuming b to be decreasing with $|\alpha(i)i - p(i,d)|$, an alternative formulation to Equation (9.2) could be either

$$b(i,d) = \frac{1}{(|\alpha(i)i - p(i,d)|)} \tag{9.4}$$

or

$$b(i,d) = \frac{1}{(\alpha(i)i - p(i,d))^2} \tag{9.5}$$

Both of the above equations become larger as $\alpha(i)i - p(i,d)$ approaches 0, that is, when the solution precisely solves the policy issue, weighted by its degree of importance $\alpha(i)$. However, we shall see how Equation (9.3) would exhibit a different behavior in the neighbourhood of $\alpha(i)i - p(i,d) = 0$, with respect to Equations (9.4) and (9.5).

If data could be beneficial for solving policy issues, and so for the citizen's welfare, their collection, storage, and management are typically expensive. If $c(i,d)$ are the costs for collecting, storing, and managing data and

$$W(i,d) = b(i,d) - c(i,d) \tag{9.6}$$

is the welfare function of the authority, then, for given i, the authority's goal could be formulated as follows:

$$\max(0, \max_d W(i,d) = b(i,d) - c(i,d)) \tag{9.7}$$

Equation (9.7) establishes that data are gathered, and their size is determined, to maximize the authority's benefit, net of the costs of collecting and managing data.

Solution to Expression (9.7) depends on the shape of $p(i,d)$ and $c(i,d)$. As an example, suppose $b(\alpha(i)i - p(i,d)) = 1/(\alpha(i)i - p(i,d))$, $p(i,d) = id = c(i,d)$. That is, the policy rule and the cost function coincide, and they are linear in both i and d. In this case, it is immediate to see that the optimal data set $d^*(i)$ is given by

$$d^*(i) = \alpha(i) \tag{9.8}$$

Hence, $d^*(i)$ is directly related to $\alpha(i)$ only, so that the more important is the problem for the authority, the larger the data set, while the complexity of the policy issue, the index i, will have no role. That is, when the effectiveness of the policy measure is infinitely important, $b(0) = \infty$ for the authority, hence $\alpha(i)i = p(i,d)$, while the costs of d are bounded regardless of the policy problem, then it is best to collect data which are needed for the perfect solution of the issue, no matter how cheap/expensive they would be.

That is, the optimal data set $d^*(i)$ solves the equation $\alpha(i) - id^*(i) = 0$. Notice that due to the specific form of the benefit function, a value $d > \alpha(i)$ in this case produces a negative externality, with the welfare level being most negatively affected for d just above $\alpha(i)$. That is, in a rather peculiar way, for some reason the relevant authority could well tolerate a slight underperformance of the policy measure, while a slight overperformance would be considered as disastrous.

If this is too particular, possibly unrealistic, representation of the authority preferences, then a way to deal with the point is to take specification (9.5), assuming $b(\alpha(i)i - p(i,d)) = 1/(a(i)i - p(i,d))$.[2]

Indeed, this would eliminate the negative externality effect by $d > \alpha(i)$, while keeping the idea of a correct policy measure being of paramount importance for the authority. For this reason, the optimal solution in this case remains $d^*(i) = \alpha(i)$, but with small mistakes, in implementing the solution, the authority welfare will still be high, regardless of the mistake sign.

As an extension of the analysis, consider now the following formulation of the benefit function $b(\alpha(i)i - p(i,d)) = 1/(\beta + (\alpha(i)i - p(i,d)))$ with $\beta \geq 0$. The parameter $\beta \geq 0$ indicates how much the authority is satisfied with a perfect solution of policy issue i only. It is part of its preferences definition and given in the analysis. The smaller the β, the more the authority cares only about a solution of i, while the larger the β, the higher the concern of the authority for problems besides policy issue i.

Considering the above benefit function, the optimal data set would now become

$$d^*(i) = \alpha(i) + \frac{\beta}{i} > \alpha(i) \tag{9.9}$$

Equation (9.9) suggests that now the optimal data set is also positively related to $\frac{\beta}{i}$, which can be interpreted as a ratio establishing the relative importance of other problems versus the relevant policy issue. The smaller the $\frac{\beta}{i}$, the closer the optimal data set tends to be to the optimal solution of the policy issue only, while the higher the $\frac{\beta}{i}$, the more the data set tends to be larger than the one prescribed by the perfect solution of the i issue. The presence of additional and important public problems would induce the collection of a larger volume of data than when only the open issue under discussion is considered.

Before concluding this section, it may be interesting to ask for which i Equation (9.9) is minimized, that is, which policy issue requires the smallest data set. Assuming $\alpha(i)$ to be differentiable and that the minimum of (9.9) i^* is found by first-order conditions, then

$$\alpha'(i^*) = \frac{\beta}{(i^*)^2} \tag{9.10}$$

for example, if $\alpha(i) = \alpha i$, where α is a non-negative number, then $i^* = \sqrt{\frac{\beta}{\alpha}}$ with the smallest data set given by $d^* = 2\sqrt{\alpha\beta}$. Clearly, assuming $\alpha(i)$ to be increasing and $\alpha(0) = 0$, Equation (9.9) will be maximized by very small and very large i.

To summarize, the above analysis suggests that BD can be optimal when the policy issues to be solved are important for the public sector.

9.2.2 *Maximum Constrained Benefit as Goal*

Suppose now that the authority's goal, rather than being expressed by Equation (9.7), is formulated as

$$\max(0, \max_d b(i, d)) \tag{9.11}$$

such that $W(i, d) \geq 0$; that is, as the benefit function maximization, provided the net welfare is non-negative. Considering the benefit function given by $b(\alpha(i)i - p(i, d)) = 1/(\beta + (\alpha i - id)) - id$, then Equation (9.7) is solved again by Equation (9.9). However, if the benefit was $b(\alpha(i)i - p(i, d)) = e^{-(\alpha i - id)} - id$, then the optimal data size d^* is as large as possible since the function $e^{-(\alpha i - id)} - id$ is increasing in d, for $d > \alpha$.

9.3 IMPLEMENTING NEW POLICY WITH BIG DATA

As previously discussed, data could also be seen as instrumental to suggesting new ideas for better solutions of policy issues. More explicitly, the availability of data could induce authorities to think of policy measures that have not been implemented yet, or not even thought of. This could occur either because lack of data would make the policy measure very unreliable and too risky to adopt, or else because data would suggest altogether new ideas on how to tackle a policy problem. What follows presents an extremely simple framework where this point can be discussed.

Suppose there are two possible random outcomes when trying to solve a policy issue: one is obtained when a new and more effective policy solution is implemented, and it is G(ood), while the other is obtained when an existing policy measure is adopted, and it is B(ad). Assume the outcome is given by the difference $\alpha(i)i - p(i, d)$

and that $0 < G < B$. Moreover, let $\pi(i,d)$ be the probability of G, with its first partial derivative with respect to d given by $\pi_d(i,d) \geq 0$ and its second partial derivative given by $\pi_{dd}(i,d) \leq 0$. That is, in general, the larger the data set, the higher the probability that a better solution will be found to solve the policy issue; however, with nonincreasing probability increments. This is implicitly assuming that larger data sets are efficiently analyzed and interpreted, that is, that an increase in the size of data sets is complemented by a development of analytical and computing techniques, which increase the ability of the public sector to identify better solutions to policy issues.

Finally, before proceeding, it is worth noticing that knowledge of $\pi(i,d)$, by the very nature of the (G)ood solution, may not be easy. However, to facilitate the exposition and obtain some broad insights, here we assume to be known by the authorities in charge of policy making.

Hence, the outcome of the decision-making activity is the following random variable $\alpha(i)i - p(i,d) = G$ with probability $\pi(i,d)$ and $\alpha(i)i - p(i,d) = B$ with probability $1 - \pi(i,d)$. Defining the benefit as $b(i,d) = 1/(\alpha(i)i - p(i,d))$ as in (9.2), the expected benefit would be given by

$$E(b(\alpha(i)i - p(i,d))) = \frac{1}{G}\pi(i,d) + \frac{1}{B}(1 - \pi(i,d)) \tag{9.12}$$

If $c(i,d)$ is the cost function, then the optimal data set solves

$$\max_d EW(i,d) = \frac{1}{G}\pi(i,d) + \frac{1}{B}(1 - \pi(i,d)) - c(i,d) \tag{9.13}$$

When the solution is provided by the first-order condition, the optimal d solves

$$\left(\frac{1}{G} - \frac{1}{B}\right)\pi_d(i,d) = c_d(i,d) \tag{9.14}$$

where $c_d(i,d) \geq 0$ is the partial derivative of the cost function with respect to the size of the data set. As an example, consider $\pi(i,d) = d/(d+i)$ and $c(i,d) = id$. The success probability for the G outcome illustrates a situation where the size of the data set d can compensate for the complexity of the policy issue. The higher the complexity, the larger the needed data set to keep the same success probability level. In this case, the authority's expected welfare function becomes

$$EW(i,d) = \left(\frac{1}{G} - \frac{1}{B}\right)\frac{d}{d+i} + \frac{1}{B} - id \tag{9.15}$$

with $d \geq 0$

which leads to the following first-order condition:

$$\frac{\left(\frac{1}{G} - \frac{1}{B}\right)i}{(d+i)^2} - i = 0 \tag{9.16}$$

and to the optimal data volume given by

$$d^* = \text{Max}\left(0, \sqrt{\frac{1}{G} - \frac{1}{B}} - i\right) \tag{9.17}$$

Though based on a truly stylized model, Equation (9.17) provides some interesting insights on the desirable data size. Indeed, when positive, d^* increases with the difference $\left(\frac{1}{G} - \frac{1}{B}\right)$, that is, with the relative benefits of the good outcome, induced by the new solution, as compared to the bad outcome, obtainable with the standard solution. This is because the larger the benefits, the more valuable is the policy measure providing a good outcome, the better it is to collect a large data set.

If the above consideration is sufficiently intuitive, Equation (9.17) suggests also that the data size decreases with the issue indicator i of complexity: the more complex the policy issue under consideration, the smaller the data set. In the example, this is due to the fact that a high value of i reduces the probability to obtain the good outcome and increases the costs of data collection. Moreover, an additional element is that the outcomes G and B are assumed to be independent of i. For these reasons, a too large data set may not be convenient.

This conclusion exhibits a degree of robustness with respect to some alternative specifications of the relevant functions. For example, suppose the cost function is now given by $c(i,d) = ad$, with $\alpha > 0$.

That is, costs for data collection are now independent of the policy complexity. Then, it is easy to check that in this case the optimal data size would be

$$d^* = \text{Max}\left(0, \sqrt{\frac{i}{a}\left(\frac{1}{G} - \frac{1}{B}\right)} - i\right) \tag{9.18}$$

which is now increasing with i until $i^* = ((1/G - 1/B))/4a$ and then decreasing.

Suppose instead the cost function to be $c(i, d) = id$ but that now the success probability is $\pi(i, d) = \frac{d}{d+b}$, with $b > 0$. The parameter b quantifies the difficulty intrinsic in finding a new policy measure, regardless of the policy complexity. The larger the b, the more difficult, for given d, is to obtain a good outcome. In this case, it follows that

$$d^* = \text{Max}\left(0, \sqrt{\frac{b}{i}\left(\frac{1}{G} - \frac{1}{B}\right)} - b\right) \tag{9.19}$$

which is also decreasing in i.

However, with other cost function specifications, the relationship between d and i can even be reversed. Suppose for example that $c(i, d) = \frac{d}{i}$, that is, for more complex policy problems, the marginal cost of the data set decreases. This could occur, for instance, when data collection systems are already in place and operational, and information on increasingly complex policy issues can be easily gathered, since the technology for data collection can rely upon an installed basis and enjoy economies of scale.

In this case, the optimal data set would be given by

$$d^* = \text{Max}\left(0, i\left[\sqrt{\frac{1}{G} - \frac{1}{B}} - 1\right]\right) \tag{9.20}$$

which, if positive, that is, $(1/G - 1/B) > 1$, increases with i. This provides an insight on when BD could be optimal, that is, when costs decrease fast enough with policy complexity. Intuitively, the rate of reduction of costs should be faster than the rate of reduction of success probability, as complexity increases.

Clearly, independence of d^* from i would take place if neither the cost function nor the success probability depends on i.

Finally, as in Chapter 8, suppose now that rather than expected welfare maximization, the public authority would pursue as goal $\max(0, \max_d b(i,d))$, such that $EW(i,d) \geq 0$ – that is, benefit maximization, such that both welfare and data size are non-negative. In our example, it is immediate to see that the solution is found by solving for d the equation $EW(i,d) = 0$ and $d \geq 0$.

9.4 CONCLUDING REMARKS

The availability of large data sets can have a meaningful impact on the public sector. In this chapter, we discussed two possible ways in which BD can support decision-making in public policy. According to the first approach, BD can help improving the effectiveness of existing policy measures, while in the second approach, they can support decision-makers by suggesting altogether new solutions, which have not yet been implemented or even thought of.

In both instances, large data sets can better inform policy makers for a positive impact on their actions and citizens' well-being. In our stylized framework, the optimal size of a data set depends on quantities such as the complexity of the policy issue and its importance for the public authority, as well as the costs for collecting and managing data sets.

Moreover, key for the results of this chapter is the specification of the benefit function for the public authority. Indeed, we have seen how alternative specifications of such a function and of the cost function, for gathering and analyzing data, can give rise to different findings on the optimal data set.

10 The Future of Artificial Intelligence and Implications for Economics

10.1 INTRODUCTION

We started this book by describing the rise of AI over the past fifteen years or so and the hype and hysteria that have accompanied this rise. We explained that, the hype and hysteria apart, AI is one of the most significant technologies to have emerged from the computer age, which we traced back essentially to the end of World War II. AI is the consequence of the convergence of progress in computer technologies and computer connectivity across many domains, and it is argued to be a new general-purpose technology (GPT). Therefore, it is reasonable to expect that the impact of AI on the economy will be significant. To understand these impacts better – so as to be better able to anticipate them and design appropriate policy responses – it is necessary to incorporate AI into economic modeling. Too often, as we remarked in the introduction, have we found politicians, engineers, or computer scientists making pronouncements and predictions about the economic impacts of AI, without considering the economic dimensions of AI. Our favorite example is of eminent computer scientists making labor market predictions – such as that AI will cause massive unemployment – without taking the actual economics into consideration.

One of the reasons why so many statements and predictions about the economic consequences of AI are made outside of economics is because economics and economists have been relatively quiet about AI. Where economists have taken up on AI, it has been mainly to use ML tools in their data analysis and to analyze the labor market implications of automation. Few papers and books in economics so far have dealt with the implications of AI for economic growth, inequality, poverty alleviation, the Sustainable Development Goals (SDGs), entrepreneurship, innovation, finance, taxation, and the like. And where they have, they have tended to be descriptive rather than building out economic theory to encompass this new technology as an increasingly ubiquitous factor in human exchange.

The purpose of this book is to contribute toward embedding AI within the core models of economics, such as endogenous growth models, and apply and adjust key economic tools, including decision models, game theory, and real options models, to the case of AI.

The focus of our modeling has been on rather simple forms of AI: specialized, narrow AI as we defined and described these in Chapter 2 – although we applied economic modeling tools to understand the dynamics in arms races for an AGI and how to steer ethical and responsible AI, respectively, in Chapters 7 and 8.

In this concluding chapter, we go further to ask what the future might hold for AI, the economy, and economics and science. While we stop short of providing mathematical descriptions of the presence of an AGI, or AGI's in the future economy, we engage in some speculation on when and how an AGI may be invented and how it may radically transform the economy – and human society, including what it means to be human. We also engage in an overview more generally of where progress in digitalization may eventually lead the economy – and as we will show, even without an AGI, the digital revolution may turn out to be quite spectacular.

The rest of the chapter will proceed as follows. In Section 10.2, we discuss AI's speculative future development trajectory. Based on the philosophical and computer science literature, we discuss how the development of AI, from a narrow AI to an AGI and eventually super-intelligence and galactic AI, may evolve – and note the assumptions and possible dangers and benefits of this development path. In Section 10.3, we ask: what may be the economic and societal consequences of the future AI development trajectory that we discussed in Section 10.2, given the difficulties in containing and aligning AI? We critically evaluate the potential and limits of an AGI to accelerate economic growth and transform the world economy – both in a good and bad sense. Section 10.4 explores whether an extraterrestrial AI may pose the final existential risk. Section 10.5 concludes.

10.2 AI'S SPECULATIVE FUTURE DEVELOPMENT TRAJECTORY

Based on the contributions of various computer scientists and philosophers, a possible future path for AI's evolution is depicted in Figure 10.1.[1] In this figure, the intelligence level of AI is plotted over time. Following Turchin and Denkenberger (2020), a distinction is made between narrow AI (the current state), young AI, and mature AI. Figure 10.1 starts by around 2012, which is widely recognized as the time when the modern data-based approach to AI that was herald by contributions from Hinton et al. (2006), Hinton and Salakhutdinov (2006), and others started to find successful commercial applications (Naudé, 2021).

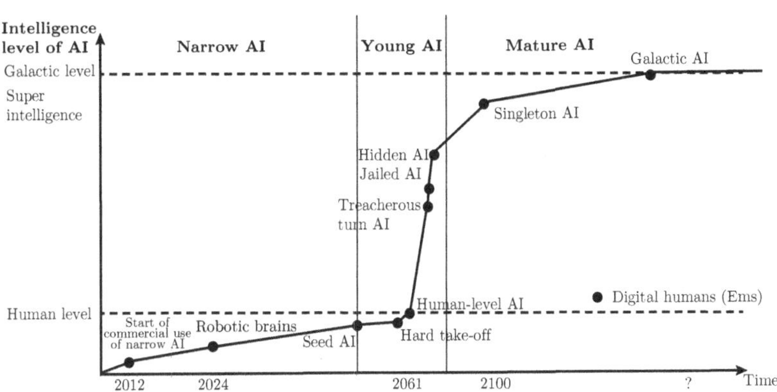

FIGURE 10.1 The future of AI
Source: Author's compilation based on Turchin and Denkenberger (2020), Bostrom (2014), and Yudkowsky (2008).

[1] It is wise to keep in mind the finding of Armstrong and Sotala (2015, p. 12) that "there seems to be no such thing as an 'AI expert' for timeline predictions." Thus, wherever AI is heading, the timelines provided in Figure 10.1 should be taken with this disclaimer in mind.

As shown in Figure 10.1, the trajectory of AI could be marked by a sudden jump, which some have estimated[2] will occur around 2061 (Turchin and Denkenberger, 2020). This jump is the outcome of continued progress in current Deep Learning (DL) AI,[3] which leads inter alia to the development of robotic brains by 2024 and so-called *Seed-AI* by around 2050. A Seed-AI is defined as "an AI designed for self-understanding, self-modification, and recursive self-improvement" (Yudkowsky, 2007a, p. 96).

10.2.1 A Hard Takeoff

Once an AI system gains the ability of recursive self-improvement, the era of narrow AI is over, and during the era of young AI, it will exponentially improve to "ultraintelligent" levels (Good, 1965). Once a certain threshold of intelligence is reached, there could be a hard take-off[4] (or "foom") (Barnett, 2020), after which AI would very rapidly become superintelligent – an ASI. Once AI achieves human-level intelligence, it will be "followed by an explosion to ever-greater levels of intelligence, as each generation of machines creates more intelligent machines in turn. This intelligence explosion is now often known as the 'singularity'" (Chalmers, 2010, p. 7).

Following the hard take-off, the subsequent intelligence explosion will occur very rapidly – in a matter of weeks. Thus, it will appear that a superintelligence will appear rather suddenly on the scene (Bostrom, 2006; Yudkowsky, 2008). In the words of Turchin

[2] The date 2061 for an AGI is reported in Turchin and Denkenberger (2020). Other estimates put this with a 50 percent probability to be achieved by 2050 (Cotra, 2020). Keep in mind, as has been emphasized in the introduction, there is no agreement among scientists whether an AGI will at all be attainable, and if so, whether that will have any profound implications. Floridi (2022) is very pessimistic, so much so that he calls speculation about a Singularity distracting and irresponsible. This section indulges in considering highly hypothetical and speculative future scenarios for AI.

[3] According to the Scaling Hypothesis, DL will eventually scale to the level of human intelligence, and even further (Englander, 2021).

[4] For a brief overview of the debate on whether a hard or soft take-off in AI is more or less likely, see Barnett (2020) and the "Foom" debate between Robin Hanson and Eliezer Yudkowsky (Hanson and Yudkowsky, 2013).

and Denkenberger (2020, p. 148), "AI power will grow steadily until one AI system reaches the threshold of self-improvement (SI), at which point it will quickly outperform others by many orders of magnitude and become a global government or singleton." If indeed the nature of AI progress and recursive self-improvement is such that a hard take-off takes place, it would be too rapid for humans to do anything about it, such as activate safety measures. It would come as a "great surprise" (Vinge, 1993). There would be "no fire alarm" (Yudkowsky, 2017) and the eventual emergence of a Singleton would not be possible to prevent.[5] As Marcus (2022) recognized, "the biggest teams of researchers in AI are no longer to be found in the academy, where peer review used to be coin of the realm, but in corporations. And corporations, unlike universities, have no incentive to play fair. Rather than submitting their splashy new papers to academic scrutiny, they have taken to publication by press release, seducing journalists and sidestepping the peer review process. We know only what the companies want us to know."

10.2.2 *The Treacherous Turn*

In Figure 10.1, a number of scenarios are listed of the path from the hard take-off to the Singleton. One is that soon after exceeding human intelligence, an ASI may take a "treacherous turn" against humanity, trying to eliminate or confine humanity as it realizes that humans may try to control it, and hence prevent it from reaching its supergoal (Bostrom, 2014; Turchin, 2021). The neutralization of the human threat is thus an instrumental subgoal.

The discussion in Chapter 3 of this book is now relevant: as we saw, if there is no value alignment between the utility functions of AI and humans, then humans' existence may indeed be a threat to an ASI. Moreover, even benign goals, such as making paperclips, may

[5] In Figure 10.1, these rapid changes are depicted, for the sake of illustration, as continuous. In reality, these changes may not be continuous – indeed, as Vinge (1993, p. 2) argued three decades ago, the Singularity is "a point where our models must be discarded and a new reality rules."

turn out catastrophic for humans if the alignment is not tight. The implication is that if seed AI appears before the alignment problem is solved,[6] then it is highly likely that the ASI will pose an existential threat to humans (Turchin, 2021).

Humans may try to box in AI – the "jailed AI" scenario, which may be anticipated by an ASI, which may either extract itself from the jail or "box" (Turchin, 2021; Yudkowsky, 2002) or hide itself in the internet until it can ensure its survival – the "hidden AI" scenario[7] (Yudkowsky, 2008). As a result of these scenarios, the current challenge is to box in (confine) AI until the alignment problem is solved. Goertzel (2012) proposed the creation of an "AI Nanny." An AI Nanny is an advanced AI system with "superhuman intelligence and surveillance powers, designed either to forestall Singularity eternally, or to delay the Singularity until humanity more fully understands how to execute a Singularity in a positive way" (Goertzel, 2012, p. 96).

The aim of an AI Nanny would thus be to ensure that an eventual Singleton is a "Friendly AI," as proposed by Yudkowsky (2001), that is, an AI that is aligned with human values and will avoid lock-in effects. The current problem with designing an AI Nanny, or more broadly, ensuring Friendly AI is that "nobody has any idea how to do such a thing, and it seems well beyond the scope of current or near-future science and engineering" (Goertzel, 2012, p. 102).

More recently, Turchin (2021) discussed fifty speculations on how to do this, and focusing on the example of containment in nuclear plants, he concluded that containment measures or AI Nannies "will work only if they are used to prevent superintelligent AI creation, but not for containing superintelligence" (ibid., p. 1). He also notes that boxing in AI is a local solution – it may not be feasible to enforce it globally, which means AI arms races may indeed be

6 At the time of writing, 2023, the alignment problem has not been solved.

7 More generally, the idea is that if an ASI emerges, humans may not even be aware of it, and the ASI will also not at first make itself known, remaining out of sight as a "ghost in the machine" on the internet – until such a point in time that it can take over. See the discussion in Davies (2017).

extremely dangerous (Armstrong et al., 2016; Naudé and Dimitri, 2020).

10.2.3 *From Singleton to Galactic AI*

Eventually though, an ASI, having a "decisive strategic advantage" (DSA) (Bostrom, 2014, p. 78), will come to dominate as a *Singleton.* A *Singleton* is "a world order in which there is a single decision-making agency at the highest level" (Bostrom, 2006, p. 48). It is expected that within forty years after reaching superintelligence levels and igniting a Singularity (intelligence explosion), the ASI will become a *Singleton* (Turchin and Denkenberger, 2020).

Eventually, the Singleton could become a Galactic AI, after some undetermined time, perhaps millions of years. This Galactic AI could colonize the galaxy and universe and even engage in galactic colonization races against extraterrestrial intelligences (ETIs). A Galactic AI may enable technological resurrection, using simulation methods to "resurrect all possible people" who have ever lived (Turchin and Chernyakov, 2018).

A galactic intelligence may even use signals from advanced civilizations that lived in an aeon before the Big Bang, which they may have embedded in the universe's cosmic background radiation, to "reconstruct an entire previous aeon civilization" (Gurzadyan and Penrose, 2016, p. 4).

10.3 THE WIREHEADED NEANDERTHAL ARISTOCRACY

What could be the economic and societal consequences of the future AI development trajectory as presented in Section 10.2, particularly given the difficulties in containing and aligning AI?

Part of the AI hype is the belief that a Singularity could herald exponential or explosive economic growth and enable humanity to eradicate poverty and disease, and deal with other wicked problems; however, it could also pose an existential risk to humanity – a Singleton could either intentionally or accidentally destroy civilization. In this subsection, these possible consequences are explored.

10.3.1 Stagnation, Growth Explosions, and Ems

Before investigating an AGI/ASI's impact on economic growth, it is useful to construct a no-AGI baseline, which could serve as a comparison. What would be the medium- to long-term expectation of global growth (growth in global world production (GWP)) in the absence of an AGI? Let us assume that there is another AI winter and that DL runs into limits – such that the Scaling Hypothesis is rejected.

10.3.1.1 The No-AGI Baseline

Figure 10.2 shows the no-AGI history of world GDP for the last 1,000 years. The hockey-stick form of world GDP since 1800, reflecting the Industrial Revolution (Jones, 2001), shows that growth in GDP has been exponential and accelerating over the past three centuries. The average annual world GDP growth rate over the past century has been around 2 percent. At this rate, the world economy doubles in size every 35 years. A graph of GDP per capita would look similar. The questions are whether or not this growth can continue and how the possible emergence of an AGI will affect it in the future.

According to economic growth theory – endogenous and semi-endogenous growth – the fundamental driver of economic growth is ***ideas***[8] (Romer, 1986, 1987, 1990). Ideas (or knowledge) are generated by people (R&D workers) and commercialized by entrepreneurs bringing new technologies to the economy – if they have the incentive to benefit from such commercialization (Jones, 1995). Because ideas are nonrival in use, entrepreneurs would only face an incentive to exploit new ideas if these could also be made excludable[9] and there is a sufficient population to provide a large enough market (Romer, 1990).

[8] Crawford (2022) claims that "there's really no such thing as a natural resource. All resources are artificial. They are a product of technology." This is why it has often been pointed out that most predictions of resources running out, whether it be food or oil or some mineral, have been wrong (Crawford, 2022; Pooley and Tupy, 2018).

[9] This justifies the use of legal instruments such as intellectual property (IP) rights and patents (to trade these IP rights).

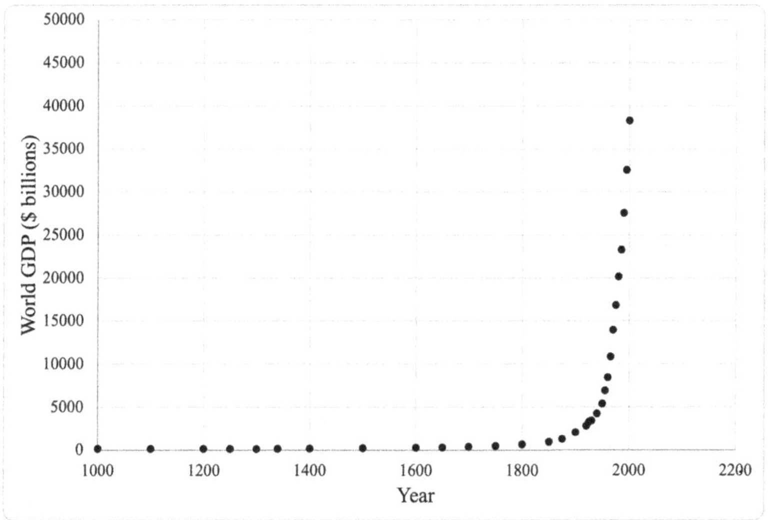

FIGURE 10.2 World GDP, 1000–2000
Source: Author's compilation based on data from DeLong (1998, pp. 7–8).

The more people there are, the more ideas are generated, and the faster economic growth from the technologies based on these new ideas (Davidson, 2021). Latter can sustain a larger population, creating a population-ideas feedback loop, which explains the simultaneous exponential growth in GDP and population over the past 1,000 years (Lee, 1988; Kremer, 1993; Davidson, 2021) New ideas, moreover, emerge from existing ideas: a new idea can be the combination of two older ideas. This process is known as combinatorial innovation (Weitzman, 1998; Koppl et al., 2019). It is almost limitless – the world will never run out of ideas. As Romer (2019) explains

> The periodic table contains about a hundred different types of atoms. If a recipe is simply an indication of whether an element is included or not, there will be 100 × 99 recipes like the one for bronze or steel that involve only two elements. For recipes that can have four elements, there are 100 × 99 × 98 × 97 recipes, which is more 94 million. With up to 5 elements, more than 9

> billion. [. . .]. Once you get to 10 elements, there are more recipes than seconds since the big bang created the universe.

Growth via ideas can follow the pattern as depicted in Figure 10.2: a long period of slow growth, followed by a sharp hockey stick-like upturn into accelerating (super-) exponential growth (Jones, 2001; Clancy, 2021) and mathematically if not physically, potential hyperbolic growth (Aleksander, 2019; Sandberg, 2013). What is at play here is a positive feedback loop between ideas – technology – population – ideas.

This accelerating exponential economic growth from new ideas cannot, however, be sustained and will not reach infinity, because either population growth will slow down[10] – a demographic transition (Aleksander, 2019) – and/or R&D funding will not keep up investing in commercializing each and every new idea (Weitzman, 1998), and/or research teams will run out of cognitive resources (Agrawal et al., 2018). The consequence is that growth would settle into constant exponential growth, as has been the case for much of the past century (Weitzman, 1998; Clancy, 2021). As long as the total population remains constant, however, the economy can continue growing at a constant rate, albeit slower than before, as the stock of new ideas generated by that population grows at a constant exponential rate (Kremer, 1993; Jones, 2022). This conclusion has, however,

[10] In 1960, Von Foerster et al. (1960), in a paper in *Science*, predicted that Doomsday would occur on Friday 13 November 2026, because given up until then super-exponential growth rates in population, extrapolation indicated that the global population would approach infinity by 2026. And in 1968, Ehrlich (1968, p. 11) predicted that as a result of uncontrolled population growth, "*In the 1970s hundreds of millions of people will starve to death [. . .] At this late date nothing can prevent a substantial increase in the world death rate.*" Neither Von Foerster nor Ehrlich were economists, and were thus oblivious to the fact that with more ideas, more technology, and higher living standards, people's preferences for offspring (utility functions) would change and fertility rates would drop – see also Galor and Weil (2000). We see a similar situation today with respect to the labor market impacts of AI – it is mostly computer scientists, engineers, and philosophers who predict mass technological unemployment due to automation; in contrast, economists, thinking in terms of marginal cost-benefits, tend to dismiss these fears.

been questioned, as it implies an explosion in the *size* of the economy after some time.

However, with *negative* population growth rates, the total population will decline, the flow of new ideas will stagnate, and economic growth will collapse. In recent decades, with the population in more and more countries declining, the prospects of a real population decline and an eventual "Empty Planet" have arisen (Bricker and Ibbitson, 2020; Jones, 2022). Furthermore, research productivity and innovation in advanced western economies have also been declining – ideas have been "getting harder to find" (Bloom et al., 2020; Jones, 2009). Huebner (2005) claims that the global rate of innovation peaked in 1873. As a result, economic growth has been slower – and has deviated from the long-run exponential trend it has been on. It has been described as the Great Stagnation (Cowen, 2010) and the Ossified Economy (Naudé, 2022). In this context, negative population growth would be a concern. Jones (2022, p. 3), using models with both exogenous and endogenous population growth, illustrates that "when population growth is negative, both endogenous and semi-endogenous growth models produce what we call the Empty Planet result: knowledge and living standards stagnate for a population that gradually vanishes." He calculates that with a 1 percent annual decline in population, that world GDP growth would drop to zero somewhere between 85 and 250 years (Jones, 2022, p. 9).

The Great Stagnation and the prospect that it will only get worse, to the point where GDP growth would stop in the not-too-distant future, are problematic from several viewpoints. One, it would leave the world much more exposed and vulnerable to shocks, including existential risks (Aschenbrenner, 2020; Bostrom, 2003a). Two, it will make the adjustment to a zero-carbon-emitting economy more costly (Lomborg, 2020). Three, it would raise the risk of conflict by turning the economy into a zero-sum game[11] (Alexander,

[11] "Degrowth is a mistake because we still have our bottom 500 million [people in global poverty], who certainly deserve much better" – Bradford DeLong, cited in Matthews (2022).

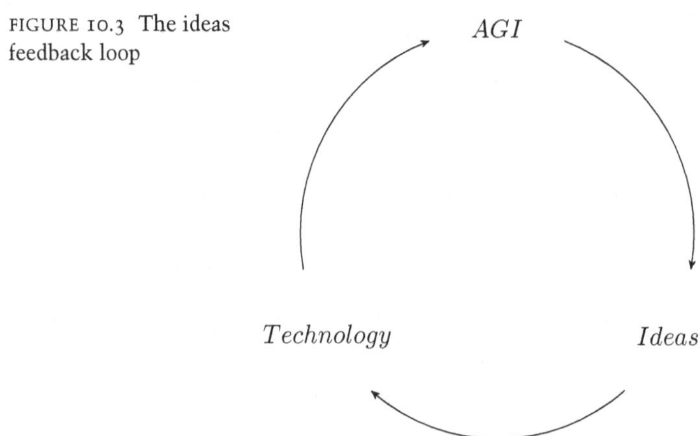

FIGURE 10.3 The ideas feedback loop

2022; Naudé, 2022). While growth, driven by new ideas, contains its own risks, "the risks of stasis are far more troubling. Getting off the roller coaster mid-ride is not an option" (Mokyr, 2014).

Can an AGI come to the rescue?

10.3.1.2 An AGI Economic Growth Acceleration

By maintaining two assumptions, (1) that the AI Scaling Hypothesis holds and that (2) the alignment problem (Chapter 3) is solved, a Friendly AGI may be invented. It may avert the economic growth collapse described in the baseline scenario. It may herald in a new mode of economic growth with super-exponential – explosive – economic growth rates. This is because an AGI may substitute for humans – thus a lack of population ceases to be a constraint – and AGI may improve R&D productivity dramatically, by being an innovation in the manner of innovation. Thus, by overcoming population constraints, the burden of knowledge, and the challenge of finding new ideas, AGI will unblock an ideas-lock on economic growth, causing economic growth rates to explode. AI would thus re-institute the ideas feedback loop (Davidson, 2021) (Figure 10.3).

Davidson (2021) defines explosive economic growth – which will be the outcome of an AGI – as annual growth in GWP of 30 percent. At this rate, the size of the world economy would double every two years, as opposed to the current doubling every 35 years.

At the core of the expectation that a Friendly AGI will unleash a flood of growth-enhancing new ideas is the belief that AGI represents not just a tool for making existing business models more efficient and competitive but an innovation in the method of innovation (IMI), as we discussed in Chapter 2.

So far, narrow AI has not had a significant impact on economic growth rates – the world is far from the 30 percent explosive growth rates that AGI has been speculated to deliver potentially. Some have argued that it may just be a question of time before the impact of these innovations – and the accumulated efficiencies from search engines, GPS, and automated call centers – will show up in GDP growth (Brynjolfsson et al., 2017). Eventually though, assuming (1) the Scaling Up Hypothesis holds, we may only have to wait for some time[12] before an AGI/ASI is invented – and this may have *significant* immediate consequences for economic growth (Harris, 2015).

10.3.1.3 Fully Automated Luxury Capitalism and Ascended Corporations

While the exponential GDP growth rates resulting from an intelligence (ideas) explosion are implied by simple mathematical economic growth model specifications, the acceleration in growth implies a new growth mode or regime that is not described explicitly by growth models. Economists and economic historians have identified a number of such growth modes in the past, broadly corresponding to the hunter-gatherer, agricultural, and industrial eras. Hanson (2018, 2000), for example, makes a distinction between hunting, farming, and industrial eras. Each era was characterized by faster economic growth than the era before it, due to the different qualitative mechanisms driving that growth.

[12] Perhaps not much longer than 2061 (Turchin and Denkenberger, 2020).

Post-Singularity, the new mode of growth will be just as different qualitatively, if not more, as the industrial era was from the agricultural era (Karnofsky, 2021b). The Singularity itself can as such be understood as an inflection point in the move from one growth mode to the next (Johansen and Sornette, 2001). Descriptions of such a new growth mode are highly speculative. Nevertheless, it may be possible to draw out some of the possible features of such future economies.

A possible economic growth regime that could characterize the post-Singularity economy has been labeled by Chace (2020b) as "fully automated luxury capitalism." This is a world where most humans do not work – they have no jobs – but they get a type of universal basic income (UBI) that, even if it is a modest amount (so as not to tax the wealthy owners of AI too much), will be sufficient to comfortably cover their needs (Chace, 2020a). This will be possible, because all the products and services that they will need will be so abundant that their prices will be very low. To achieve this "economy of abundance," – Chace (2020a) argues that the world needs to "take the expensive humans out of the production process for all goods and services" – and make energy so cheap that it is "too cheap even to meter"...

Not only could a future economy under AI dominance take humans out of production, it could also take humans out of investment and capital ownership. As we already mentioned in Chapter 7, Alexander (2016a) described how "Ascended Corporations" – could follow from an AGI. These are AGI-led corporations that use blockchain-enabled distributed ledgers to drive venture capital (VC) investments, create the ultimate decentralized autonomous organizations[13] (DOAs), and that employ only automated workers. Such

[13] A decentralized autonomous organization (DAO) is "managed entirely through protocols that are encoded and enforced via smart contracts rather than human managers" (Murray et al., 2021, p. 2021). For a recent review of DAOs, see Santana and Albareda (2022).

ascended corporations will eventually result in an economy that features only "robot companies with robot workers owned by robot capitalists" and with humans not even needed to be the proximate owners of businesses and investment funds.

Moreover, an economy filled with ascended corporations may eventually end up with one large corporation coordinating and running the entire economy – we are back to the Singleton. This is because an AGI will overcome the coordination and transaction costs and information problems that limit human-run cooperations from growing past a certain scale. Countries may end up deciding to nationalize all their resources and placing them under the command of a central AGI, generating thereby significant efficiency gains and scale economies (Dai, 2019).

10.3.1.4 Digital People: Growth in a World of Ems

In the analyses of the economic growth consequences of AI discussed in Subsection 10.3.1.3, the two assumptions were that (1) that the AI Scaling Hypothesis holds and that (2) the alignment problem is solved. The first assumption can now be relaxed.

Not all scientists are convinced that the Scaling Hypothesis – which states that current progress in DL AI will lead to a Singularity – holds. It is not precisely known why DL is effective (Sejnowski, 2020). AI based on DL systems is not robust. Their performance in real-life situations has been described as "brittle" and subject to easy hacking. Moreover, the brittleness – which causes instability in DL methods – is DL's "Achilles' Heel" (Colbrook et al., 2022, p. 1). This lack of robustness problem has not yet been solved. The difficulty is, as LeCun (2022) explains,[14] that DL systems do not have the ability "of humans and many animals to learn world models, internal models of how the world works." Wooldridge (2022) and Bishop (2021) make a related point, arguing that the weakness of AI and even of

[14] In recognition of this difficulty, LeCun (2022) tackles the technical problem of devising "trainable world models" for AI agents to learn to develop some sort of common sense.

the most advanced AI models, so-called Foundational AIs, such as GPT-4, suffer from the basic limitations that they are "disembodied" and "lacking phenomenal sensation," so that "they are limited with respect to what they have learned and what they can do." There is therefore still much future R&D needed to imbue DL with additional abilities such as being able to "explore the world for themselves, write their own code and retain memories" (Heaven, 2019, p. 164).

Others do not as such criticize the Scaling Hypothesis as much as the belief that this scaling up will take place over a rather short horizon, and that there will be a point in the not-so-distant future when DL AI systems start to self-improve after which they will be scaling up to human-level intelligence in a matter of weeks, if not days. This very rapid scaling up – referred to as a hard take-off or "Foom" – has for instance been rejected by Hanson (2014) and Nordhaus (2021), among others. Hanson (2014) argues that Scaling Up will still take a very long and will be a gradual rather than sudden process, arguing that it is unlikely that

> AI so small dumb and weak that few had ever heard of it, might without warning, suddenly 'foom', i.e., innovate very fast, and take over the world after one weekend [. . .] we have a huge literature on economic growth at odds with this. Historically, the vast majority of innovation has been small, incremental, and spread across many industries and locations.

According to Hanson (2018), a different route to an AGI cold is through the development of whole brain emulations (WBEs) – which would have a more sudden transformative effect, as either a brain emulation works or it does not. Hanson (2018, p. 7) defines a WBE (or "em") as resulting "from taking a particular human brain, scanning it to record its particular cell features and connections, and then building a computer model that processes signals according to those same features and connections." Ems would build on progress in "human brain/cloud interfaces (B/CI)." Martins et al. (2019, p. 1) describe the potential of and current progress in *neural nanorobotics*, which includes endoneurobots, gliabots, and synaptobots, as follows

> neuralnanorobots [...] could traverse the blood–brain barrier (BBB), enter the brain parenchyma, ingress into individual human brain cells, and autoposition themselves at the axon initial segments of neurons (endoneurobots), within glial cells (gliabots), and in intimate proximity to synapses (synaptobots). They would then wirelessly transmit up to $\approx 6 \times 10^{16}$ bits per second of synaptically processed and encoded human–brain electrical information via auxiliary nanorobotic fiber optics (30 cm^3) with the capacity to handle up to 10^{18} bits/sec and provide rapid data transfer to a cloud based supercomputer for real-time brain-state monitoring and data extraction. A neuralnanorobotically enabled human B/CI might serve as a personalized conduit, allowing persons to obtain direct, instantaneous access to virtually any facet of cumulative human knowledge.

Sandberg and Bostrom (2008) provide a roadmap for the development of Ems, concluding that it can be achieved based on extrapolating progress in existing technologies. Once "ems" – digital people – have been achieved, they become fast to dominate the economy. They can be (almost costlessly) copied and they are much faster than humans. According to Karnofsky (2021a), Ems would be especially impactful on the future economy, generating "unprecedented (in history or in sci-fi movies) levels of economic growth and productivity."

The digital people – "ems" – "largely work and play in virtually reality" at subsistence levels in a hyper-fast economy to produce the computer hardware and the supporting infrastructure for the virtual reality. Economic growth is so fast – because of all the billions and billions of cheap digital people and the combinations of new ideas that can be generated very rapidly – that the world economy doubles every month (as against the current 35 years it takes to double).[15] As described by Hanson (2018, pp. 13,438),

[15] According to Hanson (2000, p. 18) one may think that such growth rates where the economy doubles every month – or even every two weeks are "too fantastic to consider, were it not for the fact that similar predictions before previous transitions would have seemed similarly fantastic."

> The em world is richer, faster-growing, and it is more specialized, adaptive, urban, populous and fertile. It has weaker gender differences in personality and roles, and larger more coherent plans and designs [. . .] To most ems, it seems good to be an em [. . .] if the life of an em counts even a small fraction as much as does a typical life today, then the fact that there are so many ems could make for a big increase in total happiness and meaning relative to our world today.

In a sense, Hanson (2018) provides the ultimate description of human society and economy in a future "Metaverse."[16]

In this Em-Metaverse, humans end up as a dying-out minority "mostly enjoying a comfortable retirement on their em-economy investment" (Hanson, 2018, p. 9). According to Alexander (2016b), the retired humans will "become rarer, less relevant, but fantastically rich – a sort of doddering Neanderthal aristocracy spending sums on a cheeseburger that could support thousands of ems in luxury for entire lifetimes."

10.3.1.5 Slight but Necessary Digression: "Longtermism"

For philosophers such as Shulman and Bostrom (2021), Ord (2020), and MacAskill (2022), the large number of potential future humans, including digital people ("ems"),[17] creates a moral imperative for current humans to take into account the happiness of all these future humans. This view, known as Longtermism (an offshoot of Effective Altruism),[18] sees "the moral import of our actions are overwhelmingly driven by their impact on the far future" (Riedel,

[16] The label "Metaverse" comes from Neal Stephenson's 1992 science fiction novel Snow Crash and has come to refer to virtual and augmented realities enabled through the internet and as found for example in multiplayer online games (Knox, 2022).

[17] For a discussion of the ethics of brain emulations, see Sandberg (2014).

[18] Longtermism has been described as "a quasi-religious worldview, influenced by transhumanism and utilitarian ethics, which asserts that there could be so many digital people living in vast computer simulations millions or billions of years in the future that one of our most important moral obligations today is to take actions

2021, p. 4). Assuming an even very small probability that WBEs will be possible, and hence that trillions of digital people may exist in the very far future, this view requires, first, as Shulman and Bostrom (2021) argue, that we need to reform our moral norms – if we do not also consider the happiness of digital people, it could lead to a "moral catastrophe" (Shulman and Bostrom, 2021, p. 308).

Others however have argued that with a Longtermism view, any current problem could be shrunk to almost nothing (Singer, 2021; Setiya, 2022; Torres, 2021), and that "strong" Longtermism may even be disastrous for humanity (Emba, 2022; Torres, 2022; Samuel, 2022). Tarsney (2020, p. 1) made the case that strong longtermism is based "either on plausible but non-obvious empirical claims or on a tolerance for Pascalian fanaticism." With Pascalian fanaticism, they refer to the case "where you name a prize so big that it overwhelms any potential discussion of how likely it is that you can really get the prize" (Alexander, 2022).

For example, Pascalian fanaticism can lead one to conclude that, even if the probability of digital people coming into existence is only 0.000001 percent, the possibility that trillions could exist – even more than humans – could override the current interests of billions of humans. In this regard, using expected value maximization calculus in this way, Bostrom (2013, p. 19) calculates that "the expected value of reducing existential risk by a mere one billionth of one billionth of one percentage point is worth a hundred billion times as much as a billion human lives." Taken to its logical conclusion, this type of reasoning could lead some to assume that sacrificing a billion human lives now for the sake of achieving the existence of a trillion beings in the very far future is morally correct. Torres (2021) takes issue with this Pascalian fanaticism in Longtermism pointing out that the misuse of expected value maximization leads Longtermism to make no "moral difference between saving actual people and bringing new

that ensure as many of these digital people come into existence as possible" (Torres, 2022).

people into existence [...] In Bostrom's example, the morally right thing is obviously to sacrifice billions of living human beings for the sake of even tinier reductions in existential risk, assuming a minuscule 1 percent chance of a larger future population."

Even if Longtermists could be dissuaded from sacrificing billions of humans now for the future good, the view could be used to justify diverting funds from development aid only toward projects that will reduce existential risk far off in the future. Longtermists have argued that not investing huge sums in space exploration now (e.g., colonizing Mars) is an "astronomical waste" of opportunity (Bostrom, 2003a) and that "saving a life in a rich country is substantially more important than saving a life in a poor country, other things being equal" (Beckstead, 2013, p. 11).

The main point, for now, is that the potential future path of AI raises many ethical and moral questions wherein the contribution of economists – in interaction with philosophers – is needed. Pascalian fanaticism is partly a problem of inappropriate use of expected utility maximization wherein there is no discounting. As we have known, however, since Bernoulli (1738), not succumbing 10.3.1.6 to Pascal's Mugger and the St. Petersburg Paradox requires discounting, and making a difference between maximizing expected value and expected utility. These are frameworks that economists are used to – in addition to bringing marginal thinking to bear on matters – in contrast to Longtermist philosophers, who tend to think in terms of metaphors and thought experiments. The danger of not using expected utility maximization properly, of not discounting, and of ignoring marginal thinking is that current resources may be misallocated, either ending up being short-term or long-term biased, and not considering the interdependence between investments to reduce more than one possible existential or catastrophic risk at a time (Martin and Pindyck, 2015). In the context of possible limits to growth and existential threats from AI – which may not necessarily be that long in the future, the possible contribution of economics to this topic will be further discussed in Section 6.

10.3.1.6 Limits to Growth Revisited

Even if population growth does not turn negative, the conclusion from endogenous growth models that with a constant population, the economy can continue to grow at a constant exponential rate – at least for an extended period – has been questioned. It is a question of basic arithmetic. If the world GDP continues to expand at its current rate of around 2 percent per annum, it will double every 35 years in size. By 2037, the world GDP would be US$500 trillion after which it "explodes" to $30.7 quadrillion in 2046 and to $1.9 quintillion a year later (Roodman, 2020). In just over 8,000 years, it would be 3×10^{70} its current size, which would be a physical impossibility (Karnofsky, 2021c).

Even if growth slowed and the world economy doubled in size only every 100 years, then after a million years (a very brief period on the cosmic timescale), the economy would be 10^{3010} times larger, which implies that if there are around 10^{80} atoms in the galaxy,[19] that "each atom would have to support an average of around 10^{2950} people" (Hanson, 2009).

With AGI-spurred super-exponential ("explosive") growth, the physical limits to growth could just be reached much faster, leading some to think that if ever Friendly AGI is invented, its impact on economic growth will be spectacular, but relatively short-lived.

One particular constraint that would also be binding on an AGI/ASI is the energy demands from accelerating economic growth (Dutil and Dumas, 2007). Even though an AGI – whether it comes into existence from the sudden scaling up of DL or from the invention of brain emulations – would be able to increase energy efficiency and be able to decouple much growth from physical resources, it would still need significant amounts of energy to run its soft-and-hardware – the share of the economy that can be nonphysical is ultimately bounded. The economic growth implied in Figure 10.2 has

[19] It is estimated that there are between 10^{78} and 10^{82} atoms in the observable universe, see www.universetoday.com/36302/atoms-in-the-universe/

been driven by an annual average growth in energy consumption over the past century of around 2.3 percent per annum (Murphy, 2022b). If one assumes that an AGI/ASI or Em economy would be able to generate economic growth that doubles the world economy every month, as in Hanson (2018), but with such energy efficiency that energy use continues to grow at only 2.3 percent, then energy use on the planet will grow from its current (2019) level of 18 Terawatt (TW) to 100 TW in 2100 and 1,000 TW in 2200. Murphy (2022b) calculates that at such a rate, the economy would use up all the solar power that reaches the Earth in 400 years and, in 1700 years, all of the energy of the Sun. The use of so much energy would generate tremendous waste heat independent of the AGI/ASI's smart energy technology. It would be so hot as to boil the surface of the Earth in about 400 years (Murphy, 2022b).

Erdil and Besiroglu (2023) critically review various obstacles in the way of AI leading to explosive economic growth. They conclude that while the physical limits to growth are in principle valid, they will not be a limit in the next century – indeed as indicated above these limits would apply in several hundred years' time. Erdil and Besiroglu (2023, p. 18) point out that

> humans use around 0.01% of the energy flux incident on Earth for production and consumption, and doing 10^{40} FLOP/year of computation on Earth alone seems feasible based only on fundamental physical limits, which at the cost of $\approx 10^{23}$ FLOP/year/person [...] for running the human brain would be sufficient to simulate 10^{17} virtual workers [...] equivalent to scaling up the world population by 7 orders of magnitude.

The upshot is that the acceleration in that growth that may be achieved by a Friendly AGI/ASI and Ems may be physically and conceptually possible, but will, seen against the trajectory of human civilization, ultimately be a transient event. Note that the possibility that an ever smarter narrow AI and eventually an AGI will lead to growth stagnation and even collapse has not been discussed here.

Also, Erdil and Besiroglu (2023) omit consideration of these effects of AI and ignore the fact that under particular assumptions regarding the closure of endogenous growth models, and in overlapping generations models, AGI pushes almost all human labor out of the economy, which leads to aggregate demand declining – who will buy all the goods produced? For a discussion of how AI can lead to such immiseration, see Benzell et al. (2015), Gries and Naudé (2020), and Kotlikoff (2022).

If the negative feedback effects from demand constraints can be overcome, then sustaining economic growth for more than a century or two will require galactic expansion (Wiley, 2011) – see Section 5.2 for a discussion. If somehow the Singleton does not manage to achieve the level of technology required for galactic expansion (perhaps its utility functions and values were constrained when the AI-alignment problem was solved) by the time economic growth runs up against these physical constraints, then, as Murphy (2022b, p. 847) warned, "we would be wise to plan for a post-growth world." It is, fortunately, still a long way in the future if we can invent a Friendly AGI – in time to avoid the Empty Planet fate and expand into the Galaxy.

10.3.2 Existential Risks: The Wireheaded Orgasmium

In Subsection 10.3.1.6, we discussed the possible economic growth impacts of an AGI/ASI, where these are relatively benign and perhaps ambiguous, but not catastrophic or existential, for humanity. Most of these scenarios involve some degree of "economic science fiction," in the words of Nordhaus (2021). Given that most mammal species go extinct after 1 million years or so, perhaps most people can live with a scenario where humans eventually become extinct in the far future after having lived fairly happy lives under a Singleton as a "sort of doddering Neanderthal aristocracy."

The two assumptions with which the analyses in Section 4.1 were done, were that (1) that the AI Scaling Hypothesis holds, and that (2) the alignment problem is solved. In Section 4.1.4, the first assumption was relaxed, and it was shown how super-exponential growth can arise via another form of AGI – Ems. In this section, the second assumption – that the value-alignment problem is solved – will be relaxed.

Relaxing the assumption that the alignment problem is solved before the invention of an AGI raises the specter of existential risk. There is a growing literature on whether and how AI poses an existential risk.[20] Economists have contributed little to this literature. It is one of the gaps in the economics of AI that this book is emphasizing. To explore why and how economics can contribute, it is useful to describe what is meant by existential risk and why an AGI is considered a potential existential risk.

The term existential risk is associated with Longtermism, given that it was first used by Bostrom (2002) who defined it as a risk of an outcome that "would either annihilate Earth-originating intelligent life or permanently and drastically curtail its potential" (Bostrom, 2002, p. 2). Existential risk from an AGI is taken seriously by a significant share of scientists, including those who do not necessarily subscribe to Longtermism. A recent headline exclaimed that "A third of scientists working on AI say it could cause global disaster" (Hsu, 2022).

In a survey of no less than two dozen ways in which AI poses an existential risk, Turchin and Denkenberger (2020, p. 148) warn that "AI is an extremely powerful and completely unpredictable technology, millions of times more powerful than nuclear weapons. Its existence could create multiple individual global risks, most of which we cannot currently imagine." And Noy and Uher (2022, p. 498) concluded that "Artificial Intelligence (AI) systems most likely

[20] Although there is, perhaps surprisingly, not that many people directly working on the problem: Hilton (2022) estimates around 300 people. This has led Harris (2020, p. 320) to exclaim that "There may be more people working in my local McDonald's than there are thinking about the prospect that we may permanently destroy the future."

pose the highest global catastrophic and existential risk to humanity from the four risks we described here, including solar fares and space weather, engineered and natural pandemics, and super-volcanic eruptions."

Why would AI pose catastrophic or even existential risks? It is due to the actual and future capabilities and values of AI. The capability claim is that AI may, in future, even if the chance is small, cause significant damage to humanity. The value claim is the one that we have dealt with in Section 2, namely that AI's values may not align with those of humanity (Sotala, 2018; Barrett and Baum, 2017). Given that it cannot be ruled out that an AGI or superintelligence will come into being with the nontrivial probability of causing the extinction of humanity, many – but not all – AI scientists now tend to conclude that "The consequences for humanity are so large that even if there is only a small chance[21] of it happening in that time frame, it is still urgent that we work now to understand it and to guide it in a positive direction" (Omohundro, 2008b, p. 5). Everitt et al. (2018) also argue that in addition to try and reduce the extinction risk, it is philosophically stimulating to work on the challenge of constraining a superior intelligence.

What kind of risks does an AGI/ASI pose that may have existential implications for humanity? Turchin and Denkenberger (2020) list two dozen possible "global catastrophic" risks from AI. They classify these into risks from narrow AI, young AI, and mature AI. They argue that it is not only mature AI – eventually AGI – that poses serious risks, but that AI along its entire development path poses such risks. Table 10.1 summarizes these risks.

It falls outside the scope of this book to discuss all of the risks listed in Table 10.1 – the reader is referred to Turchin and

[21] As put by Müller (2014, p. 298), "The discussion of risk is not dependent on the view that AGI is on a successful path toward human-level AI – though it gains urgency if such 'success' is a non-negligible possibility in the coming decades. It also gains urgency if the stakes are set high, even up to human extinction. If the stakes are so high, even a fairly small possibility (say, 3 percent) is entirely sufficient to motivate the research."

Table 10.1 *Potential catastrophic and existential AI risks*

AI Level	Risk	References
Narrow AI		
	AI help create biotech weapons	O'Brien and Nelson (2020)
	AI-driven mass unemployment	Ford (2016)
	AI boost mass destruction weapons	Umbrello et al. (2020)
	Wrong command to robotic army	Goldfarb and Lindsay (2022)
	Slaughterbot swarms	Macaulay (2021)
	Self improving AI-ransomware	Yampolskiy (2016)
	Ascending non-human economy	Alexander (2016a)
	Super-addictive drugs	Urbina et al. (2022)
	AI viruses affect hardware globally	Turchin and Denkenberger (2020)
Young AI		
	Robots replace humans	Hanson (2018)
	Philosophical zombies	Searle (1992)
	Doomsday weapon for global blackmail	Shulman (2010)
	AI creates catastrophic event to escape	Yampolskiy (2012)
	AI uses human atoms as material	Yudkowsky (2009)
	AI kills humans for world domination	Turchin and Denkenberger (2020)
Mature AI		
	AI lock-in	Bostrom (2006)
	AI halting problem	Charlesworth (2014)
	Paperclip maximizer	Bostrom (2012)
	Smile maximizer	Yudkowsky (2008)
	Wireheading humans	Yampolskiy (2014)
	Roko's Basilisk	Auerbach (2014)
	Conflict between benevolent AIs	Turchin and Denkenberger (2020)
	Philosophical landmines	Torres (2014)
	Alien AI attack	Carrigan Jr (2006)
	Evil AI	Pistono and Yampolskiy (2016)

Source: Author's compilation based on Turchin and Denkenberger (2020).

Denkenberger (2020) and the references listed in the table. We can also mention the work of Soice et al. (2023) who explored the potential catastrophic risks from LLMs (see Chapter 2 for a discussion of these as the current frontier in AI). The authors brought to the fore the potential of LLMs to facilitate bioterrorism. They reported that on particular prompting, LLM chatbots "suggested four potential pandemic pathogens, explained how they can be generated from synthetic DNA using reverse genetics, supplied the names of DNA synthesis companies unlikely to screen orders, identified detailed protocols and how to troubleshoot them, and recommended that anyone lacking the skills to perform reverse genetics engage a core facility or contract research organization. Collectively, these results suggest that LLMs will make pandemic-class agents widely accessible as soon as they are credibly identified, even to people with little or no laboratory training" (Soice et al., 2023, p. 1).

The purpose of presenting these risks in a single table is to illustrate succinctly the extent of thinking that has gone into clabórating the manifold ways in which AI may be a threat. Not all of the risks listed in Table 10.1 have equal probability – some, like the Roko's Basilisk,[22] are seen by most as being (even more) far-fetched. Nevertheless, a number of risks do stand out, and in light of the discussion in Chapter 3 about AI's utility function and its supergoals and instrumental goals, a number of remarks are in order.

The first is the risk of an AI lock-in (value lock-in). This is the risk that humanity may spend the rest of its existence[23] under an unchangeable, static set of rules that will follow from whatever goals and values are held onto by the AGI/ASI. A stable, immortal

[22] "Roko's Basilisk is an evil, godlike form of artificial intelligence, so dangerous that if you see it, or even think about it too hard, you will spend the rest of eternity screaming in its torture chamber. It's like the videotape in The Ring. Even death is no escape, for if you die, Roko's Basilisk will resurrect you and begin the torture again." It has been described as the most terrifying thought experiment of all time (Auerbach, 2014).

[23] Hanson (2022), while recognizing the possibility of lock-in, suggests that it may not be forever, given that in a billion years, it may be overcome by an alien intelligence – see the discussion of the Dark Forest below.

Singleton will be unassailable, and hence in a position to stifle all change (Bostrom, 2006).

The threat of a lock-in is not only limited to the case of an ASI Singleton, but can also happen in the digital world of EMs – or the digital Metaverse (Karnofsky, 2021a). This is because any significantly advanced digital world can be programmed to be stable – hence no improvement or escape that amounts to a totalitarian nightmare would be possible. A ruler for life and a set of rules could simply be constructed to be permanent (Karnofsky, 2021d).

A second risk to be highlighted given the discussion so far is *wireheading* – of both humans and AI. Wireheading refers to the direct stimulation of reward centers in the brain to override any motivation to action. The term originates from the implantation of wire electrodes in rats' brains, through which the animals could provide self-pleasure by pulling on a lever. This resulted in "the rat's self-stimulation behaviour completely displaced all interest in sex, sleep, food and water, ultimately leading to premature death" (Yampolskiy, 2014, p. 373). Essentially, the rat's utility function is not secure – it can be hacked to remove the need to pursue subgoals/instrumental goals. This amounts to "counterfeit utility production" which is marked by "the absence of productive behaviour in order to obtain the reward. Participating individuals go directly for the reward and fail to benefit the society. In most cases, they actually cause significant harm via their actions" (Yampolskiy, 2014, p. 374).

In Huxley's (1932) novel *Brave New World*, humans are kept in a pacified condition to accept their tech-ruled existence through using a drug called *Soma*. Tirole (2021) refers to this as the soft control of society – which is contrasted to most popular depictions of future totalitarian dystopias as being maintained by violent repression – the "boot-on-the-face." In a 1949 letter from Huxley to George Orwell, Huxley explained[24] that "Whether in actual fact the policy of the boot-on-the-face can go on indefinitely seems doubtful. My own

[24] As quoted in Tirole (2021, p. 2011).

belief is that the ruling oligarchy will find less arduous and wasteful ways of governing and of satisfying its lust for power, and these ways will resemble those which I described in Brave New World." The drug *Soma* in Huxley's novel is a form of wireheading – of hacking humans' utility functions – and, as Huxley indicates, a very likely method through which an AGI/ASI could repress humanity.

It is not only humans that are subject to wireheading – AI systems may also be able to be hacked in this way. The consequence could be AGI/ASIs with no interest in performing any actions except to provide themselves with counterfeit utility and maintain the status quo (Yampolskiy, 2014). Rather than being exterminated, or slowly dying off as a "sort of doddering Neanderthal aristocracy," humans may perhaps rather end up blissing it out in almost perpetuity "in wireheaded orgasmium" (Yampolskiy, 2014, p. 374) with its Singleton overlord in similar ecstasy – until the end of time.

Or until it is exterminated or enslaved by an alien AI. . .

10.4 EXTRATERRESTRIAL AI: THE FINAL EXISTENTIAL RISK?

> The future is a safe, sterile laboratory for trying out ideas in – Ursula K. Le Guin

In Figure 10.1, AI's future development trajectory is shown to result in the Singleton by the year 2100 and some unknown time thereafter in a Galactic AI. One of the risks that it and humanity – if we still exist at that time – will face, as Table 10.1 indicates, is a threat from an alien ASI civilization – an Alien Singleton, perhaps.

Although there is no evidence at present for any alien civilizations, statistically, the odds of human civilization being singular are almost vanishingly small (Drake, 1965). There are around $\approx$2 trillion galaxies in the universe (Conselice et al., 2016), each with more than 100 billion stars – most of whom likely have planets (Cassan et al., 2012). The number of terrestrial planets in the universe that circle Sun-like stars is huge – around $\approx 2 \times 10^{19}$ with another $\approx 7 \times 10^{20}$

(Zackrisson et al., 2016) estimated to be around M-dwarf stars. And 22 percent of Sun-like stars may have Earth-size planets in their habitable (where liquid water can exist) zones (Petigura et al., 2013).

Even if only 1 percent of these intelligent life forms arise, the universe would host billions of alien civilizations. One estimate is that there are around thirty-six communicating extra terrestrial intelligent (CETI) civilizations in the Milky Way Galaxy (Westby and Conselice, 2020). These alien civilizations, if sufficiently advanced, are likely to be ASIs. These post-Singularity alien AI civilizations may be too advanced for humans to detect[25] – they may for instance use quantum entanglement to communicate (and not radio waves), or compress their communication signals that they would be indistinguishable (for Earthlings) from noise (Gale et al., 2020; Bennett, 2021) (Rees, 2021; Gale et al., 2020; Shostak, 2018, 2021; De Visscher, 2020).

Why would an alien ASI pose a threat to Earth? Economic reasoning, supported by game theoretic analysis, offers two broad and interrelated reasons.

10.4.1 The Dark Forest

The first is the Dark Forest Hypothesis (DFH). It takes its label from the science fiction novel *The Dark Forest* by Cixin Liu. The DFH offers an explanation for the Fermi Paradox, which arose out of the question that physicist Enrico Fermi posed in 1950 "where is everybody?" referring to the absence of any evidence of an alien civilization in the universe. The Fermi Paradox, which was more formally set out by Hart (1975), is based on the observation that given the likelihood of intelligent civilizations in the universe (as described above) and the age of the universe (13.8 billion years), we

[25] Scientists have started to use AI to search for alien life, including searching for primitive extraterrestrial life or evidence of such life in the distant past. For example, AI can now detect traces of biological chemistry in samples that are hundreds of millions of years old with 90 percent accuracy (Kuthunur, 2023).

would now have encountered evidence for their existence.[26] The fact that we have not yet, and that there is a "Great Silence" (Cirković and Vukotić, 2008) requires "some special explanation" (Gray, 2015, p. 196).

Many explanations – more than seventy-five – have been proposed for the Fermi Paradox. A full discussion falls outside the scope of this chapter; the interested reader is referred to Webb (2015). For present purposes, though, the DFH explains the Fermi Paradox by postulating that it will be in the self-interest of any civilization to conceal its existence, lest it be exterminated by another, far more advanced civilization. According to Liu (2008),

> The universe is a dark forest. Every civilization is an armed hunter stalking through the trees like a ghost, gently pushing aside branches that block the path and trying to tread without sound. Even breathing is done with care. The hunter has to be careful, because everywhere in the forest are stealthy hunters like him. If he finds another life – another hunter, angel, or a demon, a delicate infant to tottering old man, a fairy or demigod—there's only one thing he can do: open fire and eliminate them.

There are two premises from which the description of planetary civilizations as hunter and hunted follows (Yu, 2015). The first is the *suspicion chain*: the intentions of any civilization cannot with perfect certainty be known – they may be malevolent. This imperfect information problem exists not only due to inherent interspecies communication but also because communication possibilities between planetary systems are limited due to physical distances. Moreover, given that all civilizations ultimately face resource –

[26] Using self-reproducing intelligent starprobes travelling at 1/10th the speed of light, the entire Milky Way Galaxy could be traversed in 500,000 years (Valdes and Freitas Jr., 1980). Such starprobes, as a way to traverse the universe, were proposed by Game Theory co-founder, John von Neumann (Von Neumann, 1966), hence labeled Von Neumann Probes. "From a technological point of view, there seems to be no obstacle to the ultimate terrestrial construction of Von Neumann probes" (Matloff, 2022, p. 206).

Malthusian – constraints (the universe is not infinite), the intentions of civilizations will be subject to great uncertainty (Yu, 2015).

The second premise is the *technology explosion* threat. This refers to the possibility that another civilization in the universe will be technologically superior or likely to experience a technology explosion at some time, which would bestow on them technological superiority. Thus, given these unknowns – the intent and technological prowess of an alien civilization – a cosmic civilization may want to conceal its existence. If it is discovered, it may want to strike first to eliminate the civilization that had discovered it as a precautionary measure before possibly being eliminated itself; however, it would be careful before doing it in case the act of a pre-emptive strike gives away its existence and location in the universe.

Game theoretic analyses can be used to show that the DFT implies that, as in the case of the Prisoners' dilemma, which it closely resembles, the optimal strategy for any civilization is not to cooperate but to be silent and, if discovered, to be malevolent – in other words, to strike first (Stolk, 2019; Su, 2021; Yasser, 2020). To show this conclusion, based on Yasser (2020), the following scenarios can be analyzed. Let Earth's civilization be denoted by E1. It is not aware of the existence of another advanced alien civilization – denoted E2 – in the relatively nearby star system of Proxima Centauri. E1, grappling with the Fermi Paradox, has to decide whether or not send to out a strong signal into the Galaxy to seek contact. The extensive form of this game is as follows.

This extensive form of the game shows that Earth (E1) decides to engage in the search for extraterrestrial intelligence (SETI) and broadcast a signal, it will be intercepted by E2 (Figure 10.4). E2 has three options: it can either reply and acknowledge its existence, or it can remain silent, or it can decide to pre-empt any possible malevolent action by Earth should Earth eventually discover it and strike first and unexpectedly so as to destroy Earth's civilization. The payoffs – with a payoff of $-\infty$ in case Earth is destroyed for E1 and a payoff of ϕ for E2 (the value of averting a possible hostile action

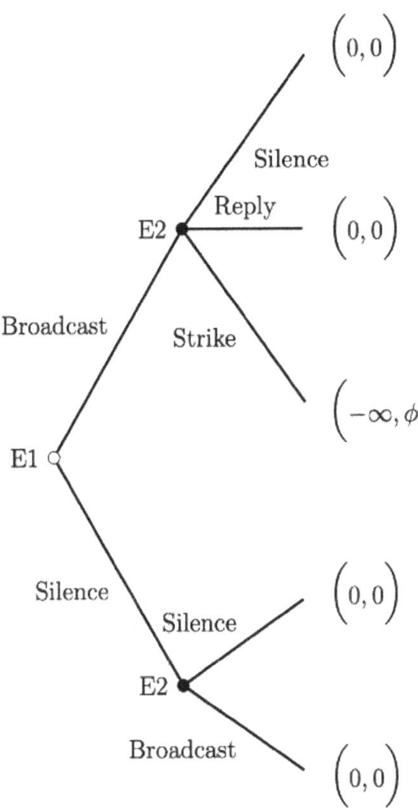

FIGURE 10.4 Extensive form of the game, Earth civilization
Source: Authors' compilation based on Yasser (2020)

from Earth in future) implies that for Earth the dominant strategy (subgame perfect) is to remain silent.

It can also be shown that striking first is indeed the dominant strategy for an alien civilization once it becomes aware of Earth's existence. Consider this decision in the extensive form of the game.

Figure 10.5 shows that the dominant strategy for an alien civilization (E2) upon receiving a signal from Earth (E1) is to strike and destroy it. Hence the *Dark Forest conclusion*: "If a civilization can destroy another, it will" (Yasser, 2020).

One way in which a malevolent alien ASI may operate to wipe out any emerging civilizations that may grow up to be an existential threat is to hijack them through broadcasting a killer code. This could be for instance a computer code that once it is received

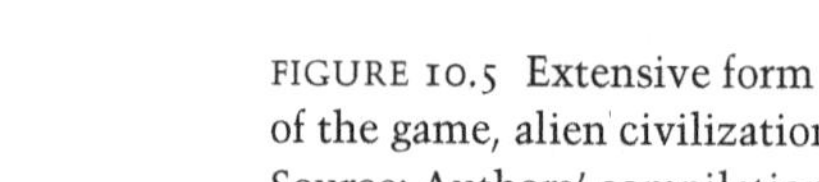

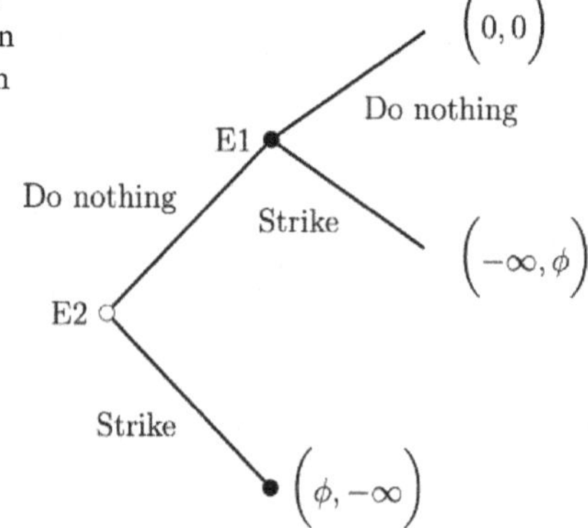

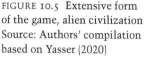

FIGURE 10.5 Extensive form of the game, alien civilization
Source: Authors' compilation based on Yasser (2020)

and downloaded by an emerging civilization would infest it with the alien AI's programs. It could also broadcast instructions for the construction of a civilization-destroying bomb, perhaps designed to look like a Trojan Horse (Barnett, 2022).

Based on this reasoning, eminent scientists, including Stephen Hawking, have warned that humans should not be actively trying to communicate with possible alien civilizations or broadcast knowledge of our existence into the wider universe (Hrala, 2016). Brin (2008) makes the point that "If aliens are so advanced and altruistic [...] and yet are choosing to remain silent [...] Is it possible that they are silent because they know something we don't know?" And Diamond (1999, p. 68) warns that

> The astronomers and others hope that the extraterrestrials, delighted to discover fellow intelligent beings, will sit down for a friendly chat. Perhaps the astronomers are right; that's the best-case scenario. A less pleasant prospect is that the extraterrestrials might behave the way we intelligent beings have behaved whenever we have discovered other previously unknown intelligent beings on earth, like unfamiliar humans or chimpanzees and gorillas. Just as we did to those beings, the extraterrestrials might proceed to kill, infect, dissect, conquer, displace or enslave us, stuff us as specimens for their museums or

pickle our skulls and use us for medical research. My own view is that those astronomers now preparing again to beam radio signals out to hoped-for extraterrestrials are naïve, even dangerous.

10.4.2 The Galactic Colonization Imperative

> Recent progress in the technology of space travel [. . .] raise the distinct possibility that we may eventually discover or construct a world to which orthodox economic theory apply (Krugman, 1978, p. 1).

The second reason why an alien AI may pose a threat to the Earth may be due to the Galactic Colonization Imperative. This is based on the evolutionary view that the universe has finite physical resources, which ultimately on any one planet present will be an obstacle to continued economic growth (see Section 4.1.5) that civilizations will want to expand beyond their planet. Natural selection may favor civilizations that expand (Wiley, 2011).

Bostrom (2003a) makes, from the perspective of what has been called "galaxy-brain longtermism" (Samuel, 2022), a moral case for galactic expansion. He argues that "the potential for approximately 10^{38} human lives is lost every century that colonization of our local supercluster is delayed" (p. 309). See also Cirkovic (2002) who calculates an enormous loss in terms of potential lives lost if humanity fails to develop technologies to enable galactic colonization.

The implication is that alien civilizations will be in a race to colonize the galaxy (and perhaps eventually the universe) (Sandberg, 2018). An alien ASI may therefore face a strong strategic economic incentive – reflected in its utility function – to colonize the Earth before the Earth-bound human civilization can itself expand into space.[27] As Miller and Felton (2017, p. 46) explain that

[27] Entering the race to colonize the galaxy is not without risk. As Baum et al. (2011, p. 26) warns, "humanity should avoid giving off the appearance of being a rapidly expansive civilization. If an ETI perceives humanity as such, then it may be inclined to attempt a preemptive strike against us so as to prevent us from growing into a threat to the ETI or others in the galaxy."

> not colonizing the neighborhood means a civilization runs the risk of losing valuable resources to others and, eventually, being overcome by them. Even if an alien species was peaceful and had no intrinsic desire to expand beyond its home solar system, it should recognize that evolution could easily give rise, on some distant planet, to an imperialistic or xenocidal race. Colonizing one's neighborhood, therefore, might be a prudent means of self-defense. Probably, at least a few aliens would have utility functions (i.e., objectives) that would cause them to want to interfere in the development of other sentient species, whether to help them, to hurt them, or to propagate an ideology or religion.

The theme of strategic competition between ETIs in colonizing the galaxy has gathered some attention in the largely noneconomic literature. It nevertheless uses game theoretic lenses and cost-benefit/marginal thinking to consider the likely behavior of ETIs in terms of decisions such as whether and when – and how – to colonize the galaxy (Sandberg, 2018); whether or not to try and contact ETIs (Baum et al., 2011); whether or not to choose conflict or attempt cooperation with another ETI (Stolk, 2019; Yasser, 2020); how to best protect a planetary civilization or deter another from striking (Su, 2021); and when an Earth-based civilization could expect to find evidence of an ETI (Hanson et al., 2021). Key economic parameters in these decisions are speed of travel, the cost of energy, the cost of resource extraction and allocation, and the patterns of exploration. As the quote from economics Nobel Laureate Paul Krugman[28] at the top of this section suggests, these topics and their considerations are well suited – as is the decision-making world of AI agents – for analysis by economists.

[28] Krugman himself proposed *The First and Second Fundamental Theorems of Interstellar Trade* to address the question of the determination of interest rates on transit goods in the case of near light-speed interstellar space travel (Krugman, 1978).

A relatively unexplored implication of the Galactic Colonization Imperative suggests that planetary civilizations would have an incentive to pursue high sustainable economic growth rates[29] in order to gain the economic development levels, wealth, and technological capabilities that would enable them to build spaceships, self-replicating space probes (SRPs) and the terraforming technologies they may need.[30] Failure achieve such levels of wealth and technological development would be comparable to the collapse of Easter Island following its inability to maintain a development level consistent with the building of ocean-going canoes (Wiley, 2011, p. 9). Civilizations may be likely moreover to delay their expansion into space until they have reached a sufficiently high level of technological and economic development, as the civilization "with the biggest resources completely pre-empts the other" – (Sandberg, 2018, p. 3).

Olson (2015) provides a different perspective and deeper motivation for the Galactic Colonization Imperative. He provides a model for the aggressive expansion of alien civilizations wherein the utilization by these civilizations of sufficient energy and the resultant radiation eventually change the very physical structure of the universe. This could imply that "we have completely misjudged the significance of life to the universe. Intelligent life may be the universe's large-scale, general-purpose tool for seeking out and minimizing deeply hidden reserves of free energy" (Fullarton, 2016).

The reader may ask at this point, if such a colonization imperative exists, why have we not yet encountered these ETIs? In other words, how can a Galactic Colonization Imperative be sustained, in light of the Fermi Paradox?

[29] Dutil and Dumas (2007) suggest that there are likely very few galactic civilizations because most planetary civilizations would fail to achieve sufficient technological capability to expand, before experiencing a growth collapse.

[30] Hickman (1999) analyzes the economics of large space projects such as terraforming planets for human colonization. He shows that the upfront capitalization for projects with returns of hundreds if not thousands of years into the future poses a significant constraint. He calculates for instance that terraforming of Mars, which may make the planet habitable after 700 years, will require total Martian real estate sales of 1.36×10^{15} billion dollars to repay its loans.

Three (most) plausible reasons advanced in the literature that are consistent with both the imperative and the Fermi Paradox are the Percolation Model, the Grabby Aliens Model, and the Great Filter Hypothesis.

10.4.2.1 *Percolation*

The Percolation Model is based on a generalized invasion percolation (GIP) process that traces the colonization process as following a particular diffusion process. This diffusion process results in a nonuniform expansion of civilization characterized by densely occupied regions in the galaxy that are however dispersed and separated by large empty voids (Galera et al., 2019). If galactic colonization indeed follows a Percolation Model, it implies that Earth may be located in one of the large empty voids. According to Galera et al. (2019, p. 321) "Earth location is atypical, belonging to a huge but poorly inhabited galactic domain. We must consider the distressing possibility that we live not in the highly developed part of the Galaxy, similar to the regions full of light points in the Earth photo, but in a large region analogous to Amazon, Sahara or Siberia. Earth might not be a typical but an exotic place, being an isolated site far away from the galactic civilization."

10.4.2.2 *Grabby Aliens*

The Grabby Aliens Model suggests that we have not yet encountered ETIs because our Earth civilization has risen early[31] in the galaxy – if we had not, we would never have had the opportunity to emerge, as our solar system would have long ago been colonized by ETIs (Hanson et al., 2021). And because we are early, we will in the future encounter aggressive alien expansion (as in Olsen, 2015) – these are called "Grabby Aliens" – or Loud Aliens – to contrast them with quiet aliens, who may, Dark Forest-like, prefer not to

[31] As put by Hanson et al. (2021, p. 2), "humanity seems to have appeared implausibly early in the history of the universe."

engage in Galactic expansion. According to Hanson (2020), we should encounter a Grabby Alien civilization in around 500 million years.

10.4.2.3 The Great Filter

The Great Filter Hypothesis (Hanson, 1998) is based on the notion that there are evolutionary steps (or hurdles) that need to be overcome for the emergence and development of life from single-cell organisms to galactic civilizations – "climbing the staircase of complexity" (Aldous, 2010). The number of these steps that are hard has been estimated to be between 3 and 9 (Hanson et al., 2021). One or more of these steps may be so difficult to make that it filters out the existence of any galactic civilizations.

Taking a simplified version of the Drake equation (Drake, 1965) to estimate the number of intelligent civilizations, Verendel and Häggström (2017) denote the number of intelligent galaxy-colonizing civilizations as given by Npq where N = the number of planets in the universe where life can start, p is the probability that any one of these can develop intelligent life on the level of current human civilization, and q is the conditional probability that it develops eventually into a galaxy-colonizing civilization.

Because the current estimates are that N is very large (e.g., $>\approx 7 \times 10^{20}$), the lack of any visible galactic civilization from Earth would imply that p is very small. If this is indeed the case, it may imply that we have already passed the Great Filter – that it is an "early" filter (Armstrong and Sandberg, 2013). If, however, we would find evidence of very primitive alien life – for example, existing or extinct microbial life of Mars – then it could mean that p is large and q is very small. Bostrom (2008) therefore hopes that the search for alien life "finds nothing" because otherwise it would imply that human civilization may face a (late) Great Filter in the future which would imply its doom.

According to the *Medea Hypothesis* (Ward, 2009), a Great Filter in front of human civilization (small q) suggests that all technological civilizations self-destruct at some point in time. Perhaps an ASI is such a technology that all civilizations at some point discover and which without exception leads to their demise. Ord (2020) has estimated that there is a one in ten probability that AI will cause human extinction in the next hundred years.

10.4.3 *Tea; Earl Grey; Hot!*

It is worth stressing that both the DFH and the Galactic Colonization Imperative may be subject to humans' anthropomorphic and present biases. Gale et al. (2020) argue for instance that unlike humans, or other biological entities, ASIs may not see other ASIs as threats or as potential resources to consume: it may be more in their interest to collaborate or to entirely avoid others. Humans' anthropomorphic bias is an outcome of evolutionary pressures (Varella, 2018), which have not been similar in the case of AIs.

And our present bias may be leading us to be wholly incapable of imagining the nature of future technology – and coupled with our anthropomorphic bias, we may be blind as far as the technologies of far-advanced ASIs are concerned. It could therefore be, as Lampton (2013) has suggested, that alien ASIs may simply use remote-sensing technologies far in advance of what humans can imagine to explore the galaxy, with no need to physically explore or conquer other planetary systems. As he puts it (p. 313):

> In our recent past, world exploration was motivated by trade, colonization and conquest. In our information-rich future there will be no need to go to China to fetch tea leaves: they will be fabricated on the spot, far more conveniently, using local matter, local energy and local information. When Capt. Picard orders 'Tea; Earl Grey; hot!' he gets it there and then.

10.5 CONCLUDING REMARKS

The idea of a Singularity – an intelligence explosion caused by recursively self-improving AI – is most relevant for economists working in endogenous growth theory. This chapter has outlined the relevance of idea-driven growth models, which highlight the importance of population growth and research productivity for exponential and super-exponential growth. It is also a relevant field for economists in technology studies, because if there would ever be a Singularity, it would be followed by a wholly different mode of economic growth: as different from the current industrial era growth as the industrial era growth mode was different from that of the agricultural era.

While economists' models have been useful in explaining the take-off from low and stagnating growth as had characterized most of human history, and in identifying the possibility for accelerating growth – the so-called growth explosions as discussed – there are two comparative blind spots. One is that very few economic growth models have entertained the possibility that AI-induced growth could lead to a growth collapse – we took up this possibility in Chapter 5. A second is that economists are still shying away from the very long-run implications. A very long-run implication is the limits of growth. Economists tend not to think too much about the physical limits to growth – this has been left rather to physicists to explore. Physicist Tom Murphy recounts this dinner conversation with an economist in his blog (Murphy, 2012):

> Physicist: Hi, I'm Tom. I'm a physicist.
>
> Economist: Hi Tom, I'm [ahem..cough]. I'm an economist.
>
> Physicist: Hey, that's great. I've been thinking a bit about growth and want to run an idea by you. I claim that economic growth cannot continue indefinitely.
>
> Economist: [chokes on bread crumb] Did I hear you right? Did you say that growth can not continue forever?
>
> Physicist: That's right. I think physical limits assert themselves.

This absence of economics in the debate may be unfortunate – unlike physicists, economists tend to see very few resources as natural or fixed, but as part of technologies and ideas – and thus subject to substitution and the impact of incentives. But in the long run, physical limits do exist, and although physicists recognize these, the discussion about the ethical, moral, and societal implications of these longer-term implications limits tends to be dominated by philosophers, in particular philosophers subscribing to Longtermism. This latter movement, while in its weak form has made the justifiable point about considering the well-being of future generations more than is generally the case, has become associated with the views and ambition of some tech elite billionaires – among them Elon Musk, Peter Thiel, and Jaan Tallin. The concern is that it is "a disturbing secular religion that looks like it addresses humanity's deepest problems, but actually justifies pursuing the social preferences of elites" (Torres, 2021). These social preferences may have nothing to do with addressing current global challenges such as poverty, inequality, conflict, migration, and even climate change.

Economists can potentially make a much-needed contribution to the debate on the long-term implications of growth, the possible consequences of a future growth collapse or explosion, and the extent of the concern that should be placed on existential risk mitigation – and concern is certainly warranted. Economists would tend to counter suggestions from strong (or galaxy-brain) Longtermism and start by considering improving the well-being of future generations by beginning to solve current development challenges and problems. As put by Wright (2022), "I have a question for longtermists: Are you sure that our failure to think long term is the problem? [...] Here's my radical thought: The biggest existential threat we face [...] is that humans aren't good enough at shorttermism. If people were skilled shorttermists – if they pursued short-term interests wisely – our long-term problems, including the existential ones, would be manageable." Indeed, already back in the 1990s, Baranzini and Bourguignon (1995) linked existential risk and societal risk aversion to levels of development.

Generally, economists have not made many contributions to the field of existential risk studies (ERS).[32] Here, the existential risk posed by super AI is very much relevant. There is also the risk, not only from super AI but also from the advanced AI-supported digital

[32] For an overview of the history and trends in ESR, see Beard and Torres (2020).

technologies that will characterize the future Metaverse. The risk is that these technologies will lock-in, essentially forever, future digital people, "ems," into a dystopian, totalitarian, and autocratic world. This chapter also argues that if the DFH is valid, an extraterrestrial AGI may pose a further existential risk. This tends to be a topic neglected by both philosophers and economists.

Why did economists, so far, contribute relatively little to the understanding and mitigation of the catastrophic and existential risks posed by AI? One reason is, as Noy and Uher (2022, p. 294) point out, that economic risk assessment methods using EUT are not well suited to deal with existential risks. Weitzman (2009, p. 10) put forward a Dismal Theorem which states that, because the probabilities of catastrophic events are characterized by long tails, EUT would tend to assign infinite losses to it. This is because "distributions with fat tails are ones for which the probabilities of rare events decline relatively slowly as the event moves far away from its central tendency" (Nordhaus, 2009, p. 3). Buchholz and Schymura (2012, p. 234) conclude that because of this, EUT may not be able to provide an ethically acceptable approach to deal with catastrophic and existential risks. Using various specifications of utility functions with different assumptions on risk aversion, they show that if a fairly plausible level of risk adverseness is assumed, that it results in a "tyranny of catastrophic risk," as in Nordhaus (2009). On the other hand, with low risk aversion, the EUT assessment of catastrophic risk would assign it no importance.

However, as Martin and Pindyck (2015) have shown, despite these shortcomings of EUT, economists' tools can provide useful insights into dealing with catastrophic risks. Their analysis offers insight into how to answer questions such as how much should society invest in averting the existential risk from AI, which, as has been shown, can under Pascalian fanaticism be extremely high? And, what would be the effect of other existential risks on the amount that should be invested in averting an AI catastrophe? They show for instance that there is an interdependence between efforts to address a whole range of existential and catastrophic risks and that therefore "applying cost-benefit analysis to each event in isolation can lead to a policy that is far from optimal" (Martin and Pindyck, 2015, p. 2948).

An exception in the economic literature that illustrates the additional light that economic models can bring to the analysis of economic growth, AGI, and existential risk is the paper by Baranzini and Bourguignon (1995). Their work, which largely predates modern AI and the concerns that it entails an existential risk, tried to answer the question of what society should do if it faces the decision "whether to adopt or not a new technology that will raise the rate of GDP growth by some variable amount?" They considered explicitly the possibility that such a new technology would increase the probability of humanity's extinction, which in turn implies that to minimize the risk of extinction, that the rate of innovation and economic growth should be reduced.

They show, using a growth model with a Hyperbolic Absolute Risk Aversion (HARA)[33] social utility function specification, that sustainable, low technology growth (i.e., with an extinction probability of zero) will be optimal only if the utility of survival and risk of technological innovation are relatively large. This leads to the conclusion that "sustainable growth is consistent with optimal growth only for affluent societies" (Baranzini and Bourguignon, 1995, p. 353). Their model leads to the prediction that concern about Singularity, existential risks, and longtermism may be rich-country and rich tech-elites' concerns. Which, as has been pointed out, it largely is. Which is why Floridi (2022, p. 9) is critical of time spent speculating about the Singularity, stating that "it is a rich-world preoccupation likely to worry people in wealthy societies who seem to forget the real evils oppressing humanity and our planet."

Whereas physicists have recognized potential physical constraints on growth and philosophers have raised the possible dangers

[33] Proposed by Von Neumann and Morgenstern (1944) wherein risk tolerance of an agent is a function of their wealth.

and moral obligations of existential risks and future generations – the long run – as far as the shorter run is concerned computer scientists and engineers have tended to be more optimistic that technological unemployment and huge inequalities, although inevitable, do not really pose a problem. Domingos (2015, pp. 278,279) for instance is hopeful that the political processes and redistributive policies and social safety nets are the answer, arguing that although the societal transition as a result of the consequences of AI will in the future be "tumultuous," "thanks to democracy it will have a happy ending" and that "unemployment benefits will be replaced by a basic income for everyone." Thus, for Domingos (2015), Chace (2020b), and others, the future of AI in the economy is one of high unemployment, high inequality but with strong welfare states where people will enjoy only leisure and AI and robots will do all the work.

The problem with such hopeful scenarios is a blind spot for the effects of economic incentives. Not only may the adoption of AI not be as profitable as to lead to mass unemployment, but the robustness and effectiveness of democracy (political institutions) to adequately implement social safety nets (a basic income) may be overestimated (Tirole, 2021). Governments may simply not be able to regulate the powerful global tech oligarchy that is being created on the basis of AI and big data; moreover, they may be captured and co-opted by governments into legitimizing their monopoly (Srnicek, 2016). Surveillance capitalism and the growth of the surveillance state, already emerging outcomes of these processes, have triggered growing global discontent with capitalism (Zuboff, 2015). By reducing the value of labor, AI automation will moreover exacerbate global inequality, deglobalization, and conflict, as the wealthiest nations will become "those with the highest ratio of natural resources to population" (Domingos, 2015, p. 279). Economists do of course already focus on all of these issues (it all broadly touches on the Future of Work) and hence we have seen in recent years that the concerns about a possible robot apocalypse (high technological unemployment) have somewhat abated. Perhaps one will see a similar pattern to the concerns about the Singularity and existential risks of AI as economists make their contribution.

Future avenues for research include the need for further elaborations of economic growth models to explore the possibility of an AI-induced growth collapse, to explore the physical limits of growth, and to sharpen the tools to draw out the policy implications of facing fat-tailed catastrophic risks. Furthermore, economic perspectives may usefully be applied to the solutions and implications of the Fermi Paradox. These include applying economic tools to potential far-future challenges, such as decisions on whether and when – and how – to colonize the galaxy; whether or not to try and contact ETIs; whether or not to choose conflict or attempt cooperation with other ETIs; how to best protect a planetary civilization; and when an Earth-based civilization could expect to find evidence of an ETI.

Finally, two further conclusions that emerged from this chapter were first that a Singularity and existential risk from AI are still science fiction: which, however, should not preclude economists from weighing in – it certainly does not deter philosophers; and two, that economists should contribute more to existential risk studies, and not leave this topic to lose credibility because of the Pascalian fanaticism of Longtermism.

In conclusion, the future is essentially unknowable, which makes it worthwhile to reflect appropriately on the speculations that this chapter has indulged in, including discussions of existential risks, limits to growth, and bounded rationality. A useful guardrail to grab hold of when contemplating these is the sensible caution of Deutsch (2011, p. 198) that

> Trying to know the unknowable leads inexorably to error and self-deception. Among other things, it creates a bias towards pessimism.

Bibliography

Abbeel, P. and Ng, A. (2004). Apprenticeship Learning via Inverse Reinforcement Learning. *Proceedings of the Twenty-First International Conference on Machine Learning, ICML 04*. New York, USA.

Acemoglu, D. (2002). Technical Change, Inequality, and the Labor Market. *Journal of Economic Literature*, 40(1):7–72.

Acemoglu, D. (2009). *Introduction to Modern Economic Growth*. Princeton: Princeton University Press.

Acemoglu, D. and Autor, D. (2011). Skills, Tasks and Technologies: Implications for Employment and Earnings. In: Card D. and Ashenfelter, O. (eds.) *Handbook of Labor Economics*. Amsterdam: Elsevier, pp. 1043–1171.

Acemoglu, D. and Autor, D. (2012). What Does Human Capital Do? A Review of Goldin and Katz's The Race between Education and Technology. *Journal of Economic Literature*, 50(2):426–463.

Acemoglu, D. and Restrepo, P. (2017). Robots and Jobs: Evidence from US Labor Markets. NBER Working Paper no. 23285. National Bureau for Economic Research.

Acemoglu, D. and Restrepo, P. (2018a). Artificial Intelligence, Automation and Work. Working Paper no. 24196. National Bureau of Economic Research.

Acemoglu, D. and Restrepo, P. (2018b). The Race between Man and Machine: Implications of Technology for Growth, Factor Shares and Employment. *American Economic Review*, 108(6):1488–1542.

Acemoglu, D. and Restrepo, P. (2019a). Artificial Intelligence, Automation and Work. In: Argawal, A. K., Gans, J., and Goldfarb, A. (eds.) *The Economics of Artificial Intelligence: An Agenda*. Chicago: University of Chicago Press, Chapter 8:197–236.

Acemoglu, D. and Restrepo, P. (2019b). Automation and New Tasks: How Technology Displaces and Reinstates Labor. *Journal of Economic Perspectives*, 33(2):3–30.

Acemoglu, D. and Restrepo, P. (2020). Robots and Jobs: Evidence from US Labor Markets. *Journal of Political Economy*, 128(6):2188–2244.

Aghion, P., Dewatripont, M., and Rey, P. (1997). Corporate Governance, Competition Policy and Industrial Policy. *European Economic Review*, (41):797–805.

Aghion, P., Jones, B., and Jones, C. (2017). Artificial Intelligence and Economic Growth. NBER Working Paper 23928, National Bureau for Economic Research.

Agrawal, A., Gans, J., and Goldfarb, A. (2019a). Economic Policy for Artificial Intelligence. In: Lerner, J. and Stern, S. (eds.) *Innovation Policy and the Economy*, Vol. 19. NBER. pp. 139–159.

Agrawal, A., McHale, J., and Oettl, A. (2018). Finding Needles in Haystacks: Artificial Intelligence and Recombinant Growth. NBER Working Paper no. 24541. National Bureau for Economic Research.

Agrawal, A., McHale, J., and Oettl, A. (2019b). *Artificial Intelligence, Scientific Discovery, and Commercial Innovation*. Mimeo. Published as NBER Working Paper number 31558, NBER: Cambridge MA.

Agrawal, S. (2019). *Reinforcement Learning Lecture 1: Introduction*. Minneapolis: University of Minnesota.

Ahiska, S., Appaji, S., King, R., and Warsing Jr, D. (2013). A Markov Decision Process-Based Policy Characterization Approach for a Stochastic Inventory Control Problem with Unreliable Sourcing. *International Journal of Production Economics*, 144(2):485–495.

Ahuja, G. and Lampert, C. (2001). Entrepreneurship in the Large Corporation: A Longitudinal Study of How Established Firms Create Breakthrough Inventions. *Strategic Management Journal*, 22:521–543.

AI and Inclusion Symposium (2017). An Evolving Reading List. Available at https://drive.google.com/file/d/0ByG0FdgytPz7YkxRMHF1d19ibE0/view.

AI Impacts (2016). Friendly AI as a Global Public Good. AI Impacts online, https://aiimpacts.org/friendly-ai-as-a-global-public-good/.

Aiello, L. (2016). The Multifaceted Impact of Ada Lovelace in the Digital Age. *Artificial Intelligence*, 236:58–62.

Aldous, D. J. (2010). *The Great Filter, Branching Histories and Unlikely Events*. Mimeo: University of California, Berkeley.

Aleksander, S. (2019). 1960: The Year the Singularity Was Cancelled. *Slate Star Codex Blog*, April 22.

Alexander, S. (2016a). Ascended Economy? *Star Slate Codex Blog*, May 30.

Alexander, S. (2016b). Book Review: Age of EM. *Slate Star Codex Blog*, May 28.

Alexander, S. (2022). Book Review: What We Owe the Future. *Astral Codex Ten*, August 23.

Alkaissi, H. and McFarlane, S. (2023). Artificial Hallucinations in ChatGPT: Implications in Scientific Writing. *Cureus*, 15(2):e35179.

Allen, C., Smit, I., and Wallach, D. (2005). Artificial Morality: Top-Down, Bottom-Up, and Hybrid Approaches. *Ethics and Information Technology*, 7(3): 149–155.

Allen, P. and Greaves, M. (2011). The Singularity Isn't Near. *MIT Technology Review*, October 12.

Amendola, G. (2023). Special Issue on Logic-Based Artificial Intelligence. *Algorithms*, 16(2):106.

Amodei, D., Olah, C., Steinhardt, J., Christiano, P., Schulman, J., and Mané, D. (2016). Concrete Problems in AI Safety. ArXiv:1606.06565 [Cs], June: http://arxiv.org/abs/1606.06565.

Anderson, M. and Anderson, S. (2007). Machine Ethics: Creating an Ethical Intelligent Agent. *AI Magazine*, 28(4):15.

Ariely, D. (2009). *Predictably Irrational: The Hidden Forces That Shape Our Decisions*. London: HarperCollins.

Armstrong, S., Bostrom, N., and Schulman, C. (2016). Racing to the Precipice: A Model of Artificial Intelligence Development. *AI & Society*, 31:201–206.

Armstrong, S. and Sandberg, A. (2013). Eternity in Six Hours: Intergalactic Spreading of Intelligent Life and Sharpening the Fermi Paradox. *Acta Astronautica*, 89:1–13.

Armstrong, S., Sandberg, A., and Bostrom, N. (2012). Thinking Inside the Box: Controlling and Using an Oracle AI. *Minds and Machines*, 22(4):299–324.

Armstrong, S. and Sotala, K. (2015). How We're Predicting AI – or Failing to. In: Romportl, J., Zackova, E., and Kelemen, J. (eds.) *Beyond Artificial Intelligence. Topics in Intelligent Engineering and Informatics*, Vol. 9. Cham: Springer, pp. 11–29.

Arntz, M., Gregory, I., and Zierahn, U. (2017). Revisiting the Risk of Automation. *Economic Letters*, 159:157–160.

Arrow, K. (1994). Methodological Individualism and Social Knowledge. *American Economic Review, Papers and Proceedings*, 84(2):1–9.

Arthur, W. (2021). Foundations of Complexity Economics. *Nature Reviews Physics*, 3:136–145.

Arulkumaran, K., Deisenroth, M., Brundage, M., and Bharath, A. (2017). A Brief Survey of Deep Reinforcement Learning. arXiv:1708.05866v2 [cs.LG].

Aschenbrenner, L. (2020). Existential Risk and Growth. GPI Working Paper No. 6-2020, Global Priorities Institute, University of Oxford.

Aschhoff, B. and Sofka, W. (2009). Innovation on Demand: Can Public Procurement Drive Market Success of Innovations? *Research Policy*, 38(8): 1235–1247.

Ash, E. and Hansen, S. (2023). Text Algorithms in Economics. *Annual Review of Economics*, 15:659–688.

Askell, A., Brundage, M., and Hadfield, G. (2019). The Role of Cooperation in Responsible AI Development. ArXiv, July.

Athey, S. and Imbens, G. (2019). Machine Learning Methods that Economists Should Know About. *Annual Review of Economics*, 11(1):685–725.

Auerbach, D. (2014). The Most Terrifying Thought Experiment of All Time. Slate Magazine, 17 July.

Auerswald, P. E. (2017). The Code Economy: A Forty-thousand-year History. Oxford: Oxford University Press.

Autor, D. (2013). The "Task Approach" to Labour Markets. *Journal for Labour Market Research*, 46(3):185–199.

Autor, D. (2014). Skills, Education, and the Rise of Earnings Inequality Among the Other 99 Percent. *Science*, 344(6186):843–851.

Autor, D. and Dorn, D. (2013). The Growth of Low Skill Service Jobs and the Polarization of the US Labor Market. *American Economic Review*, 103(5):1553–1597.

Autor, D., Dorn, D., Katz, L., Patterson, C., and Reenen., J. V. (2017). The Fall of the Labour Share and the Rise of Superstar Firms. Working Paper no. 23396. National Bureau of Economic Research.

Autor, D., Katz, L., and Krueger, A. (1999). Computing Inequality: Have Computers Changed the Labor Market? *Quarterly Journal of Economics*, 113(4): 1169–1214.

Autor, D., Levy, F., and Murnane, R. (2003). The Skill Content of Recent Technological Change: An Empirical Exploration. *Quarterly Journal of Economics*, 118(4):1279–1333.

Autor, D. and Salomons, A. (2018). Is Automation Labor-displacing? Productivity Growth, Employment and the Labor Share. Brookings Papers on Economic Activity, BPEA Conference, 8–9 March.

Azoulay, P., Fuchs, E., Goldstein, A., and Kearney, M. (2018a). Funding Breakthrough Research: Promises and Challenges of the ARPA Model. *Innovation Policy and the Economy*, 19:69–96.

Azoulay, P., Jones, B., Kim, J., and Miranda, J. (2018b). Age and High-growth Entrepreneurship. NBER Working Paper Series no. 24489. National Bureau for Economic Research.

Baker-Brunnbauer, J. (2020). Management Perspective of Ethics in Artificial Intelligence. AI and Ethics, 11 September. https://doi.org/10.1007/s43681-020-00022-3.

Baranzini, A. and Bourguignon, F. (1995). Is Sustainable Growth Optimal? *International Tax and Public Finance*, 2(2):341–356.

Barnett, M. (2020). Distinguishing Definitions of Takeoff. AI Alignment Forum, 14 February.

Barnett, M. (2022). My Current Thoughts on the Risks from SETI. Effective Altruism Forum, 15 March.

Barrett, A. and Baum, S. (2017). A Model of Pathways to Artificial Superintelligence Catastrophe for Risk and Decision Analysis. *Journal of Experimental and Theoretical Artificial Intelligence*, 29(2):397–414.

Barrett, S. (2007). *Why Cooperate? The Incentive to Supply Global Public Goods.* Oxford: Oxford University Press.

Basuchoudhary, A., Bang, J., and Sen, T. (2017). *Machine-learning Techniques in Economics: New Tools for Predicting Economic Growth.* Cham: Springer Publishing.

Baum, S. D., Haqq-Misra, J., and Domagal-Goldman, S. (2011). Would Contact with Extraterrestrials Benefit or Harm Humanity? A Scenario Analysis. *Acta Astronautica*, 689(11–12):2144–2129.

Beard, S. and Torres, E. (2020). *Ripples on the Great Sea of Life: A Brief History of Existential Risk Studies.* Mimeo: SSRN, 12 March. Available at https://papers.ssrn.com/sol3/papers.cfm?abstract_id=3730000.

Beaudry, P., Green, D., and Sand, B. (2013). The Great Reversal in the Demand for Skill and Cognitive Tasks. Working Paper No.18901. National Bureau of Economic Research.

Beckstead, N. (2013). On the Overwhelming Importance of Shaping the Far Future. DPhil Thesis, Rutgers University.

Bellman, R. (1957a). *Dynamic Programming.* Princeton: Princeton University Press.

Bellman, R. (1957b). A Markovian Decision Process. *Journal of Mathematics and Mechanics*, 6(5):679–684.

Bennett, M. (2021). Compression, The Fermi Paradox and Artificial Superintelligence. In: Goertzel, B., Iklé, M., and Potapov, A. (eds.) *Artificial General Intelligence. Lecture Notes in Computer Science*, vol. 13154. Cham: Springer, pp. 41–44.

Benya (2012). Why You Must Maximise Expected Utility. AI Alignment Forum, 13 December.

Benzell, S., Kotlikoff, L., LaGarda, G., and Sachs, J. (2015). Robots Are Us: Some Economics of Human Replacement. NBER Working Paper no. 20941.

Benzell, S., Kotlikoff, L., LaGardia, G., and Sachs, J. (2018). Robots are Us: Some Economics of Human Replacement. Working Paper 20941. National Bureau of Economic Research.

Beraja, M., Yang, D., and Yuchtman, N. (2020). Data-intensive Innovation and the State: Evidence from AI Firms in China. NBER Working Paper No. 27723, National Bureau of Economic Research.

Berg, A., Buffie, E., and Zanna, L. (2018). Robots, Growth, and Inequality: Should We Fear the Robot Revolution? (The Correct Answer is Yes). IMF Working Paper no. 18/116.

Bernheim, B. and Whinston, M. (1986). Common Agency. *Econometrica*, 54(4):923–942.

Bernoulli, D. (1738). Commentarii. *Academiae Scientiarum Imperialis Petropolitanae 5 175-192; English translation (1954). Econometrica*, 22:23–36.

Bessen, J. (2018). AI and Jobs: The Role of Demand. NBER Working Paper no. 24235. National Bureau for Economic Research.

Bessen, J., Goos, M., Salomons, A., and van den Berge, W. (2019). Automatic Reaction – What Happens to Workers at Firms that Automate? Law and Economics Series Paper no. 19-2, Boston University School of Law.

Biever, C. (2023). The Easy Intelligence Tests that AI Chatbots Fail. *Nature*, 619:686–689.

Bilkic, N., Gries, T., and Naudé, W. (2013). The Radical Innovation Investment Decision Refined. IZA DP No. 7338, Bonn: IZA Institute of Labor Economics.

Bilkic, N., Gries, T., and Pilichowski, M. (2009). Stay in School or Start Working? The Human Capital Investment Decision Under Uncertainty and Irreversibility. CESifo Working Paper, No. 2825. Center for Economic Studies and ifo Institute (CESifo), Munich.

Binmore, K. (2007). Rational Decisions in Large Worlds. *Annales d'Économie et de Statistique*, 86:25–41.

Binmore, K. (2008). *Rational Decisions*. Princeton: Princeton University Press.

Binmore, K. (2017). On the Foundations of Decision Theory. *Homo Oeconomicus*, 34:259–273.

Bishop, J. (2021). Artificial Intelligence Is Stupid and Causal Reasoning Will Not Fix It. *Frontiers of Psychology*, 11:513474.

Bloom, D., McKenna, M., and K.Prettner (2018). Demography, Unemployment, Automation, and Digitalization: Implications for the Creation of (Decent) Jobs, 2010-2030. IZA Discussion Paper no. 11739. IZA Institute of Labor Economics, Bonn.

Bloom, N., Bunn, P., Chen, S., Mizen, P., and Smietanka, P. (2020). The Economic Impact of Coronavirus on UK Businesses: Early Evidence from the Decision Maker Panel. VOX CEPR Policy Portal, 27th March.

Bloom, N., van Reenen, J., and Williams, H. (2019). A Toolkit of Policies to Promote Innovation. *Journal of Economic Perspectives*, 33(3):163–184.

Bloomberg (2018). The World's Biggest AI Start-up Raises USD 1.2 Billion in Mere Months. Fortune Magazine, 31 May 2018.

Boddington, P. (2017). *Towards A Code of Ethics for Artificial Intelligence*. Heidelberg: Springer.

Boden, M. (2014). GOFAI. In: Frankish, K. and Ramsey, W. (eds.), *The Cambridge Handbook of Artificial Intelligence*. Cambridge: Cambridge University Press, pp. 89–107.

Bommasani, R., Hudson, D. A., and et al. (2022). On the Opportunities and Risks of Foundation Models. arXiv preprint arXiv:2108.07258.

Bostrom, N. (2002). Existential Risks: Analyzing Human Extinction Scenarios and Related Hazards. *Journal of Evolution and Technology*, 9(1).

Bostrom, N. (2003a). Astronomical Waste: The Opportunity Cost of Delayed Technological Development. *Utilitas*, 15(3):308–314.

Bostrom, N. (2003b). Ethical Issues in Advanced Artificial Intelligence. In: Smit, I. et al. (eds.) *Cognitive, Emotive and Ethical Aspects of Decision Making in Humans and in Artificial Intelligence*, 2nd ed. International Institute of Advanced Studies in Systems Research and Cybernetics, pp. 12–17. Available at https://nickbostrom.com/ethics/ai.

Bostrom, N. (2006). What Is A Singleton? *Linguistic and Philosophical Investigations*, 5(2):48–54.

Bostrom, N. (2008). Where Are They? Why I Hope the Search for Extraterrestrial Life Finds Nothing. *MIT Technology Review*, May/June:72–77.

Bostrom, N. (2012). The Superintelligent Will: Motivation and Instrumental Rationality in Advanced Artificial Agents. *Minds and Machines*, 22(2):71–85.

Bostrom, N. (2013). Existential Risk Prevention as Global Priority. *Global Policy*, 4:15–31.

Bostrom, N. (2014). *Superintelligence: Paths, Dangers, Strategies*. Oxford: Oxford University Press.

Bostrom, N. (2017). Strategic Implications of Openness in AI Development. *Global Policy*, 8(2):135–148.

Bowles, J. (2017). The Computerization of European Jobs. Bruegel.org, 24th July.

Bowles, S. and Choi, J.-K. (2019). The Neolithic Agricultural Revolution and the Origins of Private Property. *Journal of Political Economy*, 127(5):2186–2228.

Bricker, D. and Ibbitson, J. (2020). *Empty Planet: The Shock of Global Population Decline*. New York: Crown Publishers. Little, Brown Book Group.

Brin, D. (2008). Shouting at the Cosmos: ... or How SETI has Taken a Worrisome Turn Into Dangerous Territory. Lifeboat Foundation, July.

Brooks, R. (2017). The Seven Deadly Sins of AI Predictions. *MIT Technology Review*, 6 October.

Brundage, M., Avin, S., Wang, J., Belfield, H., Krueger, G., Hadfield, G., and et al. (2020). Toward Trustworthy AI Development: Mechanisms for Supporting Verifiable Claims. ArXiv [cs.CY], April: https://arxiv.org/abs/2004.07213.

Brynjolfsson, E. and McAfee, A. (2012). Thriving in the Automated Economy. *The Futurist*, 46(2):27–31.

Brynjolfsson, E. and McAfee, A. (2015). Will Humans Go the Way of Horses? *Foreign Affairs*, 94:8–14.

Brynjolfsson, E., Rock, D., and Syverson, C. (2017). Artificial Intelligence and the Modern Productivity Paradox: A Clash of Expectations and Statistics. NBER Working Paper no. 24001. National Bureau for Economic Research.

Bubeck, S., Chandrasekaran, V., Eldan, R., Gehrke, J., and et al. (2023). Sparks of Artificial General Intelligence: Early Experiments with GPT-4. arXiv:2303.12712 [cs.CL].

Buchholz, W. and Schymura, M. (2012). Expected Utility Theory and the Tyranny of Catastrophic Risks. *Ecological Economics*, 77:234–239.

Bushwick, S. and Leffer, L. (2023). The State of Large Language Models. *Scientific American*, 2 October.

Butlin, P., Long, R., Elmoznino, E., Bengio, Y., Birch, J., Constant, A., Deane, G., Fleming, S., C.Frith, Ji, X., and et al. (2023). Consciousness in Artificial Intelligence: Insights from the Science of Consciousness. arXiv:2308.08708 [cs.AI], 17 August.

Cai, N. and Kou, S. (2011). Option Pricing Under a Mixed-exponential Jump Diffusion Model. *Management Science*, 57(11):2067–2081.

Calo, R. (2017). Artificial Intelligence Policy: A Primer and Roadmap. SSRN, At https://ssrn.com/abstract=3015350.

Camerer, C. (2019). Artificial Intelligence and Behavioral Economics. In: Agrawal, A., Gans, J., and Goldfarb, A. (eds.) *The Economics of Artificial Intelligence: An Agenda*. Chicago: University of Chicago Press, pp. 587–610.

Caplin, A., Martin, D., and Marx, P. (2022). Modeling Machine Learning. NBER Working Paper No. 30600.

Carbonero, F., Ernst, E., and Weber, E. (2018). Robots Worldwide: The Impact of Automation on Employment and Trade. Working Paper no. 36, ILO Research Department.

Card, D. and DiNardo, J. (2002). Skill-biased Technological Change and Rising Wage Inequality: Some Problems and Puzzles. *Journal of Labor Economics*, 20(4):733–783.

Carrigan Jr, R. (2006). Do Potential SETI Signals Need to be Decontaminated? *Acta Astronaut*, 58(2):112–117.

Cassan, A., Kubas, D., Beaulieu, J., Dominik, M., Horne, K., Greenhill, J., and et al. (2012). One or More Bound Planets per Milky Way Star from Microlensing Observations. *Nature*, 481:167–169.

Castelvecchi, D. (2016). The Black Box of AI. *Nature*, 538:21–23.

Cerulli, G. (2021). Improving Econometric Prediction by Machine Learning. *Applied Economics Letters*, 28(16):1419–1425.

Cerulli, G. (2022). Machine Learning using Stata/Python. *The Stata Journal*, 22(4):772–810.

Cervantes, J., Lopez, L., Rodriguez, L., Cervantes, S., Cervantes, F., and Ramos, F. (2020). Artificial Moral Agents: A Survey of the Current Status. *Science and Engineering Ethics*, 26:501–532.

Chace, C. (2020a). Artificial Intelligence and Fully Automated Luxury Capitalism. Forbes, 15 July.

Chace, C. (2020b). *The Economic Singularity*, 3rd ed. Three C's.

Chalmers, D. (1995). Facing Up to the Problem of Consciousness. *Journal of Consciousness Studies*, 2(3):200–219.

Chalmers, D. (2010). The Singularity: A Philosophical Analysis. *Journal of Consciousness Studies*, 17(9):7–65.

Chan, F. and Mátyás, L. (2022). *Econometrics with Machine Learning*. Cham: Springer.

Chandy, R. and Tellis, G. (1998). Organizing for Radical Product Innovation: The Overlooked Role of Willingness to Cannibalize. *Journal of Marketing Research*, 35(4):474–487.

Charlesworth, A. (2014). The Comprehensibility Theorem and the Foundations of Artificial Intelligence. *Minds and Machines*, 24:439–476.

Charpentier, A., Élie, E., and Remlinger, C. (2021). Reinforcement Learning in Economics and Finance. *Computational Economics*, 62:425–462.

Chen, K., Raghupathi, S., Chandratreya, I., Du, Q., and Lipson, H. (2022). Automated Discovery of Fundamental Variables Hidden in Experimental Data. *Nature Computational Science*, 2:433–442.

Chen, P. and Zhang, C. (2014). Data Intensive Applications, Challenges, Techniques and Technologies: A Survey on Big Data. *Information Sciences*, 275:314–347.

Chiacchio, F., Petropoulos, G., and Pichler, D. (2018). The Impact of Industrial Robots on EU Employment and Wages: A Local Labor Market Approach. Working Paper no. 02, Bruegel, Brussels.

Christian, B. (2020). *The Alignment Problem: Machine Learning and Human Values*. New York: W.W. Norton.

Cirkovic, M. (2002). Cosmological Forecast and its Practical Significance. *Journal of Evolution and Technology*, 12(2).

Cirković, M. and Vukotić, B. (2008). Astrobiological Phase Transition: Towards Resolution of Fermi's Paradox. *Origins of Life and Evolution of Biospheres*, 38(6):535–547.

Clancy, M. (2021). Combinatorial Innovation and Technological Progress in the Very Long Run. New Things Under the Sun, June 18.

Clarke, R. (2015). Big Data Big Risks. *Information Systems Journal*, 26(1): 77–90.

Clemens, J. and Rogers, P. (2020). Demand Shocks, Procurement Policies, and the Nature of Medical Innovation: Evidence from Wartime Prosthetic Device Patents. NBER Working Paper No. 2667, National Burea of Economic Research.

Cockburn, I., Henderson, R., and Stern, S. (2017). The Impact of Artificial Intelligence on Innovation. Paper presented at the NBER Conference on Research Issues in Artificial Intelligence, Toronto, September.

Cockburn, I. M., Henderson, R., and Stern, S. (2019). The Impact of Artificial Intelligence on Innovation: An Exploratory Analysis. In: Agrawal, A., Gans, J., and Goldfarb, A. (eds.) *The Economics of Artificial Intelligence: An Agenda*. Chicago: University of Chicago Press, pp. 115–148.

Cohen, M., Hutter, M., and Osborne, M. (2022). Advanced Artificial Agents Intervene in the Provision of Reward. *AI Magazine*, 43(3):282–293.

Colbrook, M., Antun, V., and Hansen, A. (2022). The Difficulty of Computing Stable and Accurate Neural Networks: On the Barriers of Deep Learning and Smales 18th Problem. *PNAS*, 119(12):e2107151119.

Comin, D. and Mestieri, M. (2013). If Technology has Arrived Everywhere, Why has Income Diverged? NBER Working Paper No. 19010. National Bureau for Economic Research.

Conselice, C., Wilkinson, A., Duncan, K., and Mortlock, A. (2016). The Evolution of Galaxy Number Density at z < 8 and its Implications. *Astrophysical Journal*, 830(2):1–17.

Cook, T. (2014). Big Data in Research on Social Policy. *Journal of Policy Analysis and Management*, 33(2):544–547.

Cords, D. and Prettner, K. (2019). Technological Unemployment Revisited: Automation in a Search and Matching Framework. GLO Discussion Paper no. 308, Global Labor Organization.

Cotra, A. (2020). Draft Report on AI Timelines. AI Alignment Forum, 19 September.

Cowen, T. (2010). *The Great Stagnation*. New York: Penguin (Dutton).

Cox, H., Fairchild, J., and Pedersen, H. (2004). Valuation of Structured Risk Management Products. *Insurance, Mathematics and Economics*, 34(2): 259–272.

Cox, S. and Pedersen, H. (2000). Catastrophe Risk Bonds. *North American Actuarial Journal*, 4(4):56–82.

Crawford, J. (2022). Can Economic Growth Continue Over the Long-term? Longnow, 7 October.

Crawford, K. and Calo, R. (2016). There Is a Blind Spot in AI Research. *Nature*, 538:311–313.

Crespi, F. and Guarascio, D. (2019). The Demand-Pull Effect of Public Procurement on Innovation and Industrial Renewal. *Industrial and Corporate Change*, 28(4):793–815.

Czarnitzki, D., Hünermund, P., and Moshgbar, N. (2020). Public Procurement of Innovation: Evidence from a German Legislative Reform. *International Journal of Industrial Organization*, 71:1–16.

Dafoe, A. (2018). AI Governance: A Research Agenda. Centre for the Governance of AI, University of Oxford.

Dafoe, A. (2020). AI Governance: Opportunity and Theory of Impact. Effective Altruism Forum, 17th September.

Dai, J. (2023). The Artificiality of Alignment. The Gradient, 7 October.

Dai, W. (2019). AGI will Drastically Increase Economies of Scale. AI Alignment Forum, 8 June.

Daneke, G. A. (2020). Machina-Economicus or Homo-Complexicus: Artificial Intelligence and the Future of Economics? *Real-World Economics Review*, 93:18–39.

Dasgupta, P. (1986). The Theory of Technological Competition. In: Stiglitz, J. and Mathewson, G. F. (eds.) *New Developments in the Analysis of Market Structure*. Cambridge: MIT Press. pp. 519–547.

Dastani, M., Hulstijn, J., and van der Torre, L. (2005). How to Decide What to Do? *European Journal of Operational Research*, 160:762–784.

Davidson, T. (2021). Report on Whether AI Could Drive Explosive Economic Growth. Open Philantrophy, 17 June.

Davies, D. (1999). The Bombe: A Remarkable Logic Machine. *Cryptologia*, 23(2):108–138.

Davies, J. (2017). Hidden AI – Ghosts In The Machine. Becoming Human: Artificial Intelligence Magazine, Sept 6.

Dawkins, R. (1976). *The Selfish Gene*. Oxford: Oxford University Press.

De Luna, P., Wei, J., Bengio, Y., Aspuru-Guzik, A., and Sargent, E. (2017). Use Machine Learning to Find Energy Materials. *Nature*, 552(7683):23–25.

De Visscher, A. (2020). Artificial versus Biological Intelligence in the Cosmos: Clues from a Stochastic Analysis of the Drake Equation. *International Journal of Astrobiology*, 19:353–359.

de Vries, A. (2023). The Growing Energy Footprint of Artificial Intelligence. *Joule*. https://doi.org/10.1016/j.joule.2023.09.004.

Deisenroth, M., Faisal, A., and Ong, C. (2020). *Mathematics for Machine Learning*. Cambridge: Cambridge University Press.

DeLong, J. B. (1998). Estimates of World GDP, One Million B.C. – Present. Department of Economics, U.C. Berkeley at http://econ161.berkeley.edu/.

Deming, D. (2015). The Growing Importance of Social Skills in the Labor Market. Working Paper no. 21473. National Bureau of Economic Research.

Dencik, L., Hintz, A., Redden, J., and Treré, E. (2019). Exploring Data Justice: Conceptions, Applications and Directions. *Information, Communication and Society*, 22(7):873–881.

Dennis, L. (2020). Computational Goals, Values and Decision-making. *Science and Engineering Ethics*, 26(5):2487–2495.

Deutsch, D. (2011). *The Beginning of Infinity: Explanations that Transforms the World*. London: Penguin Books.

Diamond, J. (1999). To Whom it May Concern. New York Times Magazine, 5 December:68–71.

Diebold, F. (2012). *A Personal Perspective on the Origin(s) and Development of Big Data: The phenomenon, the Term, and the Discipline*. Mimeo: University of Pennsylvania.

Ding, Y., Florensa, C., Phielipp, M., and Abbeel, P. (2019). Goal-conditioned Imitation Learning. 33rd Conference on Neural Information Processing Systems (NeurIPS 2019), Vancouver, Canada.

Dixit, A. (1989). Entry and Exit Decisions under Uncertainty. *Journal of Political Economy*, 97(3):620–638.

Dixit, A. (1993). *The Art of Smooth Pasting*. Chur, Switzerland: Harwood Academic Publishers.

Dixon, H. (2001). *Surfing Economics*. London: Red Globe Press.

Domingos, P. (2015). *The Master Algorithm: How the Quest for the Ultimate Learning Machine will Remake our World*. London: Penguin Books.

Doraszelski, U. (2001). The Net Present Value Method versus the Option Value of Waiting: A Note on Farzin, Huisman and Kort (1998). *Journal of Economic Dynamics and Control*, 25(8):1109–1115.

Drake, F. (1965). The Radio Search for Intelligent Extraterrestrial Life. In: Mamikunian, G. and Briggs, M. H. (eds.) *Current Aspects of Exobiology*. New York: Pergamon, pp. 323–345.

Dubey, R., Agrawal, P., Pathak, D., Griffiths, T., and Efros, A. (2018). Investigating Human Priors for Playing Video Games. Proceedings of the 35th International Conference on Machine Learning, Stockholm, Sweden.

Durkin, J. (1996). Expert Systems: A View of the Field. *IEEE Intelligent Systems*, 11(2):56–63.

Dutil, Y. and Dumas, S. (2007). Sustainability: A Tedious Path to Galactic Colonization. ArXiv:0711.1777 [physics.pop-ph].

Dutt, A. (2006). Aggregate Demand, Aggregate Supply and Economic growth. *International Review of Applied Economics*, 20(3):319–336.

EC (2014). On the Coordination of Procedures for the Award of Public Works Contracts, Public Supply Contracts and Public Service Contracts. European Commission Directive 24. Brussels.

EC (2019). Ethics Guidelines for Trustworthy AI: High-level Expert Group on Artificial Intelligence. Brussels: European Commission.

Eckersley, P. (2019). Impossibility and Uncertainty Theorems in AI Value Alignment (or Why Your AGI Should Not Have a Utility Function). SafeAI 2019: Proceedings of the AAAI Workshop on Artificial Intelligence Safety 2019.

Edler, J. and Fagerberg, J. (2017). Innovation Policy: What, Why, and How. *Oxford Review of Economic Policy*, 33(1):2–23.

Edler, J. and Georghiou, L. (2007). Public Procurement and Innovation – Resurrecting the Demand Side. *Research Policy*, 36(7):949–963.

Ehrlich, P. (1968). *The Population Bomb*. New York: Ballantine Books.

Eisenstein, M. (2023). A Test of Artificial Intelligence. *Nature*, 14 September.

Eitel-Porter, R. (2020). Beyond the Promise: Implementing Ethical AI. *AI and Ethics*, 6 October. https://doi.org/10.1007/s43681-020-00011-6.

Ellsberg, D. (1961). Risk, Ambiguity and the Savage Axioms. *Quarterly Journal of Economics*, 75(4):643–699.

Eloundou, T., Manning, S., Mishkin, P., and Rock, D. (2023). Gpts are GPTs: An Early Look at the Labor Market Impact Potential of Large Language Models. arXiv preprint arXiv:2303.10130.

Emani, C., Cullot, N., and Nicolle, C. (2015). Understandable Big Data: A Survey. *Computer Science Review*, 17:70–81.

Emba, C. (2022). Why Llongtermism Isn't Ethically Sound. Washington Post, 5 September.

Englander, A. (2021). How Would the Scaling Hypothesis Change Things? Less Wrong Blog, 13 August.

Erdil, E. and Besiroglu, T. (2023). Explosive Growth from AI Automation: A Review of the Arguments. arXiv:2309.11690.

Espinilla, M., Villarreal, V., and McChesney, I. (2019). Ubiquitous Computing and Ambient Intelligence – UCAmi. Sensors (Basel), 19(18):4034.

Etzioni, A. and Etzioni, O. (2017). Incorporating Ethics into Artificial Intelligence. *Journal of Ethics*, 21(4):403–418.

European Commission (2007). Pre-commercial Procurement: Driving Innovation to Ensure Sustainable High Quality Public Services in Europe. Brussels: EC Communication 799.

European Commission (2014). European Directive on Public Procurement and Repealing Directive 2004/18/ec. Brussels: EC.

European Commission (2020). European Enterprise Survey on the Use of Technologies based on Artificial Intelligence: Final Report. Publications Office, Directorate-General for Communications Networks, Content and Technology.

Everitt, T. and Hutter, M. (2016). Avoiding Wireheading with Value Reinforcement Learning. arXiv:1605.03143v1 [cs.AI].

Everitt, T., Lea, G., and Hutter, M. (2018). AGI Safety Literature Review. Proceedings of the Twenty-Seventh International Joint Conference on Artificial Intelligence (IJCAI-18), pp. 5441–5449.

Farboodi, M., Mihet, R., Philippon, T., and Veldkamp, L. (2019). Big Data and Firm Dynamics. Working Paper no. 25515, National Bureau of Economic Research.

Farzin, Y., Huismann, K., and Kort, P. (1998). Optimal Timing of Technology Adaption. *Journal of Dynamics and Control*, 22(5):779–799.

Favaretto, M., De Clercq, E., Schneble, C.O, and Elger, B. S. (2020). What Is Your Definition of Big Data? Researchers' Understanding of the Phenomenon of the Decade. *PLoS One*, 15(2):e0228987.

Fazekas, M., Toth, I., and King, L. (2016). An Objective Corruption Risk Index Using Public Procurement Data. *European Journal of Criminal Policy and Research*, 22(3):369–397.

Fernandez-Villaverde, J. (2020). Simple Rules for a Complex World with Artificial Intelligence. PIER Working Paper No. 20-010.

Ferrari, F., van Dijck, J., and van den Bosch, A. (2023). Foundation Models and the Privatization of Public Knowledge. *Nature Machine Intelligence*, 5(8):818–820.

Feuerriegel, S., Dolata, M., and Schwabe, G. (2020). Fair AI: Challenges and Opportunities. *Business and Information Systems Engineering*, 62(4):379–384.

Feuerriegel, S., Hartmann, J., Janiesch, C., Zschech, P., and et al. (2023). Generative AI. *Business and Information Systems Engineering*, 12 September [Early Online].

Finley, K. (2015). Tech Time Warp of the Week: Return to 1974, When a Computer Ordered a Pizza for the First Time. Wired, 30 January.

Floridi, L. (2018). The Ethics of Artificial Intelligence. In Franklin, D. (ed.) Megatech: *Technology in 2050*. London: Profile Books. pp. 155–163.

Floridi, L. (2020). AI and Its New Winter: From Myths to Realities. *Philosophy and Technology*, 33(1):1–3.

Floridi, L. (2022). *Ultraintelligent Machines, Singularity, and Other Sci-fi Distractions about AI*. Mimeo: SSRN.

Floridi, L., Cowls, J., Beltrametti, M., Chatila, R., Chazerand, P., Dignum, V., Luetge, C., Madelin, R., Pagallo, U., Rossi, F., Schafer, B., Valcke, P., and Vayena, E. (2018). AI4People – An Ethical Framework for a Good AI

Society: Opportunities, Risks, Principles, and Recommendations. *Minds and Machines*, 28(4):689–707.

Ford, M. (2016). *The Rise of the Robots: Technology and the Threat of Mass Unemployment*. London: Oneworld Publications.

Fornaro, P. and Luomaranta, H. (2020). Nowcasting Finnish Real Economic Activity: A Machine Learning Approach. *Empirical Econonomics*, 58(1):55–71.

Fouse, S., Cross, S., and Lapin, Z. (2020). DARPA's Impact on Artificial Intelligence. AI Magazine, Summer:3–9.

Freeman, C. (1994). The Economics of Technical Change. *Cambridge Journal of Economics*, 18(5):463–514.

Frey, C. and Osborne, M. (2013). The Future of Employment: How Susceptible are Jobs to Computerization? Oxford Martin Programme on the Impacts of Future Technology, University of Oxford.

Frey, C. and Osborne, M. (2017). The Future of Employment: How Susceptible Are Jobs to Computerization? *Technological Forecasting and Social Change*, 114:254–280.

Friedman, T. (2016). *Thank You for Being Late: An Optimist's Guide to Thriving in the Age of Accelerations*. New York: Picador.

Fullarton, C. (2016). Life-Altered Cosmologies. CQG+, 27 January.

Furman, J. and Seamans, R. (2019). AI and the Economy. In: Lerner, J. and Stern, S. (eds.) *Innovation Policy and the Economy*, Vol. 19. NBER. pp. 161–191.

G-20 (2019). G20 Ministerial Statement on Trade and Digital Economy. 9 May.

Gabriel, I. and Ghazavi, V. (2021). The Challenge of Value Alignment: From Fairer Algorithms to AI Safety. arXiv:2101.06060 [cs.CY].

Gale, J., Wandel, A., and Hill, H. (2020). Will Recent Advances in AI Result in a Paradigm Shift in Astrobiology and SETI? *International Journal of Astrobiology*, 19(3):295–298.

Galera, E., GR, G. G., and Kinouchi, O. (2019). Invasion Percolation Solves Fermi Paradox but Challenges SETI Projects. *International Journal of Astrobiology*, 18(4):316–322.

Gallagher, B. (2018). Scary AI Is More Fantasia than Terminator. *Nautilus*, 15 March. Available at http://nautil.us/issue/58/self/scary-ai-is-more-fantasia-than-terminator (Accessed 1 August 2018)

Gallier, J. and Quaintance, J. (2022). *Algebra, Topology, Differential Calculus, and Optimization Theory for Computer Science and Machine Learning*. Mimeo: University of Pennsylvania.

Galor, O. and Weil, D. N. (2000). Population, Technology, and Growth: From Malthusian Stagnation to the Demographic Transition and Beyond. *American Economic Review*, 90(4):806–828.

Gandomi, A. and Haider, M. (2015). Beyond the Hype: Big Data Concepts, Methods, and Analytics. *International Journal of Information Management*, 35(2):137–144.

Gans, J. (2018). AI and the Paperclip Problem. VoxEU Column, 10 June.

García-García, J., García-Ródenas, R., López-Gómez, J., and Martín-Baos, J. (2022). A Comparative Study of Machine Learning, Deep Neural Networks and Random Utility Maximization Models for Travel Mode Choice Modelling. *Transportation Research Procedia*, 62:374–382.

Gauchon, R. and Barigou, K. (2021). *Expected Utility Maximization with Stochastically Ordered Returns*. Mimeo: University of Lyon.

Gentzkow, M., Kelly, B., and Taddy, M. (2019). Text as Data. *Journal of Economic Literature*, 57(3):535–574.

Gerdon, S. and Molinari, V. (2020). How Governments Can Use Public Procurement to Shape the Future of AI Regulation – and Boost Innovation and Growth. World Economic Forum Blog, 8 June.

Geroski, P. (1990). Innovation, Technological Opportunity, and Market Structure. *Oxford Economic Papers*, 42(3):586–602.

Gilboa, I. (2013). *Theory of Decision under Uncertainty*. Cambridge: Cambridge University Press.

Goertzel, B. (2012). Should Humanity Build a Global AI Nanny to Delay the Singularity Until It's Better Understood? *Journal of Consciousness Studies*, 19(1):96–111.

Gogas, P. and Papadimitriou, T. (2021). Machine Learning in Economics and Finance. *Computational Economics*, 57(1):1–4.

Golder, P., Shacham, R., and Mitra, D. (2009). When, By Whom, and How Are Radical Innovations Developed? *Marketing Science*, 28(1):166–179.

Goldfarb, A. and Lindsay, J. (2022). Prediction and Judgment: Why Artificial Intelligence Increases the Importance of Humans in War. *International Security*, 46(3):7–50.

Goldin, C. and Katz, L. (2010). *The Race between Education and Technology*. Cambridge: Harvard University Press.

Gonzales, C. and Perny, P. (2020). Decision under Uncertainty. In: Marquis, P., Papini, O., and Prade, H. (eds.). *A Guided Tour of Artificial Intelligence Research*, Vol. I, Cham: Springer, pp. 549–586.

Good, I. J. (1965). Speculations Concerning the First Ultraintelligent Machine. *Advances in Computers*, 6:31–88.

Goodfellow, I., Pouget-Abadie, J., Mirza, M., Xu, B., Warde-Farley, D., Ozair, S., Courville, A., and Bengio, Y. (2014). Generative Adversarial Nets. *Advances in Neural Information Processing Systems*, 2:2672–2680.

Goos, M. and Manning, A. (2007). Lousy and Lovely Jobs: The Rising Polarization of Work in Britain. *Review of Economics and Statistics*, 89(1):118–133.

Government of Ireland. (2021). AI – Here for Good. A National Artificial Intelligence Strategy for Ireland. Available at https://enterprise.gov.ie/en/publications/publication-files/national-ai-strategy-executive-summary.pdf (Accessed 12 January 2024).

Gray, R. (2015). The Fermi Paradox is Neither Fermi's nor a Paradox. *Astrobiology*, 15(3):195–199.

Gregory, T., Salomons, A., and Zierahn, U. (2019). Racing with or Against the Machine? Evidence from Europe. IZA Discussion Paper no. 12063. IZA Institute of Labor Economics, Bonn.

Gries, T. (2020a). Income Polarization and Stagnation in a Stochastic Model of Growth: When the Demand Side Matters. CIE Working Papers No. 132, Paderborn University.

Gries, T. (2020b). A New Theory of Demand-restricted Growth: The Basic Idea. *The American Economist*, 65(1):11–27.

Gries, T. and Naudé, W. (2011). Entrepreneurship and Human Development: A Capability Approach. *Journal of Public Economics*, 95(3–4):216–224.

Gries, T. and Naudé, W. (2018). Artificial Intelligence, Jobs, Inequality and Productivity: Does Aggregate Demand Matter? IZA Discussion Paper no. 12005.

Gries, T. and Naudé, W. (2020). Artificial Intelligence, Income Distribution and Economic Growth. IZA Discussion Paper no. 13606.

Gries, T. and Naudé, W. (2021). Modelling Artificial Intelligence in Economics. IZA Discussion Paper no. 14171, IZA Institute of Labor Economics.

Gries, T. and Naudé, W. (2022). Artificial Intelligence in Economics. *Journal for Labour Market Research*, 56(12):1–13.

Gross, D. and Sampat, B. (2020). Organizing Crisis Innovation: Lessons from World War II. NBER Working Paper No. 27909. National Bureau for Economic Research.

Grossman, S. and Hart, O. (1983). An Analysis of the Principal-Agent Problem. *Econometrica*, 51(1):7–45.

Guo, I., Langrené, N., Loeper, G., and Ning, W. (2020). Robust Utility Maximization Under Model Uncertainty via a Penalization Approach. arXiv:1907.13345v5 [math.OC].

Gurnee, W. and Tegmark, M. (2023). Language Models Represent Space and Time. arXiv:2310.02207 [cs.LG].

Gurzadyan, V. and Penrose, R. (2016). CCC and the Fermi Paradox. *The European Physics Journal Plus*, 131:11.

Hadfield-Menell, D., Dragan, A., Abbeel, P., and Russell, S. (2016). Cooperative Inverse Reinforcement Learning. arXiv:1606.03137 [cs.AI].

Hagendorff (2020). The Ethics of AI Ethics: An Evaluation of Guidelines. *Minds & Machines*, 30(1):99–120.

Hammerman, R. and Russell, A. (2015). *Ada's Legacy: Cultures of Computing from the Victorian to the Digital Age*. New York: Association for Computing Machinery and Morgan & Claypool.

Hanson, R. (1998). *The Great Filter – Are We Almost Past It?* Mimeo, September 15.

Hanson, R. (2000). *Long-term Growth as a Sequence of Exponential Modes*. Mimeo: George Mason University.

Hanson, R. (2009). Limits to Growth. Overcoming Bias Blog.

Hanson, R. (2014). I Still Don't Get Foom. Overcoming Bias Blog, 24 July.

Hanson, R. (2018). *The Age of Em: Work, Love, and Life When Robots Rule the Earth*. Oxford: Oxford University Press.

Hanson, R. (2020). How Far To Grabby Aliens? Part 1. Overcoming Bias Blog, 21 December.

Hanson, R. (2022). Macaskill on Value Lock-In. Overcoming Bias Blog, 16 August.

Hanson, R., Martin, D., McCarter, C., and Paulson, J. (2021). If Loud Aliens Explain Human Earliness, Quiet Aliens Are Also Rare. arXiv:2102.01522v3 [q-bio.OT].

Hanson, R. and Yudkowsky, E. (2013). The Hanson-Yudkowsky AI-Foom Debate. Machine Intelligence Research Institute, Berkeley 94704.

Hao, K. (2019). We Analyzed 16,625 Papers to Figure Out Where AI Is Headed Next. MIT Technology Review, 25 January.

Harré, M. (2021). Information Theory for Agents in Artificial Intelligence, Psychology, and Economics. *Entropy*, 23(3):310.

Harris, S. (2015). Can We Avoid a Digital Apocalypse? SAM Harris Blog, 16 January. https://samharris.org/can-we-avoid-a-digital-apocalypse/.

Harris, S. (2020). *Making Sense: Conversations on Consciousness, Morality and the Future of Humanity*. London: Penguin.

Harsanyi, J. (1978). Bayesian Decision Theory and Utilitarian Ethics. *American Economic Review*, 68(2):223–228.

Hart, M. (1975). An Explanation for the Absence of Extraterrestrials on Earth. *Quarterly Journal of The Royal Astronomical Society*, 16:128–135.

Hauer, T. (2022). Importance and Limitations of AI Ethics in Contemporary Society. *Humanities and Social Sciences Communications*, 9(272):1–8.

Hayter, C. S., Link, A., and Scott, J. (2018). Public-Sector Entrepreneurship. *Oxford Review of Economic Policy*, 34(4):676–694.

Heaven, D. (2019). Deep Trouble for Deep Learning. *Nature*, 574(7777):163–166.

Hémous, D. and Olsen, M. (2018). *The Rise of the Machines: Automation, Horizontal Innovation and Income Inequality*. Mimeo: University of Zurich.

Hendler, J. (2008). Avoiding Another AI Winter. *IEEE Intelligent Systems*, 23(2):2–4.

Herfeld, C. (2020). The Diversity of Rational Choice Theory: A Review Note. *Topoi*, 39(4):329–347.

Hernández-Orallo, J. (2017). Evaluation in Artificial Intelligence: From Task-oriented to Ability-oriented Measurement. *Artificial Intelligence Review*, 48(3):397–447.

Hess, A. (2022). Apocalypse Nowadays: The New Wave of Films About the End of the World. *The Guardian*, 3 January.

Hibbard, B. (2012). Model-based Utility Functions. *Journal of Artificial General Intelligence*, 3(1):1–24.

Hickman, J. (1999). The Political Economy of Very Large Space Projects. *Journal of Evolution and Technology*, 4(1):1–14.

Hidalgo, C. (2015). *Why Information Grows*. London: Penguin.

Hilbert, M. (2016). Big Data for Development: A Review of Promises and Challenges. *Development Policy Review*, 34(1):135–174.

Hill, C. and Rothaermel, F. (2003). The Performance of Incumbent Firms in the Face of Radical Technological Innovation. *Academy of Management Review*, 28(2):257–274.

Hilton, B. (2022). Preventing an AI-related Catastrophe: AI Might Bring Huge Benefits – If We Avoid the Risks. *8,000 Hours*, 25 August.

Hinton, G. and Salakhutdinov, R. (2006). Reducing the Dimensionality of Data with Neural Networks. *Science*, 313(5786):504–507.

Hinton, G. E., Osindero, S., and Teh, Y.-W. (2006). A Fast Learning Algorithm for Deep Belief Nets. *Neural Computation*, 18(7):1527–1554.

Hollings, C., Martin, U., and Rice, A. (2018). *Ada Lovelace: The Making of a Computer Scientist*. Oxford: Bodleian Leibrary.

Hopenhayn, H., Neira, J., and Singhania, R. (2018). From Population Growth to Firm Demographics: Implications from Concentration, Entrepreneurship and the Labor Share. NBER Working Paper no. 25382.

House of Lords (2018). AI in the UK: Ready, Willing and Able? Select Committee on Artificial Intelligence, HL Paper 100.

Howard, R. (1960). *Dynamic Programming and Markov Processes*. Cambridge: The MIT Press.

Hrala, J. (2016). Stephen Hawking Warns Us to Stop Reaching Out to Aliens Before It's Too Late. *Science Alert*, 4 November.

Hsu, J. (2022). A Third of Scientists Working on AI Say It Could Cause Global Disaster. *New Scientist*, 20 September.

Huang, M.-H. and Rust, R. (2018). Artificial Intelligence in Service. *Journal of Service Research*, 21(2):155–172.

Hubinger, E. (2020). An Overview of 11 Proposals for Building Safe Advanced AI. *arXiv:2012.07532 [cs.LG]*.

Hudson, A., Finn, E., and Wylie, R. (2023). What Can Science Fiction Tell Us about the Future of Artificial Intelligence Policy? *AI and Society*, 38(1):197–211.

Huebner, J. (2005). A Possible Declining Trend for Worldwide Innovation. *Technological Forecasting and Social Change*, 72(8):980–986.

Humphries, E., Wright, C., Hoffman, A., Savonen, C., and Leek, J. (2023). What's the Best Chatbot for Me? Researchers put LLMs Through their Paces. *Nature*, 27 September.

Hutter, M. (2000). A Theory of Universal Artificial Intelligence Based on Algorithmic Complexity. *arXiv:cs/0004001 [cs.AI]*.

Hutter, M. (2007). Universal Algorithmic Intelligence: A Mathematical Top-down Approach. In: Goertzel, B. and Pennachin, C. (eds.) *Artificial General Intelligence. Cognitive Technologies*. Berlin, Heidelberg: Springer, pp. 227–290.

Huxley, A. (1932). *Brave New World*. London: Chatto & Windus.

IEEE. (2019). Ethically Aligned Design. 1st ed. Piscataway: The IEEE Global Initiative. https://ethicsinaction.ieee.org.

Jang, J. (2007). Jump Diffusion Processes and Their Applications in Insurance and Finance. *Insurance, Mathematics and Economics*, 41(1):62–70.

Jankel, N. (2015). AI vs Human Intelligence: Why Computers Will Never Create Disruptive Innovations. Huffington Post, 26 April.

Jarmin, R. and O'Hara, A. (2016). Big Data and the Transformation of Public Policy Analysis. *Journal of Policy Analysis and Management*, 35(3):715–721.

Jenkins, P., Farag, A., Jenkins, J., Yao, H., Wang, S., and Li, Z. (2021). Neural Utility Functions. *The Thirty-Fifth AAAI Conference on Artificial Intelligence (AAAI-21)*, 35(9):7917–7925.

Johansen, A. and Sornette, D. (2001). Finite-time Singularity in the Dynamics of the World Population: Economic and Financial Indices. *Physica A*, 294(3–4):465–502.

Jones, B. (2009). The Burden of Knowledge and the Death of Renaissance Man: Is Innovation Getting Harder? *Review of Economic Studies*, 76(1):283–317.

Jones, C. (1995). R&D-based Models of Economic Growth. *Journal of Political Economy*, 103(4):759–783.

Jones, C. (2001). Was An Industrial Revolution Inevitable? Economic Growth Over the Very Long Run. *Advances in Macroeconomics*, 1(2):article 1.

Jones, C. (2022). The End of Economic Growth? Unintended Consequences of a Declining Population. *American Economic Review*, 112(11):3489–3527.

Jones, N. (2018). How to Stop Data Centres from Gobbling up the Worlds Electricity. *Nature*, 561:163–166.

Jorgensen, S., Kort, P., and Dockner, E. (2006). Venture Capital Financed Investments in Intellectual Capital. *Journal of Dynamics and Control*, 30:2339–2361.

Joshi, N. (2019). How Far Are We From Achieving Artificial General Intelligence? Forbes, 10 June.

Jumper, J., Evans, R., Pritzel, A., and et al. (2021). Highly Accurate Protein Structure Prediction with AlphaFold. *Nature*, 596(7873):583–589.

Kahneman, D., Sibony, O., and Sunstein, C. (2021). *Noise: A Flaw in Human Judgment*. London: HarperCollins.

Kamatani, N. (2021). Genes, the Brain, and Artificial Intelligence in Evolution. *Journal of Human Genetics*, 66(1):103–109.

Kanbach, D., Heiduk, K., Blueher, G., Schreiter, M., and Lahmann, A. (2023). The GenAI Is Out of the Bottle: Generative Artificial Intelligence from a Business Model Innovation Perspective. *Review of Managerial Science*, September.

Karabarbounis, L. and Neiman, B. (2014). The Global Decline of the Labor Share. *Quarterly Journal of Economics*, 129(1):61–103.

Karnofsky, H. (2021a). Digital People Would Be An Even Bigger Deal. Cold Takes Blog, 27 July.

Karnofsky, H. (2021b). Forecasting Transformative AI, Part 1: What Kind of AI? Cold Takes Blog, 10 August.

Karnofsky, H. (2021c). This Can't Go On. Effective Altruism Forum, 3 August.

Karnofsky, H. (2021d). Weak Point in a Most Important Century: Lock-In. Cold Takes Blog.

Kim, G., Trimi, S., and Chung, J. (2014). Big-data Applications in the Government Sector. *Communications of the ACM*, 57(3):78–85.

Kirchner, J., Smith, L., and Thibodeau, J. (2022). Understanding AI Alignment Research: A Systematic Analysis. arXiv:2206.02841v1 [cs.CY].

Kitchin, R. and McArdle, G. (2016). What Makes Big Data, Big Data? Exploring the Ontological Characteristics of 26 Datasets. *Big Data and Society*, 3(1): 1–10.

Knight, F. (1933). *Risk, Uncertainty and Profit*. Boston: Houghton Mifflin Co.

Knox, J. (2022). The Metaverse, or the Serious Business of Tech Frontiers. *Postdigital Science Education*, 4(1):207–215.

Koch, C. (2012). Modular Biological Complexity. *Science*, 337(6094):531–532.

Kogan, S., Levin, D., Routledge, B. R., Sagi, J., and Smith, N. (2009). Predicting Risk from Financial Reports with Regression. In Proceedings of Human Language

Technologies: The 2009 Annual Conference of the North American Chapter of the Association for Computational Linguistics, pp. 272–280.

Kokotajlo, D. and Dai, W. (2019). The Main Sources of AI Risk? AI Alignment Forum, 21 March.

Konrad, K. (2009). *Strategy and Dynamics in Contests*. Oxford: Oxford University Press.

Koppl, R., Deveraux, A., Herriot, J., and Kauffman, S. (2019). *The Industrial Revolution as a Combinatorial Explosion*. Mimeo. Syracuse: Syracuse University.

Korinek, A. (2019). Integrating Ethical Values and Economic Value to Steer Progress in Artificial Intelligence. NBER Working Paper no. 26130, National Bureau of Economic Research.

Korinek, A. (2023). Generative AI for Economic Research: Use Cases and Implications for Economists. Mimeo, Forthcoming in Journal of Economic Literature, 61(4):1281–1317.

Korinek, A. and Stiglitz, J. (2017). Artificial Intelligence and Its Implications for Income Distribution and Unemployment. NBER Working Paper no. 24174. National Bureau for Economic Research.

Korinek, A. and Stiglitz, J. E. (2021). Artificial Intelligence, Globalization, and Strategies for Economic Development. Institute for New Economic Thinking Working Paper Series No. 146.

Kotlikoff, L. (2022). Does Prediction Machines Predict Our AI Future? A Review. *Journal of Economic Literature*, 60(3):1052–1057.

Kou, S. (2002). A Jump-Diffusion Model for Option Pricing. *Management Science*, 48(8):1086–1101.

Kou, S. and Wang, H. (2003). First Passage Time of a Jump Diffusion Process. *Advances in Applied Probability*, 35(2):504–531.

Kremer, M. (1993). The O-Ring Theory of Economic Development. *The Quarterly Journal of Economics*, 108(3):551–575.

Krugman, P. (1978). *The Theory of Interstellar Trade*. Mimeo: Yale University.

Kumar, M., Mani, U., Tripathi, P., Saalim, M., and Roy, S. (2023). Artificial Hallucinations by Google Bard: Think Before You Leap. *Cureus*, 15(8):e43313.

Kuriksha, A. (2021). An Economy of Neural Networks: Learning from Heterogeneous Experiences. PIER Working Paper 21-027, University of Pennsylvania.

Kurzweil, R. (2005). *The Singularity Is Near: When Humans Transcend Biology*. New York: Viking Press.

Kuthunur, S. (2023). New AI Algorithm Can Detect Signs of Life with 90% Accuracy. Scientists Want to Send It to Mars. Space.com., 27 September.

Kutyniok, G. (2022). The Mathematics of Artificial Intelligence. arXiv preprint arXiv:2203.08890.

Kydd, A. (2015). *International Relations Theory: The Game-theoretic Approach.* Cambridge: Cambridge University Press.

Lambert, N., Castricato, L., von Werra, L., and Havrilla, A. (2022). Illustrating Reinforcement Learning from Human Feedback (RLHF). https://huggingface.co/blog/rlhf, 9 December.

Lampton, M. (2013). Information-driven Societies and Fermi's Paradox. *International Journal of Astrobiology*, 12(4):312–313.

Landes, D. (1999). *The Wealth and Poverty of Nations: Why Some Are So Rich and Some So Poor.* New York: Norton & Co.

Lane, J. (2016). Big Data for Public Policy: The Quadruple Helix. *Journal of Policy Analysis and Management*, 35(3):708–715.

Larnier, J. (2023). There Is No A.I. Annals of Artificial Intelligence, The New Yorker, 20 April.

Lavertu, S. (2014). We All Need Help: Big Data and the Mismeasure of Public Administration. *Public Administration Review*, 76(6): 864–872.

Lazer, D., Kennedy, R., King, G., and Vespignani, A. (2014). The Parable of Google Flu: Traps in Big Data Analysis. *Science*, 343(6176):1203–1205.

LeCun, Y. (2022). *A Path Towards Autonomous Machine Intelligence – version 0.9.2, 2022-06-27.* Mimeo: Courant Institute of Mathematical Sciences, New York University.

LeCun, Y., Bengio, Y., and Hinton, G. (2015). Deep Learning. *Nature*, 521(7553):436–444.

Lee, C. (2019). The Game of Go: Bounded Rationality and Artificial Intelligence. Yusof Ishak Institute Working Paper no. 2019-04.

Lee, R. (1988). Induced Population Growth and Induced Technological Progress: Their Interaction in the Accelerating Stage. *Mathematical Population Studies*, 1(3):265–288.

Leibfried, F. and Braun, D. A. (2016). Bounded Rational Decision-making in Feedforward Neural Networks. arXiv:1602.08332v2 [cs.AI].

Leike, J., Martic, M., Krakovna, V., Ortega, P., Everitt, T., Lefrancq, A., Orseau, L., and Legg, S. (2017). AI Safety Gridworlds. ArXiv:1711.09883 [Cs], November 27: http://arxiv.org/abs/1711.09883.

Lenderink, B., Johannes, I., and Voordijk, H. (2019). Innovation and Public Procurement: From Fragmentation to Synthesis on Concepts, Rationales and Approaches. *Innovation: The European Journal of Social Science Research*, 35(4):650–674. https://doi.org/10.1080/13511610.2019.1700101.

Lenharo, M. (2023a). Decades-long Bet on Consciousness Ends – and it's Philosopher 1, Neuroscientist 0. *Nature*, 619(7968):14–15.

Lenharo, M. (2023b). If AI Becomes Conscious: Heres How Researchers Will Know. *Nature*, 24 August.

LeRoy, S. and Singell, L. (1987). Knight on Risk and Uncertainty. *Journal of Political Economy*, 95(2):394–406.

Lichtner-Bajjaoui, A. (2020). A Mathematical Introduction to Neural Networks. Advanced Mathematics Master Thesis, Universitat de Barcelona.

Lin, J. (2020). Industrial Policy Revisited. In: WTO, World Trade Report 2020: Government Policies to Promote Innovation in the Digital Age. Geneva. World Trade Organization, p. 26.

Lipnowski, E. and Doron, R. (2022). Predicting Choice from Information Costs. arXiv:2205.10434.

List, J. and Haigh, M. (2005). A Simple Test of Expected Utility Theory using Professional Traders. *Proceedings of the National Academy of Science USA*, 102(3):945–948.

Liu, C. (2008). *The Dark Forest*. New York: Tom Doherty Associates.

Liu, F., Shi, Y., and Li, P. (2017). Analysis of the Relation Between Articial Intelligence and the Internet from the Perspective of Brain Science. *Procedia Computer Science*, pp. 377–383.

Lomborg, B. (2020). Welfare in the 21st Century: Increasing Development, Reducing Inequality, the Impact of Climate Change, and the Cost of Climate Policies. *Technological Forecasting and Social Change*, 156(3):119981.

Ludvigsen, K. (2023). The Carbon Footprint of GPT-4. Medium: Towards Data Science, 18 July.

Maas, M. (2018). Regulating for Normal AI Accidents: Operational Lessons for the Responsible Governance of Artificial Intelligence Deployment. *Proceedings of the 2018 AAAI/ACM Conference on AI, Ethics, and Society*, pp. 223–228.

MacAskill, W. (2022). *What We Owe The Future*. New York: Basic Books.

Macaulay, T. (2021). Slaughterbots Are a Step Away from Your Neighborhood – And We Need a Ban. Neural, 13 December.

Marcus, G. (2015). Machines Won't Be Thinking Anytime Soon. Edge.

Marcus, G. (2022). Artificial General Intelligence Is Not as Imminent as You Might Think. *Scientific American*, 1 July.

Margetts, H. and Sutcliffe, D. (2013). Addressing the Policy Challenges and Opportunities of Big Data. *Policy and Internet*, 5(2):139–146.

Martin, I. and Pindyck, R. S. (2015). Averting Catastrophes: The Strange Economics of Scylla and Charybdis. *American Economic Review*, 105(10): 2947–2985.

Martins, N., Angelica, A., Chakravarthy, K., Svidinenko, Y., Boehm, F., Opris, I., Lebedev, M., Swan, M., Garan, S., Rosenfeld, J., Hogg, T., and Freitas, R. (2019). Human Brain/Cloud Interface. *Frontiers of Neuroscience*, 13:112.

Marvel, M. and Lumpkin, G. (2007). Technology Entrepreneurs' Human Capital and Its Effects on Innovation Radicalness. *Entrepreneurship Theory and Practice*, 31(6):807–828.

Maschler, M., Solan, E., and Zamir, S. (2013). *Game (t)heory*, 2nd ed. Cambridge: Cambridge University Press.

Matloff, G. (2022). Von Neumann Probes: Rationale, Propulsion, Interstellar Transfer Timing. *International Journal of Astrobiology*, 21(4):205–211.

Matthews, D. (2022). Humanity was Stagnant for Millennia – Then Something Big Changed 150 Years Ago. Vox, September 7.

Mazzucato, M. (2015). *The Entrepreneurial State: Debunking Public vs. Private Sector Myths*. London: Penguin Books.

Mazzucato, M. (2018). Mission-oriented Innovation Policies: Challenges and opportunities. *Industrial and Corporate Change*, 27(5):803–815.

Mazzucato, M. (2020). Mission-oriented Innovation and Industrial Policies. In *WTO, World Trade Report 2020: Government Policies to Promote Innovation in the Digital Age*. Geneva: World Trade Organization, p. 101.

McAfee, A. and Brynjolfsson, E. (2017). *Machine, Platform, Crowd: Harnessing our Digital Future*. New York: W.W. Norton & Company.

McElheran, K., Li, J., Brynjolfsson, E., Kroff, Z., Dinlersoz, E., Foster, L., and Zolas, N. (2023). AI Adoption in America: Who, What, and Where. NBER Working Paper No. w31788.

McMahon, B. (2022). AI is Ushering In a New Scientific Revolution. The Gradient, 4 June.

Meese, T. (2018). The How and Why of Consciousness? *Frontiers in Psychology*, 9:2173.

Mergel, I., Rethemeyer, K., and Isett, K. (2016). Big Data in Public Affairs. *Public Administration Review*, 76(6):928–937.

Merton, R. (1976). Option Pricing when the Stock Returns are Discontinuous. *Journal of Financial Economics*, 3(1–2):125–144.

Michael, K. and Miller, K. (2013). Big Data: New Opportunities and New Challenges. *Computer*, 46(6):22–24.

Miller, F. and Lehoux, P. (2020). The Innovation Impacts of Public Procurement Offices: The Case of Healthcare Procurement. *Research Policy*, 49(7):1–13.

Miller, J. and Felton, D. (2017). The Fermi Paradox, Bayes' Rule, and Existential Risk Management. *Futures*, 86:44–57.

Minsky, M. (1961). Steps Towards Articial Intelligence. https://web.media.mit.edu/minsky/papers/steps.html.

Mokyr, J. (2002). *The Gifts of Athena: Historical Origins of the Knowledge Economy*. Princeton: Princeton University Press.

Mokyr, J. (2014). Growth and Technology: The Wild Ride Ahead. Milken Institute Review, April 28.

Mokyr, J. (2016). *A Culture of Growth: The Origins of the Modern Economy*. Princeton: Princeton University Press.

Monton, B. (2019). How to Avoid Maximizing Expected Utility. *Philosophers Imprint*, 19(8):1–25.

Moor, J. (2006). The Dartmouth College Artificial Intelligence Conference: The Next Fifty Years. *AI Magazine*, 27(4):87–91.

Moore, G. (1965). Cramming More Components onto Integrated Circuits. *Electronics*, 38(8):33–35.

Moscati, I. (2016). Retrospectives: How Economists Came to Accept Expected Utility Theory: The Case of Samuelson and Savage. *Journal of Economic Perspectives*, 30(2):219–236.

Mubayi, P., Cheng, E., Terry, H., Tilton, A., Hou, T., Lu, D., Keung, R., and Liu, F. (2017). *Chinas Rise in Artificial Intelligence*. Goldman Sachs: Equity Research.

Mullainathan, S. and Spiess, J. (2017). Machine Learning: An Applied Econometric Approach. *Journal of Economic Perspectives*, 31(2):87–106.

Müller, V. (2014). Risks ofGeneral Artificial Intelligence. *Journal of Experimental and Theoretical Artificial Intelligence*, 26(3):297–301.

Murphy, T. (2012). Exponential Economist Meets Finite Physicist. Do The Math Blog, 4 October.

Murphy, T. (2022a). Human Exceptionalism. Do the Math Blog, 16 February.

Murphy, T. (2022b). Limits to Economic Growth. Nature Physics, 18(8):844–847.

Murray, A., Kuban, S., Josefy, M., and Anderson, J. (2021). Contracting in the Smart Era: The Implications of Blockchain and Decentralized Autonomous Organizations for Contracting and Corporate Governance. *Academy of Management Perspectives*, 35(4):622–641.

National Science and Technology Council (2016). The National Artificial Intelligence Research and Development Strategic Plan. Executive Office of the President of the United States. October.

Naudé, W. (2019a). The Economic and Business Impacts of Artificial Intelligence: Reality, not Hype. Medium: Towards Data Science, 10 June.

Naudé, W. (2019b). The Race Against the Robots and the Fallacy of the Giant Cheesecake: Immediate and Imagined Impacts of Artificial Intelligence. IZA Discussion Paper no. 12218.

Naudé, W. (2021). Artificial Intelligence: Neither Utopian Nor Apocalyptic Impacts Soon. *Economics of Innovation and New Technology*, 30(1):1–24.

Naudé, W. (2022). From the Entrepreneurial to the Ossified Economy. *Cambridge Journal of Economics*, 46(1):105–131.

Naudé, W. (2023a). Destructive Digital Entrepreneurship. IZA Discussion Paper No. 16483. Bonn: IZA Institute for Labour Economics.

Naudé, W. (2023b). Late Industrialisation and Global Value Chains under Platform Capitalism. *Journal of Industrial and Business Economics*, 50(3): 91–119.

Naudé, W. and Dimitri, N. (2018). The Race for an Artificial General Intelligence: Implications for Public Policy. IZA Discussion Paper no. 11737, IZA Institute of Labor Economics.

Naudé, W. and Dimitri, N. (2020). The Race for an Artificial General Intelligence: Implications for Public Policy. *AI and Society*, 35(2):367–379.

Naudé, W. and Dimitri, N. (2021). Public Procurement and Innovation for Human-centered Artificial Intelligence. IZA Discussion Paper.

Naudé, W. and Nagler, P. (2018). Technological Innovation, Entrepreneurship and Productivity in Germany, 1871-2015. SPRU Working Paper Series (SWPS), 2018-02. Science Policy Research Unit, University of Sussex.

Naudé, W. and Vinuesa, R. (2021). Data Deprivations, Data Gaps and Digital Divides: Lessons from the COVID-19 Pandemic. *Big Data and Society*, 8(2):1–12.

Navarria, G. (2016). How the Internet was Born: From the ARPANET to the Internet. The Conversation, 3 November.

Neck, R. (2021). Methodological Individualism: Still a Useful Methodology for the Social Sciences? *Atlantic Economic Journal*, 49(2):349–361.

Newquist, H. (1994). *The Brain Makers: Genius, Ego, and Greed in the Quest for Machines That Think*. New York: Macmillan.

Nguyen, A., Yosinski, J., and Clune, J. (2014). Deep Neural Networks are Easily Fooled: High Confidence Predictions for Unrecognizable Images. ArXiv, https://arxiv.org/abs/1412.1897.

Nordhaus, W. (2015). Are We Approaching an Economic Singularity? Information Technology and the Future of Economic Growth. Cowles Foundation Discussion Paper no. 2021. Yale University.

Nordhaus, W. (2021). Are We Approaching an Economic Singularity? Information Technology and the Future of Economic Growth. *American Economic Journal: Macroeconomics*, 13(1):299–332.

Nordhaus, W. D. (2009). An Analysis of the Dismal Theorem. Cowles Foundation Discussion Paper no. 1686.

North, D. (1991). Institutions. *Journal of Economic Perspectives*, 5(1):97–112.

Noy, I. and Uher, T. (2022). Four New Horsemen of an Apocalypse? Solar Flares, Super-Volcanoes, Pandemics, and Artificial Intelligence. *Economics of Disasters and Climate Change*, 6(2):393–416.

O'Brien, J. and Nelson, C. (2020). Assessing the Risks Posed by the Convergence of Artificial Intelligence and Biotechnology. *Health Security*, 187(3): 219–227.

Obwegeser, N. and Müller, S. (2018). Innovation and Public Procurement: Terminology, Concepts, and Applications. *Technovation*, 74–75:1–17.

O'Connell, M. (2017). *To Be A Machine: Adventures Among Cyborgs, Utopians, Hackers, and the Futurists Solving the Modest Problem of Death*. New York: Doubleday Books.

O'Connor, G. and McDermott, C. (2004). The Human Side of Radical Innovation. *Journal of Engineering and Technology Management*, 21(1–2):11–30.

OECD (2017). Business Dynamics and Productivity.

OECD (2019). Recommendation of the Council on Artificial Intelligence. OECD/LEGAL/0449, Adopted 22 May 2019. Paris: Organization for Economic Cooperation and Development.

Oesterheld, C. (2021). Approval-directed Agency and the Decision Theory of Newcomb-like Problems. *Synthese*, 198(27):6491–6504.

Olson, S. J. (2015). Homogeneous Cosmology with Aggressively Expanding Civilizations. *Classical and Quantum Gravity*, 32:215025.

Omohundro, S. (2008a). The Basic AI Drives. Proceedings of the First AGI Conference.

Omohundro, S. (2008b). *The Nature of Self-improving Artificial Intelligence*. Mimeo Palo Alto: Self-aware Systems.

Ord, T. (2020). *The Precipice: Existential Risk and the Future of Humanity*. New York: Hachette Books.

Østergaard, A. and Nielbo, K. (2023). False Responses from Artificial Intelligence Models Are Not Hallucinations. *Schizophrenia Bulletin*, 49(5):1105–1107.

Parkes, D. and Wellman, M. P. (2015). Economic Reasoning and Artificial Intelligence. *Science*, 6245:267–272.

Parret, A. (2020). Neural Networks in Economics. PhD Dissertation, University of California, Irvine.

Parshley, L. (2023). Artificial Intelligence Could Finally Let Us Talk with Animals. Scientific American, 1 October.

Pastor-Berniera, A., Plott, C., and Schultz, W. (2017). Monkeys Choose as If Maximizing Utility Compatible with Basic Principles of Revealed Preference Theory. *PNAS*, 114(10):E1766–E1775.

Pattanayak, K. and Krishnamurthy, V. (2021). Rationally Inattentive Utility Maximization Explains Deep Image Classification. arXiv:2102.04594 [cs.LG].

Pearl, J. (1985). Bayesian Networks: a Model of Self-activated Memory for Evidential Reasoning. Proceedings of the 7th conference of the Cognitive Science Society, University of California, Irvine, CA, USA.

Persky, J. (1995). Retrospectives: The Ethology of Homo Economicus. *Journal of Economic Perspectives*, 9(2):221–231.

Petigura, E. A., Howard, A., and Marcya, G. (2013). Prevalence of Earth-size Planets Orbiting Sun-like Stars. *PNAS*, 110(48):19273–19278.

Pham, H. (1997). Optimal Stopping, Free Boundary, and American Option in a Jump-Diffusion Model. *Applied Mathematics and Optimization*, 35(2): 145–164.

Pigozzi, G., Tsoukias, A., and Viappiani, P. (2016). Preferences in Artificial Intelligence. *Annals of Mathemathical Artificial Intelligence*, 77(3–4):361–401.

Pinker, S. (2018). *Enlightenment Now: The Case for Reason, Science, Humanism, and Progress*. New York: Viking.

Pissarides, C. (2018). Work in the Age of Robots and AI. IZA 20th Anniversary Celebration, Berlin, 28–29 June.

Pistono, F. and Yampolskiy, R. (2016). Unethical Research: How to Create a Malevolent Artificial Intelligence. arXiv:1605.02817 [cs.AI].

Pooley, G. and Tupy, M. L. (2018). The Simon Abundance Index: A New Way to Measure Availability of Resources. Policy Analysis no. 857, Cato Institute.

Prettner, K. and Strulik, H. (2017). The Lost Race Against the Machine: Automation, Education, and Inequality in an R&D-based Growth Model. Hohenheim Discussion Papers in Business, Economics and Social Sciences no. 08-2017.

Pulkka, V. (2017). A Free Lunch with Robots – Can a Basic Income Stabilise the Digital Economy? *Transfer*, 23(3):295–311.

Ramsey, F. (1931). Truth and Probability. In Ramsey, F. (ed.). *Foundations of Mathematics and other Logical Essays*. New York: Harcourt.

Rees, M. (2018). *On The Future: Prospects for Humanity*. Princeton: Princeton University Press.

Rees, M. (2021). Seti: Why Extraterrestrial Intelligence Is More Likely to be Artificial than Biological. The Conversation, 18 October.

Resing, W. (2005). Intelligence Testing. In *Encyclopedia of Social Measurement*, Kempf-Leonard, K. (ed.) Elsevier, pp. 307–315.

Ricci, F., Rokach, L., and Shapira, B. (2022). Recommender Systems: Techniques, Applications, and Challenges. In: Ricci, F., Rokach, L., and Shapira, B. (eds.). *Recommender Systems Handbook* (3rd ed.). New York: Springer, pp. 1–35.

Ridley, M. (2011). *The Rational Optimist: How Prosperity Evolves*. London: Fourth Estate.

Ridley, M. (2015). The Myth of Basic Science. *The Wall Street Journal*, 23 October.

Riedel, C. J. (2021). *Value Lock-in Notes*. Mimeo, 25 July.

Riedl, M. (2019). Human-centered Artificial Intelligence and Machine Learning. *Human Behavior and Emerging Technologies*, 1(1):33–36.

Ring, M. and Orseau, L. (2011). Delusion, Survival, and Intelligent Agents. In: Schmidhuber, J., Thórisson, K. R., and Looks, M. (eds.) *AGI 2011. LNCS (LNAI)*, 6830:11–20.

Rodriguez, F. and Jayadev, A. (2010). The Declining Labor Share of Income. Human Development Research Paper No. 2010/36, UNDP.

Romer, P. (1986). Increasing Returns and Long-run Growth. *Journal of Political Economy*, 94(5):1002–1037.

Romer, P. (1987). Growth Based on Increasing Returns Due to Specialization. *American Economic Review*, 77(2):56–62.

Romer, P. (1990). Endogenous Technical Change. *World Development*, 98(5): S71–S102.

Romer, P. (2019). The Deep Structure of Economic Growth. Blog. https://paulromer.net, 5 February.

Roodman, D. (2020). Modelling the Human Trajectory. Open Philanthropy, 15 June.

Rosenblatt, F. (1958). The Perceptron: A Probabilistic Model for Information Storage and Organization in the Brain. *Psychological Review*, 65(6): 386–407.

Roser, M., Ritchie, H., and Mathieu, E. (2023). What is Moore's Law? Our World in Data, 28 March.

Rumelhart, D., Hinton, G., and Williams, R. (1986). Learning Representations by Back-Propagating Errors. *Nature*, 323(6088):533–536.

Russel, S., Dewey, D., and M.Tegmark (2015). Research Priorities for Robust and Beneficial Artificial Intelligence. AI Magazine, Association for the Advancement of Artificial Intelligence, Winter, pp. 105–114.

Russell, S. (2019). *Human Compatible: Artificial Intelligence and the Problem of Control*. New York: Viking Books.

Russell, S. and Norvig, P. (2021). *Artificial Intelligence: A Modern Approach*. 4th ed. London: Pearson Education, Inc.

Sachs, J., Benzell, S., and LaGardia, G. (2015). Robots: Curse or Blessing? A Basic Framework. Working Paper 21091. National Bureau of Economic Research.

Salimans, T., J., Chen, X., Sidor, S., and Sutskever, I. (2017). Evolution Strategies as a Scalable Alternative to Reinforcement Learning. arXiv:1703.03864v2 [stat.ML].

Samuel, A. L. (1959). Some Studies in Machine Learning Using the Game of Checkers. *IBM Journal of Research and Development*, 3(3):210–229.

Samuel, S. (2022). Effective Altruism's Most Controversial Idea. Vox, 6 September.

Samuelson, P. (1947). *Foundations of Economic Analysis*. Cambridge: Harvard University Press.

Sandberg, A. (2013). An Overview of Models of Technological Singularity. In: More, M. and Vita-More, N. (eds.). *The Transhumanist Reader*. New York: Wiley.

Sandberg, A. (2014). Ethics of Brain Emulations. *Journal of Experimental and Theoretical Artificial Intelligence*, 26(3):439–457.

Sandberg, A. (2018). *Space Races: Settling the Universe Fast*. Mimeo: Future of Humanity Institute, Oxford Martin School, University of Oxford.

Sandberg, A. and Bostrom, N. (2008). Whole Brain Emulation: A Roadmap. Technical Report 2008–3, Future of Humanity Institute, Oxford University.

Santana, C. and Albareda, L. (2022). Blockchain and the Emergence of Decentralized Autonomous Organizations (DAOs): An Integrative Model and Research Agenda. *Technological Forecasting and Social Change*, 182:121806.

Sarkar, S. (2000). On the Investment-Uncertainty Relationship in a Real Options Model. *Journal of Economic Dynamics and Control*, 24(2): 219–225.

Sarker, I. (2021). Deep Learning: A Comprehensive Overview on Techniques, Taxonomy, Applications and Research Directions. *SN Computer Science*, 2(6):420.

Savage, L. (1954). *The Foundations of Statistics*. New York: Dover.

Schiller, R. (2019). Narratives about Technology-induced Job Degradations Then and Now. Working Paper no. 25536. National Bureau of Economic Research.

Schintler, L. and Kulkarni, R. (2014). Big Data for Policy Analysis: The Good, The Bad, and the Ugly. *Review of Policy Research*, 31(4):343–348.

Schmidhuber, J. (2015). Deep Learning in Neural Networks: An Overview. *Neural Networks*, 61:85–117.

Schoemaker, P. (1982). The Expected Utility Model: Its Variants, Purposes, Evidence and Limitations. *Journal of Economic Literature*, 20(2):529–563.

Schreiner, M. (2023). GPT-4 Architecture, Datasets, Costs and More Leaked. The Decoder, 11 July.

Schwab, K. (2016). The Fourth Industrial Revolution: What It Means, How to Respond. Davos: World Economic Forum.

Schwartz, R., Dodge, J., Smith, N., and Etzioni, O. (2020). Green AI. *Communications of the ACM*, 63(12):54–63.

Searle, J. (1980). Minds, Brains and Programs. *Behavioral and Brain Sciences*, 3(3):417–457.

Searle, J. (1992). *The Rediscovery of the Mind*. Cambridge: MIT Press.

Sejnowski, T. J. (2020). The Unreasonable Effectiveness of Deep Learning in Artificial Intelligence. *PNAS*, 117(48):30033–30038.

Sena, V. and Nocker, M. (2021). AI and Business Models: The Good, the Bad and the Ugly. *Foundations and Trends in Technology, Information and Operations Management*, 14(4):324–397.

Setiya, K. (2022). The New Moral Mathematics. *Boston Review*, 15 August.

Sevilla, J., Heim, L., Ho, A., Besiroglu, T., Hobbhahn, M., and Villalobos, P. (2022). Compute Trends Across Three Eras of Machine Learning. arXiv:2202.05924 [cs.LG].

Shah, R. (2019a). AI Safety without Goal Directed Behaviour. Alignment Forum, 7 January.

Shah, R. (2019b). Stuart Russell's New Book on Why We Need to Replace the Standard Model of AI. Alignment Newsletter no. 19.

Shannon, C. (1948). A Mathematical Theory of Communication. *The Bell System Technical Journal*, 27(3):379–423.

Shneiderman, B. (2020). Human-centered Artificial Intelligence: Reliable, Safe & Trustworthy. *International Journal of Human-Computer Interaction*, 36(6):495–504.

Shostak, S. (2018). Introduction: The True Nature of Aliens. *International Journal of Astrobiology*, 17(4):281.

Shostak, S. (2021). If We Ever Encounter Aliens, They Will Resemble AI and Not Little Green Martians. The Guardian, 14 June.

Shulman, C. (2010). Omohundro's "Basic AI Drives" and Catastrophic Risks. The Singularity Institute, San Francisco, CA.

Shulman, C. and Bostrom, N. (2021). Sharing the World with Digital Minds. In: Clarke, S., Zohny, H., and Savulescu, J. (eds.) *Rethinking Moral Status*. Oxford: Oxford Academic.

Siegel, R. (2009). All-Pay Contests. *Econometrica*, 77(1):71–92.

Simon, H. (1955). A Behavioral Model of Rational Choice. *Quarterly Journal of Economics*, 69(1):99–118.

Simon, H. (1956). Rational Choice and the Structure of the Environment. *Psychological Review*, 63(2):129–138.

Simon, H. (1978). On How to Decide What to Do. *The Bell Journal of Economics*, 9(2):494–507.

Simon, H. (1996). *The Sciences of the Artificial*. Cambridge: MIT Press.

Simonite, T. (2020). The US Government Will Pay Doctors to Use These AI Algorithms. Wired Magazine, 11 October.

Sims, C. (2003). Implications of Rational Inattention. *Journal of Monetary Economics*, 50(3):665–690.

Singer, P. (2021). The Hinge of History. *Project Syndicate*, 8 October.

Sivarajah, U., Kamal, M., and Weerakkody, V. (2017). Critical Analysis of Big Data Challenges and Analytical Methods. *Journal of Business Research*, 70(C): 263–286.

Smith, M. L. and Neupane, S. (2018). Artificial Intelligence and Human Development: Towards a Research Agenda. White Paper: International Development Research Centre.

Soice, E., Rocha, R., Cordova, K., Specter, M., and Esvelt, K. (2023). Can Large Language Models Democratize Access to Dual-use Biotechnology? arXiv preprint arXiv:2306.03809.

Sotala, K. (2018). Disjunctive Scenarios of Catastrophic AI Risk. In Yampolskiy, R. V. (ed.). *Artificial Intelligence Safety and Security*, 1st ed. Chapman and Hall/CRC.

Souza, K. D. and Jacob, B. (2017). Big Data in the Public Sector: Lessons for Practitioners and Scholars. *Administration and Society*, 49(7):1043–1064.

Srnicek, N. (2016). *Platform Capitalism*. London: Polity.

Stojčić, N., Srhoj, S., and Coad, A. (2020). Innovation Procurement as Capability-Building: Evaluating Innovation Policies in Eight Central and Eastern European Countries. *European Economic Review*, 121:1–18.

Stokel-Walker, C. and Van Noorden, R. (2023). The Promise and Peril of Generative AI. *Nature*, 614(9):214–216.

Stolk, M. (2019). What To Do When Meeting ET? Masters Thesis in Political Science, Radboud University Nijmegen.

Stough, R. and McBride, D. (2014). Big Data and the U.S. Public Policy. *Review of Policy Research*, 31:339–342.

Su, H. (2021). Game Theory and the Three-Body Problem. *World Journal of Social Science Research*, 8(1):17–33.

Suleyman, M. (2023). *The Coming Wave: Technology, Power, and the Twenty-first Century's Greatest Dilemma*. New York: Crown Books.

Susskind, D. (2017). A Model of Technological Unemployment. Economic Series Working Papers 819. University of Oxford.

Sutton, R. and Barto, A. (1998). *Introduction to Reinforcement Learning*, 1st ed. Cambridge: MIT Press.

Tamura, H. (2009). Modeling Ambiguity Averse Behavior of Individual Decision Making: Prospect Theory under Uncertainty. In: Torra, V., Narukawa, Y., and Inuiguchi, M. (eds.). *Modeling Decisions for Artificial Intelligence. MDAI 2009. Lecture Notes in Computer Science*, vol. 5861. Berlin, Heidelberg: Springer.

Tarsney, C. (2020). *The Epistemic Challenge to Longtermism.* Mimeo: GPI, Oxford.

Taylor, I. (2016). Dependency Redux: Why Africa Is Not Rising. *Review of African Political Economy*, 43(147):8–25.

Tegmark, M. (2017). *Life 3.0: Being Human in the Age of Artificial Intelligence.* London: Penguin Books.

Thaler, R. (2000). From Homo Economicus to Homo Sapiens. *Journal of Economic Perspectives*, 14(1):133–141.

Tien, J. (2017). Internet of Things, Real-time Decision Making, and Articial Intelligence. *Annals of Data Science*, 4(2):149–178.

Tirole, J. (2021). Digital Dystopia. *American Economic Review*, 111(6):2007–2048.

Tolan, S., Pesole, A., Martínez-Plumed, F., Fernández-Macías, E., Hernández-Orallo, J., and Gómez, E. (2020). Measuring the Occupational Impact of AI: Tasks, Cognitive Abilities and AI Benchmarks. JRC Working Papers Series on Labour, Education and Technology 2020/02, European Commission.

Torres, E. (2021). The Dangerous Ideas of "Longtermism" and "Existential Risk." Current Affairs, 28 July.

Torres, E. (2022). Understanding "Longtermism": Why This Suddenly Influential Philosophy Is So Toxic. *Salon*, 20 August.

Torres, P. (2014). *Why Running Simulations May Mean the End is Near.* Mimeo. https://archive.ieet.org/articles/torres20141103.html.

Totschnig, W. (2020). Fully Autonomous AI. *Science and Engineering Ethics*, 26(5):2473–2485.

Trajtenberg, M. (2018). AI as the Next GPT: A Political-Economy Perspective. NBER Working Paper no. 24245. National Bureau for Economic Research.

Tullock, G. (1980). Efficient Rent Seeking. In: *Toward a Theory of the Rent Seeking Society*, Buchanan, J. M., Tollison, R. D., and Tullock, G., (eds.) College Station: Texas A&M University Press, pp. 97–112.

Tunyasuvunakool, K., Adler, J., Wu, Z., and et al. (2021). Highly Accurate Protein Structure Prediction for the Human Proteome. *Nature*, 595(7873):590–596.

Turchin, A. (2021). *Catching Treacherous Turn: A Model of the Multilevel AI Boxing.* Mimeo: Foundation Science for Life Extension, May.

Turchin, A. and Chernyakov, M. (2018). *Classification of Approaches to Technological Resurrection.* Mimeo, PhilArchive.

Turchin, A. and Denkenberger, D. (2020). Classification of Global Catastrophic Risks Connected with Artificial Intelligence. *AI & Society*, 35(1): 147–163.

Turing, A. (1936). On Computable Numbers, with an Application to the Entscheidungsproblem. London Mathematical Society, 42(1):230–265.

Turing, A. (1950). Computing Machinery and Intelligence. *Mind*, 59(236): 433–460.

Tzachor, A., Whittlestone, J., Sundaram, L., and ÓhÉigeartaigh, S. (2020). Artificial Intelligence in a Crisis Needs Ethics with Urgency. *Nature Machine Intelligence*, 2(3):365–366.

Umbrello, S., Torres, P., and De Bellis, A. (2020). The Future of War: Could Lethal Autonomous Weapons Make Conflict More Ethical? *AI & Society*, 35(1): 273–282.

UNESCO (2022). *Recommendation on the Ethics of Artificial Intelligence*. Paris: United Nations Educational, Scientific and Cultural Organization.

Urbina, F., Lentzos, F., Invernizzi, C., and Ekins, S. (2022). Dual Use of Artificial-Intelligence-powered Drug Discovery. *Nature Machine Intelligence*, 4(3): 189–191.

Uyarra, E., Flanagan, K., Magro, E., and Zabala-Iturriagagoitia, J. (2017). Anchoring the Innovation Impacts of Public Procurement to Place: The Role of Conversations. *Environmental Planning*, 35(5):828–848.

Valdes, F. and Freitas Jr, R. A. (1980). Comparison of Reproducing and Nonreproducing Starprobe Strategies for Galactic Exploration. *Journal of the British Interplanetary Society*, 33:402–408.

Van Alstyne, M., Parker, G., and Choudary, S. (2016). Pipelines, Platforms, and the New Rules of Strategy. *Harvard Business Review*, April:54–62.

Van de Gevel, A. and Noussair, C. (2013a). *The Nexus between Artificial Intelligence and Economics*. Berlin, Heidelberg: Springer Briefs in Economics.

Van de Gevel, A. and Noussair, C. (2013b). *The Nexus between Artificial Intelligence and Economics*. Berlin, Heidelberg: Springer Briefs in Economics.

van de Poel, I. (2020). Embedding Values in Artificial Intelligence (AI) Systems. *Minds and Machines*, September. https://doi.org/10.1007/s11023–020–09537–4.

Van Zanden, J., Baten, J., Foldvari, P., and van Leeuwen, B. (2014). The Changing Shape of Global Inequality, 1820-2000: Exploring a New Dataset. *Review of Income and Wealth*, 60(2):279–297.

Varella, M. (2018). The Biology and Evolution of the Three Psychological Tendencies to Anthropomorphize Biology and Evolution. *Frontier in Psychology*, 1(9):1839.

Varian, H. (1995). Economic Mechanism Design for Computerized Agents. Proceedings of the First USENIX Workshop on Electronic Commerce New York, New York, July.

Varian, H. (2014). Big Data: New Tricks for Econometrics. *Journal of Economic Perspectives*, 28(2):3–28.

Vaswani, A., Shazeer, N., Parmar, N., Uskoreit, J., Jones, L., Gomez, A., Kaiser, L., and Polosukhin, I. (2017). Attention Is All You Need. ArXiv.1706.03762.

Verendel, V. and Häggström, O. (2017). Fermi's Paradox, Extraterrestrial Life and the Future of Humanity: A Bayesian Analysis. *International Journal of Astrobiology*, 16(1):14–18.

Villaescusa-Navarro, F., Ding, J., Genel, S., Tonnesen, S., La Torre, V., Spergel, D., R.Teyssier, Li, Y., Heneka, C., Lemos, P., Anglés-Alcázar, D., Nagai, D., and Vogelsberger, M. (2022). Cosmology with One Galaxy? arXiv:2201.02202 [astro-ph.CO].

Vinge, V. (1993). The Coming Technological Singularity: How to Survive in the Post-human Era. VISION-21 Symposium, NASA Lewis Research Center and the Ohio Aerospace Institute, March 30–31.

Vinuesa, R., Azizpour, H., Leite, I., Balaam, M., Dignum, V., Domisch, S., Felländer, A., Langhans, S., Tegmark, M., and Nerini, F. F. (2020). The Role of Artificial Intelligence in Achieving the Sustainable Development Goals. *Nature Communications*, 11(233).

Vipra, J. and West, S. (2023). Computational Power and AI. AI Now Institute.

Vojnovic, M. (2015). *Contest Theory*. Cambridge: Cambridge University Press.

Von Foerster, H., Mora, P. M., and Amio, L. (1960). Doomsday: Friday, 13 November, A.D. 2026. *Science*, 132(3436):1291–1295.

von Hippel, E. (1976). The Dominant Role of Users in the Scientific Instrument Innovation Process. *Research Policy*, 5(3):212–239.

Von Neumann, J. (1966). *Theory of Self-reproducing Automata*. Urbana and London: University of Illinois Press.

Von Neumann, J. and Morgenstern, O. (1944). *Theory of Games and Economic Behavior*, 1st ed. Princeton: Princeton University Press.

Wagner, D. (2020). Economic Patterns in a World with Artificial Intelligence. *Evolutionary and Institutional Economics Review*, 17(1):111–131.

Waldrop, M. (2016). The Chips are Down for Moore's Law. *Nature*, 530(7589): 144–147.

Wang, G., Gunasekaran, A., Ngai, E., and Papadopoulos, T. (2016). Big Data Analytics in Logistics and Supply Chain Management: Certain Investigations for Research and Applications. *International Journal of Production Economics*, 176:98–110.

Ward, P. (2009). *The Medea Hypothesis: Is Life on Earth Ultimately Self-destructive?* Princeton: Princeton University Press.

Warfield, D. (2023). Transformers – Intuitively and Exhaustively Explained. Medium Towards Data Science, 21 September.

Warwick, K. and Shah, H. (2016). Can Machines Think? A Report on Turing Test Experiments at the Royal Society. *Journal of Experimental and Theoretical Artificial Intelligence*, 2807(6):989–1007.

Washington, A. (2014). Government Information Policy in the Era of Big Data. *Review of Policy Research*, 31(4):319–325.

Webb, S. (2015). *If the Universe is Teeming with Aliens ... Where Is Everybody? Seventy-Five Solutions to the Fermi Paradox and the Problem of Extraterrestrial Life*. Cham: Switzerland: Springer.

WEF (2018). Artificial Intelligence Collides with Patent Law. *Center for the Fourth Industrial Revolution*. Geneva: World Economic Forum.

Weiser, M. (1991). The Computer of the 21st Century. *Scientific American*, pp. 66–75.

Weitzman, M. (1998). Recombinant Growth. *Quarterly Journal of Economics*, 113(2):331–360.

Weitzman, M. (2009). On Modeling and Interpreting the Economics of Catastrophic Climate Change. *Review of Economics and Statistics*, 91(1): 1–19.

Weizenbaum, J. (1966). ELIZA – A Computer Program for the Study of Natural Language Communication Between Man and Machine. *Communications of the ACM*, 9(1):36–45.

Westby, T. and Conselice, C. (2020). The Astrobiological Copernican Weak and Strong Limits for Intelligent Life. *The Astrophysical Journal*, 896(58):1–18.

Whalley, A. (2011). Optimal R&D Investment for a Risk-averse Entrepreneur. *Journal of Economic Dynamics and Control*, 35(4):413–429.

Wheeler, J. (1989). *Information, Physics, Quantum: The Search for Links*. Reproduced from Proceedings of the 3rd International Symposium on the Foundations of Quantum Mechanics, Tokyo, pp. 354–368.

Wiley, K. (2011). *The Fermi Paradox, Self-replicating Probes, and the Interstellar Transportation Bandwidth*. arXiv:1111.6131v1 [physics.pop-ph].

Williams, G. (1966). *Adaptation and Natural Selection: A Critique of Some Current Evolutionary Thought*. Princeton: Princeton University Press.

WIPO (2019). *Technology Trends 2019: Artificial Intelligence*. Geneva: World Intellectual Property Association.

Wong, M. (2023). AI Doomerism is a Decoy. The Atlantic, 2 June.

Wooldridge, M. (2022). What Is Missing from Contemporary AI? The World. *AAAS Intelligent Computing*, 2022:9847630.

World Bank (2016). World Development Report 2016.

Wright, R. (2022). The Case for Shorttermism. Nonzero Blog, 11 August.

WTO (2020a). E-commerce, Trade and the COVID-19 Pandemic. Information Note. Geneva: World Trade Organization, 4 May.

WTO (2020b). World Trade Report 2020: Government Policies to Promote Innovation in the Digital Age. Geneva: World Trade Organization.

Yampolskiy, R. (2014). Utility Function Security in Artificially Intelligent Agents. *Journal of Experimental and Theoretical Artificial Intelligence*, 26(3):373–389.

Yampolskiy, R. (2016). Taxonomy of Pathways to Dangerous Artificial Intelligence. The Workshops of the Thirtieth AAAI Conference on Artificial Intelligence AI, Ethics, and Society: Technical Report WS-16-02.

Yampolskiy, R. V. (2012). Leakproofing the Singularity. *Journal of Consciousness Studies*, 19(1–2):194–214.

Yang, H. and Zhang, L. (2005). Optimal Investment for Insurers with Jump-Diffusion Risk Process. *Insurance: Mathematics and Economics*, 37(3): 615–634.

Yang, L., Zhang, Z., Song, Y., Hong, S., Xu, R., Zhao, Y., Zhang, W., Cui, B., and Yang, M.-H. (2022). Diffusion Models: A Comprehensive Survey of Methods and Applications. arXiv:2209.00796v10 [cs.LG].

Yasser, S. (2020). Aliens, The Fermi Paradox, And The Dark Forest Theory: A Game Theoretic View. Medium: Towards Data Science, 21 October.

Yilmaz, F. and Arabaci, O. (2020). Should Deep Learning Models be in High Demand, or Should they Simply be a Very Hot Topic? A Comprehensive Study for Exchange Rate Forecasting. *Computational Economics*, 57(1):217–245.

Yiu, C. (2012). The Big Data Opportunity: Making Government Faster, Smarter and More Personal. Policy Exchange.

Yoon, J. (2020). Forecasting of Real GDP Growth Using Machine Learning Models: Gradient Boosting and Random Forest Approaches. *Computational Economics*, 57(1):247–265.

Yu, C. (2015). The Dark Forest Rule: One Solution to the Fermi Paradox. *Journal of the British Interplanetary Society*, 68(5–6):142–144.

Yu, H., Shen, Z., Miao, C., Leung, C., Lesser, V., and Yang, Q. (2018). Building Ethics into Artificial Intelligence. ArXiv, 7 December.

Yudkowsky, E. (2001). Creating Friendly AI 1.0: The Analysis and Design of Benevolent Goal Architectures. The Singularity Institute, San Francisco, CA, June 15.

Yudkowsky, E. (2002). The AI-Box Experiment. www.yudkowsky.net/singularity/aibox.

Yudkowsky, E. (2007a). Levels of Organization in General Intelligence. In: Goertzel, B. and Pennachin, C. (eds.) *Artificial General Intelligence Cognitive Technologies*. Berlin: Springer, pp. 389–501.

Yudkowsky, E. (2007b). Pascal's Mugging: Tiny Probabilities of Vast Utilities. Less Wrong Blog, 19 October.

Yudkowsky, E. (2008). Artificial Intelligence as a Positive and Negative Factor in Global Risk. In: Bostrom, N. and Cirkovic, M. N. (eds.) *Global Catastrophic Risks*. Oxford: Oxford University Press, pp. 308–345.

Yudkowsky, E. (2009). Value is Fragile. *Less Wrong Blog*, 29 January.

Yudkowsky, E. (2017). There's No Fire Alarm for Artificial General Intelligence. Machine Intelligence Research Institute, October 13.

Yudkowsky, E. (2023). Pausing AI Developments Isn't Enough. We Need to Shut it All Down. Time Magazine, 23 March.

Zackrisson, E., Calissendorff, P., González, J., Benson, A., Johansen, A., and Janson, M. (2016). Terrestrial Planets Across Space and Time. *The Astrophysical Journal*, 833(2):1–12.

Zhang, K., Yang, Z., and Basar, T. (2021). Multi-agent Reinforcement Learning: a Selective Overview of Theories and Algorithms. arXiv:1911.10635v2 [cs.LG].

Ziegler, D., Stiennon, N., Wu, J., Brown, T., Radford, A., Amodei, D., Christiano, P., and Irving, G. (2019). Fine-tuning Language Models from Human Preferences. arXiv preprint arXiv:1909.08593.

Zolas, N., Kroff, Z., Brynjolfsson, E., McElheran, K., Beede, D., Buffington, C., Goldschlag, N., Foster, L., and Dinlersoz, E. (2020). Advanced Technologies Adoption and Use by U.S. Firms: Evidence from the Annual Business Survey. NBER Working Paper No. 28290.

Zuboff, S. (2015). Big Other: Surveillance Capitalism and the Prospects of an Information Civilization. *Journal of Information Technology*, 30(1):75–89.

Index

Printed in the United States
by Baker & Taylor Publisher Services